Bike Touring

Sierra Club Outdoor Adventure Guides

Land Navigation Handbook

The Sierra Club Guide to Map, Compass & GPS
by W. S. Kals
Completely updated, with new text by Clyde Soles

Simple Foods for the Pack

More than 200 all-natural, trail-tested recipes
by Claudia Axcell, Vikki Kinmont Kath, and Diana Cooke

Walking Softly in the Wilderness

The Sierra Club Guide to Backpacking
by John Hart

Bike Touring

The Sierra Club Guide to
Travel on Two Wheels

Second Edition

Raymond Bridge

Illustrated by John Lencicki

Sierra Club Books
San Francisco

The Sierra Club, founded in 1892 by author and conservationist John Muir, is the oldest, largest, and most influential grassroots environmental organization in the United States. With more than a million members and supporters—and some sixty chapters across the country—we are working hard to protect our local communities, ensure an enduring legacy for America's wild places, and find smart energy solutions to stop global warming. To learn how you can participate in the Sierra Club's programs to explore, enjoy, and protect the planet, please address inquiries to Sierra Club, 85 Second Street, San Francisco, California 94105, or visit our website at www.sierraclub.org.

The Sierra Club's book publishing division, Sierra Club Books, has been a leading publisher of titles on the natural world and environmental issues for nearly half a century. We offer books to the general public as a nonprofit educational service in the hope that they may enlarge the public's understanding of the Sierra Club's concerns and priorities. The point of view expressed in each book, however, does not necessarily represent that of the Sierra Club. For more information on Sierra Club Books and a complete list of our titles and authors, please visit www.sierraclubbooks.org.

Published by Sierra Club Books
85 Second Street, San Francisco, CA 94105

Sierra Club Books are published in association with Counterpoint (www.counterpointpress.com).

SIERRA CLUB, SIERRA CLUB BOOKS, and the Sierra Club design logos are registered trademarks of the Sierra Club.

Book and cover design by Lynne O'Neil
Composition by David Van Ness

Library of Congress Cataloging-in-Publication Data

Bridge, Raymond,
    Bike touring : the Sierra Club guide to travel on two wheels / Raymond Bridge; illustrated by John Lencicki. --2nd ed.
        p. cm.– (Sierra Club outdoor adventure guides)
    Includes bibliographical references and index.
    ISBN 978-1-57805-142-7 (alk. paper)
        1. Bicycle touring–Guidebooks. I. Lencicki, John, ill. II. Sierra Club. III. Title.
    GV1044.B75 2009
    796.6'4–dc22   2009001216

Printed in the United States of America on Rolland Enviro 100 acid-free paper, which contains 100 percent post-consumer waste, processed chlorine free

Second Edition

Distributed by Publishers Group West
13 12 11 10 09
10 9 8 7 6 5 4 3 2 1

*This book is for
Lucas, Jessica, and Justina–
potentially the next generation
of touring cyclists*

Contents

Touring

Resources

Preface

It has been three decades since the original edition of *Bike Touring* was published, and it is interesting to note how much has changed since then and how much remains essentially the same.

This book is completely different from the original, though the approach has hardly changed. There are many more active cyclists today who are interested in bike touring, and good equipment is easier to find and less expensive (adjusted for inflation). However, it is still true that generally unsuitable bicycles are often sold as touring bikes. And there is still a real need for a book that covers the basics for people who want to prepare for long trips exploring the countryside via bicycle.

The changes in this book reflect the evolution of bicycle touring over the last few decades. Most important are the changes in equipment. Increased interest in cycling generally, along with globalization of manufacturing and distribution, has made much better bikes available at reasonable prices. Drive trains even on inexpensive road bicycles today are better, more durable, and easier to maintain than expensive, elite systems of thirty years ago. The same is true of many other components.

Mountain bikes did not even exist at the time the first edition of this book was written. The first custom mountain bike was built around that time. These days more people have mountain bikes than road bikes (though, of course, they mostly ride them in town). Along with many other factors, this has expanded the world of bicycle touring. You can now sign up for a commercially run mountain bike tour in Mexico's Copper Canyon, or put together your own trip on a mountain bike riding from Alaska to Patagonia. Some cyclists prefer to use mountain bikes even for touring mainly on pavement. More important for bicycle touring is that the mountain bike marketing explosion has made many high-quality, low-cost components available for touring.

This book touches on mountain-biking options, but its main topic is tours via paved roads using road bikes, covering the basics you need to know about equipment, skills, and styles of travel. It also contains discussions of tours on trail systems that have sprung up on old towpaths, railroad beds, and similar networks in locations from Missouri to Quebec. It discusses the basics of extended mountain bike tours, but those are not its main emphasis.

This book, like its predecessor, concentrates on the equipment, technique, and training that are important for anyone contemplating multiday trips by bike, on tours that are close to home, that explore some other part of the United States, or that visit some interesting area abroad. However, though the book concentrates on tours you plan yourself, there are many more supported tours available these days, so the book includes some discussion of them. Because mountain bikes provide many interesting touring possibilities for travel away from the pavement, they also get some consideration.

The emphasis in this book, however, is on touring with road bicycles, either staying at motels or hostels while carrying moderate amounts of baggage (sometimes called credit-card touring) or carrying camping gear and other necessities for self-contained touring.

This book assumes that most readers already have some bicycle skills acquired from recreational, commuting, club, or sport riding, so the sections on riding skills and techniques emphasize aspects that are specific to touring or to improving conditioning and training for riders used to either short rides or serious local club riding.

Considerable space is devoted to equipment, even though the equipment is really secondary to the experience of bike touring. In general, the book emphasizes modern, moderately priced road bikes. There are innumerable specialized machines that are prized by some experienced bicycle tourists, ranging from folding bikes to recumbent bicycles, tandems, classic road bikes with components older than their riders, and other fascinating modes of locomotion. Complete discussions of such specialized machines would take us too far afield, so they are mentioned only in passing. For most readers the most suitable touring bike, at least for a time, is one that can be purchased from a shop with only a few modifications. After you've been on a few tours, you will have met riders who have all sorts of opinions about the ultimate touring bike, and you'll be able to evaluate their arguments for yourself. You may also have acquired enough enthusiasm for touring that you'll be interested in pursuing your own ultimate touring bike.

Oversights, errors, and mistakes in emphasis in this book are strictly my responsibility, but the underlying experience of what works and doesn't in bike touring, as presented here, is the product of the bicycle touring community, a fascinating, knowledgeable, opinionated, and generous group. I am particularly grateful to the "Phreds," the Internet bicycle touring discussion group moderated by Alex Wetmore. I am also indebted to my editors at Sierra Club Books—Diana Landau, Edward Wade, Marianne Lipanovich, and Kelly Ryer—who have made this a far better book than it would have been without their discerning eyes.

Introduction

Bicycle touring has much in common with backpacking, kayaking, canoeing, ski touring, and mountaineering. All are forms of self-propelled, lightweight travel
that bring the participant into close contact with the
natural world, in both its gentle and its harsh moods.
There is a special appeal to bicycle touring, however,
that makes it unique: the bicycle is a practical means of
transportation as well as a recreational vehicle.

The convenience factor in bicycle touring makes
it extremely attractive, particularly for those who live
in densely populated regions a long way from large
tracts of public land. When the closest good backpacking trail is a couple of hundred miles away, a weekend
backpacking trip involves a tiresome, time-consuming,
and expensive amount of driving, as well as inducing pressure and fatigue because of the tight schedul-
ing needed to mesh the normal work week with the
weekend's recreation. Especially for those with busy
schedules, the logistics of driving from San Francisco
to the High Sierra or from Boston to northern New
Hampshire are likely to limit the number of such trips
to just a few each season.

By contrast, pleasant bicycle tours can begin at
most people's front doors or, at worst, a few miles
from home. If you are exploring another part of the
United States or a faraway country, you can start your

tour from a major transportation terminus instead of dealing with complex travel arrangements to get to the trailhead, river put-in, or shoreline departure point. Thus, if you are traveling from New York to Europe, you can start your bicycle tour from the Frankfurt airport rather than having to take additional transport to the Bernese Oberland before beginning your actual climbing or backpacking trip.

In our world of limited resources, cycling also offers important advantages to those concerned about the consumption of nonrenewable energy sources. Many of us who consider ourselves environmentalists are quite pious about the fossil fuels wasted in daily commuting, criticizing people who drive to work every day without passengers rather than using public transportation, carpooling, or riding a bike. At the same time, we are complacent about our own use of fuel for recreation. A commuter who drives 15 miles to his or her job travels 150 miles in a normal work week. But a wilderness lover who drives 200 miles to the mountains and back every other weekend is using more gasoline, all other things being equal, even if he or she rides a bike or a bus to work. A single vacation drive to Alaska may easily require more fuel than a commuter consumes in an entire year.

I wll not belabor this comparison, but in terms of fuel conservation, there is clearly a good case for taking some bicycle tours that start close to home in preference to wilderness treks that require long drives. Even bike trips that start some distance from home often are easier to reach by public transportation than are backpacking, ski touring, kayaking, mountaineering, or canoeing destinations. Wilderness jaunts generally begin far from heavily traveled transportation corridors, while bicycle tours can start at the nearest freeway interchange, wherever an interesting side road winds away from the main thoroughfare.

For these reasons and others, it seems particularly appropriate that the Sierra Club should publish a book on bicycle touring. Besides its attraction as a challenging recreational activity, bicycle touring enables us to enjoy open country with minimal negative impact on the Earth.

The Rediscovery of the Bicycle

Few Americans in today's automobile-dominated culture are aware of how popular the bicycle was in the United States at the beginning of the twentieth century. Bikes were a major form of both transportation and recreation at that time. Bicycling clubs were tremendously popular everywhere; the bicycle built for two was a standard vehicle for courtship; and bicycle racing was a major spectator sport. American roads were first paved for bicyclists, not for automobiles.

So it is ironic that in the United States, which was once the center of innovative bicycle design and manufacture, bikes were reduced for many years to being just children's toys. Even now, there are only a couple of major manufacturers of high-quality bicycles in the United States, and most of the accessory components on today's American-made bikes are imported from Asia.

The bicycling renaissance that began a few decades ago will almost certainly continue to flourish as more people discover the bicycle as a practical means of transportation and as the basis of a satisfying and healthful recreational activity. Consider the bicycle's advantages: it is relatively cheap and very economical of resources; it does not consume fossil fuels, except for the relatively small amounts needed to build it, ship it, and manufacture replacement parts; it is compact to store, can be easily picked up and carried into a house or other building, and is readily taken along on any well-designed means of public transportation; it is a personal vehicle, like a car, so it is ready to go when and where you are; and it is fast enough and efficient enough to cover considerable distances in reasonable time periods, with typical speeds of 10 to 20 miles per hour, depending on circumstances.

If we removed the current incentives for sprawl in our major population centers and introduced a

1. Touring bicycle from a century ago.

few minor reforms, within a few years the bicycle could again become one of our major forms of everyday transportation. For many of us that can happen today.

Many people who buy touring bicycles as recreational vehicles soon find that their bikes are the best way to get around the rest of the time too. For traveling reasonably short distances, a bike is often faster than a car and a lot less frustrating. Riding to work or school can help you stay in shape for longer weekend rides, while providing a welcome form of relaxation at the beginning and end of each day. In contrast to automobile commuting, which often leaves the driver tense and out of sorts, riding a bike to and from work is usually pleasant. Finally, because of the bike's practical uses, purchasing a costly, good-quality bike actually may save you money in the long run, unlike most other purchases of recreational equipment. And good touring bikes generally make good commuting bikes.

Styles of Bicycle Touring

Bicycle touring covers a lot of ground, both literally and figuratively. Tours can range from 15-mile Sunday-morning jaunts down the road from home to cross-continent trips covering thousands of miles. Riders who tour include casual cyclists who never ride more than 10 or 20 miles a day and stay near home and dedicated athletes who ride several hundred miles a week through most of the year. For multiday touring, camping cyclists carry everything they need on their bikes, while other riders prefer to stop at hotels every night. Some large group tours are followed by a "sag wagon," which hauls the group's luggage and picks up any riders having trouble.

Bicycle touring refers to traveling by bicycle simply for the pleasure of riding the roads, as distinct from using a bike as a commuting vehicle or for bicycle racing. A lot of touring consists of one- or two-day weekend rides that cover a circuit fairly close to the cyclist's home, perhaps with longer trips on holiday weekends or vacations. The variety of touring that can be enjoyed even close to home is amazing. Since good cyclists are quite likely to cover 50 or a 100 miles on a day's trip, there is a wide range of possibilities starting from your own doorstep, and if you use public transportation or shuttle to get to or from the ride itself, the menu of available routes becomes enormous.

From my house, for example, a day's ride can take me well out onto the Great Plains, along rolling foothills country, or into the mountains, across the Continental Divide and back. As you tour more and more, you are likely to discover near your home more interesting country seamed with delightful back roads than you ever imagined.

Cycling Equipment

Any how-to book of this sort necessarily devotes much space to equipment, because questions about gear naturally preoccupy anyone starting out in a sport. Mistakes in choosing equipment can be disheartening as well as expensive. Bicyclists in general tend to be even more equipment-oriented than other self-propelled travelers, because of the nature of the sport. The touring bicycle is a precision machine that is highly sophisticated in design, and the cyclist is dependent on its proper functioning. Hence, much of this book consists of information about bikes and accessory equipment, even though the essence of bicycle touring is the experience, not the hardware.

The cyclist's concern with equipment is not frivolous. The backpacker's ability to travel is not really affected by the design of the pack carried, providing it doesn't completely fall apart. One pack may make carrying a load somewhat easier, particularly for an out-of-shape novice, but an experienced backpacker will not double his or her mileage by trading in an old rucksack for the newest pack design on the market.

By contrast, the touring cyclist is far more dependent on equipment. You can have a lot of fun riding around on an old clunker, but you are ill advised to use it for a long tour. Good equipment does not make you a good cyclist, but even the best cyclist cannot ride well with poor equipment. Light weight is more important to the cyclist than it is to the backpacker, simply because far more ground is covered; the additional work required to move a few extra pounds is quite significant. Hence, touring cyclists are often obsessed with reducing weight, whether on bicycle components, camping equipment, or conveniences for the trip. Safety considerations are also important. Making a fast downhill run can be suicidal on a bike that is weak or that brakes poorly because of dented wheel rims. The history of cycling includes many riders who traversed the United States or the wilds of Central Asia on primitive machines, but equipment is still central to the activity.

Nevetheless, it is important to keep your main goals in mind. Good equipment simply provides a means of having a good time, directly experiencing the world around you, and enjoying the companionship of friends, all in a way that does not waste valuable resources. These goals make bicycle touring worthwhile; don't lose sight of them among the shiny bicycle parts and fancy touring bags. The information included in this book on technique, conditioning, and equipment is intended to help you to plan interesting tours, get out on the road with a minimum of fuss, and enjoy some good riding and touring.

Other Resources and Opinions

Some recommended books and generally useful Web sites are listed in the Resources section at the end of the book, and Web references are also included throughout the book to provide different points of view or illustrative stories that you may want to consult. General-interest information is listed in the Resources section as well. Sources and suppliers for specific topics or products are often listed in the text, but not necessarily repeated in the Resources section. Keep in mind that resources on the Web can be transient and may have disappeared or changed by the time this book is published.

Getting
Started

1

Varieties of Touring

Bicycle touring means different things to different people, and the style of touring that you prefer will depend on your personal proclivities, the particular tour, and perhaps your physical limitations or current mood. Bike touring is definitely about a feeling of freedom, independence, and direct connection with your environment. But what style best promotes this experience? It depends.

For some bicycle tourists, camping in the woods or the desert under the stars is the very essence of touring. But what about touring in regions where there aren't many public lands, where the landowners are not open to the idea of people camping on their property, where the authorities are mostly hostile to travelers, or where the campgrounds are all paved for motor homes and are as expensive as motels? Aren't the styles of touring appropriate to these locales just as much a part of the essence of bike touring? Many bicycle tourists frequent the urbanized northeastern United States, sometimes staying in motels, sometimes lodging with hospitable fellow cyclists, and sometimes managing to find places to camp.

In much of the United States, where things are spread out, you can find places to stay that are inexpensive and well suited to the touring cyclist, and that can connect you in interesting ways with the

2. A typical touring bike with panniers suitable for carrying equipment for any style of travel. The Bruce Gordon panniers are panel-loading and have compression devices to minimize packed size.

places where you are traveling. Struggling motels in towns that have been bypassed by the interstates can provide you with both fascinating social connections and a hot shower. Rooms for let in English villages provide a dimension to your trip that you could not experience any other way. Stopping at an accommodation in Latin America that caters to student travelers may prove far more interesting than finding a campground, and it may keep you from having to carry too much gear.

Many touring cyclists enjoy their trips far more as social occasions than as solitary treks. This is mainly a matter of taste, and different styles of touring are not mutually exclusive. Some prefer solo tours, while others prefer to travel with a dozen friends. On a well-planned tour with a small group, everyone will become friends after the first day or two. (On a badly planned trip, however, group dynamics can turn ugly in short order.)

Many people also thoroughly enjoy large group events, which are often organized as benefits for worthy causes. These large group rides, lasting anywhere from a long weekend to several weeks, have attractions all their own. Someone else does the organizing, you get all the advantages of a supported trip, you are riding with a group large enough to be partly immune to most traffic hazards, and you get to ride with people at your own level of fitness and skill, with the option of switching riding companions when you choose to do so. Such groups may be the perfect introduction for people who want to start bicycle touring without having to handle all the details on their first few trips. For others, however, such events are just too crowded and busy.

This first chapter is meant to present a wide range of bicycle-touring styles, enough to suit anyone who is taken with the general idea of traveling propelled by the power of his or her own legs, whether traveling around the world or on a circuit close to home. If you are intrigued by the idea and are willing to undertake a little physical exertion, there is a touring style that will suit you. (Chapters 17 and 18 go into more detail on specific styles of touring.)

A Real Roof over Your Head— Credit-Card Touring

Well-planned "credit-card" tours give you a roof over your head and a shower every night and allow you to carry lighter and more compact luggage. They are also guaranteed to put you in contact with a wide variety of people.

For example, a typical credit-card tour through southern England and Wales could be planned using "B roads," as designated on Ordnance Survey maps (maps created by Great Britain's national mapping agency). B roads wind through the countryside and carry reduced traffic. You can travel short distances each day, staying in a different town each night, in a bed-and-breakfast or a room for let, and taking in cathedrals, castles, and other sights along the way. Pub lunches, an occasional restaurant meal, or a salad made in your room from purchases that day can allow you to follow a personal schedule. You can vary the trip by taking a train to Wales, where a line of castles marks the English fortifications built to contain and then suppress the rebellious Welsh.

This is not to say that credit-card tours are always casual and easy. Quite the contrary. This type of touring can easily be ambitious and strenuous enough to challenge an endurance athlete. If you want to do a really extensive tour in the western United States, covering 100 to 200 miles a day through the mountains and deserts, you should travel light and follow one of these two basic approaches: either use ultralight, spartan camping gear or plan to stay in motels. The two approaches turn out to be similar in many ways. The costs won't be that different—nor will the style or rigor of the trip. The big issues in either case will be carrying water, getting food at the right times, reaching your goal for the day before dark, and dealing with exigencies. The approaches are equally strenuous and demanding, and are prone to the same risk of unplanned discomfort.

For less extreme travelers, the advantages of staying in standard accommodations are obvious: they are slightly easier to plan, they usually come with some amenities like showers and potable water, they are more likely to be associated with sources of food, they provide shelter from the elements, and they are accepted without question by law enforcement as legitimate places for dubious individuals like bicyclists to stay. None of these advantages should be taken lightly. The contention of this book is that bicycle touring should be fun. No matter how much of an individualist and loner you are, there are times when these advantages will make enjoyable a tour that would otherwise be stressful at best.

The main point here is that styles and varieties of touring reflect a variety of preferences, abilities, and ambitions. Some touring cyclists consider credit-card touring to be a derogatory term. This is silly. Many athletic and independent tourists prefer a self-contained style, and many equally athletic and independent cyclists prefer to cover more ground per day and crash with a roof over their heads. You may also choose to enjoy both styles at different times.

Self-Contained Touring (Camping)

Self-contained touring cyclists vary in their preferences for camping. Some opt for organized campsites, either on public lands or in private commercial campgrounds. Unfortunately, such campgrounds have become progressively less suitable for tent campers over the last few decades. To accommodate motor homes, trailers, and pickup-mounted campers, they tend to have large gravel pads into which it is often impossible to drive a tent stake, and you often end up paying for utility hookups that you can't use and don't want. The noise, lack of privacy, and semi-urban atmosphere can be unpleasant for many cyclists.

Many touring cyclists prefer to find small camping locations in the woods or elsewhere off the beaten path, like the one shown in Drawing 3, following the practice that some refer to as "stealth camping." Depending on the region in which you are cycling, campsites may be easy to find and clearly legal, as with many National Forests in the western United States, or they may require a resourceful nature and occasionally a bit of diplomacy to access. Tips and tricks are discussed in Chapter 18.

Supported Tours

Supported tours include a variety of styles and associated costs. You can travel with a group of friends accompanied by a station wagon or van loaded with your gear and share the driving. This works well for anything from a weekend trip within a few hundred miles of home to a longer trip to which you either fly or drive, and it works whether you are camping (as shown in Drawing 4 on page 16) or staying in commercial accommodations. You might also find a friend or spouse who is willing to drive the vehicle, traditionally known as the "sag wagon."

3. Camping on a bicycle tour can give you the ultimate freedom of the road or trail.

For a group of a half-dozen cyclists, another approach is for the riders to take turns driving the sag wagon, which can be a rental vehicle for far-flung trips. Each cyclist gets to ride most of the time, and the vehicle doesn't have to follow the riders directly—it just has to come last. The driver of the moment can sleep in or spend time in a coffee shop catching up on reading, keeping a journal, or surfing the Web before catching up to the group at a prearranged time.

At the next level of support are a variety of prearranged tours offered by various touring companies or organizations that allow you to guide yourself. These may include accommodations; they may be self-contained tours where you carry your own gear but campgrounds or hotels are prearranged; or they may be tours with expert leaders who accompany each group of cyclists, perhaps including sag wagons to deal with

4. Accommodations on supported tours can range from picturesque hotels to prearranged campsites.

mechanical problems or riders having difficulties. Some commercial organizers provide bicycles as part of the package, so if you are willing to use a rented bike of the style they offer, you don't have to deal with the cost and trouble of transporting your own. This is also a way for those who don't have suitable bikes to get a taste of touring in a distant and fascinating location.

The variety of supported tours available from commercial organizers these days is astounding. Want a trip on the coast of Ireland on which you guide yourself, but the bike, meals, and a nice place to stay every night are all prearranged? You can find it—at a price, of course. Some die-hard cycling tourists would scoff at this kind of trip, but people have different preferences, budgets, available time, and levels of experience.

Common in many parts of the country these days are large group tours on which you may camp or stay in motels and most of your gear is hauled in sag wagons. There are typically hundreds of participants on these tours, but people break into groups of similar riding ability during the day, sometimes with stronger riders taking longer routes that end up at the same locations at the end of the day.

If you want to get an idea of the general style and organization of some of these trips, take a look at the "Ride the Rockies" tour in Colorado at www.bicycle-tourcolorado.com, the "Cover Indiana Tour" tour at www.habitatindiana.org/biketour, or the "Touring Ride in Rural Indiana" tour at www.triri.org. For a more complete list of such tours, see the Resources section at the end of the book.

Mountain Bike Tours

As with tours on paved roads, mountain bike tours cover an enormous variety of styles and levels of difficulty. Some road tourists use mountain bikes, perhaps with a few modifications like smooth-tread tires, for all their touring, waxing enthusiastic about the more forgiving ride and the versatility.

Many cyclists who ride routes with a lot of gravel surfaces, like the Katy Trail in Missouri, the Route Verte in Quebec, or the American Discovery Trail, prefer mountain bikes, such as the one shown in Drawing 5 on the next page, because of their comfort and stability on unpaved roads. We'll discuss this in more detail in Chapter 4.

The overwhelming majority of cycling tourists undertaking tours on long gravel roads in Alaska and northern Canada, as well as adventurers heading to remote parts of Asia, South America, or Africa, take mountain bikes, though this is not a universal choice. Nearly everyone planning a trip on long routes with a lot of single-track trails—like the Great Divide Trail, which roughly parallels the Continental Divide from Mexico through the United States and extends a couple hundred miles into Canada—will choose a mountain bike.

5. A mountain bike equipped for touring on unpaved roads. Note that this bike has a front fork with shock absorbers, so only small panniers are attached to the front rack.

There are now many companies that offer supported tours throughout the world using mountain bikes, either rented bikes or your own, so there are plenty of opportunities to tour in whatever style suits you. If you are doing mountain bike tours, however, pay some attention to the potential environmental impact (see "Environmental Ethics" on page 356).

2

The Bicycle Tour of Your Dreams

What kind of bicycle touring trip fires your imagination? Do you dream of pedaling the roads of the largely unpopulated parts of the western United States, camping under the open skies and taking in mountain vistas, pristine lakes, and desert hoodoos? Do you want to tour regions of Europe, visit medieval castles and cathedrals, and stay in rooms let by local families? Is a North American transcontinental route the challenge that most inspires you? Are you most interested in developed trails that follow old carriage roads, towpaths, and other routes that avoid automobile traffic almost completely? Or are you most inspired by a long mountain bike trip over rough terrain or a sojourn of several months in Africa, Asia, or Latin America?

Of course, a serious touring cyclist can aspire to all these sorts of trips at some point in her or his life, but it makes sense to have a specific goal in mind when you start bike touring. It will motivate you and help you focus on developing a healthy training regimen, buying the right equipment for your needs, and planning out the trip.

Setting Your Goal

You should pick a dream trip that works for your personality and circumstances. Would you be most inspired by a trip you might take in six months or one that has a goal that is years away—the dream trip of a lifetime? Only you know your own personality well enough to decide.

Training and equipment choices derive from the tours you want to do. If you dream of taking a four-month sojourn in West Africa, you may not be starting anytime soon, unless you are extremely driven and energetic and have an extraordinarily flexible schedule. However, if this is your goal, you probably won't choose to work up to it with short, fast rides on good highways; you probably won't choose a modified road-racing bike. Rather, for your equipment—pointing toward West Africa—you should concentrate on rough and durable choices, and you should focus on acquiring a working knowledge of first aid, water purification, tropical diseases, and serious bicycle maintenance. By contrast, if you are interested in touring the California wine country or European museums, you'll be more interested in a good road bike and clothing that is readily adaptable for mingling with urbane groups.

Bicycle touring means different things to different people, and if you think about what trips you would *really* like to take, both in the near term and on your dream vacation, you'll have a better idea of the direction you should go in choosing everything from a bike to camping gear. It's easy to get bogged down in the minutiae of equipment choices or training regimens without even having formed a clear idea of what should be driving your choices. Thinking about trips you want to make is a good way to begin learning how to plan serious tours and to tie your training and equipment choices to those goals.

What's Realistic

Every plan for real bicycle tours has to be grounded in reality rather than fantasy. Your dream tour should fire your imagination but also be achievable within your planning horizon. You can always revise your objective along the way, but you shouldn't pick one that doesn't match your basic personality and resources—of time, physical ability, and budget.

If you basically prefer the comfort of soft beds and hot showers, and you're afraid of insects and snakes, you might want to forget about that four-month tour in West Africa. And if you really want to do one of the transcontinental tours at a fairly fast clip, but you're 60 years old, you're out of shape, and you've never ridden more than 20 miles at a time, you should definitely plan on working your way up through progressively longer and more arduous tours over a stretch of several years—and don't forget to keep up with regular training. If you think you can get back in shape in a couple of months, you will be rudely disappointed, and you probably will quit before riding your first "century" (a 100-mile day). Like much of life, goals in bicycle touring should be an exercise in reconciling your dreams with reality.

Working Up to the Trip of Your Dreams

Having some larger goals is a good way to motivate yourself and a very useful way of planning and direct-ing intermediate steps in getting to your desired long-term goal. If you are working toward that trans-continental trip and start planning it out, you will soon have a good idea of the daily mileage you want to cover, the style in which you plan to travel, and the kinds of shorter trips that will provide a suitable preparation.

If you want to follow a transcontinental route that is about 4,000 miles in length, and you think you can reserve two months of vacation time for the trip a couple of years hence, start by doing the arithmetic: you'll find that you'll need to approach 70 miles a day on average. As a realistic trial beforehand, you should plan to do a couple of weeklong trips on which you comfortably cover more than 100 miles a day, follow-ing the same general traveling style. On your transcon-tinental tour, you'll become more fit as you go along, but you will also encounter problems, including accu-mulated fatigue. So, if you plan for a daily mileage that is close to the maximum you can ride on a weekend trip, you will give up long before the halfway mark on your big transcontinental, and the experience will be disappointing rather than rewarding.

Choosing Your Style of Adventure

The underlying motivation for this book is to inspire readers to experience some of the remarkable rewards that cycling can provide to anyone with an adventurous nature who enjoys physical activity, the experience of the natural world, and the process of overcoming challenges that are both unique and personal.

Extreme Challenges

Consider serious mountaineering, for example. This classic adventure sport can take you to places like the Yukon, Nepal, or Patagonia. It can't be surpassed in physical and technical challenges, demands for teamwork, or the satisfaction achieved when a really momentous objective is achieved. Whitewater kayaking and extreme backcountry skiing have many of the same characteristics, combined with the aesthetic pleasure of kinetic linkage with natural forces. Either of these activities can take you to remote and exotic parts of the world, and you may encounter very interesting people once you get there.

Cycling, even in the modern world, can offer similar challenges for those who seek them out. At the extreme-challenge end of the spectrum is the trip undertaken by Richard and Nicholas Crane and described in their book *Journey to the Centre of the Earth*. They defined the center of the Earth as the point farthest from the sea in every direction, and they rode modified road bicycles from the Asian Pacific coast to a point in central Asia north of the Gobi Desert that they picked from a map. They began by hiring a canoe to take them upriver from the Bay of Bengal in Bangladesh and started cycling toward the center of Asia, crossing the Himalayas and heading into the

Gobi Desert, making for a point equidistant from the Indian Ocean, the Yellow Sea east of China, and the Arctic Ocean coast of Siberia.

Riding very strong custom road bikes weighing 22 pounds each, and carrying only about 18 pounds of luggage apiece, they bicycled 3,500 miles while climbing 17 vertical miles over bad roads, rugged trails, and barren wilderness, traversing high-altitude passes (up to 17,000 feet) and traveling through some of the most remote regions on Earth outside Antarctica. But the Cranes' encounters with the people of these regions were totally different from the typical high-altitude mountaineering expedition. They had to make friends everywhere; negotiate with locals for food and shelter; deal with bureaucrats at borders; endure the occasional arrest; and handle conditions ranging from desert sandstorms to mountain cold and snow, tropical heat, humidity, and insects. (An account of the Cranes' adventure can be found at web.archive.org/web/20041211045554/ http:/www.koopmann.lightup.net/crane.)

Most of us are satisfied with far less extreme challenges. A week touring the wine country of California or France might be just the thing! This example is mentioned to make two points:

- Bicycle touring can provide a greater variety of experience than any other self-propelled activity. It can also present opportunities for adventure to people with much more modest physical conditioning, risk tolerance, and schedule flexibility. You can choose your style of adventure.

- If you are interested in a challenge to your character or a variety of experience, whether physical, intellectual, or cultural, bicycle touring has unique potential.

Mixing Civilization with Adventure

Aside from extreme challenges like those chosen by the crazy cousins Crane, bike touring allows you to mix challenge and culture to your own taste. While many cyclists enjoy wilderness experiences, others prefer cycling through Europe: visiting museums, castles, and cathedrals; meeting interesting people in both city and country; and shuttling from one cultural center to another using the excellent train system. Latin America can be a great place to visit by bicycle—taking buses to remote villages with the bike tossed on the luggage carrier on top of the bus, and riding with the workers, mothers, children, and chickens up a bumpy road to a highland village before starting off on your bike.

Cycle-touring possibilities are limited only by your imagination and your spirit of adventure. Wherever you go, you'll find that your mode of transportation allows you to travel independently, but it also provides an instant introduction to the residents of the places where you are riding. Almost everyone is willing to chat with a touring cyclist. So, find a story or a dream that inspires you, and start pedaling toward its fulfillment!

3

Training and Riding Techniques

Cycling is a sport and a physical activity, so enjoying it requires developing the appropriate riding skills, together with the strength and conditioning to ride the distances you want to cover. Fortunately, compared with other activities, cycling allows a much wider range of people to experience real enjoyment and accomplishment. You can have a great time and reap great benefits in conditioning and health over a much wider range of skill level and fitness than in any other self-propelled sport.

Furthermore, you can train for serious bicycle touring by just riding your bike. Your first long tour will be much more enjoyable if you have a routine of riding regularly. For anyone who is reasonably healthy and without serious physical impediments, cycling is good, healthy exercise, entailing minimal risk of injury, as long as you avoid close encounters with automobiles. There are limits and cautions to be observed, but if you start at a moderate level—"moderate" being defined on your own terms—you can get in shape for bicycling by just bicycling. You are much less likely to experience activity-related injuries along the way than with running, for example. Cycling is easy on the joints, and levels of effort are simple to control. As with any form of endurance exercise, you need to avoid overuse injuries, but they are easy to identify and avoid.

What Kind of Rider Are You?

And what kind do you want to be? You won't become a really strong cyclist without doing a lot of riding. Even if you are in very good shape from some other activity— a serious marathoner, for example—general conditioning will only take you so far. As with every sport and endurance activity, cycling entails both general conditioning and specific muscle training. A sub-three-hour marathoner will be able to prepare for difficult bicycle tours much more quickly than someone who has never run a marathon, but cycling-specific conditioning and skills will still take time to develop. You need to spend time on a bicycle to be able to do long rides without getting saddle sores and specific muscle pains.

Nothing other than riding a bike will get your seat used to a bicycle seat, and cycling stresses your leg muscles in different ways than running or hiking. The muscles of your trunk may need to be strengthened to maintain a comfortable riding position on long rides and to avoid putting too much weight on your arms.

Cycling ability is a combination of physical conditioning and skills, and it is important to work on both with a view to the kind of touring you want to do. If you are planning to do serious single-track touring on a mountain bike, you need a whole set of mountain bike skills that are not necessary for road riding. By contrast, a regular bicycle commuter may acquire traffic-handling skills unknown to even the most agile mountain biker.

So, depending on the kinds of tours you want to do, you should work on building up the conditioning you need along with the skills required. In terms of conditioning, this means covering daily mileages, at least on weekends, that are perhaps 140 to 150 percent of the daily mileage you plan on the tours to which you aspire, preferably with similar climbing demands. (That is, if you want to average 75 miles a day on tour, you need to ride 105 to 115 miles a day in training, sometimes with touring loads.)

At least occasionally, you need to do day rides carrying luggage that is similar to what you will need to carry on your tours—primarily to become accustomed to the differences in bike handling, but also to gauge the effect on your daily mileage and climbing capability. You should also do some rides that otherwise match the conditions you expect. If you are training for a solo tour, for example, you should do some solo rides—drafting in the pack on a club ride is quite different, because you aren't doing the work against wind resistance. (See "Drafting" later in this chapter for more details.)

Mountain bikers, in particular, need to do a little practice for the special challenges of self-contained trips. Bike handling on a particular technical level of single track is very different when you are burdened with nothing more than a hydration pack compared to pulling a trailer or carrying even the lightest panniers together with a modest day pack.

Of course it is possible to do a transcontinental tour with very little prior training if you start with low mileages and gradually build your fitness on the way. However, it is likely to be discouraging, and most people would give up after a couple of weeks. It is much more enjoyable to be ready for the tour so that you can appreciate the experience.

Styles of Training

The most critical aspect of training for bicycle touring is to find a routine that gives you the incentive and the consistency to ride regularly and to accumulate significant mileage. Thus, if you commute every day, even for ten or twenty miles, it will help a lot with your riding fitness, and you can add weekend and evening rides as you can fit them into your schedule.

Club and Other Group Rides

There is no better training than regular rides with a local group or club, as shown in Drawing 6 on the next page. Local bike shops are a good place to ask about

6. Club rides are the best training you can find.

group rides. You'll want to start with people who are at least within range of your own level of fitness. Some group rides encompass wide ranges of capability, simply breaking into different levels at the beginning of a scheduled ride, but others consist only of hard-core riders. If you are just starting, a group that does a fast 60-mile ride in the evening is not what you are looking for—you'll be dropped from the back of the pack almost immediately.

One of the big training advantages of group rides is that the pace is much faster than you can manage on your own. When you are riding in a pack or a pace line, the trailing riders have the advantage of lower wind resistance, because they are riding in the slipstreams of those ahead. This means that the overall pace is consistently faster than anyone could manage alone for a comparable distance. The stronger riders alternate taking the lead, each one peeling off after a few minutes pulling at the front, and then rejoining the pace line at the end. Weaker riders simply drop back almost immediately after reaching the front. Riding with such a group, once you are fast enough to do so, will allow you to develop a consistently fast cadence (the number of revolutions of the pedals per minute), which makes for more efficient riding. It will also do wonders for your bike handling, but it is important to develop reasonable bike handling skills before trying to ride in a fast pace line.

A rider "drafting" in a pace line rides with his or her front wheel inches from the rider in front, usually overlapping somewhat to take advantage of the lowest possible wind resistance. (See "Drafting" later in this chapter.) If you accidentally touch your front wheel to the rear wheel of the rider in front, you will probably crash, and you'll often cause several riders behind to do so as well. This is generally considered to be bad form, so you'll want to build your skills gradually with riders of similar ability.

Warnings of road hazards ahead are normally passed back from the front of the pace line with hand or voice signals, so that everyone can move smoothly around breaks in the pavement, broken glass, or grates. When you are drafting behind a number of other riders, your view of the road ahead is obstructed, so communication along the line is important.

Training for All Seasons

Of course, you can get basic physical conditioning (but not technique) just as well from long rides by yourself or with a companion, and regularity is always the single most important aspect of training. The best training for long tours is simply to ride regularly and often. Putting in moderate regular mileage every week is far more effective than doing longer rides every few weeks.

If riding in the winter is impractical where you live, getting a trainer on which you can ride your bike is a useful alternative. The most common and least expensive trainers are set up to clamp the fork blades with a quick release, while the rear wheel rides on a single narrow roller, often attached to a fan to provide resistance that increases with speed. This type is relatively inexpensive, but it still allows you to train on your own bike. (For a few photographs of some types of trainers, take a look at www.minoura.co.jp/trainer-e2.html and www.blackburndesign.com/trainers.html.)

The best trainer is a set of rollers on which you actually ride the bike rather than clamping the fork onto a pillar. The front roller is driven by a belt attached to the rear rollers, which are in turn driven by your pedaling. It takes a little practice to learn to ride rollers, particularly when you are getting started, but it is most similar to actual riding. Rollers are also significantly more expensive than other trainers, and cheap ones are rarely a bargain, since the roller cylinders need to be perfectly true, and the rest of the apparatus has to be well made to be of any real use.

If you're training by riding alone or using a trainer, you won't have an easy way to develop pedaling with a higher cadence, so you should work on this aspect consciously (see "Cadence and Pedaling Technique" later in this chapter for more details).

The key to training is to find some combination that you enjoy and that fits into your routine so you will regularly put in the miles. If it isn't fun, you won't do it. Commuting may be a big help, but finding regular rides that are also fun will help to ensure that you ride enough before a big tour that you don't waste the entire trip getting into shape.

So, find some riding diversions that you enjoy enough to make them a regular habit. Whether you take an early-morning mountain bike ride on a trail or a late-afternoon club ride on the roads, or both, the important thing is to find riding that you enjoy enough to make it a regular habit.

Improving Your Riding Skills

Bike handling skills are an important part of the touring cyclist's repertoire, of course, and they are mostly acquired by doing a lot of riding. Some training tips are worth mentioning, however, and this section covers a few that might not be obvious.

Think Like a Vehicle

While there are some very interesting tours that allow you to stay well away from traffic, most bike touring requires that you share the road with automobiles and trucks, so it is important to learn to handle yourself comfortably in traffic. If you commute regularly in a place that doesn't have an extensive network of bicycle paths, you may already be adept at merging smoothly with cars. If not, a few points are worth considering.

Many experienced cyclists oppose separate systems for cyclists in general, contending that it is far safer for vehicles to share the road as a normal routine than to have different streams of traffic crossing one another. (This is a topic of constant dispute in the cycling community. See John Forester's *Effective Cycling* for the point of view that is generally opposed to bike paths.)

When you are on the highway or street with automobiles and trucks, the most important habit to develop is to behave in a predictable way, like other vehicles, and to follow normal traffic laws and rules of the road. Cyclists are always more vulnerable in accidents than motorists, of course, but experienced riders who can ride confidently and predictably in traffic are far less likely to be involved in accidents than those who are intimidated by traffic.

State traffic laws vary, as do interpretations by the courts, but in general as a cyclist you have the same right to use the road as motorists, along with the same responsibility to obey the traffic laws. You should act accordingly. Typically, if you obey the traffic laws and ride confidently, courteously, and predictably, motorists will yield the right of way when they should and will treat you like any other vehicle. There are exceptions: cyclists are generally not allowed on interstate highways and similar throughways, and they may be

locally prohibited from riding on some types of roads.*
Frequently, bridges and tunnels prompt local authorities to close roads to cyclists on the grounds of safety or expediency. You sometimes have to do research in advance to avoid such closed segments of road on a tour, and the published rules are not always the ones that are enforced locally.

Here are a few situations that require special attention:

- Avoid the far right edge of the road when there is a lot of debris, frequent potholes, or dangerous grates. In these situations you may have to ride farther left to be on consistent, reasonable pavement, and this may irritate motorists who think you should be farther right. The safest course is to ride along the general line of good pavement, so that you are not forced to swerve out unpredictably. If you follow a straight line along the correct path, motorists will usually adjust appropriately. In the worst situations, you may want to find an alternative route.

- Watch out for expansion joints on bridges; they can be dangerous tire-catchers.

- Be aware of cars that are passing and making right turns. Many drivers are unskilled at judging the speed of bicycles, which they view as stationary objects, like lampposts. Once they have passed you, they think they can safely turn right, and may accidentally run you down. It is worth being alert to this hazard, which is the result of driver inexperience.

- In cities and downtown areas, be aware of drivers in parked cars who might open a door in front of you.

---

* Bicyclists have successfuly fought such restrictions—for example, when they have been prohibited from using a U.S. highway and there was not an adequate alternative route—but it is obviously impractical to do so in a community where you are just passing through.

- Don't ride in tandem on the highway when cars are approaching from behind, particularly on mountain roads where it is difficult for them to pass. It's frequently illegal to ride abreast in these circumstances, it is unnecessarily discourteous, and it can create hazards for everyone. For large group rides this can cause significant local conflict; courtesy and good sense will go a long way toward heading off such problems before they create major contention. Develop a convention with fellow riders for moving to single file when you hear or see a car approaching. It is worth remembering that when such conflicts escalate, cyclists tend to come out on the losing side, so diplomacy and discretion are prudent. The club-ride pack shown in Drawing 6 on page 28 is not appropriate when there are cars following. You should move to single file to avoid obstructing drivers.

- Be aware of cars turning when you are riding on a bike path in town. One of the hazards of bike paths generally is that cars making right-hand turns don't notice parallel bike paths and therefore don't pay attention to who has the right of way, whether there are warning signs or not.

Braking

There are a lot of misconceptions about braking, of which the most prevalent is that if you brake hard with the front brake, you are in danger of pitching over the handlebars. While it is possible to do this in some circumstances, it will never occur if you are braking correctly and your bike is in good repair. This is a dangerous myth, because most of the time you should brake mainly using your front brake.

Anytime you are braking hard, you should be leaning forward with your hands in the drops (on a standard road bike), so that your center of gravity is as low as possible and your arms are firmly braced. In this position, when you are stopping as quickly as possible, the center of gravity (of you and the bike combined) tends to move forward but is restrained by the friction of the brakes against the rims and of the tires on the road. At maximum stopping force, the rear wheel is nearly unweighted, and all the force is concentrated on the front wheel.

For maximum braking, therefore, you should be doing all your braking with the front brake. Force applied to the rear brake does not help you to stop, but it will cause the rear wheel to skid, especially if you are turning. The best technique is usually to brake lightly with the rear brake so that you are aware if it begins to lose traction, but apply force to the front brake as hard as you can. Nearly all the braking is achieved with the front brake.

There are exceptions. On long, steep downhill grades, you want to control your speed, so you will brake a lot. In this situation, you don't want your brakes to overheat or your front-brake hand to tire, so you should alternate, taking care not to allow the rear to skid. On slippery surfaces or where there is loose sand or gravel on the pavement, you need to use both brakes more evenly, and take great care not to brake too hard, particularly in turns. If your front tire goes flat or you have dents in the front rim, you need to use the rear brake (and repair your bike!). And, of course, if you've allowed your front brake adjustment to become too loose, so that the lever bottoms out against the handlebar, you may need to use the rear brake too. In any of these circumstances, however, your ability to slow down will be greatly reduced, because the rear brake is far less effective.

Note that certain handlebars generally put the rider in a more upright position—mountain bike bars, albatross bars, moustache bars, and similar ones—but the same rules apply. Your center of gravity is a bit higher, so your braking will be slightly less efficient than with drop bars, but you'll still get most of your braking power from the front brake. During mountain bike descents on loose gravel, you'll have to brake more evenly and cautiously, using both brakes. On

7. Trucks pose a major hazard to long-distance cyclists, particularly on highways with minimal shoulders.

steep trails and those with loose gravel, distribution of braking depends on which wheel is on a surface that provides some traction.

On the Open Road

Dealing with traffic away from town is not usually different than it is for bicycle commuters, except that traffic passing you is generally going a lot faster. Holding a straight, predictable line is the most important practice to follow. Apart from the occasional yahoo, most drivers will pass safely.

One phenomenon that you'll have to learn to handle, however, is trucks passing at speed on older U.S. highways and similar roads (see Drawing 7). The slipstream of the truck can suck you out into the road after the truck passes unless you are alert—it acts like a sudden gust of wind from the outside. Obviously, this can be dangerous, particularly if another truck is following close behind the first. As long as you are expecting it, you can brace yourself and hold a steady line. Note that most truck drivers are experienced and careful—they will leave enough room, and they won't try to pass at dangerous points like some automobile drivers—but truckers don't realize the effect that their wind blast and slipstream have on a bicycle.

Cadence and Pedaling Technique

Like most bad habits, poor pedaling style becomes ingrained, so you should make an effort to train yourself to pedal efficiently and in a way that minimizes the likelihood of injuries. The biggest mistake that most beginners make is to pedal slowly in a high gear, putting a lot of effort into each stroke. This is inefficient because the body can do far more work if the legs move quickly, making less effort with each individual revolution.

When you aren't used to it, a fast cadence seems unnatural and ineffective. Persevere! If you watch racers or accomplished touring cyclists on the road, you will see them spinning the pedals at what appears to be a very fast rate. Racers typically spin in the vicinity of 90 to 100 revolutions per minute, while strong touring cyclists usually turn the cranks at 70 to 90 rpm. You should rarely drop much below 60 rpm, unless you are on a steep hill and already in your lowest gear. The brisk tempo will be inefficient at first, because it takes time to learn to turn your feet in little circles, but once you have learned, you will be able to maintain such speeds for long periods without tiring.

Another important reason you should learn to cycle at a relatively fast cadence is that pushing higher gears at slower speeds is very hard on your knees. Sore knees rarely bother cyclists who pedal at fast cadences, even when they are riding day after day over long distances. (This assumes that your bike is properly fitted—see Chapter 10.) Even strong, experienced cyclists can experience knee trouble from cycling in excessively high gears at slower cadences.

The most effective cadence varies from person to person, but it is largely a function of training. Simply try to concentrate on pedaling at the maximum comfortable rate for a while. When you encounter a headwind or start up a hill, try shifting down and pedaling faster rather than pushing harder at a slower cadence. Once you have had a reasonable amount of practice pedaling at fast rates, you will be able to determine the best cadence for you and develop a feel for it.

Beginning cyclists tend to exert pressure on the pedals only when they are pushing straight down. In fact, you probably will find that when you push down with one leg, you actually are resting the other leg completely on the pedal, so that your working leg is not only pushing the bike forward but lifting the weight of your other leg at the same time. Try to pedal all the way around the circle. Start pushing forward when the pedal reaches the top of its path and continue pushing back at the bottom. Most important, lift the leg that is on the upstroke rather than allowing it to hang like a dead weight on the pedal.

There are different ways to pedal all the way around the circle made by your feet, depending on cadence. When you angle your feet to push backward at the bottom of a stroke and forward at the top, so that the muscles and flexing of the ankles play a significant part, it is known as *ankling*. Generally, ankling is done at fairly slow cadences and disappears at higher rpm's. Racers who are sprinting or standing up on the pedals to climb hills (see "Climbing" below) may pull up on the rear pedal as well as pushing on the forward one. (Step-in pedals and shoes with cleats, toe clips, or Power Grips are necessary for this, but are not necessary for efficient pedaling generally; see "Pedals" on page 130.)

The important thing to concentrate on is not ankling or trying to power the bicycle with your trailing leg, but simply moving both feet in circles rather than just up and down. You can feel the greater efficiency immediately whenever you do this, and eventually it will become habitual. When you pull your back leg up instead of letting the pedal push it up, you do not eliminate the relaxation period for the working muscles. An entirely different muscle group is used to lift the leg than to extend it. By sharing the load of powering the bicycle between muscle groups, you can ride much more effectively and will tire less quickly.

The only way to develop good cadence is to practice. One or two days' riding can give you the idea, but it is not sufficient to ingrain the motions in your muscles and nervous system so that you can pedal for hours at a fast cadence, moving your feet in those efficient circles that eat up miles and hills. When you are riding for fun, check your cadence occasionally and concentrate on it. Try riding for ten minutes at a faster cadence but not at a faster speed. Drop down a gear and pedal faster. Relax your legs and attempt to spin fast without having them tense up. The cadence at which you can pedal efficiently will improve gradually with practice. There are bicycle computers that include a cadence reading for those oriented toward numbers and equipment, but you can also use a watch and occasionally count your crank rotations if you want a number. The point is to work on efficiency, however, and for that you don't really have to know your cadence accurately. There is no need to keep constant track of cadence. The objective is simply to train yourself to pedal at faster cadences until you reach your most efficient rate.

When you are riding up a hill and your legs begin to tire, you will almost always find that you are letting your back leg be pushed up by the pedal. Lift it during the upstroke, even if you only pull up hard enough to lift the weight of the leg. You'll find that the grade suddenly becomes easier because the load on the quadriceps (the muscles at the front of your thighs) has been reduced. The same trick works if you feel the soles of your feet becoming numb during a long ride. The reason for the numbness is that you have weight on your soles all the time. By pulling up slightly on each upstroke, you can take pressure off the balls of your feet during part of each rotation of the cranks. This almost always relieves the numbness.

8. Honking up a hill—standing up on the pedals with your weight forward—can be an efficient way to climb hills, but only if you've conditioned yourself to have good stamina and pace yourself so that you don't use too much of your reserves.

Climbing

There is no one right way to climb hills for either touring cyclists or racers. There have been great climbers in the Tour de France who sat most of the time while climbing hills and others who stood in the pedals for most climbs. It's worth getting some practice climbing while standing ("honking," see Drawing 8) to see whether it works for you. Generally, honking up a hill, rather than sitting and pushing hard, is more strenuous but easier on your knees. However, this depends on your gearing, conditioning, and physique. If your gearing isn't low enough to be able to climb without pushing very hard, you should train yourself to honk to avoid hurting your knees. With lower gears you'll be able to climb at a reasonable cadence so that you don't have to stand while climbing.

Touring cyclists, of course, are not in good enough physical condition to climb like a Tour de France rider, sitting or standing. Particularly with a loaded touring bike, you should rely on shifting to a low enough gear to be able to maintain a consistent level of effort without tiring.

Once you are in fairly good cycling condition, however, it is a good idea to occasionally honk up a short hill or stand up for a little while on a long hill. Standing up on the pedals can relieve the pressure on your bottom for a little while, and changing the muscles you are using to climb can be helpful. This practice will also improve your conditioning and technique, as long as you don't get too tired.

Descents

Steep descents require practice. Even if you've had lots of practice in the hills on day rides, there are some differences when you're riding with a fully loaded bike. The bike will handle differently, and you need to get used to this before you let the bike get going very fast. With a loaded bike, you have to develop a whole new sense for the effectiveness of your brakes, and hence for the degree to which you can approach corners at speed. The way you load the bike will affect the handling and steering, cornering agility, and safety on turns. You may need to experiment with how weight distribution between front and back affects the downhill stability of the bike.

Your brakes will heat up the tire rims if you don't have disc brakes, and the rims will in turn heat the tires. The heat generated by a long descent with a fully loaded bike could cause a tire to blow out. Until you know how your equipment behaves, you should beware of this possibility. Skinny tires carry the highest risk, because you run them at higher pressures and there is a smaller amount of air to absorb the transmitted heat.

Until you've developed a feel for doing descents with your bike fully loaded, the rule of thumb to follow is to keep your speed down. Unfortunately, that often means that you won't be able to follow the best line in your descents. Providing you have adequate control, it is usually best during steep descents to take your lane, since you can often travel faster than cars on mountain descents and staying in the center of the lane is

9. If you are riding with other people, drafting greatly reduces the energy needed to cover significant distances. The first rider is the only one to encounter full air resistance, and the lead is traded off frequently.

usually safer—you aren't trapped on the outside, where there may be loose sand and you may suddenly have to make sharp turns.

If traffic forces you to travel far to the right, where there may be loose gravel and sand, you must be even more conservative in controlling your speed. Mountain bikers with luggage also need to slow down until they have developed judgment about the effect of the weight on bike handling during descents.

Drafting

When you are cycling with others, you can save a lot of energy by taking turns at the front, with the second rider drafting behind the first (see Drawing 9). You can't get the advantage that club riders or racers do in a pace line, because with loaded bikes it would be quite unwise to follow with your wheel a few inches from the wheel of the rider ahead of you. Nonetheless, the second and following riders gain significant advantage from having the lead person creating a wind shadow, particularly when there is a headwind.

The normal rule is that when the lead person gets tired, he or she pulls out to the left (checking first for traffic), and the next person moves up. If you have a number of riders, you get a long rest before you have to take another pull. With only two riders, you'll need to switch more often.

Bonking and Avoiding the Bonk

While you are touring, you should rest before you are tired, drink before you are thirsty, and eat before you are hungry. "Bonking" is well known to all endurance athletes. Even if you are in very good shape (in fact, especially if you are in very good shape), you can be riding along at a good pace, feeling just fine, when your muscles just give up and you suddenly feel very weak. This occurs when you run out of immediately available blood sugar and you suddenly have to move to a much slower process of utilizing stored (mainly fat) reserves.

It is easier for cyclists, particularly touring cyclists, to avoid this problem than it is for marathoners, for example. This is because a bicyclist can digest food while riding and absorb liquids, both of which can be harder for distance runners. Carry snacks and nibble them regularly. Experiment to determine what works best for you.

The same applies to liquids. Drink a lot and find out what liquids work best for you, particularly in hot weather. You need to replace electrolytes as well as water, so occasional sports drinks or fruit juice may work well, though it is often best if they are diluted a lot. The reason that bananas are a longtime favorite snack of cyclists is because they are rich in potassium, resupplying that electrolyte in the bloodstream. (When you perspire, you lose potassium along with sodium, but it is harder to replace—table salt has sodium but not potassium. Sports drinks became popular for athletes trying to replace electrolytes in balanced proportions. Other sources of electrolytes or minerals can be just as effective, but they require a little more thought.) Again, find out what works for you. As you become acclimatized to exercise and heat, your sweat will become more dilute—perceptibly less salty—as your body learns to conserve electrolytes.

Bike-Fit Issues and Chronic Pain

The methods for fitting your bike are discussed in Chapter 10, but if you develop chronic pain in your neck or back from riding, the bike probably does not fit. Chronic numbness in your hands that is not relieved by using padding on the bars and regularly changing hand positions indicates that you may have too much weight on your hands because of bad fit. Knee pain can be caused by a poor fit or by riding with an excessively slow cadence.

Bicycles and Equipment for Touring

4

The Touring Bicycle

This chapter discusses the characteristics of a good touring bike. Bicycle touring is primarily about the experience, and people have successfully toured on every kind of bicycle: heavy 1950s "paperboy" bikes and "three-speeds," lightweight road-racing models, and full-suspension mountain bikes. Nonetheless, most experienced touring cyclists gravitate to a few types of bicycles that have proven versatile and that make it more likely that tours will be enjoyable experiences. I emphasize bikes that are well suited to touring on paved roads and graded bike paths, but later in the chapter some other styles of bikes will be discussed as well.

Most of you will begin touring with a touring-style road bike made by one of the major bike manufacturers, perhaps with a few components changed out for a better fit, improved performance, or better suitability for carrying loads and handling a variety of surfaces. This chapter therefore emphasizes moderately priced bikes that are well built and equipped for long-distance touring.

We'll concentrate on what is widely available, including modifications you might want to negotiate. While there are some deficiencies in currently available mass-produced machines, you can still get a far better bike for a reasonable price (inflation-adjusted) than you could when the first edition of this book was published almost thirty years ago.

Shopping: Local Shops and Other Sources

There are many good reasons to buy your touring bike from a local shop, rather than shopping for the apparently best deal from an online source. For a bike purchased online to be a good deal typically requires that you be a reasonably competent bicycle mechanic, have tools available, preferably have a miscellaneous parts box, and be willing to take the time to do whatever setup and changing out of parts might be required. Most people won't want to do this, at least for their first touring bike. If you save $100 on a bike by buying it from a mass retailer or an online supplier and end up having to pay $150 to have it fixed and adjusted correctly, you haven't saved money, even assuming you haven't had to change out some components that aren't quite right. If you do have to change a significant number of components, the costs will add up very quickly.

Here are some good reasons to purchase your touring bike from a local bike shop ("LBS"):

- Supporting local businesses is always a good thing. In this case, it is a particularly good thing because you will have someone who knows how to work on your bike who has an incentive to do a good job. Moreover, a good local bike shop puts a significant amount of work into assembling the bikes they sell. A high-quality assembly makes a lot of difference in how well the bike works and holds up. For an example of how one good shop assembles a bike, see www.rideyourbike.com/bikeassembly.html.

- The personnel in good bicycle shops have been trained in both fitting and setting up bikes. Both are critical for ensuring an enjoyable start in touring.

- You can negotiate accessories, component changes, and tools as part of the deal. This will often make the final price tag much lower than you could have achieved otherwise.

- You have someone you can ask about how to maintain the bike and how to make emergency repairs, among other useful things.

Of course these advantages don't apply to all circumstances, but they are definitely worth keeping in mind. If you find exactly the right machine on eBay for a third of the list price, you may want to grab it, but you'll still want to establish a relationship with a good local bike shop. Moreover, either you have to acquire the tools and skills for making adjustments and possible component changes or you'll need to take the bike to a good mechanic, preferably one who can help make sure it fits and is adjusted correctly. And you have to take on the inherent risks of making a purchase on eBay.

Major big-box and online retailers are rarely a good source for decent touring bikes. If you already have one of the lower-quality bikes they sell, it may be worth using it for a few moderate tours to get started, but it would be a poor investment to buy one specifically for touring. The frame will be of poor quality, regardless of the components you install, and you'll probably be ready to spring for a better bike in short order.

Some retailers specializing in self-propelled sports, like Recreational Equipment Inc. (REI), Eastern Mountain Sports (EMS), or Mountain Equipment Co-op in Canada (MEC), may be sources for touring bikes, but unless there is a nearby outlet that has an in-house bike shop, you should be wary. Prices are usually similar to those of local bike shops, and without knowledgeable people to set up the bike and fit you, you could end up paying far more in the long run.

Internet and mail-order bike specialists, like Performance Bicycle (www.performancebike.com), Jenson (www.jensonusa.com), and Bike Nashbar (www.nashbar.com), sometimes offer good bargains, but you need to consider the costs of shipping and whether you are capable of checking or completing the setup. In general, Internet sources are a better possibility for experienced touring cyclists and tinkerers, who are already knowledgeable. Beginners should usually rely on local shops and plan to test-ride as many bikes as necessary.

The only good alternative that will save you money in the long run is to buy a secondhand bike with a good frame and build it up with a good set of components. While this can be practical and fun, the learning curve is steep, and this approach is not recommended for most novices. Even if you are mechanically adept, there is a lot to learn about compatibility issues, and many specialized tools are needed that will eat into the money you save. This is a project best saved for your *second* touring bike.

What Makes a Good Touring Bike?

Any of the "touring" models from the major manufacturers will provide a superior riding experience for the kind of touring described in this book, compared with either conventional high-quality club, sport, or racing bicycles or older utility bikes. This book concentrates on the choices among conventional mass-produced bicycles, adjusted to fit properly. You can have a great experience touring with one of these. Then, if you become a fanatic, you can either build a bike that exactly suits you (or, more likely, several bikes), starting with a well-chosen frame, or you can go to one of the many great frame builders who can provide you with a semi-custom or custom machine.

Semi-custom, in the sense I'm using it, means bikes stocked in a number of frame sizes and proportions to fit a variety of body types that are then built up with components to accommodate the exact needs of the cyclist buying the bike. Such bikes will generally cost two to four times as much as stock bikes, but they will serve the needs of almost all riders, even the most demanding ones and those with odd body proportions. A true custom bike is designed and built specifically for your measurements and touring preferences. Custom and semi-custom bikes are designed with particular kinds of riding and particular body types in mind, and they are produced in small numbers, so you can get a bike that exactly matches your needs. (Always remember that any bicycle involves many design compromises. A bike chosen to be very comfortable on the road and usable for moderate trail riding will necessarily be marginal at best for serious single-track mountain biking.)

Frame Geometry

In general, a good touring bike is longer, uses somewhat heavier tubing, has more braze-ons (fittings for attaching components and accessories), and is designed with more generous clearances than a typical club-riding road bike. Racers and aggressive club riders prefer stiffer frames and quicker handling than what is ideal for long tours with luggage. Such club-riding bikes usually use short-reach caliper brakes, which don't allow enough clearance for the larger-diameter tires that are desirable on rougher roads, let alone fenders. Chainstays are frequently too short to mount rear panniers without pushing them so far back as to degrade bike handling. Steering geometry is often not conducive to mounting front panniers or to good handling of a bike loaded with luggage for a tour.

It is good to have these issues in mind when you are comparing bikes. The generally excellent quality of mass-produced bikes aimed at serious cyclists is the result of careful shaving of costs by manufacturers, along with techniques for quality control of large-scale production. This inevitably means that compromises and changes are made that will appeal to large numbers of customers. This year's "touring" model may suddenly be equipped with a quite different frame than last year's, even if the name and model number are the same, perhaps with a geometry more suited to a racer than someone doing long-distance tours.

An important factor for touring that is often ignored is wheel clearance. If you want to be able to tour comfortably on unpaved roads, bike trails, and moderate multiuse trails, you'll want to use tires that are fatter than those intended for fast rides on smooth pavement. Be sure that the bike you are considering can accommodate the tires you want to use. Many experienced tourists use fenders to reduce spray in wet weather, and these require extra clearance in addition to that needed for tires. Clearance also dictates what brakes can be used (see "Brakes" later in this chapter).

The point is that if you're buying a bike specifically for touring, there are a number of subtle differences in frames compared to bikes intended mainly for fast club rides. Issues that surround using a club-riding bike that you already have for touring are discussed later in this chapter. If a local bike shop salesperson is trying to sell you a sport-riding bike for touring and shows no understanding of the differences, find another bike shop.

Gearing

Models sold as touring bikes these days typically have three chainwheels (chainrings) in front, but some of them don't include a low enough gear ratio for pedaling a heavily loaded bike up long hills. In general, I strongly recommend that you make sure that the lowest gear on any bike you are considering be *much* lower than is typical on club-riding bikes.

Gearing is discussed in more detail in Chapter 6, but as a first check, I'd suggest that the lowest gear ratio (number of small front-chainring teeth divided by the number of teeth on largest rear cog) should be approximately 0.75 or less (in other terminology, a 20- or 21-inch gear, or 1.7 meters development with 700C wheels). That is, the "granny gear"—the smallest front chainwheel—should have three-fourths as many teeth as the largest cog in the back.

Late in the day your legs will probably be tired, and if you have a steep hill to climb with a heavy load before reaching your campground or lodging, you'll be very grateful for the granny gear. Even if you are in extremely good shape, you can experience the bonk. Finally, if you take some trips on rugged terrain, you'll be grateful for the low gears.

Consideration of many other gearing issues is worthwhile when you're buying a bike, but with 27- and 30-speed systems becoming the norm for all new bikes, you'll usually have all the gears you need, as long as the bike shifts smoothly through all the ranges and the lowest gear is adequate. More detailed gearing recommendations can be found in "What the Gears Do" on page 117.

If you've found a model in a shop that fits and rides well, the best time to negotiate a change in the gearing is *before* you buy the bike. This is true for several reasons beyond the fact that you are in a better bargaining position. There are limitations in chainring availability for different cranksets, and there are constraints in the capacity of derailleurs and shifters that are not obvious, so that several components may have to be swapped out to achieve the gearing you need while still allowing smooth, reliable shifting through all the gears.

You don't want to buy a new bike and then find that you need to pay hundreds of dollars for component changes to get the gears you need. Negotiate the changes you need as part of the purchase price. Your local bike shop may be willing to swap component sets at a modest cost at the time of purchase but not after you've ridden the bike.

Components

It is worth comparing all the components—shifting systems, brakes, and included accessories like luggage racks—among bikes you are considering, though you'll find that most will be generally comparable among bikes in the same price range, and the components on new bikes will usually be very good. Many more details about various components are discussed in subsequent chapters, but some that are particularly worth noting are covered here. Certain items, like pedals, may not even be included on the bike because people have different needs and preferences. Items like saddles are always included on complete bikes but are often of poor quality because they are so often replaced. While you're shopping, figure out the extras you would need for each bike you're considering and compare the prices for the final bikes rather than weighing apples against oranges.

Most road-touring bikes use drop handlebars, while most world-touring bikes are equipped with mountain bike bars or Euro-style touring bars. Each of these bicycle types provides a good starting point for the style of touring intended. Various nuances are discussed in later chapters for those who might want to consider changing the standard setup.

In general, the difference between component sets from the same manufacturer—say the difference between Shimano LX components and Shimano XT ones—is that the better grade will last a lot longer and be more trouble-free. Hence if you are comparing two bikes and the first has mostly Shimano LX components, while the second has XT ones, the second is a better bike. That said, the components you find on stock touring bikes these days are nearly all quite good and will give you years of satisfactory service, providing they fit your basic requirements.

Racks and fittings. A few of the bikes marketed as touring bikes come with rear racks as standard equipment, but most do not. You should compare different models after adding the cost of equipping them with both front and rear pannier racks, and if possible test-ride them with panniers attached and preferably with some load. The test ride will give you a feeling for the handling with luggage and tell you whether the panniers will interfere with your feet. If the bike is designed for touring, it should have eyelets for attaching racks on both the front and rear dropouts (the slotted pieces at the ends of the fork and at the rear into which the wheel axles are clamped). It should have brazed-on cable housing stops for the brakes and derailleurs you are getting, so that housing lengths are minimized.

If you plan to ride very much in rainy areas, it is preferable to have two sets of eyelets so that you can also mount fenders easily. If you want to use fenders, it is critical to pay attention to clearances—a typical sport-riding frame doesn't have enough clearance for touring tires or fenders. Bosses (threaded attachment points that are brazed or welded to the frame) for two or three water bottles are useful.

Saddle. Make sure the saddle is comfortable. The time to get it swapped out is when you are buying the bike. If you want to get a Brooks leather saddle or any other premium seat, you'll pay extra, but you should try to get a discount for the saddle being replaced. Those that come standard on commercial touring models are fine for test rides, but they usually need to be replaced for actual touring or even long training rides.

Brakes. The reach or the construction of the brakes should allow enough clearance for larger tires, as well as for fenders if you are considering them. As discussed in Chapter 8, this will usually mean choosing between cantilever or V-type brakes. "Long-reach" sidepull brakes are sometimes used successfully. Disc brakes eliminate clearance issues, but they have their own complications (see the discussion of disc brakes on page 166).

You need to be able to brake effectively with your hands on the handlebar drops (assuming you have the conventional handlebars for a road bike), as well as with your hands on the brake hoods. If you have small hands and have a hard time reaching the brakes, you should consider asking about levers with shorter travel that you can reach easily. If you are a more experienced rider and you want a differently-shaped handlebar—which may also require different shifters, brake levers, and/or derailleurs—it is also best to negotiate these changes when you're buying the bike. Such changes can inflate the cost of the bike rather rapidly, and the labor required to build up the bike will be lower if everything you want is specified from the start.

Wheels. Designs and materials for rims improve constantly, but there is always some trade-off between strength and weight. The weight of rims and tires is particularly important to the cyclist because they constitute rotating mass. More work has to be done to accelerate mass on the wheels than the same mass elsewhere on the bike. Nonetheless, the touring cyclist should usually choose strength over savings in weight. The lightest wheels will not hold up under the stress of a heavy load and the road hazards that accompany touring. For the same reasons, you should be wary of wheels built with fewer than 36 spokes—many touring cyclists prefer 40 or even 48, especially on the rear wheel. A broken spoke on a wheel with 32 or fewer spokes will cause the wheel to warp more than a wheel with more spokes, and temporary truing adjustments made on the road will be less effective and less reliable.

The most common wheel size for high-quality road bikes in the United States and Europe is 700C, and the widest selection of good tires is available in this size. Most mountain bikes have somewhat smaller wheels, called 26-inch, as do many bikes built for smaller riders, particularly those with semi-custom frames. This is because of the constraints of frame geometry, discussed in Chapter 5. Some specialized frames use even smaller wheels, particularly on the front.

Quite a few experienced touring cyclists, particularly those who travel to Latin America, Africa, or Asia, prefer 26-inch wheels because the tires (though not high-performance ones) are available everywhere. That way they don't have to carry spares—or at least not as many. A 26-inch wheel is also inherently stronger than a 700C wheel with the same number and thickness of spokes.

As a novice, you don't need to pay a lot of attention to the nuances of wheel size. You do need to understand, however, that changing wheel size is a big deal, because brakes, geometry, tire sizes, and many other factors are dependent on it. Putting 26-inch wheels on a bike designed for 700C ones would usually not be a good idea. A bike is designed around a particular wheel size.

A note on tire sizes. Only a few sizes are specifically described here. Twenty-seven-inch tires (ISO 630 mm) were standard on touring bikes a few years ago but are now uncommon. If you have an older touring bike and use 27-inch tires, you probably won't find replacements at all bike shops. They are still made and can be ordered, but the selection is limited and the quality is often poor. The most common size for touring bikes is 700C (ISO 622 mm), referred to as 29-inch on mountain bikes. A few touring bikes for smaller riders use 650C tires (ISO 571 mm), and an increasing number use 26-inch tires (ISO 559 mm). All these designations refer to the nominal outside diameter of the tire. (The 700C is nominally 700 mm in diameter, and the 650C is nominally 650 mm.) The trailing "C" is a width designation equivalent to about an inch (650B tires are wider than 650C ones). See "Tire Size" on page 155 for a more detailed discussion.

Frame Size

For initial shopping, you need to know the approximate frame size (seat tube length) for your body. Start with your crotch height or inseam—an actual measurement, not the size of your pants. Some discussions refer to this measurement as PBH—pubic bone height.

You need to get someone to help you, because trying to measure your own crotch height is likely to result in an inaccurate number. Get a thin book with a stiff cover, stand in your stocking feet with your back flat against the wall, the book between your legs, and the book edge against the wall. Have the person helping you push up on the book so that it compresses the soft tissue in your crotch, just as sitting on the bike seat will, and measure the distance from the top edge of the book to the floor.

Two-thirds of this measurement is *approximately* the right frame size. In addition, the standover height (just what it sounds like), if the manufacturer lists it, needs to be significantly less than your crotch height. The most important dimension for the actual bike fit, assuming the standover height is okay, is the top tube length, but we'll get into that in the next chapter.

There is a host of subtleties associated with sizing a bike. The measurements discussed here are just to get you started; they give you a basis to use the sizes listed by manufacturers. Fitting issues are discussed in more detail in Chapters 5 and 10, as are frame sizes. Sizes listed by different manufacturers should *not* be assumed to be measured the same way. There are many variations in specifying them. This ballpark estimate of your frame size can be used as a starting point, however.

The models sold by the largest manufacturers are, of course, optimized for average body proportions. Since women generally have a shorter torso for a particular leg length than men do, a common fitting problem is that the combined length of the top tube and stem is too long for many women. While some adjustment can be achieved with different stem lengths or by picking a slightly smaller frame and raising the seat and handlebars, these often won't result in a good fit, especially for smaller women. A few of the major manufacturers have smaller frames in some models (e.g., Specialized Sequoia, Novara Safari, and Surly Long Haul Trucker). If your crotch height is less than 25 inches, you should definitely look at specialty lines, like Terry Bikes, which are designed specifically for women.

Others who commonly have problems getting bikes that fit properly are tall people and those with body proportions that are not average, such as unusual ratios between torso and leg length. If you have a hard time finding a stock bike that fits you, you may need to go to a shop that has sophisticated custom fitting systems to get recommendations. There is more on fitting in Chapter 10, and there is an excellent detailed discussion in *Zinn's Cycling Primer*. You can also consult the Web sites in the Resources section at the end of the book.

Good Models to Consider

A number of widely available touring bikes are mentioned in this section. It is worth carefully looking at some of them in the store and test-riding them to compare with other bikes you are considering. Test-riding and comparison of features and size are the most important steps. I have not included a table with direct comparisons, because manufacturers may change both components and frame geometry from year to year, for reasons that may have as much to do with marketing considerations as functional design. Different manufacturers' measurement methods diverge wildly, and different-size frames of the same model can differ in riding characteristics. Because a particular model can change radically from year to year, with significant changes in geometry and components, looking at and riding the bike should be your final test.

Road-Touring and World-Touring Styles

Two main styles of bikes are sold for touring: "road-touring" bikes like the Trek 520 or Fuji Touring, which have frames that are variations of normal road bikes, usually equipped with drop handlebars; and "world-touring," or expedition-touring, bikes like the Novara Safari or the Thorn Raven, with frames derived from mountain bike frames, usually equipped with Euro touring bars (see Drawing 26 on page 188). The exact equipment on each style varies somewhat, and experienced tourists often choose equipment that mixes the two to reach some compromise set of characteristics. Road-touring bikes are generally preferred by those who spend most of their time on paved roads. World-touring models are chosen by cyclists with ambitions to travel in more remote surroundings.

Road-touring bikes:
> Cannondale Touring 1 and Touring 2
> Cannondale T800, T2000 (older models)
> Trek 520
> Fuji Touring
> Specialized Sequoia
> Specialized Sequoia Elite
> Specialized Tricross Sport
> Novara Randonee (from REI)
> Bianchi Volpe (up to 2007)
> Jamis Aurora
> Raleigh Sojourn
> Kona Sutra
> Terry Valkyrie Tour (women)

World-touring bike:
> Novara Safari (from REI)—a mountain bike with no front or rear suspension, aluminum frame, steel fork, disc brakes, a rear rack standard, and Euro touring handlebars

One possibility worth investigating is the small builder Surly Bikes, which generally fits into the semi-custom category (see "Custom and Semi-Custom Touring Bikes" later in this chapter). Surly Bikes makes frames but also sells some models as complete bikes. It is owned by and distributed through one of the largest bicycle component distributors in the United States. Many of its local dealers build up complete bikes, while experienced bike tinkerers use the frames to build their own. The Surly Long Haul Trucker has been widely praised as an excellent touring bike, comparable in performance to most of the semi-custom ones, but it is at the low end of the price range of the production bicycles mentioned above.

Most good bike shops can get Surlys, but it would be a rare shop that actually had the right size in stock

10. A semi-custom touring bike from Bruce Gordon.

so that you could try it out. With a little extra effort, you can get a Long Haul Trucker with excellent components at a price comparable to production bikes. The component set offered with the complete Surly is better than what is found on production bikes that cost significantly more.

Custom and Semi-custom Touring Bikes

Many longtime tourists are happy with the same stock bikes for tens of thousands of miles of touring, making only an occasional upgrade or repair to components. Others are constantly in search of the ideal bicycle, tinkering with outfitting and modifications, building up bicycles from acquired frames and parts, or seeking out the perfect touring machine from a custom or semi-custom builder.

The most important reason for going to a custom or semi-custom builder is that you can't find good fit in a stock frame or that you have a problem with chronic pain caused by a bad fit that can't be remedied with available adjustments. While such problems are not common, they do sometimes occur, even more for seasoned athletes than for beginners. If you are having some chronic problem, however, the problem is more likely to be something straightforward that can be identified by a good check of fit and remedied by changing the seat position, stem height or length, cleat position, or crank length.

Aesthetics are a major reason that some cyclists consider a semi-custom or custom bike. The design, lug work, and finishing of the best builders cannot be replicated in a production bike. This level of craftsmanship comes at a price, of course.

A few builders to consider:

Bruce Gordon
Rivendell Bicycle Works
Co-Motion
Zinn Cycles
Bob Jackson (British builder, imported by World Class Cycles)
Waterford Precision Cycles
Robert Beckman Designs (Sakkit bikes)
Tout Terrain Bikes (sold in the United States by Peter White Cycles)
Kogswell (The Porteur/Randonneur is an excellent touring frame and a good value, but you'll have to get your bike shop to build it up or do it yourself. Kogswell doesn't sell complete bikes. And the wheel size is unusual.)

Adapting a Club-Riding Bike

Should you adapt your club-riding bike for long tours? As always, of course, it depends.

If you have a bike that you enjoy riding on local rides during evenings and weekend days, your first thought when you decide to try touring will naturally be to use the bike you already have and enjoy riding. It is always possible to do this, but whether it is the best choice depends on a number of factors. If you want to start off with sub-24-hour overnight (S24O) trips like the ones suggested by the folks at Rivendell Bicycle Works, then you can certainly figure out a way to use your club-riding bike. Similarly, for supported rides, where you don't need to carry more than snacks, rain gear, and a few other lightweight items, your club-riding bike would not need any modification beyond possibly changing the gearing.

On the other hand, if you are working toward a transcontinental trip on which you are planning to camp, this may not be the optimum solution. It all depends on your finances, the kind of touring to which you aspire, what modifications you are willing to make to your fast, agile road bike, and so on. You also need to decide whether a bike that is comfortable on local rides will be fun to ride over long distances with the loads you are planning to carry. The section below is not intended to discourage you from using your current road bike, but it does raise some issues you should consider.

What Would You Have to Change?

The most important question you need to consider is whether the geometry and durability of your road bike are appropriate for the tours you want to do. Road bikes intended for racing or club riding generally have steeper angles, shorter seatstays, and more sensitive steering geometry than bicycles intended for long-distance touring. The weight of camping equipment may overstress the frame and will probably change the steering for the worse. Well-built frames have the steering geometry (head-tube angle, caster, trail, and fork flex) designed for a particular load and weight distribution. Touring loads will significantly change these factors.

Braze-on fittings. Most well-thought-out touring machines have braze-on bushings and other fittings for bar-end shifters, cantilever brakes, front and rear racks for panniers (eyelets on dropouts), preferably fenders, and as many water bottles as can be managed with the frame geometry. Most of these can be replaced with clamp-on substitutes, but collectively they point to some important design issues. For example, you may be limited in your choice of racks to those (like Old Man Mountain) that are designed for bikes without threaded fittings on the lugs and upper attachment points. Such racks may incorporate other design compromises like those intended to compensate for full-suspension mountain bikes. You can certainly find a rack that will work, but it may not be optimal. If your bike doesn't have braze-on fittings for mounting racks, you'll have to use clamps with some padding to try to avoid damaging the paint, and the load-carrying capacity will be lower than that of the best racks.

Chainstay length and rack-pannier clearance. Agile club-riding bikes nearly always have shorter chainstays to go with their generally tighter and more upright geometry. Aside from general geometry issues, this means that the rear rack and panniers will ride farther forward than they would on a frame designed for touring, and your heel may tend to hit the pannier. The remedies include using smaller rear panniers, finding panniers with a shape that cuts out the lower front corners, and mounting the panniers farther back on the rack. The last solution may allow the rear pannier corner to swing into the spokes under stress. As with the other issues presented here, these problems are not insoluble—some racks project farther to the rear than others—but they can be quite annoying, and solving them may be challenging.

Brakes and wheel clearance. This is probably the most fundamental issue. Frame design and geometry are fixed, and they determine the types of brakes that can be used, as well as tire and fender clearance. Most bikes intended for road racing or sport riding will have short-reach sidepull brakes (see Chapter 8) and narrow-profile 700C tires. There will not be enough clearance to change these significantly. Your tire choice will be limited, and you won't be able to mount fenders. This might work fine for credit-card touring or supported rides on good pavement, but it is unlikely to be suitable for carrying camping gear on rough roads.

Wheels. The wheels on most road bikes these days are marvels of strength and light weight; they are also aerodynamically efficient. However, they are not typically robust enough for many of the demands of touring. If they are traditional spoked wheels, rather than molded composite ones, they will probably use fairly light rims with 24, 28, or 32 spokes on each wheel. (American road riders typically stick to smooth pavement, and even European road races rarely include bone-jarring cobbles these days, except for a few of the classics.) Besides having extra strength, wheels with 36 or more spokes are easier to true temporarily on the road. (See "Fixing Broken Spokes" on page 238.) They are heavier, of course, and generate more air resistance. Wider rear hubs, which may be part of a well-designed touring bike, also make for slightly stronger wheels.

Gearing and shifting system. In line with the recommendations for gearing in Chapter 6, your club-riding bike will probably be geared too high for touring. You may, of course, choose not to agree with those suggestions. If you are young, ambitious, and fit, you can do fine with higher gears. If you are older and stubborn, you can at least pretend to do so. Nonetheless, the virtues of having really low gears when you are climbing long mountain grades with a full touring load should not be underestimated.

If you do want a wider and lower gear range, you need to seriously consider the complications of achieving them. Both front and rear derailleurs have built-in limitations both for the high- and low-gear sizes they can manage and for the total range they can handle. (The rear derailleur arm has to take up the slack in the chain that results from the difference between the highest and lowest gear combinations.) Shifters have complementary limitations, and of course indexed shifters have to be compatible with the chain, number of cogs, and cog spacing on the rear hub.

So, as an example, you might be very happy with the Campagnolo setup on your road bike, including the Campy Ergo combined brake lever and shifter (or "brifter") combination. But you might find that to get the gearing you want for touring, you have to go to Shimano components. And Shimano brifters work in the opposite direction from the Campy ones you're used to. So you either have to switch the levers and the way you are used to shifting or do a custom conversion that allows the Campy shifters to work with the Shimano rear derailleur. This specific incompatibility is offered simply as an illustration of the issues that can arise. Such changes are not cheap, and they may compromise your enjoyment of your road bike on regular rides.

You may be very happy doing some types of tours with minor modifications of your sport-riding bike–perhaps adding a lightweight rack and some panniers and substituting a rear cassette with a wider range. Just don't expect to end up with a bike that will easily carry full camping gear for a transcontinental trip or a month-long adventure in Patagonia.

Resurrecting Older Bikes and Frames

Many serious touring cyclists have either resurrected favorite old touring frames or purchased classic ones and built new bikes with them using modern components. Completing such a project can result in a great touring bike and be the source of enormous satisfaction. If you have the temperament and the time, this approach is heartily recommended. Unless you are already an experienced bicycle mechanic, however, don't plan on being able to do it quickly and inexpensively.

Consider that in addition to the problems mentioned above, you'll probably need to deal with obsolete components and mounting methods. You might have to bend the frame (cold-setting) to change the width between the rear dropouts, while ensuring that alignment remains good. You might need to have a frame builder attach new brazed-on fittings, which also will require repainting. And so on.

It is usually a delusion to think that you can save money this way, even if you ignore the value of your time. If you enjoy this sort of project, you will find it enormously satisfying, and you will always be able to fix your bike on the road in case of problems. But if you don't enjoy being a mechanic, ferreting out obscure information, and solving strange problems, trying to build a bike this way will not leave you with happy memories.

A possible exception is converting a used or obsolete mountain bike for touring, if the kind of touring you want to do calls for a mountain bike (see "A Secondhand Mountain Bike for Touring?" later in this chapter). If you know what to look for, you can often get a real bargain in a used mountain bike, particularly if you don't need or want full suspension. You may not have to replace too many components, and you will learn a lot along the way.

Before you decide to build or rebuild a bike, it is important to assess both your own abilities and all the actual work and parts that are needed. Many long-time bicycle tinkerers have boxes of accumulated spare parts, along with specialized tools and obscure skills. They know what to look for in purchasing a particular component on eBay. Working on a project like this is almost guaranteed to move you along the path to becoming a member of this group. But if you aren't already there, you need to start by investigating all the issues from stem to bottom bracket to derailleurs, so that you can make a realistic list of what you need and what has to be done. If that doesn't intimidate you, rebuilding a bike may actually be your cup of tea! (You'll still encounter a lot more issues along the way, however.) The Resources section at the end of the book will get you started on the nuances of cog compatibility, different bottom-bracket threads, and styles of headsets and stems.

In terms of the nitty-gritty details, one important consideration in repurposing older frames to modern touring is dropout spacing (see the illustration at www.sheldonbrown.com/frame-spacing.html). Frames that were originally built for five-cog freewheels can't just have new wheels with ten-cog freehub cassettes installed, because the latter are significantly wider. The details of all the possible permutations are far too complicated to review here, and if you are contemplating such a conversion, you should consult some of the references in the Resources section at the end of the book. In general, steel frames can be adjusted without too much worry to accommodate the wider hubs of modern equipment. If you are adventurous you can do it yourself; if you are more conservative, you can get someone competent to do it for you. Aluminum frames are in a different category. It is *not* safe to widen the dropout spacing of an aluminum frame—aluminum is simply not as malleable as steel.

Mountain Bikes and Their Kin

Mountain bikes have changed the face of bicycle touring in the three decades since they were introduced. Three influences in particular stand out:

First, mountain bikers who are interested in bicycle touring bring an entirely different perspective and set of experiences.

Second, mountain bikes are standard equipment for people interested in trekking through remote regions of the world, from Africa to Latin America to Siberia. While properly built and equipped road-style bikes can be used in these circumstances, mountain bikes are the natural choice, and models that are rugged enough to handle expedition cycling are relatively inexpensive. Tires are widely available worldwide. Such bikes—usually with no rear suspension, and often without front suspension—are typically known as expedition touring bikes or world-touring bikes.

Finally, components derived from the mass production of mountain bikes have filled important gaps on road bikes built for touring. Where well-designed gear combinations for road-style touring bikes used to be esoteric, hard-to-find equipment, they are now commonplace. Triple cranks used to be rare, but they are standard on mountain bikes, and derailleurs that handle wide gear ranges are now easy to find. Triples are usually supplied with smaller chainwheels than the cranksets on standard road bikes, making it easier to achieve the gear combinations ideal for touring.

Well-constructed cantilever brakes are another contribution of mountain bikes, even though mountain bikes now rarely use them. Well-designed cantilevers were initially produced for mountain bikes, and now they remain in production for touring bikes—the tooling costs have already been absorbed by the manufacturers, so the relatively small touring market can now benefit.

Other components were developed because mountain bikes exposed design weaknesses in older components—threadless headsets are an example.

There is no clear dividing line between road bikes and mountain bikes, nor should there be, except for the fluctuating distinctions in the typical retail lines. There are custom and semi-custom builders who make rugged road bikes that can be ridden on rough trails. Bikes built for cyclocross racing have affinities both with standard road bikes and with standard mountain bikes. Many touring cyclists who commonly ride on old towpaths, dirt roads, and converted railroad grades, such as the fine trail systems in Quebec and Missouri, prefer mountain bikes to road models.

There are also innumerable hybrids. Some tourists have modified full-suspension mountain bikes for the road, contending that suspension and wider tires make for much more comfortable touring and are far better suited to dealing with road hazards. Bicycle tourists are a diverse, innovative, and opinionated group. There are lots of good solutions to the challenges of touring, and the varying opinions on the best approaches provide fodder for animated discussions with other cyclists.

Basic Differences between Mountain Bikes and Road Bikes

Even though it's possible to mix and match components to get just the right bike for your own preferences, and though some touring cyclists ride road bikes on single-track back-country trails, there are quite a few differences between the components normally found on road bikes and those on mountain bikes. This section discusses a few of them.

Handlebars, brake levers, and shifters. Handlebars on mountain bikes are usually nearly straight (see Drawing 26 on page 188). This results in a normal riding position similar to riding on conventional dropped bars with the hands in the center or on the brake hoods, but with the hands spread a little wider. Many mountain bikers and most tourists who use straight bars add bar-end extensions to provide an additional riding position and better leverage for climbing. Other variations are discussed in Chapter 9.

Because of the different handlebar shape, brake levers and shifters are mounted and designed differently, and they are often parts of a single apparatus on each end of the bar. Note that because they typically use a different style of handlebars, mountain bikes normally have longer top tubes than similarly sized road bikes.

Wheels and tires. Most mountain bikes have 26-inch wheels, which are always initially equipped with fairly wide knobby tires designed for inflation of 60 to 70 psi.* This combination is fine for basic trail riding, but both serious single-track riders and tourists will typically change them to tires more specifically suited to their needs. See Chapter 7 for a more detailed discussion of tires.

Gear range. Mountain bikes are more likely than road bikes to come equipped with a gear range suitable for touring, because of their intended use. The smallest chainwheel is likely to be a real granny gear, and the

---

* Some mountain bikes these days feature "29-inch" wheels. This is a marketing name for 700C wheels on a mountain bike. The rims of 29ers are wider than 700C road rims. The term is unrelated to the wheel size of the old 29-inch utility bikes.

highest gears will be lower than what's typically found on stock road bikes. The shifting system is likely to have been designed for a wide range of gears, so even if you want to swap out a couple of gears, this will often be straightforward.

Brakes. Stock high-end mountain bikes are most likely to be equipped with disc brakes and low-end ones with V-type brakes (see Chapter 8 for a discussion of brake types). These are both eminently suitable for touring. Disc brakes are more of a concern if repairs are needed in remote locales, but they are less problematic than suspension systems.

Frame differences. Frame-sizing issues are similar to those encountered with road bikes, but mountain bikes are usually designed so that the standover height is lower than with a similar-size road frame, because mountain bikers encounter more variable terrain, so frame designers employ slanted top tubes more commonly than they would with a road frame. Mountain bikes are usually made with fewer frame sizes. These characteristics make it easier for smaller people to find bikes that fit, but they also make it easier to mistakenly buy a frame that only seems to fit. Make sure you check the fit just as carefully as you would with a road bike.

Suspension (shock-absorbing) systems. While suspension systems are rare on road bikes in the United States, they are very common on mountain bikes. (One sees them frequently on touring and commuting bikes in parts of Europe where cobbled streets are common.) Front-suspension systems (shock absorbers on the fork blades) are ubiquitous on medium-quality mountain bikes, and rear-suspension systems are increasingly standard on high-quality models. Whether this is a good thing depends a lot on the kind of touring you want to do.

Most mountain bikers who like to ride technical trails prefer full-suspension bikes. A bike with a good-quality full-suspension system and appropriate tires

11. A mountain bike set up for touring on rugged terrain. This one is equipped with rear panniers. The shock-absorbing fork (front suspension) is incompatible with most front racks. The rider wears a hydration pack.

can be ridden directly into a 7-inch rock step or log and will climb over it readily without the rider having to make a significant effort to lift the wheel. Traction is better on loose surfaces, and riding on rough trails is far more comfortable and efficient.

Mounting panniers is problematic on bikes with suspension systems, though some of the newer racks available for mountain bikes may make it easier. At the time this second edition was written, the best racks were made by Old Man Mountain. Their sizes and mounting systems are specifically intended for mountain bikes. However, there is enormous variation in the frames of full-suspension mountain bikes, so you'll have to determine whether there are any racks and panniers that can be successfully fitted to the bike you are considering. These difficulties are one reason why many tourists who use mountain bikes are firm advocates of using trailers for carrying luggage (see "Trailers" on page 289). Others travel very light, using a rear rack bag, a set of small panniers, or a saddlebag, along with a light backpack.

Cyclists who are more interested in long-distance travel than in bicycling on technical trails use mountain bikes without any suspension or with front shocks only (known as "hard tails" in the mountain bike community). Compromises that provide some shock absorption are special stems and seat posts with shock absorption built in, such as the Softride Powerstem and the Cane Creek Thudbuster seat post. Shock-absorbing seat posts are still readily available, but shock-absorbing stems are no longer popular, so they are hard to find and fit. (Some Thudbuster models are designed for moderate travel and are suited for touring, while the longer-travel models are intended for mountain biking on very rough trails.)

For serious mountain bikers, the quality of suspension systems has increased dramatically in the last few years. Modern shocks are adjustable for many variables. These systems are heavy and expensive, and a thorough discussion is far beyond the scope of this book; they are also changing at a rapid rate. For touring, however, it is always important to consider what can go wrong, what you can do about problems in the field, and whether the advantages are worth the potential problems. Full-suspension mountain bikes are not recommended for touring because of repair problems, but there are many mountain bikers who would disagree.

A Secondhand Mountain Bike for Touring?

Tons of mountain bikes have been produced over the last 15 years, including many that are of very high quality. Many have hardly been used, having spent years collecting dust in garages, and many others have been replaced by more up-to-date models, as equipment has changed and avid riders have upgraded to newer bikes.

Thus, while good touring bikes are not exactly plentiful on the secondhand market, decent mountain bikes are common, and they can often be acquired at bargain prices. You have to be willing to do a little research in exchange for getting a good price.

Mountain bikes make good choices for those who are interested in the style of touring in which they excel, such as expedition-style trips to remote locations, rides in areas where there are a lot of unpaved roads and towpaths, or moderate trails. Serious mountain bikers who like to ride technical terrain are not likely to be happy with an older bike that is not equipped with full suspension and disc brakes. For many types of touring, however, this deficiency is an advantage rather than a hindrance. If you are headed to remote areas in Asia or Latin America, the risk of malfunction associated with modern, complex components should be taken quite seriously.

For touring mainly on the road, some cyclists prefer the slightly more forgiving ride and upright riding posture of a mountain bike, particularly if it is equipped with low-rolling-resistance tires. The best news is that the most suitable expedition touring bikes are old-fashioned hard-tail bikes that most of today's mountain bikers are anxious to dump. This provides a great opportunity for someone looking for a high-quality touring bike.

In judging the quality of an older mountain bike, online research can be useful. Various specialty sites are run by fans of particular makes of bicycles. One clue for the garage-sale shopper is the quality of the bike's component set. If the bike was originally equipped with one of the better-quality component sets from Shimano, for example, those components are likely to have held up well, barring serious abuse, and they are also probably indicators that the frame is of good quality. Bike manufacturers don't pay for top-of-the-line component sets to put on mediocre frames.

Obviously, with a secondhand purchase, it is important to both ride the bike and check it out mechanically. If you aren't adept enough to check the bike fairly thoroughly, it is worth taking it to a bike mechanic to have it checked out. You need to look for dimples in the frame that might signal a crash, verify the frame alignment, check all the bearings for problems, and examine the cogs for wear that can be caused by a worn (stretched) chain. Such cogs have to be replaced, along with the chain and possibly the chainwheels.

In the typical garage-sale bike, having to scrub a lot of mud off the frame should reduce the price but not be a cause for concern. However, rusted wheel bearings mean that you have to replace the hubs, which is not an inexpensive proposition. Take your tools to the garage sale if you're shopping for a bike.

In terms of features, on an older bike you definitely don't want rear suspension. It is likely to cause trouble. Shocks on the fork are more typical on an older bike, but you should check to see whether the fork can be replaced at a reasonable price, should that become necessary. With the rapid changes in production components, this is not always easy. For example, newer bikes and forks are designed for 1⅛-inch threadless headsets. Older ones use threaded headsets or 1-inch threadless ones (and sometimes other sizes). Forks and stems are not interchangeable between these variations.

You should be aware that mountain bikes have significantly shorter chainstays than do road bikes, especially touring bikes, so equipping a mountain bike with racks and panniers will probably require getting equipment made specifically for mountain frames, and this may dictate more expensive racks and luggage. The racks are likely to have weight capacities that are lower than the best standard touring racks. These issues are more likely to plague tall cyclists with large feet. None of these limitations is serious, but you should be aware of them if you decide to build your touring bike from an older mountain bike. Mountain bikes, except for special expedition models, hardly ever have a full complement of braze-ons for touring accessories, but some at least have eyelets on the rear drop-outs for racks, and this is a positive feature. Any other braze-ons and bushings, as discussed above, are helpful in converting the bike for touring.

Finally, older mountain bikes typically use integrated brake-and-shifter systems that have to be replaced completely if anything is broken or if you want to install a wider gear range on an indexed system (for example, from a 7-speed cassette to a 10-speed one). This is not terribly hard to do, but you need to consider it when you are calculating your final cost.

Tandems

Tandems constitute another specialized group of bikes that is discussed only briefly here. Many touring cyclists are dedicated tandem riders; however, because their numbers are small, quality tandems are expensive.

A tandem is usually a diamond-frame bike with an elongated front triangle and a seat tube for the front rider (the captain) crossing and bracing the front triangle. A bottom tube connects the two bottom brackets. Both riders pedal using the same drive train, so they have to pedal at the same cadence. The front rider typically has a single chainwheel on the left side of the crankset, which connects to a single chainwheel on the left side of the rear crankset. At the right of the rear crankset is a conventional triple set of chainwheels. Shifters and brake levers both have to be in front so that it is possible for one person to ride the bike alone and still operate all the controls.

A lot of tandem components need to be stronger than those on single bikes. Wheels are customarily built with more and heavier spokes and sturdier, wider rims. Many tandems were equipped with disc brakes long before they became common on mountain bikes.

A high-quality tandem touring bike can cost two or three times what a comparable single bike would. Most people won't get one as a first touring bike, and it's wise for two people considering tandem touring to first do some tours together on separate bikes.

In general, tandem riders gain a lot of efficiency on flatlands, because they have two people providing power but wind resistance is not much greater than that experienced by a single rider. Tandems encounter more of a challenge climbing hills than do single riders, and on descents they need good brakes and technique. For couples, tandem touring can be a great experience, but it can also seriously test a relationship. Some couples happily tour together for years but wisely decide that separate bikes work best.

If you want to familiarize yourself with tandems, some good places to start are at www.thetandemlink .com, www.tandemclub.org, and www.co-motion.com, the site of Co-Motion Cycles, which makes some of the best tandem machines. There are lots of good photos and tandem-trip narratives at several of the sites listed in the Resources section in the back of the book, such as Crazyguyonabike (www.crazyguyonabike.com).

Folding and Take-Apart Bikes

Many tourists have been great fans of folding bikes since their introduction into the market; many others think that folders are nice for some commuting and other specialized uses but are unenthusiastic about using folding bikes for real touring. Take-apart bikes come with the same options included on standard touring bikes, but they can be taken apart and put back together with S&S couplers or other mechanisms. These systems give you a fairly portable, high-performance, but expensive bike that can be taken apart and put in a medium-sized traveling case that usually can be brought along as standard luggage.

Folding Bikes

Folding bikes, also called "folders," have been made by a number of companies over the years, and many that haven't been manufactured for over a decade still have aficionados. All use smaller wheels than conventional 700C road bikes or 26-inch mountain bikes. For the rider of the folding bike, this can mean that the ride will be more jarring when going over small bumps in the pavement, because, everything else being equal, smaller-diameter wheels drop into depressions that larger wheels manage to span. Some folders incorporated high-pressure tires and suspension systems to deal with this problem long before suspension systems were used on mountain bikes. (The original bicycle-suspension design was part of the 1962 Moulton bicycle, which used small wheels with high-pressure tires and paved the way for folding bikes of similar design.)

In general, folding bikes suitable for touring are more expensive than roughly comparable standard frames. They also have some inherent disadvantages, as in braking on steep downhill runs, where they are less stable than conventional frames. Tires may be available only from specialized dealers, as are many other components. However, the best folding bikes are very good touring bikes, so they should be considered as viable alternative machines for touring cyclists.

Types of folders. Folding bikes can be categorized in a number of ways. One is simply to consider the ease of folding and the folded size. Naturally, bikes with smaller wheels and tires can be constructed to fold into a more compact size. The longtime standard in the 16-inch-wheel, very-compact size is the Brompton bike, designed and built in England. The Brompton bike has suspension systems and a range of models all the way up to full-titanium touring frames with a variety of accessories, gearing, and luggage. Birdy bikes, made in Germany, use 18-inch* wheels and have

---

* The sizes listed in the text are the terms commonly used by the manufacturers and by enthusiasts, which conceal a host of incompatibilities. *Most* Bike Fridays use ISO 406 mm wheels, which is the same size used on BMX bikes, so tires are available worldwide. This is also true of *most* Dahons. Bromptons use ISO 349 mm tires and Birdys 355. You should not purchase a folder unless you know what the wheel/tire size really is and what the availability of tires is. These issues are inevitable for specialty bikes, and they don't reflect badly on folding-bike makers. You must consider the same issues with a manufacturer like Kogswell, which uses 650B tires, also not widely available.

full-suspension frames at a little lower price than the Brompton bike.

The next size up uses 20-inch wheels, and many enthusiastic users feel that the better bikes in this category make quite good touring bikes. Though you can't count on finding tires of this size (especially high-quality ones) at a shop along the road, a wide variety is available from Web sources. The most commonly recommended bicycles of this size are those from Bike Friday, which offers bikes with a variety of options, generally starting at a price range a little above a high-quality conventional production touring bike. The most common model chosen by touring cyclists is the New World Tourist, but all new Fridays are assembled to customer specifications. Because of Bike Friday's popularity, there are many used models available, as well as a lot of accessories. Bike Fridays fold very easily and will fit in readily available (and cheap) suitcases for air travel. That is, you don't have to buy a custom case—you can buy the bike and find a relatively inexpensive hard-sided suitcase to carry it.

Also in the 20-inch-wheel category are a host of other manufacturers, the largest being Dahon, which makes some bikes that are quite suitable for touring and others that are not. (Dahon also has models with smaller and larger wheels, but the great majority has 20-inch wheels.) Some 24-inch folders, like the Airnimal, are quite nice—and quite pricey. The 24-inch folders usually cannot fit in a standard luggage bag for air travel without having the wheels removed. That is, if you get a folder with larger than 20-inch wheels, don't count on being able to take it on airlines without an extra charge, unless you're willing to spend more time in the disassembly-reassembly process, as with the take-apart bikes discussed later in this chapter.

Choosing a folder. People are interested in folding bikes for many reasons, and the criteria are often incompatible. The principal design issue is whether easy, quick folding is the most important feature, or whether the quality of the ride takes precedence. Many folders are purchased mainly for commuting—a bike you can use to ride to the bus or the train, that will quickly fold, and that will fit under your desk in the office.

For readers of this book, the greatest advantage of a folder is that you can pack it easily in a piece of luggage that you can carry as checked baggage on a plane without paying oversize charges, then take it out at your destination and use it for enjoyable touring. For this purpose the packed size is important, but the speed of folding and unfolding is not so critical. And if you really want to be able to tour at your destination, the bike should ride well and be able to carry whatever luggage you need for touring.

While you can come up with reasonable compromises between these somewhat contradictory requirements, it is important to decide what your main needs are before you go folder shopping. This book naturally emphasizes touring requirements. A related requirement is the gear range. Many commuters don't need much of a shifting range, whereas for a folder that you are going to use for touring, the requirements are the same as for any touring bike—with the exact gears adjusted for smaller wheel size.

In general, you should look at the Bike Friday, because it meets many of the touring-end folder requirements, has a wide and enthusiastic user community, and provides excellent support and a wide range of touring options. Even if you don't get a Friday, you'll be able to compare other offerings if you've familiarized yourself with the Friday—see the Web site at www.bikefriday.com. Besides making very good folding bikes for touring, Bike Friday provides excellent support and information, whereas some folder companies don't bother.

Dahon makes a wide variety of bikes, and some of their models are very suitable for touring and reasonably priced, but their support is reported to be marginal at best. If you are interested in a Dahon, take a look at www.travelbybike.com. This is a small shop specializing in Dahon bikes that has lots of information about touring and is strongly oriented to customer service.

As noted earlier, tire sizes are a confusing mish-mash of seemingly definitive numbers that really conceal a mass of contradictions. This is particularly problematic with folders, because they use less-common sizes. You should consider the availability of tires for your folder before buying one. Twenty-inch (ISO 406) tires are the most widely available and have the largest selection, because they are the most common BMX tires. Knowing that you can obtain replacement tires only from the company store is not a comforting thought as you nurse a bad tire while pedaling toward the nearest town somewhere in South Asia. Of course you should carry spares, but you have to carry more if the size is unusual, and having to take along a bunch of tires reduces the advantages of a compact folder.

Note also that folders, because they have small wheel sizes, generally need better-quality tires than conventional bikes. This is because folders need better-quality sidewalls to compensate for smaller diameters while maintaining the same performance. Thus, if you rely on local supply in case of problems, you'll be better off with a commonly available 26-inch replacement than a 20-inch one when buying a low-quality replacement somewhere in Latin America, for example. This is not a critical issue, but it is one you should understand.

Take-Apart Bikes

The old-timer of take-aparts, which is often listed among folders, is the Moulton, but it does not actually fold. Moultons are very popular among their advocates, but the Moulton is more a high-performance (and high-priced) compact bicycle than a folder.

More recently, many high-end builders have begun to offer couplers as an option for their best bicycles. Various schemes have been used over the years to allow frames to be disassembled, but with the advent of S&S couplers this can finally be done without compromising either the performance or the strength of the frame. This is a triumph of technology. When the first edition of this book was written, other coupling systems existed, but none was remotely comparable in performance or reliability to S&S couplers.

Whether a take-apart bike is worthwhile or not depends completely on your needs and finances. If it is a feature you want and can easily afford, it may be an easy choice. However, if you are getting a custom touring bike built and are trying to decide whether the feature is worthwhile in terms of expense and convenience, the choice is more complicated.

From a strictly monetary point of view, a bike with couplers that will fit into airline-legal standard baggage saves you a surcharge with every flight. If you only sometimes fly with your bike, you probably will not save enough in baggage surcharges to pay for the couplers. If you take your bike on a lot of trips, the extra cost may be saved in a year or two. But with the airlines constantly changing luggage rules and surcharges, spending a thousand dollars for a (currently) airline-legal solution may seem less an investment than a spin of the roulette wheel.

Adding S&S couplers to an existing bike has a lot of complications, so consider the points below and then talk to the bike builder who would do the work. For a new custom or semi-custom bike, you need to consider the advantages and disadvantages:

- S&S couplers add significantly to a bike's price. As of this book's publication, it costs more than $600 to add the feature—significantly more for titanium frames and tandems. This premium is going up all the time.

- More is involved than the couplers alone. For a take-apart frame, all cable paths—shifting and brakes—have to separate, which entails extra bosses, extra hardware, and complications during disassembly and assembly.

- A bike that separates using couplers takes longer to disassemble and reassemble than a folding bike or a conventional bike that has been broken down enough to fit in a bike box. The inconvenience this imposes is a matter of subjective judgment. For some it is a huge task; for others it is a minor inconvenience.

- Hard cases for carrying disassembled take-apart bikes are not cheap, and you have to be able to store them at your destination or ship them to the endpoint if you are ending the tour at a different location. If you are flying into a city, staying in a hotel, and doing a circuit tour that ends in the same place, this is not a big problem—you just store the case in the hotel baggage room or some equivalent. If you are returning from a different location, you may be better off paying a supplementary air charge for a cardboard bike box, throwing it away, and finding another bike box at the end of the trip in which to send your bike back.

So, as with many other bike choices, there is no universal answer as to whether a take-apart bike has major advantages. It depends on your individual circumstances.

Recumbent Bicycles and Trikes

These kinds of bikes make up another specialized group that can only be touched on here. This is particularly true because of the wide range of recumbent designs, each with strong partisans among the limited group of recumbent riders.

The basic idea of the recumbent is that the rider is positioned low, in a more aerodynamic posture than on a standard bike. This is an uncontestable point, but most of the other advantages of recumbents are matters of significant disagreement. For example, recumbent advocates argue that the position of the recumbent rider allows him or her to use the large leg muscles more efficiently, but many cyclists who have used both recumbents and standard bikes extensively do not agree. None of these disagreements is new. Recumbents were made and advocated at the same time as the development of the "safety bicycle" in the Victorian era.

Different recumbent designs, which have different handling characteristics, impose different stresses on the body and have many other subtle advantages and disadvantages. Even the few shops that specialize in recumbents are rarely experts in all models and makers, and some highly touted models are no longer made, so they can only be purchased second-hand. There are models that are *long wheelbase* (LWB), *compact long wheelbase* (CLWB), and *short wheelbase* (SWB—not usually used for touring). The location and arrangement of steering and controls varies. Possibilities for carrying luggage vary.

Recumbents are less visible to drivers. The rider is typically below the field of view of a driver looking across the passenger side. A flag is essential and helps enormously, but visibility can still be a problem. (Many recumbent and trike riders would contend that with a flag they are as visible as a bike, and that drivers, for whatever reason, give them room and are less inclined to drive too close. Whether visibility is a problem is therefore another issue on which opinions differ.)

Trikes are made with a single steering wheel in the front (delta configuration) or in the back (tadpole configuration). Trikes have the advantage of not requiring the rider to balance on long hill climbs, so with appropriate gearing they can be ridden very slowly. All recumbents and trikes are less vulnerable to wind gusts than standard touring bikes. Trikes have the additional attribute of being wider, so that the rider has to take possession of the lane more frequently.

The most highly charged controversies comparing trikes and recumbents with conventional bikes tend to be over comfort, their relative tendencies to cause overuse injuries, and related issues. Many recumbent riders find that "bents," as recumbents are commonly termed by their fans, are much easier on their backs, necks, and hands than standard frames. Other cyclists have reported that recumbents have resulted in back injuries.

There is really no single correct answer to the advantages/disadvantages dispute. People's bodies and training are different, as are the techniques that have been used to fit their bikes of whatever style. Those who have had trouble achieving a comfortable ride for long tours after making significant efforts to get a good fit and to train properly may want to try recumbents as a possible solution. There is a strong community of advocates who believe recumbents to be the answer to everything from numbness in the hands to neck and back pain to stock market fluctuations. There are some specific injuries and disabilities that may dictate a recumbent (in many cases a trike) as the only possibility for bicycle touring.

A good place to get some background (from a decidedly pro-recumbent point of view) is at www.recumbentcyclistnews.com. For varied opinions, pro and con, do a search on "recumbent" at the touring list archive, accessible at search.bikelist.org. For one good journal example of a long recumbent touring trip, take a look at Andrew and Joanne Hooker's tales at www.where2pedalto.com. Another source of useful information is www.calhouncycle.com.

Also bear in mind that riding skills are somewhat different, as is training. If you are switching to a recumbent, you'll have to learn basic bike-handling skills all over again. Depending on the speed at which you adapt, this may take a week or more. From stopping at intersections to braking, emergency maneuvers, and mountain descents, the skills are a little different. The balance of muscle strength and endurance is also different, so you need to allow time for conditioning to a new activity.

5

Frames

If you've already figured out from the preceding chapter how you will go about buying your touring bike, you may not care about the nuances of tubing types, materials, and frame geometry. In that case, you could skim this chapter and rely on your local shop, your judgment of the bike's ride (based on test rides), and the reputation of the manufacturer, rather than worrying about the details of frame geometry and materials. Chapter 10 covers bike fit in detail, so make sure you take time to read it closely—you'll be glad you did.

Nevertheless, because the frame is the most important part of the bike, you may want to learn more about how it works and is constructed, even if you aren't quite ready to specify your own frame geometry. Besides, frames are a topic of endless discussion when cyclists get together, so having a little knowledge may be a worthwhile social skill. This chapter is an introduction to bicycle-frame design with an emphasis on touring requirements.

If you are spending the money and effort to get a semi-custom or custom-made bike, you're paying for and should rely on the expertise of the frame builder. He or she knows more about the nuances of putting together a good bike than you or I will ever know. Most importantly, a good frame builder knows how to measure for fit and how to evaluate what you need based on

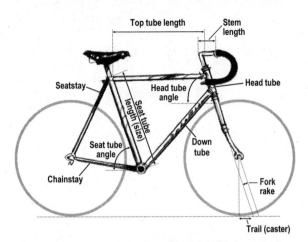

12. Frame measurements and geometry for a traditional road-touring bike. Note that manufacturers measure dimensions differently, so don't assume that nominal sizes and measurements are comparable between bike makers or are identical to those shown here. Stem length (reach) is measured horizontally, regardless of the angle of the stem extension.

your style of riding, body type, training, and personal preference. The only associated caveat is that you must tell your frame builder what kind of riding you actually do or are about to do, rather than what your fantasy persona would do. It is also important for the frame builder to have an interest in and knowledge of touring bikes.

We'll concentrate on traditional diamond frames made of steel tubing. I then briefly discuss alternative materials, and finally some of the common variations in geometry. The design considerations discussed at the beginning apply equally to frames built with steel, aluminum, titanium, or composites like carbon fiber. The specialized bikes mentioned in Chapter 4—tandems, folding bikes, recumbents, and trikes—are not considered in this chapter.

Frame Geometry

Over the years, many geometries for bicycle frames have been tried, but modern touring bikes typically use one of just two types: either the standard diamond frame or

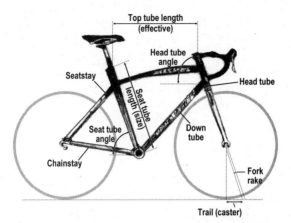

13. Frame measurements and geometry for a road-touring bike with compact geometry. The most obvious difference from the more conventional frame shown in Drawing 12 is that *effective* top tube length is required for comparison with other frames. Fork rake in the frame shown is achieved by angling the blades from the crown, rather than bending the ends forward. Most mountain bikes use compact geometry.

a variation that features a sloping top tube. This configuration is usually referred to as "compact geometry." The two types are illustrated in Drawings 12 and 13.

The Diamond Frame

The basic configuration of the single-rider bicycle frame (as shown in Drawing 12) has remained nearly the same for a long time, and it continues as the basis of most modern bikes, with a few variations that are discussed later in this chapter. Many alternatives have been tried, but most touring bikes still use the traditional diamond frame—originally known as the safety bicycle (see Drawing 1 on page 4), as designs evolved from the earlier "ordinaries" or "big wheels" (see Drawing 16 on page 119).* The same diamond-frame

---

* Fans of recumbent bikes note that this dominance is at least partly the result of arbitrary rules. Shortly after a world speed record was set on a recumbent in the 1930s, the UCI—the governing body of bicycle racing—ruled that a recumbent wasn't a bicycle, so it wasn't legal for racing or records.

design, developed at the end of the nineteenth century, is used in most of the bikes ridden today in the Tour de France and the European classics (prestigious races run over traditional routes), as well as most touring bikes or road bikes used for club riding. This frame geometry provides a great deal of strength where it is needed while using minimal materials and providing a practical and efficient riding position.

The traditional configuration is built around a front triangle formed by the seat tube, which goes from the seat at the top to the bottom-bracket shell at the bottom; the top tube, which connects the seat tube with the head tube; and the down tube, which goes down and back from the head tube to the bottom-bracket shell. This front triangle supports the rider and connects with the steerer and the fork holding the wheel at the front, the bottom bracket holding the cranks and pedals at the bottom, and the rear triangle(s) holding the rear, or drive, wheel at the back.

The bottom-bracket shell forms the lower apex of both the main and the rear triangles, and the head tube truncates the main triangle at the front between the top tube and the down tube. (Note that both the head tube and the bottom-bracket shell provide rigid tubes in which bearings are mounted for rotating components—the fork and the crank axle, respectively.) The rear triangle of the diamond frame actually consists of two triangles, one on either side of the back wheel, each sharing the seat tube as the leading side, and comprising the seatstays and the chainstays on the two trailing sides. Each apex of the seatstay–chainstay triangle is joined by a rear dropout, which forms a joint and provides a mounting bracket for the rear-wheel axle plus—on the right side—the rear derailleur.

The differences between most standard frames are subtle. A novice would not see much difference between a touring frame, a road-racing frame used in the Tour de France, and a track bike used for sprints on steep oval racing tracks. The seat tube for any of these should be longer for a taller rider, and the lengths of other tubes should be sized to fit the rider, to provide

rigidity where it is needed, and to meet other requirements. All the dimensions, including invisible tubing
thicknesses and material selection, work together to
produce the riding characteristics of the frame—which
obviously need to be quite different for each of the
bikes mentioned—and to mount equipment (the track
bike doesn't need brakes or derailleurs).

Frame Components and Some Factors
Affecting Frame Dimensions

The obvious assumption is that in building frames for
larger or smaller riders, one simply needs to scale the
frame up or down, changing all the dimensions proportionally. However, things are really much more
complicated than that. Consider just a few examples of
the constraints and complications:

Most obviously, the rider needs to be able to straddle the top tube with a few centimeters of clearance to
avoid crushing delicate body parts. She or he should
also be able to pedal comfortably and efficiently from
a seat height that is within the range of adjustment,
using cranks of appropriate length.

Wheels come in a few discrete sizes, and for a
standard racing or club-riding bike using short-reach
sidepull brakes (see "Sidepull Brakes" on page 171),
the distance from the front dropouts to the fork crown
is determined mostly by the wheel and tire size, as
is the distance from the rear dropouts to the bridge
between the seatstays. The clearances can be increased
somewhat by the designer, but wheel size is always a
critical constraint. Wheel size constraints are especially
problematic for touring bikes because odd tire and rim
sizes can't be found in remote locations.

To fit the rider, the distance between the seat and
the top of the handlebars has to be just right. Ignoring
exact seat positioning and head-tube angle for the
moment, this distance is the sum of the top tube
length (as shown in Drawing 12 on page 86) and the
distance that the stem extension projects beyond the
head tube, a total measurement known as *reach*. This

means that the top tube length is constrained by the upper body size of the rider. A person with a short torso (compared to leg length), like most women, needs a shorter top tube, and a person with a longer torso needs a longer one. Thirty years ago this problem was ignored, but it is extremely important. Very long or short stem extensions and extreme seat positioning were formerly used to compensate for mismatches, but today's riders will no longer put up with such ill-fitting frames. (Basically, frames were built to the proportions of typical male European racers, and all bike sizes had the same top-tube length. Stems, seat tubes, and head tubes were lengthened or shortened to "fit" riders of different sizes.)

If the top tube is too long, the rider will have to stretch out, his or her arms will be overextended, and too much weight will rest on the hands and the locked elbows. The rider's back and neck will be unnaturally contorted, and road shocks will travel up the straight arms to the shoulder muscles. These misalignments will cause pain and can result in chronic injuries, particularly for touring cyclists who ride many miles day after day.

If the top tube is too short, the rider's torso will be bent excessively and will project ahead, the overall center of gravity will be too far forward, and the bike's handling will be degraded. The rider will also have to crane his or her neck up for visibility or will look mainly at the pavement below. Neither the neck pain nor the accidents that result are acceptable. If these deficiencies are compensated for with an excessively long stem reach, bike handling will be adversely affected.

For an optimum frame, tube dimensions and the resultant stiffness need to change in order for heavier or stronger riders to experience the same handling characteristics as lighter, more diminutive riders. Thicker tubes or tubes with larger diameters, and tube-wall thickness extending farther from frame joints, result in stiffer, stronger frames. (However, if walls are too thick, they result in harsh, punishing, unresponsive frames.)

If the seat tube is lengthened for a rider with longer legs and the angles of the seat tube and the head tube are maintained, the head tube will be significantly longer, changing the flex and stiffness of the main triangle. This change will also affect steering.

Special Considerations for Women

The frame builder must also consider many other types of constraints and interactions. For example, a bike with 700C wheels that fits and has good handling characteristics is impossible to design for small women, particularly a touring bike. Georgena Terry, who is deservedly famous as a designer of bicycles for women, therefore uses 24-inch (ISO 520) front wheels for smaller frames. Other dimensions and angles have to change accordingly to enable proper handling.

Lennard Zinn, who is known for designing bikes both for women of all sizes and for especially tall riders, has built bikes with similar variations. Both Terry and Zinn sponsored women's racing teams for many years and had the opportunity to fine-tune their designs for riders who did not fit the prejudices of earlier prestigious frame builders. (The tradition of the European frame-building masters was that if you didn't have the body proportions of Jacques Anquetil or Eddy Merckx—well-known European cycling champions— you didn't deserve to have a bike that fit!) As a result, Terry and Zinn bikes became legendary among women cyclists. A few of the mass manufacturers have recently started to follow their design precepts.

The interactions among the various subtle changes in shape, along with tubing and other specifications, are extremely complex, and they are all interdependent. Guidelines mentioned later in this chapter are therefore very rough. Master frame builders spend their entire careers learning to balance these and other factors. This chapter merely mentions a few of the considerations that go into the design and construction of the perfect frame.

Important Frame Design Considerations

The bicycle's basic design really is amazingly efficient: the bicycle frame easily carries a load ten times its weight with strength to spare. Its exact structure is always a compromise, however, and many of the arguments about bike design result primarily from disagreements concerning which features should predominate. The characteristics most desired in bike design are that (1) the bike support the rider in the optimum position for delivering power; (2) as much power as possible be translated into forward motion, rather than being dissipated in rear-end whip and other deflections; (3) road shocks be cushioned; and (4) the bike be both maneuverable and stable, even with touring loads. Clearly, the touring frame must be strong enough to support the rider and any luggage with no danger of failure on bumpy mountain roads or after tens of thousands of miles of cumulative road shocks.

What Doesn't Matter

Compromises among these features are inescapable in any specific design, but a design may also be influenced by prejudices that aren't truly relevant to the function of the machine. For touring cyclists, the problematic biases relate to features that may be desirable for racers or serious sport riders, but that compromise durability, load-carrying capacity, and comfort for long tours. Some of those biases aren't even always well advised for high-performance road riding.

One example is the common misconception surrounding the idea of stiffness. A stiff frame, in the positive sense, refers to one that has a lot of side-to-side rigidity in the rear end, so that there is little whip as the rider pushes down hard on the pedals, particularly when power is needed for hill climbing or for sprinting during a race. Another advantage to a low-whip rear end is that it is less susceptible to accidental gear shifts due to sideways movement of the dropouts and rear derailleur.

Unfortunately, the same qualities that contribute to rigidity, and thus to a more efficient transfer of power, also tend to make the bike transmit the bumps of the road directly to the cyclist's body. Consequently, some riders influenced by current racing and sport-riding fashions irrationally seek a harsh, uncomfortable ride, because a "stiff" frame is identified with high performance. The desirable feature is not the harsh ride but rather the efficient power transfer. In fact, some frames that have a very harsh ride are not particularly efficient, so the rider of such frames gets the worst of both worlds—an uncomfortable ride and poor power transfer.

What Does Matter

Some genuinely desirable characteristics do entail clear-cut choices to be made by the rider from the beginning. For example, it is always desirable for a bike to track straight if you ride with your hands off the handlebars. It is also essential for the rider to be able to maneuver a bike well. The criterium racer or points racer on the track, who must make tight turns at high speed while maneuvering within a pack of riders, needs a bike that can turn on a dime and is very responsive to the rider. Such a rider doesn't care much whether the bike can be easily kept on course with relaxed and casual steering—she or he wants stability at speed but will not be relaxed and casual while maneuvering in a pack at 20 to 40 miles per hour.

If you are a tourist, however, you need very different steering characteristics. You don't want a bike that needs constant attention to the steering. You want to be able to ride down the road with your hands in the middle of the bars and look at the scenery without the bike tending to turn into a ditch in response to the slightest variation in the pavement. There is a definite difference, therefore, between the ultra-quick steering found on a criterium or track bike and the more stable feel of a good touring bike; in terms of steering design and many other factors, a well-designed road-racing bike is likely to fall between the two. Some of the specific design decisions influencing these characteristics are discussed in the section titled "Steering" later in this chapter.

Design Trade-Offs

You may need to trade one desirable design feature for another to meet your needs. Everyone would like to eliminate whip and also have plenty of cushioning, but in balancing the two, a racer concentrating on hill climbing is likely to be more concerned with torsional rigidity, while the long-distance tourist will be more interested in comfort, load-carrying capacity, and stable handling. The bicycle designer has a limited number of variables to work with, and tolerances are close. For example, the differences in frame angles among various bicycle designs are minimal. The angle of the steering tube to the horizontal might be 74 degrees in a rather uncompromising criterium racing bike and 70 to 72 degrees on a soft, easy-riding touring machine. These are small differences, but they produce major changes in handling. The seat tube angle will also influence these riding characteristics, and looking at this number alone, you can easily find that the same frame—designed to have the same ride and feel—has angles varying from 72 to 75 degrees for different sizes (seat tube lengths). The average person, looking at the frames, wouldn't even be able to tell the difference without taking exact measurements. None of these numbers by itself is indicative of performance or feel.

A number of important frame dimensions should be dictated mainly by your body measurements, and secondarily by your riding style and the kind of cycling you do. The length of the seat tube cannot be increased more than a small amount from the ideal for a particular individual, because you have to be able to reach the pedals from the seat and to stand on the ground while straddling the top tube. (Compact geometry—which uses a sloping top tube—gives the designer a little more flexibility; see Drawing 13 on page 87.) Similarly, the length of the top tube should be determined primarily by the length of your upper body, with only small adjustments possible using the length of the stem extension and movement of the seat. Wheel size is usually fixed, or at least constrained to a few choices. The builder has to work within all these limitations in designing the frame.

The main variables with which the builder can work are the stiffness of the various tubes (see "Tubing" later in this chapter), the angles of the seat tube and the head tube, the fork rake, the length of the chainstays, the length and possibly the slope of the top tube, the length of the down tube, and the height of the bottom-bracket shell above the ground. Each of these variables interacts with the others.

To obtain a forgiving ride, for example, several things can be done. The wheelbase can be lengthened a bit by extending the chainstays and the top tube, the angle of the headset can be lessened, and fork rake can be increased. The fork rake (see Drawings 12 and 13) is the distance produced by the forward bend of the fork on traditional forks and the forward angling of the fork blades at the fork crown on some new designs. It is measured from the center of the axle to the steering axis, which is a line projected along the axis of the head and steering tubes. The more rake and the more the fork is inclined from the vertical by a decreased head tube angle, the more it deflects in response to the shock from a bump. Similarly, longer chainstays deflect upward more, and they also bring the rear wheel farther back and less directly under the rider. Each of these modifications has other consequences, however. Increasing fork rake, for example, has major effects on the quickness and stability of steering.

Frame Size, Seat Tube Length, and Top Tube Length

This section, though it is mainly concerned with frame design, mentions a few fit issues, because they inevitably affect design and your choice of a particular design. For example, the smaller frame sizes of the Novara Safari, the Rivendell Atlantis, and the Surly Long Haul Trucker have different wheel sizes and substantially different geometry than the larger sizes. Detailed fitting recommendations are covered in Chapter 10.

While several dimensions of the frame affect the suitability of a bike for a particular rider, one of the most important is the length of the seat tube. The frame size of a bike is the distance between the center of the bottom-bracket shell and the top of the top tube. (It is important to note that there is a lot of variation in the way this is measured, and often manufacturers and builders don't specify their method, even changing method without mentioning that fact. Many also don't acknowledge the differences.) The traditional measurement was from the centerline of the bottom bracket and the crank axle to the very top of the seat tube. Of course this meant that otherwise identical frames would be labeled with different sizes depending on the length of any stub projecting above the top tube. Most frame makers seem to be gravitating toward a sensible standard of measuring to the top edge of the top tube, or where the upper edge of the top tube would be if it were horizontal. (Some measure from the center of the bottom bracket to the center of the top tube.) For an approximate size, figure approximately two-thirds of your crotch height (see "Frame Size" on page 56). If you are taller than 6 feet, you should also consider slightly larger frames.

One critical dimension that derives partly from the frame size is the standover height—the distance from the ground to the top tube just in front of the seat. You really want to be able to straddle the bike comfortably when you are standing still, and if you ride on rough terrain, you want a little extra clearance, because the bike may be above the ground on which you are standing on occasions when the trail drops off to that side. Standover height is determined by a number of frame dimensions, but also by the size of the wheels and tires you are using. Standover height is rarely a problem for an otherwise properly sized frame these days, because mountain bikes and bikes for smaller riders are often made with sloping top tubes (see Drawing 13 on page 87), also called compact geometry.

Clearances

There are several important clearances incorporated in every frame design, and it is important that the ones on the frame you select match your needs. The clearance between the tires and the fork crown in front and the brake bridge in back can vary enormously. Most road bikes are designed for racing or club and sport riding, and they won't accommodate either fenders or larger-profile tires. Many touring cyclists would like both. The main reasons for the tight clearances are connected with the choice of brakes (more discussion in Chapter 8), but there are other factors. In any case, for versatility in touring, you want much larger clearances than those on a sport-riding bike. Whereas the typical club rider will probably be riding something like 700C × 26 (ISO 26-622) or even narrower tires, tourists are likely to want 700C × 32 (ISO 32-622) or even larger profiles, as much as 700C × 50 (ISO 50-622). For those who plan on traversing a significant amount of rough terrain, much larger widths are in order. These are impossible to mount on conventional road bikes.

If you want fenders, you need even more clearance. Designs optimized for touring, such as the Rivendell Atlantis, Bruce Gordon bikes, and the Surly Long Haul Trucker, will accommodate a tire width of at least 45 mm, for example a 700C × 45 (ISO 45-622). Unfortunately, most major manufacturers don't bother to list this information, because they are not tuned into touring requirements. Every touring bike description should include maximum tire size, with and without fenders.

The wheel or tire size may be an important design characteristic in itself when you are looking at touring bikes, because availability of tires varies widely, particularly in less-developed countries and in places far from the nearest bike shop. This issue is discussed in Chapter 7.

Heel clearance for panniers is important unless you are using a trailer or a luggage arrangement that does not include rear panniers. Better heel clearance is achieved by bikes with relatively longer chainstays.

Finally, the clearance between the front tire and the toe clip or the toe of your shoe is of some importance. For racers, this determines whether you risk hitting the wheel during tight cornering or maneuvering. For tourists, it is an issue in climbing situations when you are slowly climbing a hill with a lot of luggage and making steering corrections. Hitting the front wheel with your toe in either case can be quite unpleasant.

Several factors in frame design and component choice affect this clearance, which interacts with your shoe size. Steeper head tube angles, reduced fork rake, longer cranks, and larger wheel sizes all make this interference more likely. This is an issue worth checking on test rides. It doesn't usually present a problem, because one rarely turns the front wheel very far, but the occasions when it does occur can be dangerous, or at least unnerving. You don't want to take a tumble while you are pedaling slowly up a mountain grade with traffic on your left.

Another important dimension for those who plan to tour on trails like the Great Divide Trail is the height of the bottom bracket above the ground (listed by some manufacturers as bottom-bracket height). This affects clearance on rocky terrain and helps to determine cornering when you are pedaling through steep turns on the road. The frame dimensions affecting bottom-bracket height are not definitive; fatter tires result in more bottom-bracket height, so a better dimension is bottom-bracket drop, the distance from a line between the front and rear wheel axles (centers of the drop-outs) to the center of the bottom bracket. Some bikes originally designed for cyclocross are popular choices for touring, like the Surly Crosscheck. They tend to have high bottom-bracket clearance (short bottom-bracket drop).

Steering

The steering characteristics of a bike are complex, and everything from the weight of the rider to the height of the bottom bracket has some effect on them. The main elements, however, are the head tube angle, the fork length, and the fork rake (see Drawing 12 on page 86); these must be carefully balanced to achieve the desired handling. Replacing one fork with another of the same length can radically change the steering if the second fork has a 1¼-inch rake instead of a 2½-inch one.

All bicycles are built so that the front wheel has some caster or trail, meaning that the actual point where the wheel makes contact with the ground is behind the turning axis (see Drawings 12 and 13 on pages 86 and 87), so that there is a self-correcting bias in the steering. If you extend a line down from the axis of the head tube, around which the fork, stem, and handlebars turn, the line reaches the ground in front of a line dropped verti-cally from the center of the axle. The distance between these points is the caster, or trail. If a bike had no caster, it would be almost impossible to steer. In a turn, the bike would tend to turn more and more sharply. Caster produces the self-steering tendency you use when you ride with your hands off the bars, but it also makes the steering stable when you are riding normally. (For some good illustrations of the interactions between trail and fork rake, see Tom Matchak's article at www.phred .org/~alex/bikes/Fork%20Re-raking%20Summary.pdf and Josh Putnam's article at www.phred.org/~josh/ bike/trail.html.)

A bike built with a vertical head tube and a straight fork would have zero caster. As the angle of the head tube (shown in Drawings 12 and 13) decreases from 90 degrees, tilting the wheel forward, caster increases, but it is reduced by the introduction of fork rake. Increased fork rake and steeper angles both reduce caster and quicken the steering. Thus, if a builder wants to increase rake in order to soften the ride, he or she must decrease the angle of the head tube at the same time; otherwise the steering would become erratic. Increasing the fork length also increases the caster.*

A correct balance between the head tube angle, fork length, and rake is essential if a bike is to have proper handling characteristics. Touring models usually have more moderate head tube angles, and they also usually have less rake. This design feature is harder to spot visually with modern bikes than it was on traditional ones, because rake is often achieved in modern bikes by angling the fork blades from the fork crown. In traditional bikes all the rake was accomplished with the forward curve of the fork ends and was much more apparent.

Recommended Frame Dimensions

Most frame dimensions should be a function of general suitability for touring, and the proper configuration depends on the way the whole bike is designed, so fixing on a couple of numbers is usually not helpful. The overall combination determines fit, which is discussed in Chapter 10. Most touring cyclists should pay attention to a few specific dimensions, however.

Chainstay length is the main determinant of whether you'll be able to mount rear panniers reasonably without having your heel hit the pannier. Your foot size and crank length, as well as the pannier shape and rack construction, figure into this issue, but it makes sense to look for chainstays that are more than 44 cm. (17⅓ in.). Long chainstays are also one component in producing longer wheelbases, which are generally

---

* The interaction between caster and handling characteristics is complex. It depends on speed, tire width and pressure, and loading of the bike, among other factors. If you want to see how some of this works out in practice, take a look at the *Vintage Bicycle Quarterly* article comparing identical bikes with three different forks, reproduced at www.kogswell.com /KogswellPR.pdf.

desirable for touring—they make for better stability, a softer ride, and more relaxed steering. Regardless of other frame dimensions, tourists carrying panniers will always have to be concerned with chainstay length (those using trailers don't need to be as concerned).

A few other dimensions may be useful in evaluating whether a bike appears to have the right general geometry for touring. The head tube angle should probably be in the range of 72 to 72.5 degrees. Seat tube angles vary with the size of the frame but typically would be 72.5 to 75 degrees in a well-designed touring frame. The wheelbase on small-size frames (50 cm or less) should be at least 104 cm. Some large touring frames have wheelbases of more than 110 cm.

It is highly desirable for the steering tube on the fork to extend well above the top of the head tube (assuming a threadless headset), so that the optimum positioning of the stem can be determined before the tube is cut—an exposure of around 300 mm is a good length. Most touring cyclists are happier with handlebars at or above seat height (as in Drawing 12), rather than below (Drawing 13), and an uncut steering tube provides this latitude. Unfortunately, the steerers come precut very short on many touring bikes, so that an extension has to be mounted to clamp the stem at the correct height.

Frame designers adjust the seat tube angle concurrently with the top tube length to achieve a fit for riders with torsos of a certain length. An unfortunate marketing trend in mass-produced bikes is the use of compact geometry (slanting top tubes) to reduce the number of frame sizes offered by a manufacturer, so that the same size frame can be sold to a wider range of cyclists. People with different leg lengths can then straddle the same frame, but other proportions might not fit so well. This means that you need to pay close attention to fit, particularly top tube or effective top tube length.

In researching this section, I looked at the dimensions of several bikes that had small sizes and standover heights, making them suitable for small women, one would have thought. But the top tube lengths were completely out of comfortable range for most women of the height that would require small sizes. Tall people also fall out of the range of normal bike sizing, and they should be particularly attentive to fitting issues.

Tubing

Steel with a very high tensile strength (about 100,000 pounds per square inch, or psi) is used to make the tubing in most good-quality touring bicycles. The maker of the tubing must choose an alloy that is strong and can be assembled by the frame builder without losing its strength. Different characteristics may be required for joining by brazing than by welding, and thinner tubing sets intended for special racing uses may not be available to all frame builders. (Racing bikes are increasingly made of carbon fiber, discussed later in this chapter, but the principle is the same.)

The steels generally used for bicycle tubing are chrome-molybdenum ("chromoly") and molybdenum-manganese alloys. More malleable steels are used for lugs and similar parts. The strength and rigidity of a tube are dependent upon the composition of the steel, the tube diameter, and the thickness of the tube walls. Because the greatest stress in a bicycle frame occurs at the ends of the tubes near the joints, a lighter and livelier bike can be fashioned if the tubes are thicker at the ends, where the extra strength is required. Thicker ends lend extra rigidity where distorting stress is greatest and allow a larger margin for error against weakening the metal through overheating. The extra thickness also accommodates variations in stress at the joint caused by tiny irregularities in the brazing or welding, as well as smoothing the inherent thickening at the joint, which would otherwise cause a rapid change in the distribution of stress in the tubing (known as a stress riser).

Tubing with thicker walls at each end is called double-butted tubing. The extra thickness is inside the tubes and cannot be seen externally. Such tubes are difficult and expensive to make, so they naturally cost more than tubing of uniform thickness. The butting is achieved by compressing the tube with great force around an interior shaped bar called a mandrill and then running the tube between rollers that spring open one end momentarily while the mandrill is drawn out. A different process is used in high-quality seamed butted tubing, which is drawn over a mandrill (DOM), a process used, for example, by the manufacturer True Temper. (Seamed tubing, contrary to rumor, is not inherently weaker than unseamed.)

Traditional makers of quality double-butted tubing have developed a well-deserved reputation. The most prestigious have long been Columbus (Italian) and Reynolds (British). Thus a decal on the bike that certifies it is made from Columbus SL or Reynolds 531 has always held significant prestige. And there are varying decals indicating which frame members are made with the specified material (resulting in significant heartburn for cyclists who have their frames repainted—it's tough to replace those classic decals!). As a practical matter, name-brand tubing commands a name-brand price. You will pay more for the Reynolds and Columbus decals. You need to judge whether you also get a better bike.

Many tubing manufacturers, including True Temper, Oria, Tange, Ishiwata, Falk, Vitus, and others, now make superb products. Today, it makes no sense for an individual cyclist to delve very deeply into the details of tubing manufacture or wonder if a particular fork is made of butted tubing. Plenty of good tubing manufacturers and many variations in characteristics now exist. If you are buying a production bike from Trek, Fuji, Miyata, or another major manufacturer, you are relying on their engineers and quality-control departments to ensure proper tubing selection and adequate quality control of the joints.

Types of Tubing

Most companies use numbering or letter systems to distinguish between different types of tubing. Reynolds decal indicates whether the bike is made from 531 or another specified alloy. If the decal specifies only the brand and alloy number, the tubes are not butted. The decal also indicates whether only the three main tubes are butted or rather the tubes, forks, and stays are all butted. (Seat tubes, stays, and fork blades are always tapered rather than double-butted.)

Many specification numbers are commonly used by marketers in discussing tubing, and you should mostly ignore them and rely on builders and engineers. Assertions are frequently made about chromoly 4130 or some other combination of names and numbers. Unless you know all the details, don't take these claims too seriously. Some may claim, for example, that some alloy, like SAE 4130 (the actual specification for chromoly) is "stiffer" or "less stiff" than some other alloy, like Reynolds 531 or Reynolds 953. In general, all steels and steel alloys have the same stiffness. The differences between alloys are in tensile strength and hardness. Steel with higher tensile strength can be formed into tubes with thinner walls that have the same strength as much thicker-walled and heavier tubes of cheaper steel but produce frames that are both lighter and livelier. There is also variability in resistance to fatigue and in characteristics that affect ease of brazing or welding (see "Joining the Tubes—Lugs, Brazing, and Welding" below).

Ultimately, the quality of the bike does not depend on the specific alloy used to make it, but on whether the frame builder or bicycle manufacturer has chosen the best materials to match the bike design and used the best techniques to make it. What you want is construction that will be durable and as lightweight as possible—a combination dependent on the material, the joining techniques, and skill and quality control. You inevitably rely on the frame builder. The best choice for reliable construction of a mass-produced frame will probably be different than for a hand-built frame put together by a master builder. One will probably be joined using welding and the other with lugs and brazing, with the type of construction dictating the materials used.

Joining the Tubes—Lugs, Brazing, and Welding

Frame tubes are cut to size and mitered to fit together properly as part of the initial preparation, whether they are manufactured en masse or custom built. Then they are joined together using some method of melting and bonding the metal surfaces at temperatures a little above 800 degrees Fahrenheit (for brazing with bronze—an alloy of copper and zinc). Brazing melts only the joining material—either bronze or a silver alloy, while welding also melts the surface of the tubing.

Lugs. Traditionally, the joints are made with lugs—junction parts made of softer steel that fit around the tubes being joined. Lugged joints are brazed with either a bronze or silver alloy, and they form very strong joints. The brazing material fills the thin space between the lugs and tubes, as well as the tube junctures, and the brazing metal and the flux interact with the surface layers of the tubes to form a very strong bond. This occurs at a much lower temperature than the melting temperature of the tubing steel, so there is less danger of changing the crystalline structure of the tubing and weakening it.

Lugless joints can be made either by brazing or by welding. Forming lugless joints with brazing is often called fillet brazing. Welding, which can be done in several ways, melts the two metal parts together into a single unit, normally with the addition of some additional filler or joint-strengthening material of a similar steel (welding rod or wire). The joint material has to be chosen to work with the tubing used. Brazing fills the joint with a different metal—typically brass or a silver alloy—that bonds to the two parts and fills any gaps.

Brazing. Brazing requires skillful craftsmanship to create strong joints, but it has inherent advantages when properly done. Most cyclists also feel that a well-brazed lugged frame is aesthetically the most attractive method of construction. There are heated arguments about the relative advantages of bronze and silver alloy brazing, which are too esoteric to cover in this book.

Welding. TIG (tungsten inert gas) welding is the most common technique for joining modern steel frames. It is a type of arc welding in which a tungsten electrode heats the metal of the tubes and an inert gas, such as argon, surrounds the joint during the welding process to prevent atmospheric contamination while the metal is hot and reactive. The tubes being joined are heated to the melting point, and filler steel (wire or welding rod) is supplied and melted to form a solid joint.

TIG welding, when it is properly controlled, forms joints that are just as strong as the best brazing, but the process demands very tight quality control. Mitering has to be very close, temperatures have to be perfectly controlled to prevent weakening of the tubing, and the steel alloys used in the tubing have to be certified for TIG welding—many tubing sets are not—or the steel of the tubing will recrystallize during welding and may be weakened. TIG welding normally requires very precise jigs, so it is generally better suited to mass production than to custom frame building. There are some excellent custom builders who use TIG welding, however.

A good TIG-welded frame is just as serviceable as a brazed, lugged one. The relative aesthetics are a matter of personal preference. Some cyclists contend that an advantage of a lugged, brazed frame is that after a crash in which a frame tube has been bent, the damaged tube can be replaced by a skilled frame maker, whereas this really can't be done with a welded frame. This statement is true, but the argument is a real stretch; you can almost certainly buy a brand new TIG-welded frame for less than the cost of the repair to the lugged one.

Semi-custom frames are produced using both methods, but high-quality lugged frames will generally cost twice as much as high-quality TIG-welded ones.

Custom frames are also built using both methods, although most of the best custom frame builders use brazed lug construction, for reasons of aesthetics or design choice. One important factor is that adjusting frame angles to specific individual measurements is easier with lugged construction.

Finish and Extra Features

Many fancy extras can be incorporated in a bike frame, and some are very useful for the touring cyclist. Some special features are a matter of fashion more than anything else, however, and you must decide for yourself whether they are worth the money.

Finishes

A good finish on a bike may give some indication of quality in other areas, though the relationship does not always hold. The tougher the finish and the better it is applied, the easier it is to keep the bike clean and untarnished. There are a number of ways of applying a quality finish, ranging from new technologically sophisticated methods like powder coating to old-fashioned spraying, sanding, and baking of many coats, along with hand detailing of lug work. If the dropouts aren't chromed, you can take a sharp object and test the adherence of the paint where the wheel clamps on, an area that is going to lose its paint anyway.

A chrome finish requires the least care if it is well applied, but it is heavy and does not appeal aesthetically to many cyclists. Chrome makes excellent sense when applied to areas that normally receive a lot of dirt and wear, such as fork ends, chainstays, and dropouts.

A lot of modern frames, both production and custom, are powder-coated. Powder coating is a painting process that does not start with a suspension of pigments in liquid, but instead uses particles of plastic or other polymer along with pigments, which are deposited on the frame electrostatically and then cured (baked on). Powder coating can produce amazingly durable paint layers, is environmentally more sound, and is more easily applied to small numbers of frames than traditional painting. Of course, a tough coat still requires good surface preparation before application, or some parts of the frame will be vulnerable to attack by rust, and this is a process issue you can't see. A high-quality powder-coated finish is at least as tough as chrome and is quite attractive, but because the coat itself is so strong, bad surface preparation may not show up immediately and may cause major flaking when it does occur.

Fancy cutout work and filing on the lugs of traditionally made bikes are often the marks of a fine bike, though the weight saved is negligible. (If you want to see some attractive and functional lugs, take a look at photos on the Web sites of Rivendell Bikes (www.rivbike.com/products/list/bicycle_models #product=50-990) and Bruce Gordon (www.bgcycles .com/lugged.html). Sadly, lug work is relevant to fewer and fewer of us, because mass-produced bikes are made with TIG welding and have no lugs or cutouts.

One final finishing step that is worthwhile but rarely included in assembling a bike is the inside treatment of the steel-frame tubes. Spraying the interiors with Boeing Boeshield, JP Weigle Frame Saver, linseed oil, LPS 3, or motor fogging oil will prevent rust from developing inside the frame from the inevitable moisture buildup. Perhaps you can get the bike shop where you bought the bike to do this as part of the purchase deal. You can do it yourself by disassembling the bike but it is a messy job, so paying the shop to do it as part of the setup is well worth a few dollars. All steel frames should have this treatment as standard preparation, but it is rarely included because it's so messy.

Fittings and Features

More important to the tourist than finish are the various fittings on the bike. The fork ends and dropouts should have threaded eyelets for attaching racks. It is a nuisance to mount luggage carriers without them, though Blackburn, Old Man Mountain, and others make some fairly effective clamp-on fittings for attaching racks to mountain bikes, as well as axle attachments to substitute for eyelets and other attachment bosses. These clamps and axle hangers will also work for club-riding bikes that lack braze-on bosses, and they can be improvised if necessary. It is convenient to have double eyelets on the dropouts for mounting fenders in addition to racks, but this can be managed with single eyelets. Fittings that attach under quick-release ends to substitute for eyelets will work, but they are far less desirable.

The best touring frames include a host of extra braze-ons—bosses, posts, and fittings, which may be either brazed or welded to the frame tubes to eliminate the need for clamps. Such clamps are weaker and less reliable than bosses, and they mar the paint when they slip. Of course, the extra braze-on bosses are indispensable when you need them, while the unused ones are extraneous and sometimes annoying. Unless you're having a true custom frame built, it is hard to find the optimum configuration.

Most important are the fittings for brakes and derailleurs. A brake bridge cable stop between the seatstays is useful for the rear brakes. Most touring bikes should have posts on the forks and the seatstays for mounting cantilever brakes (or V-type brakes if you are using a straight handlebar, like those typically used on mountain bikes). The highest-quality cantilever brakes require these posts. Touring bikes should also have bosses for water-bottle mounts and cable stops for both brake and derailleur cables. (Routing of cables depends on components and other fine points, so the placement of these features presupposes some specific component choices.)

The best-thought-out touring frames have down-tube posts that act as cable stops for brifters or bar-end shifters, or as mounting posts for down-tube shifters. Finally, there are mounting braze-on posts on the fork blades and the seatstays for mounting front and rear racks, respectively.

Other commonly used fittings include brake cable stops on the top tube, a cable stop for the derailleur on the right chainstay, derailleur cable guides above or below the bottom bracket, and a stop at the appropriate place for the front derailleur (ideal location varies with the model of derailleur). These all reduce the number of clamp-on fittings and the length of cable housing required to complete the bike.

Alignment

Any bike frame should be perfectly aligned, although there is often no way to tell whether some corrections have been made by bending a frame after construction. The simplest overall alignment test is to ride the bike with no hands. A properly aligned bike tracks easily, rather than pulling to one side or feeling as though it is about to swerve out of control. There are other tests that you can make quite simply. If the wheels are properly trued, the rims should be equidistant from the fork blades (front) and the chainstays (rear). If one side is closer than the other, reverse the wheel to see whether the fault is in the wheel or in the frame. If the short side remains next to the same frame member, the frame is misaligned.

The wheels should be easy to mount and remove without pressing in on the fork ends and chainstays or spreading them apart (except for the effects of depressions or "lawyer lips" typically included on newer dropouts). With someone holding the bike and pointing the front wheel straight ahead, sight along the two wheels from the front and back. They should line up perfectly in exactly the same plane. The head tube and seat tube also should line up precisely in the same plane.

Stretch a string around the front of the head tube and back on either side of the bike to the rear dropouts. The string should be the same distance from the seat tube on each side. The cranks should pass the seat tube and down tube at exactly the same distance on each side; otherwise either the bottom-bracket shell is not oriented exactly at a right angle to the plane of the main triangle or the bottom-bracket assembly is not correctly positioned within the shell (the bearing assemblies are screwed too far to the left or the right).

Alternative Frame Materials and Construction

Many alternatives to steel have been used to make bicycle frames, ranging from bamboo to exotic metals and composite materials that use epoxy or polyester resin to bond fibers of graphite or other materials. This section considers the most commonly used alternatives to steel for frames and forks.

Aluminum

The most common material, other than steel, suitable for touring bikes is aluminum alloy. Cannondale has made touring bikes from aluminum alloy since 1983, and these frames have a host of very experienced devotees. Many original users are still touring on early Cannondale bikes that have covered tens of thousands of miles. Furthermore, many mountain bikes are made from aluminum. It is clear from this record that solid, durable touring bikes can be constructed with aluminum and that one can confidently use these bikes anywhere on Earth. (Among the models suggested in Chapter 4, only the Cannondale models and the Novara Safari are aluminum.)

Aluminum frames tend to be quite stiff, but they have several advantages. They do not rust, even if the paint is chipped, and there is no reason to consider having the inside of the frame tubes sprayed with rust-preventive treatments, as you should do with steel frames. Though aluminum doesn't rust, serious corrosion can occur on aluminum bikes where steel and aluminum meet, as with headsets and bottom brackets, where steel-aluminum contacts that are not properly lubricated can form a bimetallic bond that is worse than rusting. You also have to be more careful about cross-threading other components into aluminum. These are minor problems, however, and they can be prevented by proper design and maintenance. Though there are individual horror stories, issues associated with steel-aluminum contacts are easily avoided with standard lubrication practices.

Aluminum frames are welded, similarly to TIG-welded steel frames, though the temperature and the details are different. Virtually all aluminum frames are production frames. Aluminum is significantly lighter than steel, but larger-diameter tubes with thicker walls are generally used, and when all is said and done, aluminum bikes generally weigh about the same as comparable steel ones. Aluminum bikes that are suitable for touring typically have steel forks.

Most experienced tourists prefer steel frames. Two principal reasons are usually cited. One is that aluminum is less ductile and fatigues more easily than steel—if it is bent, it is prone to crack, and it is usually not safe to repair. For example, with an older steel frame that you want to adapt to a newer, wider wheel, a steel frame can be safely cold-set to the new width; an aluminum one cannot. Cyclists headed to remote corners of the world note that village welders can sometimes make repairs to a damaged steel frame, but this is not true of aluminum. I don't find these arguments wholly convincing. Very few touring cyclists have actually had their bikes repaired by welders in Bangladesh or Patagonia, and craftsmen at primitive airstrips can often do as well with aluminum. Compared with other remote field-repair issues, this seems to be an unlikely one. Most touring cyclists, however, simply like the ride of steel frames better. Steel feels springier and livelier to most riders, but this is a subjective question.

Titanium and Magnesium

Titanium is an excellent material for bicycle frames. It is very strong and very light, but titanium frames are quite expensive. It is used by a few semi-custom builders, but their market is for racing or sport-riding bikes. In general, a custom titanium frame will cost twice as much as a custom steel frame. A titanium touring bike would be an extravagance, and I've never met a tourist who actually had one. If you are interested in this possibility, you should also be aware that bimetallic corrosion and bonding problems are issues with titanium bikes.

And, if a titanium frame isn't exotic enough for you, the next step is magnesium. It is even lighter than titanium, but for touring bikes, saving a couple of pounds in the frame makes little sense. There are several custom builders who work with magnesium, and the price range is similar to that for titanium.

Composites (Carbon Fiber)

Composite materials are strong, stiff fibers that are bonded together with plastic resins. Over the last few decades, the technology for building structural products with composites has become quite sophisticated. Composites are used to meet special requirements in the aerospace industry. Under the right circumstances, composites can replace metal, providing adequate strength with a considerable weight reduction. Additionally, creating molds and curing tools for composite construction has become cheaper than the typical tooling, casting, forging, and machining for metal frame parts, so building a composite bike of a new design for large-scale production is often cheaper than doing the same thing with steel or aluminum.

In cycling, the shorthand for composite material is carbon. Carbon fiber and graphite (a form of carbon) fiber bonded with epoxy resins are very strong and very stiff. The lightest production racing and sport-riding bicycles use carbon or graphite fiber composite frames and components.

Composites have disadvantages, though. They are not at all ductile. They develop microscopic fatigue cracks when stressed beyond their design capacity or simply subjected to the repeated stresses and vibrations of cycling. They degrade with age and can fail catastrophically. For bicycle tourists, carbon fiber frames are not a viable option (that's a good thing), because all current carbon frames are made for racing and sport riding. Carbon fiber components, such as handlebars, stems, or cranks, do show up on touring bikes, but they are not particularly recommended.

6

The Drive Train

The drive train comprises all of the bicycle components used to transmit power from your legs and feet through the pedals, cranks, chainwheels, chain, and rear cogs, along with the shifting systems that change the mechanical advantage, so that you can vary the distance traveled with each rotation of the pedals. The large gears on the front are usually referred to as chainwheels, and those at the rear as cogs, or the rear cluster. The shifting mechanisms are derailleurs, and the mechanisms that move the derailleurs, via cables, are shifters. The general quality of the derailleur and shifter systems included on modern production bikes is truly phenomenal, and this chapter concentrates on them. It is worth noting, however, that other alternatives, which are discussed briefly at the end of the chapter, are also available.

If you buy a new bike for touring, it should have three chainwheels at the front and a cluster of eight, nine, or ten cogs at the rear, yielding a 24-, 27-, or 30-speed system. This provides more combinations than you will ever need, but the number of usable combinations is often far less, for a variety of reasons. There are often many duplicate or near-duplicate ratios, and some combinations don't operate well mechanically, so they are often avoided. Hence, while you may have a bike that is nominally a 30-speed, the practical number may be far smaller.

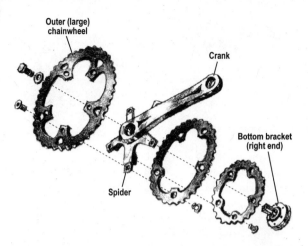

Outer (large) chainwheel

Crank

Bottom bracket (right end)

Spider

14. A typical crankset. The two larger rings are attached with special bolts and screws to either side of the spider. The inner chainring is held on with a separate set of bolts.

The Drive Train and Shifting System

Though modern engineers have greatly improved the materials and the details on bicycles sold today, the basic functioning of the drive train is quite simple and has not changed in any fundamental way for many decades. (Note that this book ignores single-speed, fixed-gear bicycles, which are fun bikes for a number of purposes but would not be a good choice for any but the most extreme touring cyclists.)

You transmit the driving power for the bicycle through pedals mounted on two cranks, which are part of the crankset (see Drawing 14). The crankset is made up of the cranks, a connecting axle, bearings that run in the bottom bracket of the frame, and two or three chainwheels.

A chainwheel is connected via the chain to one of a cluster of gears at the rear of the bike, and the cluster of gears is, in turn, attached to the rear wheel using a free-hub or freewheel—a ratchet device that allows power to be transmitted to drive the bicycle forward while the

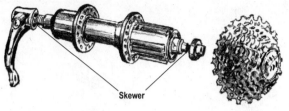

15. A freehub and cassette.

chain and pedals are free to move backward unencumbered. The chain is free to flex around the gears, but it is fairly rigid from side to side.

The front derailleur allows the rider to shift the chain back and forth between the chainwheels attached to the crankset. The rear derailleur moves the chain between the cogs attached to the rear wheel, and it also includes a spring-loaded arm designed to take up slack in the chain, which thus remains tight regardless of which combination of gears is being used.

The derailleurs are controlled by using two shifters, which work by increasing or reducing tension on cables that connect the shifters to the derailleurs. Normally the front derailleur is controlled by the left shifter and the rear by the right shifter. Fixed segments of cable housing are used to allow tension on a cable to be transmitted along curved paths. Modern shifters use indexed shifting, so that you can easily shift from one gear to another by simply moving the shifter by a single click. Shifters come in a variety of designs and mounting positions, and are discussed toward the end of this chapter.

The final important aspect of the drive train is the mechanism for attaching the cluster of rear cogs to the hub of the back wheel. This is most commonly done with a freehub (see Drawing 15), which incorporates a ratchet and all bearings into the freehub, and which has a set of splines onto which the cogs fit. The cogs are held on by a lockring. (Freewheels, which you may find on older bikes, have the ratchet and some bearings in a separate unit. You can find a photograph showing the difference at www.sheldonbrown.com/gloss_e-f .html#freewheel.)

What the Gears Do

As with an automobile, the purpose of the gears is to allow the engine (you) to operate efficiently while moving the wheels at a speed appropriate to the resistance. If you try to drive a car forward in high gear, especially up a steep grade, the engine will stall. You need a low gear to attain momentum before shifting into a higher gear. The other gears, whether manual or automatic, are designed to allow the engine to operate at reasonable efficiency under widely varying loads.

You need more gears on your touring bicycle than on a car, because your body generates power efficiently over a narrower range of speeds and you will find yourself climbing hills at least as steep as you do when you are driving a car, pedaling against wind resistance that is proportionally greater and moving loads that vary widely. Your gearing system should accommodate all these requirements effectively, allowing you to rack up the miles on windless flat segments of roads but also to climb mountain grades without becoming exhausted or hurting your knees.

Ideal gearing would have these characteristics:

- A low enough gear to allow you to pedal up the steepest grades at an efficient cadence and without stressing your knees too much.

- A high enough gear to allow you to pedal at a reasonable cadence on mountain descents, if you want to or need to.

- Evenly spaced steps between gears, requiring the use of only one shifter (rather than, for example, having to shift down in the front while shifting up in the rear). The steps should be close enough that you always have a gear just above the one you are using and one just below, so that you can pedal at the cadence that is most comfortable.

Other requirements are technical ones associated with the drive train. The rear derailleur has to have a long enough parallelogram cage to accommodate the largest cog and a long enough arm to take up the chain length needed to cover the difference between the highest and the lowest gears. But it still needs to be rigid enough to shift crisply and accurately. The front derailleur has to be designed to handle the largest and smallest chainwheels. Finally, of course, all the components have to be available and to work together flawlessly.

These requirements are often contradictory, and there is an enormous range of possibilities. The detailed sections that follow consider the main choices you should focus on, concentrating on newer bikes.

What's in a Gear? Some Contradictory Terms

Serious cyclists often refer to *gearing* in a host of conflicting ways. Gears on a bike enable you to adjust the distance the bike travels for each stroke you make on the pedals. They provide a multiplying effect that causes the bicycle to go farther for each revolution of the pedals. The old-fashioned "ordinary"—the big-wheel bikes of the late nineteenth century (see Drawing 16)— went exactly the same distance for each revolution of the pedals, a distance equal to the wheel diameter × π, just like a child's tricycle.

Today's bikes often come with thirty possible gear combinations—each defined by a chainwheel–rear cog combination. A person may refer to a specific gear pairing by the number of teeth in the chainwheel and cog: "52-12," for example, would mean a 52-tooth chainwheel at the front connected by the chain to a 12-tooth cog in the rear. This same gear could be referred to by the ratio (number of teeth on the smallest chainwheel divided by the number of teeth on the largest rear cog), 52÷12, or 4.33; by its *development* or *rollout* (the distance traveled for each revolution of the pedals), 9.14 meters; or by the gear, 114.5 inches. Both the development and the gear inches are dependent on the diameter of the

16. Expressing gear ratios in inches derives from the diameter of the wheel of an 1890s "big-wheeler," which would go the same distance with each revolution of the pedals.

wheel, which is affected by both the rim size and the size of the tire mounted on it.

All these methods, except for the ratio, are a bit peculiar. A 52-24 gear has exactly the same effect on distance traveled and effort required as a 26-12, so it is really only a useful way of talking about gears for people who use the same sets of chainwheels. A person with a large front chainwheel of 48 needs to do some mental calculation to decide that this is roughly a 48-22. The development measurement is rarely used in the United States, but referring to gears in inches is very common.

Besides being dependent on tire size, this terminology harks back a century to the days when the pedal cranks were connected directly to the axle of the front wheel. The distance you could travel with one revolution of the pedals was directly proportional to the size of the wheel, so bikes were made and bought with the biggest wheel the rider could straddle. The gear in inches was the diameter of the equivalent wheel (see Drawing 16 on page 119). Of course, no one could straddle a 114.5-inch wheel, which would have required an inseam of nearly five feet. Higher gears like a 114.5 required a system incorporating mechanical advantage, like modern bikes.

How Many Speeds? Theory and Reality

Referring to a bike as a 27- or 30-speed implies that the rider has that many distinct gears from which to choose on a ride. Let's look at a practical example of the gears available. One of the widely available bikes mentioned in Chapter 4, the touring bicycle, with fairly well chosen gears for touring, has 48/36/26 chainwheels and a 9-speed cassette in the rear, made up of cogs with 11/13/15/17/20/23/26/30/34 teeth. The following gear chart for a touring bike with tires you might use for club rides (700C × 25) shows gears in inches for each combination:

Teeth	11	13	15	17	20	23	26	30	34
48	115.3	97.5	84.5	74.6	63.4	55.1	48.8	42.3	37.3
36	86.5	73.2	63.4	55.9	47.6	41.3	36.6	31.7	28.0
26	62.4	52.8	45.8	40.4	34.3	29.9	26.4	22.9	20.2

If you look carefully at this chart, you'll see that you don't really have 27 meaningful "speeds." The 36-15 and the 48-20 combinations yield exactly the same gear, 63.4, and it is very close to the 26-11 combination. What the large number of combinations that are standard on today's bikes really buys you is not 27 or 30 unique gears, but rather enough of them that you have comfortable shifting sequences in many different situations, without having to make awkward shifts or memorize all your gears. Providing you choose a gearing setup that meets a few important criteria, shifting sequences should be simple and effective. For a 24-, 27-, or 30-speed system, the important criteria are:

- Your lowest gear—the chain positioned on the smallest chainring and the largest rear cog—should be a real hill-climber, something that will get you up a steep final climb to a campground or motel, even with a heavy load and after a long day when you may have bonked. You'll be grateful for a true granny gear like this, even in less extreme circumstances. I recommend that your lowest gear have a ratio of around 0.75 or less. The setup in the gear chart above has a ratio of 0.76, which is close enough. This recommendation works out to a low gear of around 20 inches.

- The jumps from one rear cog to the next while the chain is on a particular chainwheel should be reasonable and fairly even. The proportions going from one gear to the next in the example given above range from 1.13 to 1.18. Neither the variation nor the numbers should be much larger than this, and in this case the 1.18 ratio occurs only when shifting to the largest gear, which is higher than really needed.

The most common deficiency in the standard gearing on most of the touring bikes mentioned in Chapter 4 is that the lowest gear is not low enough. If a bike is satisfactory in every other respect, you can change gears later, but it is a good idea to consider this issue before buying the bike, because you should be able to negotiate a swap-out to the right set of gears as part of the purchase.

Compatibility Issues

The limitations on gear combinations are often not obvious. When the first edition of this book was published, getting a good gearing arrangement for bicycle touring was often a significant challenge. Fortunately, on modern bikes it is possible to get good gearing and components, largely thanks to the advent of mountain bikes, which require wider ranges and are popular enough that component manufacturers have worked out the problems. If you are modifying an older bike, however, you may have to delve into the details.

The first issue is associated with the number of speeds. As the number of speeds has increased, chains have been made narrower, cog spacing has changed, the width of the frame between the two rear dropouts has been widened, and the tooth thickness for both cogs and chainwheels has narrowed. For indexed shifting, the shifters have changed to accommodate more speeds and sometimes different spacing. The number of potential incompatibilities is truly mind-boggling, but with a new bike, you should be able to keep things pretty simple. Just buy parts that are specified to work with the components you have. If you are heading into the weeds of modifying an older bike, some sources of information are suggested in the Resources section at the end of the book, or you can consult one of Lennard Zinn's maintenance manuals.

Both the front and rear derailleurs have to be physically constructed to work with the largest and smallest gears at their respective ends of the drive train. The rear derailleur also has to have a long enough arm to take up the chain length between the largest and smallest gear combinations. None of these factors should be taken for granted. When components are being designed for, say, a 20-speed road-racing bike, the cage on the front derailleur will be just long enough to handle the expected gear range, lending it a little extra stiffness for crisp shifting. The rear derailleur will have short dimensions for optimally quick and smooth shifting, and it will be able to handle neither the larger cogs you will want nor the gear range you will need.

There are many other potential compatibility issues. For example, chainwheels have to be made to fit the rest of the crankset. Chainwheels may have a varying number of mounting holes, varying distances between the holes, and a varying number of arms in the spider (see Drawing 14 on page 115). Cogs have to be made for your specific freehub. Freewheels and freehubs are made very differently, and successive generations of each require different cogs, spacers, locknuts, and so on. But again, with a newer bike you'll seldom have to deal with such issues, unless you are changing components and gearing yourself.

Shifting Patterns

With the limited gear ranges and component availability that prevailed a couple of decades ago, touring cyclists paid a lot of attention to shifting order, and the resulting patterns were sometimes pretty complicated. Some people still pay a lot of attention to shifting pattern and order. The goal is to maintain pedaling efficiency by being able to smoothly shift to either the next highest or lowest gear without much fuss. For example, with the gear system illustrated in the gear chart on page 120, if you are climbing a long, moderately steep hill with the 48-26 combination (48.8 inches), and you feel the need for a slightly lower gear, the best option would be to shift to 36-20 (47.6 inches), a change by a factor of 1.03. This shift would also have the advantage of putting you in the middle of the 36-tooth gear range, giving you a number of easy shifts to lower and higher gears if the grade changes. However, this change requires you to shift down one step with your front derailleur and up two steps with your rear derailleur, which is both a little awkward and nearly impossible to remember. The more obvious change, which is what most people will make, is to shift one step lower with your rear derailleur to the 48-30 combination (42.3 inches), a somewhat larger factor of 1.15.

Because gear choices used to be rather constrained, many theories developed for dealing with the problems of achieving an efficient set of ratios, remembering the order, and making the sometimes awkward shifts. One style was the crossover system, which uses widely spaced chainwheels and closely spaced rear cogs. The general shifting scenario was to start with a particular chainwheel (large chainwheel for flat conditions, middle chainwheel for more difficult ones, and small chainwheel for steep uphill and headwinds) and shift up and down with the rear derailleur for most changes. Somewhere near the end of each range, or at a convenient point, you switch chainwheels and enter a different range. The example in the gear chart on page 120 is a typical crossover design, and it is the style of most touring setups. Another favored system was the half-step approach, with closely spaced chainwheels and a shifting pattern that alternated in regular steps between the rear gears and the chainwheels.

With current equipment, crossover systems allow you to find or specify a gearing setup that works very well, is inexpensive and easy to obtain, and is easy to use and remember. In other words, the range and functionality of modern systems makes the easy, lazy solution more than adequate, so I will not discuss half-step systems and other complex possibilities.

I don't mean that you should assume that whatever gears come with your bike are okay. Most are not. Many of the stock setups are poorly designed, and you should try to get your bike shop to change them without charge. Let's consider the standard setup on one of the touring bikes mentioned in Chapter 4. The following gear chart shows standard gearing (700C × 28mm tires):

Teeth	11	12	14	16	18	21	24	28	32
52	124.9	114.5	98.1	85.9	76.3	65.4	57.2	49.1	42.9
42	100.9	92.5	79.3	69.3	61.6	52.8	46.2	39.6	34.7
30	72.0	66.0	56.6	49.5	44.0	37.7	33.0	28.3	24.8

The principal problem with this system is that the lowest gear is not low enough—the ratio is 0.94, compared with a preferred one of 0.75 or lower. The highest gear is far higher than necessary. The proportions going from one gear to the next using the rear derailleur are quite reasonable, however, because the rear cogs are spaced in moderate steps.

When you are buying a bike, unless the gears are fairly close to optimal on the stock model, you should find out what you can get changed at no cost or with minimal charge. If you order the bike with a changed set of gears or components, ride it before you accept it to make sure everything works smoothly all the way through the shifting range.

For example, if you got the setup shown above changed so that the chainwheels were 48/36/26 instead of 52/42/30, the gears would look like this:

Teeth	11	12	14	16	18	21	24	28	32
48	115.3	105.7	90.6	79.3	70.4	60.4	52.8	45.3	39.6
36	86.5	79.3	67.9	59.4	52.8	45.3	39.6	34.0	29.7
26	62.4	57.2	49.1	42.9	38.2	32.7	28.6	24.5	21.5

This is still not perfect. The ratio changes using the rear derailleur only range from 1.09 to 1.17, which is reasonable. The high gear is still higher than necessary, and the low gear is 0.81, still not quite as low as recommended but getting close. Ideally, you would also want to make the gears in the rear cluster a little larger throughout, but if the derailleurs won't accommodate this or the change in the front is all you can get the shop to do, this setup would be reasonable.

Gear choices are always a compromise, but they are more expensive to change after you've bought the bike, so have an idea of what you want before shopping and make sure you have modifications made, if necessary, at the time of purchase.

Chains

Modern bicycle chains are quite simple in basic design, but they are a marvel in engineering and manufacturing execution. The chain consists of a series of links, each exactly twice the length of the spacing between the teeth of the chainwheels and cogs of the bike's gears, so that the chain precisely meshes with the gears. A link has two overlapping plates on each side, an outside set and an inside set (Drawing 29 on page 223). The ends of each set of plates are joined with a rivet or pin. Each rivet connects an outer plate, an inner plate, a roller, the opposite inner plate, and the opposite outer plate.

The rivets mushroom out slightly at each end so that they hold at the end of each outer plate. This is done at a precise length, so that the inner plates and the roller can rotate freely around the rivet with very little play.

As the chain wraps around one of the gears, the links must pivot with minimal friction as they wrap around the chainwheel or cog, but the length of each link must be held very precisely, so that the chain can transmit force between the gears without stretching and riding up over the teeth. Finally, the side-to-side stiffness of the chain allows the derailleurs to deflect it, moving it from one chainwheel or cog to the next.

Chain Lubrication and Cleaning

All of the leg power required to move the bicycle forward is transmitted through the chain, and it has to move smoothly whenever you are pedaling. Any friction in the chain will reduce the power transmitted, and you will have to do more work to move the bike forward. To convince yourself, just try pedaling a bike with an old rusty chain!

Furthermore, any friction in the chain causes the links to stiffen and ride up as they go around the gears. This will tend to make the chain skip, to make pedaling rough, and to make shifting spotty and unreliable—either the chain will hesitate to shift when you try to do so or it will start to shift when you don't want it to do so.

Smooth operation of the chain is probably the single most important and frequent maintenance goal to keep your bike in good operating order. It is impossible to have your chain too clean or too well lubricated. As a result, opinions and credos abound on the best practices for chain cleaning and lubrication. Some recommended practices are outlined in "Maintaining Chains" on page 215, but the best thing to keep in mind is that if you keep your chain clean and well lubricated, your bike will operate well and you'll avoid other costly repairs.

Chain Wear and Stretch

A chain that is dirty or poorly lubricated (usually both) will result in excessive friction between the rollers and pins and between the rollers and the teeth of the gears. The two go together: if the rollers don't rotate smoothly on the pins, they stick and rub against the teeth of the gears. At the same time, friction between the rollers and the pins produces wear on the outside diameter of the pins, causing the chain to lengthen, or "stretch." When the chain lengthens, the links become longer than the spacing between the teeth of the gears. The chain then rides up on the gears and wears the driving sides of the teeth down. The teeth become asymmetrical, the chain rides higher, and soon it starts to skip and shift badly.

Riding a bike for a few hundred miles with a chain that has become worn and lengthened will ruin the teeth of at least some of its gears. Replacing the chain alone at that point will not help, because the gear teeth have already been reground to the wrong shape and spacing. Chain skipping and bad shifting can be caused by poorly adjusted derailleurs, but they are usually (and more seriously) associated with an elongated chain—and, necessarily, worn and distorted gear teeth. Once the wear has occurred, you have to replace both the chain and the worn chainwheels and cogs.

Cranks, Chainwheels, and Front Derailleurs

A touring crankset (see Drawing 14 on page 115) normally has three chainwheels, which bolt to a set of radiating arms, called the spider. The spider is part of a single unit with the right crank arm. The crank arms fit on either end of the axle and are held tight with bolts. The spider may have four, five, or six arms, with five arms being the most common.

The quality and weather tightness of the bearings of the crankset are important for durability and low maintenance, but the most evident design limitation is the chainwheels that are available. The principal determinant is the distance between the bolt holes.

For a touring bike, the critical limitation will be the size of the granny gear that can be accommodated, which is determined by the diameter of the inside bolt circle. The dimensions are usually described with "BCD" values, meaning bolt circle diameter, so a triple crank might be described as 110/74 mm BCD, meaning that the diameter of the bolt circles of the two larger rings is 110 mm and that of the granny gear is 74 mm. The smallest-size granny gear for this BCD would be 24 teeth. (A 110/74 five-arm crankset is the most common size for mountain and touring bikes.)

Cranks are made of aluminum alloy. Chainwheels may be made of aluminum alloy or steel. Steel wears longer, and aluminum alloy is lighter. Note that in addition to the gear teeth, chainwheels often have pins and ramps on the sides to catch the chain and facilitate shifting.

Front derailleurs are designed to handle either double or triple chainrings in particular size ranges. If you are considering any changes in chainrings, you also need to be sure the front derailleur you are using will work with the new combination.

Rear Derailleurs

Rear derailleurs (see Drawing 17, opposite, and Drawing 33 on page 242) have capacities that limit both the largest cog they can handle and the total range of differences in gears they can accommodate. A derailleur has to have a longer jockey arm to handle larger ranges of gears, because it has to take up the slack chain that is freed when you shift to the smallest chainwheel and smallest rear cog. Thus, the required jockey arm length is dictated by the total gear range, front and back.

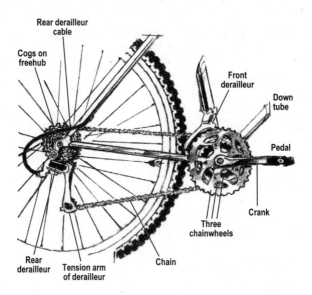

17. The drive train and shifting system of a typical touring or mountain bike.

Note that when you are riding, it is generally best to avoid either of the extreme chain angles—smallest chainwheel to smallest cog or largest chainwheel to largest cog. These positions tend to result in greater chain and gear wear.

The vast majority of rear derailleurs operate by moving to larger (lower) gears when the tension on the shift cable is increased. One counterintuitive result is that the right shift lever (rear derailleur) results in a lower gear when it is moved back (more tension), while the left shift lever (front derailleur) results in a lower gear when it is moved forward (less tension).

A few shift systems have reversed the movement of the rear derailleur, so that the low-high direction of the two levers is the same. The most recent system of this type is the Shimano Rapid Rise (also known as low-normal). A spring moves the derailleur left (to the largest cog), so the derailleur shifts to the lowest gear if the cable breaks, rather than shifting to the highest. Opinions vary as to the efficiency of shifting in this system, but it works well enough that there is no clear winner.

Freehubs, Freewheels, and Cogs

New bicycles will be equipped with a freehub that includes all bearings and the ratchet mechanism in the hub. Cassettes (sets of gears that slide onto the free-hub) can have 7, 8, 9, or 10 cogs (11-cog ones are now available), and these cogs will fit the same hubs, but for indexed shifting they have to match the shifters on the bike. The gears slide onto a set of splines. In place of a cassette, some older hubs take freewheels that screw onto the hub. Freewheels include bearings and the ratchet for the gears in the body of the freewheel.

Note that the widths of rear hubs vary. You need to make sure that any wheel or rear hub you buy matches the distance between the rear dropouts of your frame.

Pedals

Pedals are your connection to the power train. All the energy you use to propel the bike has to be transmitted through the pedals, so they are clearly important components. If you buy a complete bike, it will come either without pedals (unless you've negotiated their inclusion in the purchase price) or with fairly cheap generic pedals that you'll want to replace. This is because cyclists prefer different pedal systems, and pedal selection is closely associated with shoes, so manufacturers don't want to raise the price of the bike by including costly pedals when they may be immediately replaced.

Clipless Pedals

Most experienced touring cyclists use clipless pedals. The advantages of these pedals are that once you've spent a little time getting the cleats properly positioned on your shoes, when you clip in, your feet are always in the right place for efficient pedaling. You can get extra power on occasion by pulling up on the pedals—this not critical for touring cyclists, but it can occasionally be helpful. Many cyclists find it easier to learn to pedal efficiently and to keep their feet correctly placed on the pedals if they are clipped in. It definitely helps in slippery conditions, when your feet might otherwise slide off the pedal.

The term "clipless pedals" derives from historical usage and doesn't make a lot of sense. Traditionally, toe clips were used by serious riders to hold the foot in position and lock a grooved cleat on the bottom of the shoe to the back edge of the pedal. When pedals began to be made with spring-loaded devices that hooked onto specially shaped cleats, eliminating the clips and straps, they were called "clipless pedals."

Today "clipless pedals" generally refer to pedals like that shown in the middle example of Drawing 18 on the next page. They clamp onto a shoe cleat and hold the feet more or less rigidly in position, thus—in the experience of many riders—allow more efficient pedaling. Of course, platform pedals are also clipless, but they are not referred to that way. More accurate terms for most pedals used today that attach to cleats are "step-in" or "clip-in pedals," although these terms are not often used.

"Road" clipless pedals will not be discussed here, because they are rarely favored by tourists. On the bike they work just as well as any of the others described here, but because road-style clipless pedals require large, slippery cleats, the shoes are miserable for walking. It is nearly mandatory to carry extra shoes or sandals for walking if you use road-style step-in pedals.

Most experienced touring cyclists use step-in pedals with cleats that have drill patterns compatible with Shimano Pedaling Dynamics, or SPD. Note that cleats are not interchangeable between SPD and alternative SPD-compatible systems, but the drill pattern and screw holes are the same (such pedals always come with one set of cleats to fit the specific pedals).

With stiff-soled shoes, step-in pedals can be quite small and light, because the shoes provide a platform. The SPD pedal shown in the center of Drawing 18 is an example, and the "eggbeater" pedals made by Crank Brothers are even more minimalist. They essentially

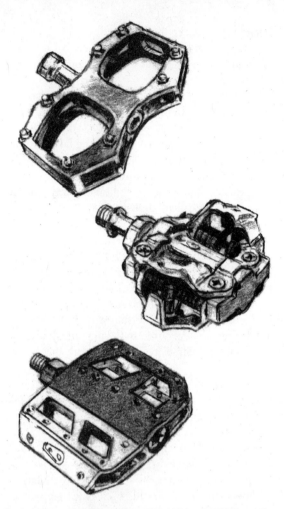

18. A platform pedal (top), an SPD pedal (middle), and a BMX/downhill-style platform pedal with pins to prevent slipping (bottom).

just clip the soles of your shoes to a sealed set of bearings connected to the pedal axles.

Disadvantages of step-in pedals, even the popular SPD-compatible ones, are worth mentioning here. Good-quality, properly adjusted step-in pedals are easy to get out of, once you are used to them—much better than the old clip variety, on which you needed to loosen the strap before pulling out—but beginners are still likely to have a few incidents when they have a hard time releasing their feet from the step-in pedals. Even very experienced riders occasionally take falls, particularly on trail rides, when a foot is trapped due to some awkward situation. This problem can be largely eliminated with appropriate practice and adjustment of release tension, especially when getting used to a new set of pedals.

While many riders find that step-in pedals reduce overuse injuries by allowing them to assume the best position with proper placement of the cleats, other riders have just the opposite experience. They find that riding on platform pedals without cleats results in far more injury-free miles, because the feet are free to move around a little, and the most comfortable shoes can be chosen, without regard for pedal compatibility and sole rigidity.

The fact that a step-in pedal locks your foot in a specific position may cause discomfort and numbing when you ride long distances, particularly if your shoes don't fit comfortably, if the bike it not fitted perfectly, or if you haven't set up the cleats optimally.

Most step-in pedals are not suitable for riding long distances with any shoes other than those designed for them, and they may not work well even for short distances. If you want to use different shoes for any reason, this is a major disadvantage. As a result of these disadvantages and others, there is a growing contingent of touring cyclists who prefer to use some alternative to the common SPD-type pedals like those discussed below.

There are hybrid versions of SPD-type pedals that are favored by many tourists. Shimano and other manufacturers make pedals that have SPD step-ins on one side and regular platform pedals on the other; at the expense of a little practice and slightly slower entry time when you are using the step-in side, you have the advantages of both. A number of other pedals, like Crank Brothers Mallet models, have clamp mechanisms that don't project very far, so you can ride comfortably with step-in-equipped shoes, hiking shoes, noncycling sandals, and other shoes that don't have overly thin soles.

Platform Pedals

The simplest alternative is a basic platform pedal like the one illustrated at the top of Drawing 18 on page 132. Platform pedals have enough weight-bearing surface area to be comfortable in a variety of shoes, without the need for soles that are sufficiently stiff to distribute pressure. This means you can wear whatever shoes you find comfortable that are suitable for other aspects of a tour—hiking, camping, walking, or whatever. Your feet can move around slightly while pedaling, so there is less likelihood of numbness or other types of overuse injuries. You eliminate both the disadvantages and advantages of step-in pedals.

One downside of regular platform pedals is that they can be slippery when they are wet or muddy. Ideally, platform pedals should have fairly large surfaces so that they don't dig into the soles of your feet, even if you are wearing shoes with relatively flexible soles. Variations on platform pedals include those with raised projections to provide some traction in wet conditions. Some, like the Grip Kings sold by Rivendell, are indented on the sides to have maximum clearance in turns.

Other Alternatives

If you choose not to use step-in pedals but you want some grip, pedals made for BMX, downhill, or freestyle bike riders may be just what you need. They have studs or pins, sometimes replaceable, that are intended to provide purchase for your soles. They don't position your feet the way step-in pedals do, but they prevent your foot from sliding around, even in wet or muddy conditions. One current example is the Crank Brothers 5050 pedal, shown at the bottom of Drawing 18 on page 132. If you want this type of pedal for touring, especially to use with shoes that have relatively soft soles, look for pedals that have a fairly large surface area for adequate foot support.

One final alternative favored by some tourists is platform pedals supplemented by Power Grips, nonstretch straps that mount diagonally across each pedal. They are a fixed length after mounting, so you flip the pedal up with your toe and slide your foot in. The motion is the same as with traditional toe-clips, but there is no metal cleat to hold your shoe in a particular position. Power Grips prevent your foot from sliding off the pedal to the side, and they allow you to pull up on the pedals on the rare occasions when this is desirable. They work with older rat-trap-style pedals and with some platform pedals. A few riders use old-style clip pedals and straps but dispense with the cleats. This approach provides most of the advantages of Power Grips and is significantly cheaper.

Shifters

Shifters have a simple basic function: they are used to tighten or loosen the cable connected to the front or rear derailleur so that the chain is moved onto a different chainwheel or rear cog. This changes the number of revolutions made by the rear wheel each time you turn the cranks, which is how gearing works on a typical multispeed bicycle.

Most modern production bikes, road and mountain, are equipped with indexed shifting—you move the shifter in click stops, and the mechanism positions the chain automatically to the correct orientation over the cog or the chainwheel. With traditional friction shifting, a friction device holds the shifter in position after you move it, and you change gears by feel and sound. Friction shifting has some advantages and is really no more difficult once you are used to it. Note that all bar-end and down-tube index shifters can be converted to friction shifting by simply twisting an adjuster. Left-hand bar-end shifters (for the front derailleur) are typically set for friction rather than click shifting. It is a good idea to learn to do this, because indexed shifting

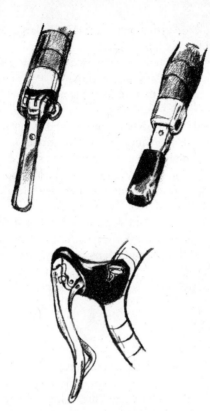

19. Two styles of bar-end shifters and a brake-lever shifter.

is sensitive to cable stretch and damage. Being able to switch to friction shifting can be a useful trick if you have shifting problems on the road.

The two styles of shifters most commonly used by touring cyclists with road bars are bar-end shifters, or "barcons," and integrated brake-shifter combinations, both shown in Drawing 19. The majority of tourists who use drop handlebars use bar-end shifters. They are easy to use, reliable, and fairly easy to service if something goes wrong.

Devotees of shifters that are integrated in brake levers ("brifters") like the convenience of being able to shift without moving their hands while riding on the brake hoods. The problem with these complicated devices is that they are often difficult or impossible to service, so if one fails on a tour, you're stuck until you can get to a bike shop, and then you may have a rather expensive repair to deal with.

There are a few other alternatives that you may encounter. For example, if you are beginning with a mountain bike or are changing to mountain-style bars, you'll probably have thumb-operated trigger shifters.

Other Shifting Systems

Hubs with internal planetary gear systems* have been around for a long time. They were used in the "3-speed" utility bikes that were ubiquitous in the United States up until a few decades ago, and they are still the norm in many parts of the world. There are several versatile variants available today, of which the best is the German-made 14-speed Rohloff hub. Shimano and the venerable Sturmey-Archer make 8-speed hubs, and SRAM makes a 7-speed. These are more practical for serious touring than you might think, because the gear ratios can be evenly spaced over the range of the hubs, so that the number of usable ratios available is the same as those on many 27- or 30-speed derailleur systems—at least for the Rohloff.

Note the advantages of internal-gear hubs: they are practically weatherproof, they are less vulnerable to damage than derailleurs, and they can be shifted more quickly—even when the bike is not moving. Reliability

---

* A planetary gear-drive system consists of a central gear (the "sun" gear), several smaller gears (the "planet" gears) that mesh around the sun's circumference and roll around it, and, outside these, a "ring" gear with interior teeth that mesh with the planet gears. The planet gears can be considered a unit, and their axes are usually connected with some sort of frame. All three system components are interconnected but move at different speeds; if two move with respect to each other, the third is driven. A three-speed hub uses this type of system with a clutch that connects different combinations to change gears. The gears themselves are always connected and move in the same relation to one another; only the linkage to the bike's sprocket changes.

and internal power losses are a concern, though the Rohloff hubs, at least, are very efficient and almost indestructible. A Rohloff also costs more than a moderately priced touring bike. I have not seen enough tests on the lower-priced hubs to know how reliable and efficient they are. Internal-gear hubs require very little maintenance—a good thing, because if they fail, you can't do much.

The biggest disadvantage to the internal-gear hubs is that they are specialty items for touring bikes; their main use is on BMX bikes. Adapting the hardware may be fun if you like to mess around with bikes, but if you aren't inclined to do that, you'll have a hard time finding someone to do it. Information on hubs and parts can be found at sheldonbrown.com/harris/hubs-internal.html, and general articles at sheldonbrown.com/internal-gears.html.

7

Wheels, Tires, and Fenders

Bicycle wheels are marvels of simple but elegant engineering. Their basic design has been around since about the second half of the nineteenth century, though there have been constant improvements right up to the present day. The wheel is supported by wire spokes under tension.

On the outside, of course, is a pneumatic tire, which provides contact with the pavement (or gravel or trail), with enough friction to allow you to brake, steer effectively, and accelerate, and enough springiness to cushion the bumps. The pneumatic tire was invented at the same time as the diamond frame. Most tires used today are clinchers, which have a cross section like a smoothed-out capital omega (Ω). The tire encloses a separate inner tube that holds the air pressure. The tire is held on the rim by a lip edge that fits into the depression in the tire adjoining the bead (see Drawing 20 on the next page). It is the lip that "clinches" the tire and therefore provides the name "clincher."

The rim, usually made of a hard aluminum alloy, is circular, forming the actual wheel on which you roll, and is protected and cushioned by the tire on the outside while its shape is preserved by the tension of the spokes that attach it to the hub. The rim has to be strong enough to hold the beads of the tire, to

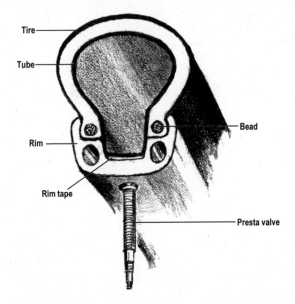

20. Cross-section of a rim and tire. The Presta valve shown here is preferred for bicycles.

withstand the air pressure that tends to spread the tire, and to keep the spoke nipples from ripping out, even though the spokes are under high tension.

The Magic and Mechanics of the Bicycle Wheel

The bicycle wheel is an example of what is known by engineers as a "prestressed structure." The most common use of the term is in prestressed concrete. Think about a highway overpass. To hold up the overpass, the most obvious structural element to provide a horizontal support is a steel I-beam, which is strong in both compression and tension but heavy and expensive. Under the weight of the structure and the traffic, as the beam resists deformation, the top of the beam is compressed and the bottom is under tension. In the right situations, concrete can be used instead of steel to provide the horizontal support. Concrete alone is very strong and inelastic under pressure but very weak under tension (it cracks and fails catastrophically). The way concrete beams can be used to span an overpass is to prestress them—steel cables or rods are embedded in the concrete and are tightened so that the whole concrete beam is under pressure that exceeds any forces of tension that are exerted upon it, such as when used as an overpass. This means that when the beam is used, the lower part is put under tension by the weight of the bridge and crossing vehicles, but the tension only reduces the compressive forces exerted by the prestressing.

That is how the bicycle wheel works. Your weight is borne by the spokes extending down to the road, just as if you were on an old-fashioned wooden-spoked wagon wheel. Of course, the spokes are only thin wires, and if they were simply inserted in place with no tension, they would immediately collapse under your weight. Prestressing the wheel places each spoke under a tension force that far exceeds even a fraction of the weight that it will have to bear. So, when you put your weight on the bike, the tension on the lowest spokes is reduced by the portion of your weight that they have to carry.

The weight-bearing property is only part of the story—spokes also have to resist sideways pressures, transmit the force of pedaling to the rims, and, to a lesser degree, transmit some of the braking forces when you are slowing down. These issues are further discussed under "Spokes and Lacing Patterns" later in this chapter. The dominant forces on the spokes, however, are the radial forces—the ones that hold you and the bike up above the road and that keep the rims nearly perfect circles.

The final wheel components are the hubs. Their function is to hold the inner ends of the spokes (hence the hub flanges have to withstand high tension), to provide rigid center structures for the wheels, and to rotate with virtually no friction on axles that can be attached rigidly to the frame. The rear hub also has to have a provision for the freehub or freewheel, a feature described in "Freehubs, Freewheels, and Cogs" on page 130. The best hubs have bearings that run very smoothly, are well sealed against the elements, and hold up for many thousands or tens of thousands of miles. The flange has to be strong enough to hold the spoke heads, with enough of a margin to withstand metal fatigue and some wear from the spoke ends.

Hubs

Hubs form the centers of the wheels, the points of attachment between the wheels and the bike, and, at the rear, the connection for the drive train. They provide the axes of rotation for the wheels, so they are one of the primary sources of potential friction on a bicycle. Along with the chain and rear derailleur, hubs are critical for lubrication, maintenance, and attention to design. A little friction in the hubs can generate a huge amount of effort as the miles add up on a tour.

At the most elementary level, the hub is part of the basic wheel design. A 36-spoke wheel has to have a hub with 18 holes in each flange (18 on the right and 18 on the left). A 48-spoke wheel has to have 24 holes in each flange.

The two critical functions of the hub are to turn freely around the axle, which requires bearings that are as friction-free as possible, and to anchor the spokes. There are many subsidiary design issues like the position of the bearings. Only a few of these nuances are discussed here. In general, it is better for hubs to be strong, rigid, and failure-free. The hollow axle of the hub is normally clamped between the dropouts or fork ends with a quick-release device: a skewer that goes through the axle with a cam-action lever on one end and a nut on the other.

One historical distinction was between low-flange (smaller diameter) and high-flange (larger diameter) hubs. The division was always arbitrary in terms of actual measurements, and many of the justifications for high-flange hubs have disappeared. High-flange hubs are now mostly confined to a few track-racing bicycles and tandems. The two differences between

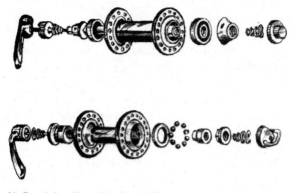

21. Front hubs with cartridge ("sealed") bearings (above) and with "cup-and-cone" bearings (below).

low- and high-flange hubs are the angle of the spokes and the clearance for the rear sprocket or cluster, which allowed spoke replacement without removing the gears. With modern equipment, these considerations are mostly obsolete, so the usual low-flange hubs supplied on most modern bikes are assumed in this book.

The biggest difference between various hubs you are likely to see in high-quality production bikes is between "cup-and-cone" hubs ("loose bearings") and cartridge ("sealed-bearing") hubs (see Drawing 21). The distinction these days is far less important than it was when the first edition of this book was published three decades ago.

Four important hub characteristics relate to bearing design. The first, and by far the most important, is that the wheels should run as close to friction-free as possible. The second is that the bearings should be as impermeable to the weather (moisture) as possible. This feature can be hard to evaluate, because it depends on the weather in which you ride and your maintenance habits. Third, the hub should be as easy to maintain as possible. This is also a subjective characteristic, depending on your habits, your skills, and your priorities, along with the climate. Fourth, you should consider the lateral stability and strength of the hub. Unfortunately, this is also an issue that has subjective elements.

Dynamo hubs for the front wheel are a specialized hub for riders like randonneurs, who anticipate needing lights for extended periods. (Randonneur rides—brevets or randonées—are events in which participants ride a predefined route of a specified distance, unsupported, for personal times. They are endurance rides but not competitive. Many randonneur riders are also touring cyclists.) The dynamo constantly produces electric power, so that batteries are not needed. They are discussed under "Dynamo Systems" on page 270.

Cup-and-Cone Hubs

Cup-and-cone hubs are the traditional hubs in high-quality bicycles, and there is no reason to avoid a bike that uses them. They are arguably just as easy to maintain as sealed bearing hubs. Weather and moisture issues are contingent on the way you maintain the hubs.

Cup-and-cone hubs use loose ball bearings that rotate between a cup race (groove) that is part of the body of the hub, and the cone—a threaded nut that forms the outer race for the ball bearings and is adjusted by screwing it along the axle. A second (lock) nut screws on the same thread to lock the cone at a specific position. The adjustments are made using cone wrenches—thin, open-ended wrenches.

Cartridge-Bearing ("Sealed-Bearing") Hubs

The other type of hub is the cartridge-bearing hub, typically referred to as a sealed-bearing hub. The bearings are enclosed between two sleeves and are not designed to be serviced; cartridges are standard industrial parts that are replaced when servicing is required. The best cartridge-bearing hubs are very durable and relatively watertight, but they are not truly sealed—they can be penetrated by moisture just as cup-and-cone bearings can. The best ones, like Phil Wood hubs, are favorites of touring cyclists because of their durability, reliability, and good resistance to water penetration. Ease of service varies with manufacturer, but the bearings themselves can be found in good hardware stores and automotive-parts houses, because they are not specific to bicycles.

Hub Width

In general, hub width is not something you will determine. Front hubs are generally 100 mm, measured locknut to locknut, but rear hubs are variable. Hubs have to be the right width to fit between the frame or fork dropouts. If you've bought or resurrected an older bike with a five-, six-, or seven-speed freewheel or freehub, the length of the axle (and the distance between the rear dropouts of the frame) will be 120 or 126 mm. Modern road bikes use 130 mm axles, and that's what your bike will have if you buy one of the production bikes mentioned in Chapter 4. Mountain bikes use 135 mm spacing, and some builders of custom and semi-custom touring bikes advocate this width, especially for heavy riders, because it requires less extreme dishing of the wheel (see "Rudiments of Wheel Building" later in this chapter), so it makes broken spokes less likely. Rivendell makes frames with 132.5 mm spacing, so that either 130 or 135 mm hubs can be mounted without causing problems.

Rims

The most important criteria for rims on touring bikes are that they be strong and durable and that they be wide enough to accommodate the tires you want to use. Many 700C rims are intended for narrow, lightweight road tires for sport riding or road racing. These are typically around 20 mm in width, and they may not accommodate touring tires in the 35 to 40 mm range, which are recommended to absorb bumps. (The feasible tire size, regardless of rim width, will be governed by your frame clearance and by whether you are using fenders.) Rims have to be drilled for the same number of spokes as the hubs. For touring bikes, 36 or more holes are generally recommended, as discussed in the section titled "Spokes and Lacing Patterns" later in this chapter.

It should be noted that 700C tires and rims can be hard to find outside the United States, Canada, and some western European countries. Usually only a limited selection is available. The tires are likely to be narrow and the rims probably only available in limited drilling patterns. Thirty-six-hole, 26-inch rims are ubiquitous almost everywhere because mountain bikes have become so common worldwide. This means that if you are doing a tour in rural Latin America or Asia and you manage to damage a wheel, you could probably find a usable replacement. You could also find a replacement tire that would work.

The "rim strip" is the rubber, plastic, or cloth strip that covers the spoke holes on the inside of the rim. Some also use fiberglass strapping tape instead of a rim strip. Most rim strips work fine. After patching a tire or replacing a tube, it is important to make sure the rim strip covers the spoke holes properly. Otherwise a sharp edge can gradually wear a hole in the tube.

Spokes and Lacing Patterns

Extensive discussion of wheel-building issues is beyond the scope of this book, but every touring cyclist should have some basic understanding of the way bicycle wheels are constructed. A typical spoke pattern for a touring wheel is illustrated in Drawing 22.

Overall, it is best for touring wheels to have 36 or more spokes to ensure durability, reduce the likelihood of broken spokes, and simplify emergency retruing in case of a broken spoke or damaged wheel. Some tourists insist on 40 or 48 spokes, particularly on the rear wheel. Heavier riders and those who carry more luggage should err on the side of caution and choose or build wheels with more spokes rather than fewer.

Spokes exert tension between the hub and the rim. The hub end of the spoke is secured by a swaged

22. How a bicycle wheel is laced. The lacing pattern shown is for a 3-cross front wheel (each spoke crosses three spokes going in the opposite direction). A high-flange hub is shown for clarity, though low-flange wheels are standard on all modern touring and road bikes.

head, like the head of a nail. It is held in the rim by a spoke nipple, which screws onto the threaded end of the spoke. The tension in the spoke is determined by turning the nipple with a spoke wrench. If you look at the spokes extending from the hub, you'll note that they alternate in direction—one spoke slants to the left and the next one to the right. In contrast, the simplest spoke lacing is radial spoking, where every spoke extends perpendicularly from the hub to the rim. Radial spoking is used occasionally for very specialized wheels—it is a very strong and efficient arrangement for wheels that don't need to accelerate the bike forward or slow it down. For example, it works well for the front wheels of track bikes that have no brakes.

It would be unwise to equip any touring bike with a radially spoked wheel, either front or back, and it is worthwhile to understand why. A radially spoked wheel is the strongest possible configuration for supporting your and the bike's weight when you're not braking or accelerating by pushing on the pedals and the drive train, but it is a poor choice for general use. When you are standing still or rolling without pedaling or braking, weight is transmitted vertically through the spokes from the hub to the rim. But if you push on the pedals, you're accelerating the hub with respect to the rim. When you apply the brakes, you're decelerating the rim with respect to the hub. With either of these actions, force has to be transmitted through the spokes between the hub and the rim, or vice versa. This force is transmitted through the spokes. A radially spoked wheel has to distort in either of these cases, and the tension on the spokes will be very high, so the likelihood of broken spokes or cracked hub flanges is great.

For most kinds of riding, the wheel is laced so that the spokes meet the hub and the rim at an angle, thus transmitting the forces between the two without extreme changes in spoke tension. Each alternate spoke is angled in the opposite direction from those on either side, so that the forces balance, and each crosses one or more spokes going in the opposite direction. Wheel-lacing patterns are usually described by indicating the number of opposite-direction spokes that any one spoke crosses: 1-cross, 2-cross, 3-cross, or 4-cross.

If you want to understand the nuances of different patterns, take a look at the Resources section at the back of the book. In general, for touring bikes with 700C or 26-inch wheels, a pattern with 36 spokes laced 3-cross works well. Riders with more body weight and tandems sometimes prefer 40 or 48 spokes.

In general, the best wheels for touring use butted (thinner in the middle than the ends) stainless steel spokes, typically 14-16 gauge (2.0 mm-1.8 mm-2.0 mm) or 14-17 gauge (2.0 mm-1.5 mm-2.0 mm), with nickel-plated brass nipples. Aluminum nipples are a bad idea for touring wheels, because they can crack over time. Straight-gauge spokes (14 gauge) are typical on complete bikes even though they weigh a bit more. If you decide to indulge in hand-built wheels, you should get butted spokes. Butted spokes, contrary to intuition and some advertising claims, make stronger wheels than straight-gauge spokes. A good choice for touring bikes is 14-16 gauge spokes rather than the slightly lighter 14-17 ones. (Technically, modern spokes have metric dimensions, but the old gauge terminology, now an approximation, is still most commonly used in the United States.)

Finally, you should understand that rear wheels on most touring bikes are *dished*. That is, the spokes on the right-hand side of the wheels are under more tension and go from the hub to the rim at a different angle than the ones on the left. This is necessary because space has to be left for the gear cluster. Since the right spokes are under more tension and they are on the rear wheel, which carries a heavier load, the drive-side spokes on the rear wheel are the most likely spokes to break. And because the spoke heads going through the hub flange are behind the gear cluster, these spokes are also the hardest to replace—a perfect example of Murphy's Law.

There are a few exceptions. Internally geared hubs like the Rohloff don't require dished wheels. Bikes with disc brakes require dished front wheels and a change in the dishing of the rear.

Rudiments of Wheel Building

If you are buying a complete bike, unless you are having it built to your specifications, it will come with machine-built wheels, which these days are pretty good. Depending on your local shop's standard preparation, they may do virtually nothing to these wheels: whoever assembles the bike may just give the wheels a spin to make sure they are (more or less) true, check them quickly for major discrepancies in spoke tension, or, if they are very conscientious, they might retension the spokes—basically, put the wheel in a truing stand and tweak each of the spokes to make sure they are evenly tensioned and that the nipples are not frozen. If the wheel components are reasonable for your intended use, you can expect that they will give you good service. The machines that lace current wheels have gotten far better.

That being said, nearly all experienced riders agree that hand-built wheels laced by competent wheel builders are still superior to machine-built ones. This may be partly mystique, but there are good reasons to believe that it is true. When you are building a wheel, you create the round, centered structure in increments so that the final wheel is very evenly tensioned, making it much more resistant to being distorted and weakened by impacts from potholes, rocks, and other road hazards. So there are good reasons why dedicated cyclists will pay a premium for hand-built wheels or take the time to build them personally.

At the next level of quality and expense, wheels built by master wheel builders will, of course, be very unlikely to incorporate mistakes, small or large. The best builders make a host of subtle choices in matching components and putting them together in the optimum way. Those who know how to build merely adequate wheels cannot match this experience—it comes from having built thousands of solid wheels, observing the effects of small differences, and incorporating those into the next set of wheels. If you want to get a feel for some of the differences, read the wheel-building books listed in the Resources section or take a look at the various sections on wheels at the Peter White Cycles Web site at www.peterwhitecycles.com.

Should You Do It Yourself?

Most touring cyclists have never built a bicycle wheel, so it is clearly not an essential skill. It is worth trying if you are mechanically inclined, however, even if you only build a few. Truing or repairing a wheel, whether on the road or in your garage, will be a lot easier and more reliable if you've built a few wheels. It is also very satisfying to ride on wheels you've built yourself.

The actual process of building a wheel is not hard to understand. Obviously, the materials have to be assembled first, including spokes of the correct length, separated into groups when appropriate. (Wheels that are dished, with the spokes forming a different angle with the vertical to allow for the rear cogs or a disc brake to fit on one side of the wheel, require different length spokes for each side of the wheel. Different cross patterns require different spoke lengths. Different hub–rim combinations require different spoke lengths.)

Once the materials are assembled, the builder lubricates the spoke nipples and the rim holes and then does the basic lacing of the wheel. This is not difficult, but for those who don't do it every day, it requires following a step-by-step process. Start with the spokes on one side going in one direction, then those on the same side going in the opposite direction, and then repeat the process on the other side. Once the wheel is completely laced, it is stable, and you can gradually tighten it.

Complete step-by-step instructions are not included here. The books listed in the Resources section or Sheldon Brown's Web-based instructions will tell you what you need to know. For touring, build 36-spoke wheels, or perhaps 40- or 48-spoke ones for the rear if you are heavy, you're carrying heavier than normal loads, or you're building wheels for a tandem. Build wheels that are 3-cross on both sides.

Tools and Supplies

You will need a few tools. The most important is a truing stand. It doesn't have to be an expensive one—you can build wheels that are just as good with a basic stand. It takes a little longer, but beginners should take their time building wheels. You also need a good spoke wrench that is the right size for the nipples you are using, a screwdriver (or, better, a nipple driver), and a dish gauge.

It is quite possible to build a wheel using a fork as a truing stand—it just takes longer and may be rather inconvenient. You can build your own, very good, truing stand and dish gauge using the directions in Roger Musson's book, listed in the Resources section.

Don't fool around with exotic materials or wheel designs for your first wheels—if you can't control yourself, you can always do that later. You need good hubs, the best quality you can afford or justify. The same is true for rims. You want rims that are strong and true. You can't easily measure the roundness of a rim before it is incorporated in a wheel, so you have to rely on the manufacturer's quality control. Get 14-16 double-butted stainless steel spokes (2.0 mm in diameter at the ends, but 1.7 mm in the center). These are not only lighter than straight-gauge spokes, but they make stronger wheels. Use nickel-plated brass nipples.

You must be completely sure of the correct spoke lengths before ordering spokes. The spoke length is determined by the lacing pattern (3-cross, 4-cross, etc.). If you are buying hubs, rims, and spokes from a shop or other dealer, they should be able to provide the right lengths. You can look them up in the reference books listed in the Resources section at the end of the book or use one of the online spoke calculators listed there. For rounding spoke lengths, round to the longer figure.

Once you have the materials, follow the directions in one of the wheel-building resources. A few steps may be a little confusing if you are just reading the instructions, but they become clear as the wheel takes shape.

Exotic Wheels

Classically spoked wheels continue to dominate cycling generally, and this dominance seems unlikely to change soon. Spoke patterns have changed for some uses—as rims and spokes have become stronger, racers and sport riders can use wheels with fewer spokes, particularly on good roads, reducing weight and wind resistance. As discussed in "Spokes and Lacing Patterns" earlier in this chapter, cycling tourists are advised to take a conservative approach in adopting wheels with fewer spokes.

More radical are disc wheels and composite wheels with a few cast spokes. Disc wheels have had some success in very specialized events—time trials on flat courses with no side winds, and time-trial and pursuit events on the track. Disc wheels are heavy and a disaster when wind is gusting, making them unsuitable for bicycle touring. Composite wheels made of carbon or graphite fiber and epoxy resin with three, four, or five spokes have found occasional favor in high-performance racing bikes. Such designs can sometimes achieve a small advantage in aerodynamic efficiency for time trials, with lower weight penalties than disc wheels, but they are expensive and cannot be repaired, so they make no sense for touring. They had largely disappeared from the racing scene as well at the time this was written.

Choosing Tires

Tires are really one of the simplest components of a bike and one of the easiest to choose, but there tends to be a lot of misinformation and many misconceptions about them. Another difficulty is that tire size presents a classic example of one of the worst vices of the bike industry—its tendency to avoid standards even when they would be easy to adopt.

As noted at the beginning of this chapter, most tires on today's touring bikes are clinchers. Tubulars, another tire type, use very different rim designs and have some advantages, but they are rarely used today and therefore won't be discussed in detail. Specialized tubeless tires are also not covered—they are not used by touring cyclists and are still confined to mountain bike racing. It remains to be seen whether their various problems can be solved, making them more practical. Their main attraction at the moment is to permit riding on trails with relatively low pressure while still avoiding "pinch flats." Pinch flats occur when the wheel hits an obstruction causing the tire and tube to be momentarily compressed against the rim, pinching the tube and making a small cut. Pinch flats can occur on rocky trails or after hitting a pothole in pavement, but they are more likely when tire pressure has been reduced to provide better traction on trails.

Tire Construction

The main structure of the tire is provided by two circular beads (Drawing 20 on page 140), usually made of steel wire but sometimes Kevlar (the generic term is aramid fiber) or another synthetic material, with a fabric casing connecting the two beads. The casing is impregnated and covered with rubber, but the fabric provides the structural strength. The beads are designed to barely fit over the rim before the tire is inflated, and their edges are pressed into channels on each side of the rim when the tire is inflated with an airtight inner tube.

The beads and the casing provide the principal strength of the tire. The rubber is there to glue the rest into place, to protect from sunlight and abrasion, and to provide adequate grip on the pavement. The threads of the fabric normally run diagonally between the beads (on a bias), and there are several layers—hence they are called bias-ply tires. Designs are often highly sophisticated and have additional features, such as tough layers of aramid fibers in a belt below the tread to resist punctures.

Aramid beads are lighter than steel ones and more flexible, so they are used to make foldable tires, and they are particularly popular for spares. Though steel-beaded tires are a little heavier, they are usually cheaper, so they are widely used. A steel-beaded tire can also be folded into a small enough package to easily fit in a pannier, but they need to be folded carefully to avoid kinking the beads (see "Folding a Spare Tire" later in this chapter).

Tire Tread

The tread on road tires is mainly cosmetic. It doesn't provide a better grip or reduce rolling resistance, though people tend to expect it. Bicycle tires do not hydroplane in wet weather, as car tires can, because the pressure on the patch that contacts the road is high and your speed is far too low. Thus tread is only of significance if you are riding on dirt, especially soft dirt, or if you are riding a heavily treaded mountain bike tire on pavement, where it may generate significant drag.

A few multisurface tires are designed with tread on the sides and a smooth ridge in the center. The theory is that the ridge provides low rolling resistance on pavement, and the tread on the sides gives you traction on dirt. Whether this strategy works is a matter of dispute. Probably the most important feature of tires for varying surfaces is their width—fat tires do better on trails, fire roads, and other loose surfaces.

Tire Size

After the invention of the safety bicycle near the end of the nineteenth century, most bicycles came with wheels with the largest diameter possible that worked with the design, only a little larger than the size used on most road bikes today. The size was generally labeled with the diameter of the tire mounted on the wheel. The pneumatic tire, invented by John Dunlop at about the time of the origin of the safety bicycle and patented in 1888, was one of the most important innovations in the development of the bicycle—and later the automobile.

The nomenclature for tire (and wheel) sizes is enormously confusing, because it has evolved over the years to describe often inconsistent "standards." Historically, each of the important cycling nations developed its own system, along with its own terminology. Consider that there are at least five incompatible sizes of 26-inch tires and at least four incompatible 16-inch sizes. The International Standards Organization (ISO) determines the standards for specifying tire sizes. The purpose of this is to eliminate ambiguity as a result of the different systems within various countries, but the most commonly used nomenclature does not follow the standard, and some tire manufacturers still don't bother to put the ISO sizes on their products. Unlike some other areas of bicycle design, where proprietary innovations drive the lack of standardization, inconsistent labeling of tire sizes has no real justification.

The most common sizes for touring bikes are 700C (ISO 622) and 26-inch (ISO 559). In this case, "26-inch" refers to the widely available mountain bike size—there are other, completely incompatible 26-inch sizes. The ISO sizes are always more reliable. They also include widths (diameter of the cross section of the tire), such as 40-722 or 40-559 for tires that are 40 mm wide. Note that given the material from which tires are made, these figures do not have the precision of measurements of metal parts. The cross-sectional diameter tends to be less precise than the radial diameter, so that if you are looking at a tire from one manufacturer that is labeled 37-622, it might actually be larger than another maker's 40-622. Both will fit the same rim, however.

Another number is added to the common terminology that indicates the width of the cross section of the tire in millimeters—700 × 28C (ISO 28-622), 700 × 32C (ISO 32-622), 650 × 30B (ISO 30-571), and so on. A larger second number indicates a wider, heavier, typically more durable tire.

Wider tires are heavier, and the weight has to be accelerated more than the bike because you have to provide the angular momentum. That is, you have to supply the energy required to get the mass on the outside of the wheel rotating. However, this is far less consequential for a tourist, who mostly rides at a steady pace for long distances, than for a road racer who has to accelerate frequently to go into a sprint.

A narrower tire under high pressure on very smooth pavement or on a track has lower rolling resistance than a fatter one. But the high pressure actually results in more required effort for the rider as the surface becomes rougher. The thinner tire has less air drag, but it is considerably less comfortable, and relatively high pressure has to be maintained to prevent pinch flats, particularly on gravel or rough pavement, and especially with touring loads.

Generally, for long-distance touring with variable surfaces, wider tires are more comfortable, durable, and resistant to damage. Requirements vary due to a number of factors, but I'd recommend touring tires be at least 30 mm, if they will fit on your bike, or more, up to 50 mm.

Rim Size and Tire Diameter

In general, the ISO diameter designation can be trusted for matching rims and tires, though you should be alert for mismatches if you are replacing either. The ISO diameter refers to the diameter of the inside of the tire bead and the corresponding surface on the rim. However, some rims have higher flanges than others, so a few tires may be hard to mount on some rims, and some tires may pop over a rim with a relatively low flange if they aren't perfectly mounted. Tires too wide for the rims on which they are mounted risk rolling off and blowing out on descents. Pay attention to these issues and compensate for them if necessary. I won't use a tire that comes off the rim too easily. Tight fit generally just requires unbreakable tire irons and good mounting technique (make sure that as you are trying to get the last few inches of the tire over the rim, the opposite side of the bead is all the way down in the center depression of the rim).

Rims should also have the width specified, for example, 20 mm or 24 mm. This measurement typically refers to the outside measurement. Clearly, the rim must be compatible with the tire. A lightweight 19 mm rim intended for road racing will not work properly with a 50 mm tire. (A rim with a 19 mm outside measurement would probably have an inside width of about 15 mm.) There is significant flexibility in this match, however. A 20 mm rim will work fine with tires ranging in size from 26 to 32 mm, but would be unsuited to much wider tires. A 24 to 25 mm rim will work well with tires 32 mm and wider.

Tire Pressure

Tires are marked on the outside with a pressure rating, but this number is not particularly useful, because it represents marketing considerations rather than practical information for the cyclist. Nearly all tires will be perfectly safe with much higher pressures than this number, but frequently the optimum pressure is less than the one marked on the tire.

To determine the right tire pressure for your bike with a particular set of tires, you need to experiment. The optimum pressure will be higher when the bike is carrying panniers with a full load of gear for self-contained touring. It will be higher if you are heavier. Since the rear wheel almost always carries more weight, it will typically be inflated to a higher pressure (approximately 10 percent higher) than the front tire.

The ideal is to achieve a pressure that inflates the tire enough so that it has very little rolling resistance but still provides a comfortable ride. The limitation on the low end is that a tire that is too soft is vulnerable to pinch flats, particularly for narrow tires on rough terrain. In general, fatter tires should be inflated to a lower pressure than skinny ones, because they need less pressure to hold you and your luggage up with negligible rolling resistance. Skinny tires have to be inflated harder to avoid pinch flats.

Signs of an overinflated tire include a rough ride and a tendency to skitter from minor road irregularities. Signs of an underinflated tire include bottoming out when you hit potholes and other irregularities and squirminess, particularly with the front wheel when cornering. Note that as long as your tires are fat enough that they won't get pinch flats, you'll normally want to reduce the tire pressure on rough roads, on soft surfaces, on trails, and on gravel. It's more comfortable, and you'll have better traction and control.

It is worthwhile to experiment to get the pressure right, and then record the numbers or memorize them. If you carry a tire gauge on tour, this will allow you to quickly and confidently adjust the tire pressure for different conditions.

Tubes, Valves, and Puncture Reduction

Usually, if you get matching tubes when you buy tires, there isn't much question about the right size. Because tubes are designed to stretch freely, unlike tire casings, replacing a tube with a smaller cross-section tube of the same diameter will usually work fine, except that the undersized tube will lose pressure every couple of days, instead of every few weeks. Oversized tubes and tubes intended for larger-diameter tires will also work in a pinch, but they do entail problems. A significantly oversized tube will typically form some folds when you install it in the tire, and under pressure these create wear points and opportunities for blowouts. They should be avoided except in emergencies, and they should be replaced at the earliest opportunity.

For cycling, Presta valves (see Drawing 20 on page 140) are far superior to Schrader (conventional automobile) valves, because their pumps are more efficient, and because there is no internal spring pushing on the valve—only air pressure and the lock nut assist the seal, and the release mechanism is easily accessible.

There are a few issues with Presta valves, however. The valve actuator can be bent or broken, so you need to carry a spare tube. You have to carry an adapter (very cheap and lightweight) to be able to use gas station inflation hoses. Most important, if you are headed to places far from United States, Canadian, or western European bike shops, you may have a hard time finding tubes with Presta valves. In these situations, you can drill the stem hole of your rim to accept Schrader valves and install easily available rubber grommets so that you can use Presta-equipped tubes except in emergencies. Some frame-mounted bicycle pumps can handle both.

Tire liners, such as Mr. Tuffy, Panaracer Flat-Away, and STOP Flats, are strips placed between the tube and the inside of the tire to reduce the number of flats. They work, at the expense of additional weight, and I have found them very useful in the past. However, with modern puncture-resistant tires, they seem superfluous. If you're willing to run wheels that are a little heavier to avoid most flats, it usually makes more sense to get tires that incorporate puncture-resistant bands.

Folding a Spare Tire

Most tourists who carry spare tires choose Kevlar-beaded tires, because the material used to make them is more flexible than steel, making them easy to fold and pack. However, it is perfectly feasible to fold a steel-beaded tire without kinking the cable in the bead. Hold it in front of you with your hands grasping the top two quadrants (at 10 o'clock and 2 o'clock). Move your hands together until they cross, with your left hand next to you and the right away from you. The tire will form a figure eight. Hold the junction together with your right hand and grab the bottom of the larger loop with your left. Twist it gently in the opposite direction than the first twist. You will now have three loops forming a cloverleaf, and you can coax these into a package of three adjacent loops of the same size with no kinks in the bead. (Do all this slowly—kinking the bead will damage the tire.) This can easily be packed in a pannier. Any short strap can be used to keep the tire from unfolding accidentally, but it is best not to store it folded when you get home, since the bends will become permanent.

It takes a little practice to get the knack of doing this, but it's easy once you do. If you want an illustration, there is a video of the process at sheldonbrown. com/video/tire-folding.html.

Recommended Tires

There is a host of reputable tire brands that have firm devotees among experienced tourists. These include Specialized, Avocet, Vredestein, and Vittoria. Tires that consistently get particularly good reviews from experienced tourists are Schwalbe Marathons, Continental Contacts, and Panaracer Paselas. All are available in the usual touring sizes and with different tread designs for various kinds of tours, with and without puncture-resistant belts, and with steel or aramid beads.

Careful shopping among models is worth your time. Sizes and features change constantly and are designed for different requirements. As of this writing, Continental Contacts and Schwalbe Marathons make over a half-dozen models each in a variety of sizes and widths. These models change over the years, so nobody tries more than a few, making a full and fair comparison impossible. After all, a good set of touring tires will last thousands of miles—you don't need to replace them very often unless you made a bad choice. For reliable recommendations, however, consult either the touring list at search.bikelist.org or a tire vendor that specializes in touring, like Peter White (www.peterwhite cycles.com).

Fenders

Cyclists who tend to ride mainly in areas where rain is occasional and rarely long-lasting may choose either to leave the fenders at home or never to get them at all. If you are doing tours where you can expect to ride for days in the rain, however, you should equip your bike with fenders if you possibly can.

Fenders add weight, wind resistance, and inconvenience to tasks like boxing your bike for air travel. However, they make it far easier to put together a set of rain gear that actually works—you eliminate the extra stream of water (and dirt) being kicked up from the road, so you can concentrate on protecting yourself from rain that is falling or being driven by the wind.

In general, on many tours in arid parts of the American West, you can leave the fenders at home and rely on good rain clothing. But in locations where you can anticipate the possibility of a lot of rain, life will be much happier with fenders.

Construction and Fit

Good fenders can be made from plastic (Planet Bike), aluminum (Velo Orange, Honjo), stainless steel (Berthoud), carbon fiber (Berthoud), or an aluminum–plastic laminate (SKS, Berthoud). Some are more durable than others, but because treatment and type of riding affect durability, differences are often hard to pin down when one solicits opinions from experienced touring cyclists. Aesthetics play a large role in individual choices.

The fenders have to fit your bike, the wheel size you are using, and the tire width. Basic clearance issues (tire to bridge, brake, and fork crown) have been discussed in a number of places already (see "Rims" earlier in this chapter, the sections on brake types in Chapter 8, and "Choosing a Frame for Fit" on page 195). If your bike is designed for very tight clearances—for example, if it is a sport-riding or racing model with short-reach caliper brakes—you won't be able to equip it with fenders. Similarly, if you are running tires that are large enough to barely clear the brakes or the frame, you won't be able to squeeze fenders in.

Assuming that vertical clearance is not a problem, measure the space between the seatstays above the tire and the fork crown between the fork blades. This is the maximum width of fenders your frame can accommodate. If your brakes have a narrower clearance—side-pull brakes or V-brakes may be narrower—then the width of the fenders will be limited by that. You may be able to cheat a little by squeezing the fenders, but not much. Note that fenders have to clear the tires vertically by a moderate amount, or road debris will jam in the intervening space.

The fenders should be designed for the size wheels you are riding—typically 700C, 26-inch, or 650B. They should be five-sixteenths to one-half inch (8 to 12 mm) wider than the width of your tires, so that spray doesn't come around the sides and road debris doesn't catch between the tire and the fender.

Longer fenders give you more protection against spray. A front mud flap further reduces spray on your feet. A rear mud flap may be appreciated by a companion riding behind you. If your fenders don't come with mud flaps, or if they are too short, it is easy to cut them from flexible rubber or plastic material like stair treads or vinyl cove base (baseboard). You can then attach the homemade mud flaps with screws.

8

Brakes

You need to be able to slow and stop your bike quickly and smoothly, so it is important to make sure the brakes on your touring bike are up to the demands, and that your technique can handle difficult situations. Your life depends on your brakes and on your ability to use them effectively.

Brakes are important in all kinds of cycling, apart from velodrome racing. Racers and fast club riders need to be able to adjust speed very quickly and precisely, even in tight corners, when they are riding in tight packs with their front wheels inches from the riders ahead. Fortunately modern bicycle brakes are very good, and the performance of the brakesets on all high-quality bicycles is as good as the top-of-the-line components from a few years ago. Wet weather is the major limiting factor for most modern rim brakes.

Touring does impose some special demands, however, and it is important to understand them when you are evaluating and using brakes. At the most fundamental level, braking reduces the kinetic energy of your body, the bike, and your luggage by converting it to heat through the friction of the brake pads against the rims and of the tires on the pavement. If you are in control, all the heat dissipation is through the pads and rims. When braking, you want to stay within the limits of the adhesion of the tires to the pavement: when the tires start sliding on the asphalt, your control diminishes rapidly.

The heat generated while braking on a steep mountain descent can be great, even for lightly equipped sport riders and racers. Generating enough heat to blow tires is not unknown. Consider that a touring cyclist has a bike that is a few pounds heavier than a sport-riding model, body weight that is probably greater than a racer's, and possibly 40 pounds of luggage or more, and you should conclude that there is a lot of additional energy that must be dissipated. Larger tires reduce the danger somewhat, but the main lesson is that you should keep your speed moderate during steep mountain descents, particularly in hot weather, and especially if you are riding high-pressure, narrow tires. In extreme cases, you may want to stop partway through the descent to allow your rims to cool.

Braking Basics

All braking systems on bicycles operate by slowing one or both wheels, and this fact imposes some fundamental limits on the slowing force that can be applied. Because the brakes do not have any direct contact with the ground, they ultimately depend on the friction of the tires against the road surface as the first link in the chain of forces that slow the bicycle and rider. No matter how efficient other elements of the braking system may be, the slowing force can never be greater than the maximum adherence of the tires to the road. If you are riding down a gravel road or down a single-track trail in the mountains, the limiting factor in your ability to stop is a function not of the design of your brakes but rather of the loose surface of the road or trail itself (though brakes that grab or don't allow you to apply force evenly will cause you to lose control prematurely).

The limit of adherence of the bicycle tire to the road is even more important with bicycles than with automobiles. When a car starts to skid because of too much pressure or uneven pressure on the brakes, it is more difficult to control and braking is less effective, but a competent driver usually can control the skid. Because the bicycle is a two-wheeled vehicle, any skid that is not stopped immediately will cause a crash (apart from low-speed controlled skids on mountain bikes).

One other important basic characteristic of all bicycle brake systems is that most of the braking power is transmitted through the fork and the front wheel and tire. This is a consequence of basic physics. When you begin to brake, the rotation of the bike's wheels is reduced, and the tires exert frictional force on the pavement. The center of gravity, around which forward momentum is concentrated, is somewhere in your body, high above the bike. This center of gravity tends to pitch forward, rotating around the front axle, lifting the rear wheel and putting most of the pressure on the front wheel. Thus, nearly all of the braking power comes from the front brake, and if the rider squeezes the rear brake too hard, the rear wheel will quickly lock and skid.

The braking force you can exert is limited by the adherence of the front tire to the road and the force needed to pitch you up over the handlebars into a face plant on the pavement. You must keep the braking force below both those limits. It is easy to learn to do this with practice, but beginners need to err on the side of cautious descents until they have a feel for the brakes and the handling of the bike, particularly with loaded panniers or trailer. It is also vital to position yourself low in the handlebar drops, which lowers your center of gravity, requiring more force to pitch you over the front wheel, and thereby allowing you to brake harder. (If you are using nondrop bars, you can lower your center of gravity by bending your elbows and moving your posterior farther back.)

It is important to note that the overwhelming importance of the front brake is not as great with mountain bikes on trails, for two reasons. Here, the limits on braking force have far more to do with the limits of adhesion to the trail surface, so you need a lot of help from both brakes. And the surface varies, so sometimes you get traction from the tire that is on a good surface like rock or packed dirt, while the other is on loose gravel.

The standard brakes for touring bicycles are caliper-rim brakes, which squeeze pads of rubber or composite material against both sides of each wheel rim, using one of several methods of leverage. Cables are used to transmit the force from the brake control levers to the brakes themselves. The various types of caliper-rim brakes include sidepull brakes, centerpull brakes, cantilever brakes, and V-type brakes, all of which are discussed later in this chapter. (Technically, one can argue that a caliper brake is one that uses a single mechanism to move both brake pads against a rim or a disc. This book classifies cantilever brakes as caliper brakes, and discusses disc brakes separately.)

The only other significant type of brake used on touring bicycles is the disc brake, which is now standard for many high-end mountain bikes, as well as some tandem road bikes. Disc brakes are considered by some as an upgrade for road touring bikes, but they will not be discussed in detail here. They have three major advantages:

- They generate all the heat of energy dissipation in the pads and discs, and can be designed to tolerate high temperatures. Because the wheel rims do not heat up, there is no danger of blowing out tires from the energy generated in braking.

- Braking capacity usually is not reduced by wet weather. Conventional caliper brakes rely on friction between the pads and the wheel rims, which are constantly rewetted in hard rain and have to be "wiped" before the rider gets any reduction in velocity at all. The discs have a much smaller surface area so they are wiped dry quickly, and they are farther from the road surface and are hotter, so they stay dry. Thus disc brakes are much more reliable in the rain; the only degradation in the ability to stop results from the tendency of tires to slide on the wet pavement.

- Disc brakes are unaffected by dented rims or warped wheels, and they prevent wear of the rims, especially in muddy conditions.

In general, disc brakes should be used only on bikes designed and built for them. Putting disc brakes on a standard touring bike is unwise. Wheels have to have hubs with disc attachment flanges. A fitting has to be welded on the rear chainstay or seatstay for brake attachment. The fork must be designed to take the additional stress and the asymmetric forces of the brake near the fork end—conventional road forks are not. There are also some subtleties about dropout orientation. With conventional caliper brakes, replacing cables, brake pads, and levers is quite simple; even if you damage or break other parts, chances are good that a local bike shop can replace them, enabling you to continue without major incident. But if you dent or warp a disc, getting it repaired is much more difficult outside of urban areas with specialized and sophisticated bike shops (mainly in the United States or some parts of Europe), so you have to have the parts, tools, and skills to do it yourself.

Most conventional caliper brakes use cables sheathed in a plastic and metal housing to transmit braking force from the rider to the brake. Conversely, most disc brakes are operated with hydraulic systems, in which the power is transmitted by fluid pressure in enclosed tubes, as with all brakes in modern automobiles (though there are disc brakes that are cable activated and caliper-rim brakes with hydraulic systems). Cables have the advantage of simplicity and ease of repair, while hydraulic systems are inherently more efficient (and complex). There are other subtle disadvantages to disc brakes that will not be detailed here.

Any type of brake has to be anchored to the bike so that the force to stop the movement of the wheel can be transmitted from the frame or fork. With caliper-rim brakes, this is done at the front through bosses high on the fork or attachments to the fork crown. At the rear, the anchors are similarly located. For disc brakes, attachment points are provided near the hubs on bikes designed for disc brakes, and the dropout openings are directed so that the torque exerted on the hub does not dislodge the axle. Any conversion of a bike not built for disc brakes has to have attachment methods that serve these functions. Not all conversions are safe. Most modern front-disc brakes are mounted on the rigid lower arms of suspension forks. Most nonsuspension forks are thinner and more flexible, so they are not suitable to handle the forces involved unless they are specifically designed for disc brakes. Because most of your braking is necessarily done with the front brake, a disc brake only on the rear would be of little use, except on tandems.

In general, unless your bike comes with disc brakes, I would recommend avoiding them, unless you have a special need for them, as when you are riding a tandem or mountain biking where you encounter a lot of mud and wet grit. Only two of the models listed in Chapter 4 come equipped with disc brakes.

If you tour with disc brakes, you should probably carry spare disc rotors as part of your repair kit. A warped rotor can be caused by overheating and is not repairable. You also need to pay attention to servicing requirements and special tools that may be needed for any disc braking system.

Mechanical Advantage and Cable Travel

To understand the trade-offs that affect brake design and brake choices, it is important to keep a few things in mind. First, there are efficiency considerations. Friction in the system reduces the force that is transmitted from your hands and the brake levers to the pads as they are squeezed against the wheel rim (or the rotor in a disc brake). High-quality brake systems transmit the force with less friction, so more of it reaches the calipers and pads. Hydraulic systems are used in modern cars because they have virtually no friction, but they are still rare on bikes except for disc braking systems, and they have a few disadvantages of their own.

Cable systems use plastic-encased coiled steel housings to cover the cables. These transmit the equal-and-opposite force along the path of the cable. (To transmit force, the cable has to pull against something. Force has to be transmitted in both directions.) The housings are designed to resist compression, so that maximum braking force is transmitted. They may also include internal sheathing that reduces friction between the cable and the housing. (Note that while brake cables look the same as shift cables externally, the two are not interchangeable. The brake cable housings are designed to withstand much more force.)

Any stretching of cables or compression of cable housings results in loss of some of the force exerted by your hands on the brake levers. (Hydraulic systems also eliminate most of this problem.) The reason that braze-on brake housing stops are attached to the top tubes of high-quality touring bikes is to reduce the length of cable housing, thus reducing both friction and housing compression. Similarly, a brazed-on bridge between the seatstays is often installed on better bikes as a cable stop for the rear brake. This reduces cable play by eliminating the inevitable flex in a bracket attached to the seat tube.

After the friction and cable play are reduced as much as possible, the remaining factors that are most important in brake design and choice are mechanical advantage and its flip side—cable travel. Cable travel refers to the amount of cable that is taken up when you squeeze the brake levers. Brake levers with more leverage or mechanical advantage move the cable a smaller distance, and brake levers with less leverage or mechanical advantage move the cable a greater distance.

Mechanical advantage, or leverage, is a basic principle of physics. If you think about a playground see-saw, moving the pivot in one direction from the center means that the person sitting on the long end of the see-saw can be lighter in weight and still balance the heavier person on the other end. But the lighter person will travel farther up when her end goes up. The lighter person can balance the heavier one by moving a greater distance. Similarly, with a block-and-tackle pulley system, more force can be exerted on the moving block at the cost of pulling much more rope through the system for a small amount of contraction between the two blocks. The basic principle of mechanical advantage is that more force can be applied at one end of the system if the force at the other end travels farther, and conversely that making one end travel farther requires more force at the opposite end. The two are always precisely linked and reciprocal.

So, if you want brake levers that don't travel as far—if you have small hands, for example—you'll have to squeeze harder to achieve the same amount of braking. If your system has a mechanical advantage of 10, then applying 10 pounds of force to the brake lever will result in 100 pounds of force on the rims from the brake pads (ignoring friction loss), and they will move one-tenth as far as the lever.

The main point is that because the two are reciprocal, the designs of various parts of the system are closely interdependent and can't always be changed independently. For example, the mechanical advantage of most sidepull and V-type brakes is fixed, so the amount of cable travel required at the brake levers is also essentially fixed. Sidepull brakes are designed for road bikes, and most brake levers intended for drop handlebars are designed to have the amount of cable travel required by sidepulls. On the other hand, most brake levers on mountain bikes with straight handlebars produce about twice the cable travel as those on road bikes, and V-type brakes, which are all designed for mountain bikes, need about twice the cable travel as sidepulls, so they won't work with most road bike levers without installing a special converter that changes the cable travel and mechanical advantage.

Cantilever brakes are different because the mechanical advantage can be adjusted, within certain limits, by changing the length of the transverse cable, along with the height of the cable yoke (see the middle example in Drawing 23 on the next page). Disc brakes may have variable or fixed mechanical advantage, depending on the design, but most are fixed, and they are mostly designed for the travel of mountain-bike levers.

The practical consequence of all this is that brake lever design must be compatible with the design of the calipers, and in general mountain bike systems assume greater cable travel than road bike systems.

Types of Brakes

The various types of conventional caliper-rim brakes use different mechanisms for transmitting braking power from the brake levers mounted on the handlebar to the pads that squeeze the rims of the wheels. It is worth understanding their strengths and weaknesses when you are choosing or modifying a touring bike.

Note that any of the caliper-type brakes may come with quick-release levers where the brake cable attaches. These are always useful. They allow tension to be released in the brake cable for easy removal of the wheel without having to unclamp the cable. These quick releases are not related to the axle quick releases. Brake quick releases can also be incorporated in the levers.

Sidepull Brakes

Sidepull caliper brakes are the most common brakes on high-quality racing and club riding bikes (see the top example in Drawing 23 on the next page), and they have been for decades. They are simple, lightweight, reliable, and tend to have a very good, nuanced feel, allowing precise control. They can be constructed with very little play from cable stretch, cable housing compression, and brake arm flex. The best models, like the top-of-the-line Campagnolo and Shimano brakesets, set the standard by which all other brakes are judged.

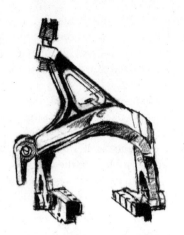

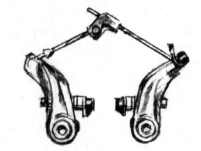

23. Top, a typical high-quality caliper (sidepull) front brake; middle, a centerpull cantilever front brake; bottom, a front V-type brake.

The disadvantage of sidepulls for a touring bike is that the standard designs have very tight clearance for the wheels. Thus, with top-of-the-line sidepull models, larger-diameter tires may not fit, and fenders are out of the question. This is partly a function of the basic mechanics of the design. Sidepull brakes designed with a somewhat longer reach may alleviate this problem, but the frame has to be designed to accommodate the longer reach. (Reach refers to the distance between the center of the brake mounting bolt and the center of the brake pad and rim. For an illustration, see www .sheldonbrown.com/gloss_ra-e.html#reach). Given a particular frame and wheel size, this can't be changed, so if a bike is designed for short-reach sidepull brakes (39–49 mm), you can't just put on longer-reach brakes to allow fenders and larger tires (see Chapter 5). There are also inherent limits on the reach of sidepulls, because they work with simple lever arms—if you make the reach longer, either you have to make the brakes more difficult to squeeze (not good for those with hands of moderate strength), or the brake levers have to travel farther (not good if you have small hands).

A few less-popular, "medium-reach" brakes (47–57 mm) that still provide all the benefits of sidepulls but allow a bit more room for larger tires and fenders are available. (Examples are the Shimano A-550 and the Tektro 521 AG. These are sidepulls, but they use a modified design.) There are also a few "long-reach" (55–73 mm) sidepull brakes (Tektro R556). Cyclists with small hands may have difficulties using these, because the brake-lever travel has to be greater.

Centerpull Brakes

Some of the clearance problems of sidepulls were once dealt with using centerpull brakes that mounted, like sidepulls, from a single hole in the fork crown or the bridge at the rear. These are now obsolete, because modern bikes sold for touring have braze-on mounts for cantilever brakes (they are also centerpulls), which are far superior to the old centerpulls in performance and ease of adjustment. Club riding or racing bikes are typically designed for sidepull caliper-rim brakes, and the frames will not have the clearance for larger tires or fenders, so there is no reason to replace the sidepulls for which they were designed. If you tour with a bike designed for short-reach sidepull brakes, you'll have great brakes, but you'll have to give up the possibility of using larger tires or mounting fenders.

Cantilever Brakes

Cantilever brakes are generally the best choice for touring bikes with standard dropped handlebars because they have the best combination of features for the purpose. Great cantilever brakes are available today (see the middle example in Drawing 23 on page 172). A few years ago the cantilever brakes available were not well designed or constructed, but the advent of mountain bikes resulted in a wide range of excellent cantilever designs. Normal cantilever brakes use single cables going through a brazed-on bridge or bracket (rear) and a bracket mounted at the base of the stem or on the fork crown (front). Each cable attaches to a transverse cable going to separately pivoted arms for each brake pad, typically mounted on pivots brazed to the seatstays or the fork.

Cantilever brakes are simple and reliable, and they can be constructed to accommodate any clearance, so it is easy to allow for larger tire sizes and fender clearance, and the leverage and brake lever movement can be designed independent of the needed clearance. Finally, cantilevers are a bit more forgiving of rim irregularities than sidepulls. The disadvantages of cantilevers compared with sidepulls are that they are heavier, trickier to adjust, and somewhat less precise.

V-Type Brakes (Sidepull Cantilevers)

V-type brakes were introduced in the late 1990s and rapidly became the dominant choice for most of the better mountain bikes (see the bottom example in

Drawing 23 on page 172). They are not yet common on touring bikes. They have all the advantages of cantilevers (minimal clearance problems, design flexibility for lever travel, and excellent leverage), and they have less cable stretch and better control in centering the brakes than cantilevers. Models are made by Shimano, Dia-Compe, and others, but current models are designed for compatibility with mountain bike levers.

Retrofitting V-type brakes to road bikes is a little tricky, because they are designed for more cable movement than cantilever brakes or sidepulls, so you either have to get levers that are designed for them or install a special adapter. Some V-type brakes are also incompatible with fenders. (Regular length V-type brakes require special brake levers that pull more cable; mini-V-type brakes will work with most road-style brake levers, including brifters, but they don't provide much clearance.) If brake levers that pull more cable are used, they may not work for people with small hands.

Brake Levers

Basic brake levers for road bikes have not changed much in the decades since the first edition of this book, except for improvements in the quality of affordable models. The levers pull the cables that are routed (inside housings) to the front and rear brakes. There may be tensioning-adjustment devices at either or both ends of the brake cable housing, and they are often a part of the brake levers. Quick releases (for the brakes, not related to quick releases on the axles of the wheels) can be part of the levers, the brakes, or both, and they greatly simplify removing the wheels and adjusting the brakes.

Standard Levers

Mountain bikes use simple brake levers, often integrated with shifters at the ends of the handlebars ("bar ends"), while the brake levers for road bikes are mounted at the curves of the bars, high enough that you can comfortably ride on the hoods (rubber covers) of the brake levers and still brake. You can also reach them while gripping the drops. The latter position is the most efficient riding position on a road bike. It ensures the lowest center of gravity and allows maximum braking leverage, so it is always used when you really need to stop. Mountain bikers have access to the levers from the standard hand position, but they need to tuck as much as possible to lower their center of gravity.

Many modern road bikes incorporate the shifters into the brake levers: Campagnolo Ergopower, Shimano STI, and SRAM Double-Tap systems—often called brifters (these are discussed under "Shifters" on page 135). They are very convenient, but they introduce complications (maintenance on the road, gear ranges) for bicycle tourists, and you should consider these issues before getting a bike that has them or adding them to a bike you already have.

In-Line Levers

Supplemental bar-top levers originally were made to connect to the main brake levers. They had a deservedly bad reputation as extremely dangerous. They bottomed out under hard braking, so they provided a false sense of security.

The supplemental levers made today, however, if properly installed, work very well and are recommended if you feel the need for brake levers that are accessible when you are riding on top of the bars. They are variously known as "in-line" levers, "cross interrupter" levers (from cyclocross racing use), and other variants. They are installed in the line of the brake cables and housing.

This type of lever, either by itself or in conjunction with a second set, is commonly used by those who opt for a less conventional style of handlebar, such as Euro touring bars or moustache bars (see Drawing 26 on page 188). Most cyclists who ride with drop bars find them unnecessary, taking up handlebar real estate without conferring a real advantage, because braking is usually done from the brake hoods or in a position in the drops. But it's a matter of personal preference. If, after you've put in some miles on your touring bike, you feel the need for brakes on the bar tops, it may be worth installing them.

Cables, Braze-Ons, and Adjustments

Small but important attributes of brake systems derive from the routing of the brake cables. These usually work flawlessly (or almost flawlessly) when you bring the bike home from the shop. You should look at cable routing at the very beginning, however, with an eye to maintenance. Later on, you have to actually do the maintenance.

Cables stretch. It is in their very nature. Cable housings compress, which is also inherent. The longer the cables, the more stretch will occur over a period of use. Many bikes use braze-on fittings to reduce housing length (and therefore compression), because straight sections of the cable route along the top tube can then be spanned with bare cable, often reducing the length of housing needed for the rear brake by a foot or more. Instead of running the housing for the rear brake the full length of the top tube, the housing goes to a cable stop at the front, and the cable runs bare to another stop at the back, saving about a foot of housing. This reduces the need for adjustments and lubrication, but it increases the number of fittings on the frame that are vulnerable to damage. (If a fitting breaks off, you have to replace the cable and housing—not a devastating repair, but still annoying and time consuming.) Fancy and expensive custom routing of cables inside the frame instead of outside can make for more responsive brakes and fewer adjustments, but if you have to replace a cable and reroute it in the middle of a tour, this can be a major (sometimes impossible) endeavor.

Thus the nicest touring bikes have well-thought-out and judiciously placed braze-ons for brake cables (and for brakes), but you should look at these with caution and judge them based on the kinds of trips you plan to take. Bikes that are tossed atop buses in Latin America, South Asia, or Africa may well be subject to broken or bent braze-ons. You should weigh the convenience and elegance against possible needed repairs and the size and weight of a repair kit.

Adjustment barrels at each end of every cable are very convenient, because they allow adjustments without loosening bolts and screws. When they break, however, they are a huge annoyance. Plastic and nylon adjusters eventually break, so metal ones are preferable.

Modern brake cables are usually equipped with Teflon-lined sleeves inside the housing to minimize friction between the housing and cable. This simple addition has significantly improved performance and reduced needed maintenance. Adjusting brakes and replacing pads and cables are discussed under "Maintaining Brakes" on page 226.

9

Saddles, Seat Posts, and Handlebars

Your connections with your bike are the pedals (see "Pedals" on page 130), the seat (saddle), and the handlebars. Both the saddle and the bars have a lot to do with whether you are comfortable on long tours.

Saddles

Longtime touring cyclists are typically opinionated about a lot of subjects but none more so than saddles. Before discussing materials and makers, we should note a few basics. Saddles are supported by two longitudinal rails, which are clamped by the seat post to hold the saddle securely and allow adjustments in its position. The rails attach to the rest of the saddle frame. The structure of the saddle itself ranges from all leather to molded plastic padded with foam and covered with leather or synthetic material. Springs may be incorporated in the frame for some shock absorption. Traditional leather saddles consist of rather stiff, shaped cowhide that is suspended from the frame and molds itself to the rider's anatomy over time. More modern molded saddles incorporate a lot of structural form in the body of the saddle, along with anatomical shaping and foam padding, and this composite shape attaches to the frame.

One reason that opinions on saddles are so varied and so strong is that people have differently shaped

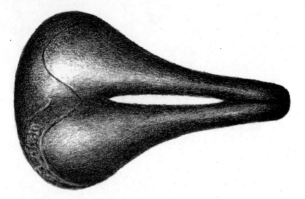

24. A split saddle of the type favored by many women cyclists. This one is made by Terry, and is widely praised by a host of riders. Terry also makes men's saddles that have a lot of devotees. Many excellent modern saddles for both men and women feature an indentation or opening in the center to reduce pressure on delicate tissue.

butts. Individuals also favor different riding positions, which result in pressure being applied differently to the sit bones—the ischial tuberosities—and to nearby delicate tissue. As an obvious example, women's pelvises are wider than men's, so women typically are comfortable with wider, shorter-profile saddles. This shape accommodates ishial tuberosities that are spaced farther apart and sensitive soft tissue that is farther back. Traditional Brooks leather saddles have women's models that are shorter in length and wider at the rear. The most popular Brooks among bicycle tourists for decades has been the B17. The equivalent women's model is the B17S, standing for "short," because the women's model is shorter. Similarly, the women's model of the B68 is the B68S. In molded saddle types, specific models are designed and manufactured for women (see Drawing 24).

A saddle should support your weight through your sit bones, not your soft tissue. It should also cause a minimum of friction as you pedal. These requirements are best accommodated by a fairly firm, but not unyielding, saddle. The wide, cushy, padded saddles that look to complete novices as though they would be comfortable fail both these tests. They are completely

25. A Brooks leather saddle, still the favorite of many touring cyclists.

unsuitable for long rides. Despite a variety of opinions, by far the most popular saddle among experienced touring cyclists is the venerable Brooks leather saddle (see Drawing 25). Traditional leather saddles have such a strong following that many tourists still use Ideale leather saddles, buying them on eBay, though they are no longer made. Some new leather models based on traditional styles are also making their appearance. For these, look at www.velo-orange.com.

Historically, the replacement for traditional leather saddles was molded plastic. It was lightweight, weatherproof, and inexpensive. It was also brutally unfriendly to the human posterior. Compromises then appeared that took advantage of modern materials but attempted to accommodate themselves to our anatomical limitations.

A host of very good saddles have appeared that use relatively rigid plastic bases attached to metal frames and rails but incorporate shaping to eliminate unfortunate pressure points, add fairly durable foam or gel compartments to support your sit bones, and are sheathed with leather or synthetic coverings that wear well and allow moisture to pass through as it should. Such composite saddles are very popular among many cyclists. Some of the manufacturers with the best reputations are Terry (see Drawing 24), Avocet, and Selle Italia (particularly the Anatomica and Regal models).

In general, the tradeoff between traditional leather saddles and the better designed modern ones is that the best modern saddles are shaped so that they provide just the right amount of firm support where you need it and avoid creating pressure where it is undesirable. When they fit your posterior perfectly, they are hard to beat, though they will not last as long as traditional saddles.

By contrast, traditional leather saddles provide a modest number of shapes and stiffnesses. Beyond their initial very approximate shape, they rely on the fact that leather will ultimately conform to your shape over time. After a year or so, your leather saddle will fit you perfectly. No molded saddle will ever do this. The modern saddle might fit perfectly at the beginning, but if it doesn't, it will never get better.

As a final remark on choosing a saddle, it is important to note that there is no single solution that will work for all cyclists. Variations in pelvis shape mean that no saddle will fit everyone well. You need to find one that is comfortable for you. If you are a novice, you may have to spend some time riding before you'll be able to judge well. But if you regularly do rides of over 50 miles, your rear should be acclimatized enough to allow you to make a better initial evaluation of whether a particular saddle works for you.

If you're buying a new touring bike and aren't sure about the saddle, the one that comes stock will probably be good enough to get you started, but it probably won't be something you want to take on a transcontinental ride. If you're more experienced, you may want to try some saddles at your local bike shop and specify the saddle as part of your bike purchase.

Here are the rules of thumb for fit:

- The saddle must support your sit bones. If it's too narrow, so that they slide down on the sides, the saddle will bruise or numb delicate tissue. If it is too wide, your thighs will chafe and you may end up having to shift from side to side while pedaling. This will produce real discomfort over touring distances.

- If you typically ride in a more upright position, your seat will shift so that more of your weight will be supported by the saddle, and you will usually need a slightly wider saddle. Conversely, racers and sport riders who spend a lot of time in the handlebar drops are likely to want narrower saddles.

Choosing a Saddle

If you know from experience what kind of saddle you want, you'll be able to specify it when you purchase the bike. Otherwise, make sure the bike frame fits before you spend money to get a new saddle. Then take some time picking a saddle. Be patient—it's worth the effort. Once you get a saddle that is exactly right, you will probably use it for a long time, often over many bikes.

Apart from the basic form of the saddle, which is the most important characteristic, there are a number of other criteria and materials choices. The majority of touring cyclists prefer leather saddles, but a strong contingent has found that molded designs using laminated layers of plastic, leather, fabric, foam, and/or gel suit their needs perfectly. The advantage of leather saddles is that they gradually stretch and mold to fit your seat. The advantage of molded saddles is that they can be designed readily to conform to a particular shape—and if that form is exactly right for you, with the soft and firm areas in the right places, then the saddle may be perfect. A molded saddle always has the same shape. If it works for you, you can keep buying the same model. If it doesn't quite fit, it still won't fit five years hence.

The best-rated saddles are not cheap. Leather saddles are dominated by Brooks, though there are a few competitors. Several new lines have recently been introduced. For laminated, molded saddles, there are some inexpensive variations that many riders have found quite satisfactory, but beyond the best-known names, the off-brand molded, laminated saddles change every year. Their designs are revised based on mass-market manufacturer requirements, not customer needs and loyalty.

Most saddles have steel rails and frames; a few of them save a little weight by using aluminum alloy rails and frames. As indicated in Chapter 4, miniscule reductions in the weight of touring bikes are not worth pursuing. Lighter-weight materials can be used for the rails and frame, but the small savings in weight is rarely worth the increased cost.

Trying out various saddles at your local bike shop is the best way to get a feel for what you want. You may also find that the shop has an inexpensive version of one of the name saddles or a slightly used returned one that is just right for you. Actually riding a saddle is the only way to evaluate it. Ideally, of course, you'll want to ride for a long distance, preferably several full-day rides.

If, because of your location or other factors, you get your saddle from a catalog or Internet source, it is wise to try to find a supplier who will accept a return if it doesn't fit. Wallingford Bicycle Parts allows the unconditional return of any Brooks saddle for up to six months from the time of purchase. Terry Saddles has a 30-day return policy wherever they are purchased. Their Liberator models are designed for touring and come in men's and women's models. For a discussion and advice on saddles (and shorts) for women, look at Pamela Blalock's Web site at www.blayleys.com/articles/womensfit/index.htm.

Brooks Saddles

Because they are the most popular saddles among touring cyclists, Brooks leather saddles warrant some discussion. Desirable models depend on your own body shape and your typical riding position. A wide range of widths is available. Touring cyclists tend to gravitate to the B-17 and its many variations, but there are many wider models for those who ride in a more upright position and narrower saddles for those who spend a lot of time in the handlebar drops or who position their handlebars below the level of the saddle.

Avoid the Brooks "double-rail" and "triple-rail" models. These are intended for very old-style straight seat posts, for which they use a separate clamp. To mount one on a modern seat post, you have to use a special adapter. "Single-rail" models are designed to fit all modern seat posts.

Many of the Brooks designs can be found with or without springs. For example, the Champion Flyer is essentially a B-17 with springs. The springs are fairly hard and don't move much during normal riding, but they provide some cushioning on rough pavement or trails. Some riders love them; others find them annoying and too heavy.

Because one of the advantages of leather saddles is that they gradually stretch and mold themselves to your shape, there may be a break-in period while the saddle adjusts and conforms to your sit bones. However, if the saddle doesn't feel fairly comfortable from the start, do not endure too much discomfort on the assumption that it will feel better once broken in. There are various techniques that have been recommended over the years for softening the saddle either temporarily (with water) or permanently (with various oils). These are inadvisable; they will void the warranty on the saddle, and if they are needed, it means the saddle doesn't really fit.

Basic care of leather saddles includes keeping them reasonably dry, treating them occasionally top and bottom with a preservative wax—Brooks has a beeswax-based one called Proofide—and avoiding leaving them in the sun for extended periods. You can use a lightweight waterproof saddle cover in the rain, which can also be stretched onto the seat if the bike is parked in the hot sun for a long time. If the saddle has gotten wet, let it dry out slowly in the shade or ride it. Don't set it out in the hot sun. You can always improvise a temporary cover on the road using a plastic grocery bag.

Seat Posts

If you are buying a new bike, evaluating the seat post is a simple matter. You should check to be sure that the seat angle is readily adjustable over small increments.

Posts with serrated contacts that make rather large jumps in angle are irritating. Murphy's Law clearly holds that the angle you want will be in between two steps. Ideally, you'll want a post with a mechanism that allows the seat angle to be finely adjusted and then reliably clamped in position. If you're specifying a saddle, make sure the clamping mechanism of the seat post permits the seat to be moved significantly fore and aft from the initial position, so that you'll be able to fine-tune the adjustment. Seat posts with a single clamping bolt are easier to adjust, but some riders prefer the additional strength they infer from two clamping bolts.

For fine-tuning the angle of the seat, a micro-adjusting seat post like the Nitto Jaguar is invaluable. If you are having a hard time getting just the right seat angle, you may need to find one. Seat posts with increased clamp setback to the rear are sometimes necessary to achieve the ideal saddle position. Fortunately, those available generally have micro-adjusting clamps. See page 204 for some specific models.

If you're replacing a seat post, the new one has to be the right diameter to fit inside the seat tube. It should insert easily but without significant play. The post must be long enough that the highest adjustment you might make does not require the post to be positioned above the minimum insertion line marked on the post. Grease the post and the binder bolt or put on anti-seize compound before tightening. Removing a corroded seat post is a challenge you never want to encounter. Tighten the binder bolt or the quick release enough so that you can't turn the seat with one hand—don't overtighten.

Handlebars and Stems

The handlebars, along with the seat and the pedals, provide one of your major points of contact with the bike. The most important function of the handlebars is to give you a range of comfortable positions for your hands, while providing good control of steering and braking. The bars also serve as the attachment point for brake levers, most shifters, and a host of accessories like bike computers, headlights, handlebar bags, and so on.

Most touring cyclists are happy with standard road bars like the top two in Drawing 26 on the next page, so unless you have good reason to want a different style, you should start with one of them. These provide a number of different riding positions and hand grips, and they have proved themselves over the years. Experienced riders can argue for hours over subtleties in different bends—for example, a shallower drop may be indicated if you find you don't want to lean forward quite as much when you are in the drops—but most such differences are minor. You'll develop your own preferences with experience, but the variations don't matter enormously. Make sure that the brake levers are positioned correctly and that you're happy with the aesthetics and feel of the bar tape. Some like one or two layers of cloth tape, some prefer leather or cork, and some like to use padded tape or to put gel or foam padding on the tops of the bars before wrapping.

The old rule of thumb for fitting road bars is that they should be the same width as the distance between the bony ends of your shoulders, and this is a pretty reasonable place to start. (Note that catalog sizes of bars are not always exactly comparable—some manufacturers measure edge to edge and others center to center.) Some touring cyclists prefer bars somewhat wider than shoulder width, contending that they provide better leverage for climbing. The height at which you have the bars mounted depends on the riding position you prefer and a lot of other issues of fit. The majority of touring cyclists prefer the top of the bars to be a ½ inch to 1½ inches above the level of the saddle.

Once you've chosen and fitted a set of standard bars, it's best to get used to them first or to at least test them on an extended ride before you try alternative shapes. Keep in mind that different kinds of bars will typically have to be fitted differently. They may need

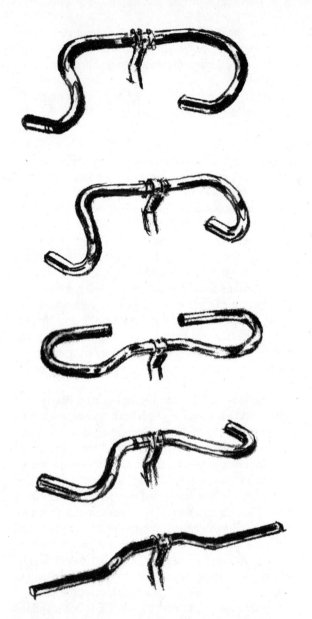

26. Several examples of touring handlebars. The two upper bars are among the many variations on the standard drop handlebar, which is preferred by most touring cyclists. In the center is a Euro touring (butterfly) bar, and below that are a moustache bar and one variation of a mountain bike handlebar. Other styles are discussed in the text.

to be positioned at a different height or mounted with a different stem, and they may require different shifters and brake levers. Introducing all these variables simultaneously is unwise until you really know what you want.

Handlebar Variations

As noted above, most touring cyclists choose regular drop road bars, but some prefer one of a number of other available types. Some cyclists, for example, prefer a more upright riding position. Before considering changing bars, you need to think about other changes that might be required. Brake levers and shifters may need to be mounted in different locations or changed altogether. If the new bar has a clamping area that is a different diameter than the original bar, you'll either have to add a shim or change the stem to one designed for the new bar. The clamp should be exactly the right size as a matter of safety. Similarly, if the new bar positions your body differently, you may need a longer or shorter stem or one with a different rise to achieve the same fit.

Some riders prefer variations on the drop bars that came with their bikes. Standard road bars can have curves that project farther forward (increased reach) or farther down (increased drop). Some have flat areas on the bar tops or in the area just above the brake levers that some riders find more comfortable. Some riders like bars with much less drop, like the On-One Midge bar and the WTB Mountain Road Drop bar (see the photograph at www.wtb.com/products/components/handlebar/mountainroaddropbar).

Relatively upright bars that still allow for a number of positions include moustache bars, second from the bottom in Drawing 26, and various versions of albatross bars (see the photograph at www.rivbike.com/products/list/handlebars_stems_and_tape?page=2 #product=16-127).

One type of bar that has a significant number of advocates is the Euro touring or Euro trekking bar (see the middle example in Drawing 26 on page 188), which is fairly flat vertically but goes into extended forward curves and then back to provide a straight set of grips closer to the rider. Inexpensive versions are sold by Bike Nashbar and Harris Cyclery. Variations are known as butterfly bars.

Mountain bikes come with some variation of straight bars—the lowest bars illustrated in Drawing 26. Because these result in a body position that is less stretched out than with standard drop road bars, mountain bikes usually have longer top tubes than road bikes of the same size, to compensate. That is, if you grip the bars on a typical mountain bike where the controls are located, you'll be less stretched out than you are in the drops of road bars. The longer top tube results in your hands being placed similarly to the way they would be on a road bike. So if you switch to a completely different type of bar on your mountain bike, you may have to change to a different length of stem to get the same fit and the same riding position.

If you tour with some variation of mountain bike bars, you will almost certainly want to add clamp-on extensions ("bar ends") to the ends of the bars. These extend at right angles, providing an additional hand position and better leverage for climbing. Bar ends are widely available and inexpensive. They are typically mounted so that they jut up and forward at a 45-degree angle.

Handlebar Real Estate and Extensions

One important peripheral issue associated with handlebar selection and setup is real estate on the handlebars. Many accessories (bike computers, lights, handlebar bags, GPS systems, and more) have convenient mounting hardware included or readily available for attaching to the handlebar. Of course, these are only convenient when they aren't competing for space with other accessories and with your hand positions. So, whenever you're considering some convenient gadget, ask yourself whether it needs handlebar space and whether it could be mounted elsewhere. Could the light be mounted on the fork or the front rack? Would a rack-top bag do as well or better than a handlebar bag?

There are also other ways to get extra space. On threadless headsets, which are the norm on all new bikes, it is frequently possible to mount an extra stem in place of a spacer below the one holding your bars. The second stem points forward below the one hold-ing the handlebars and is used to hold a piece of tub-ing, a dowel, or a cut-off center handlebar section, which, along with an extra stem, can often be obtained cheaply from most shop parts bins or bike swap sales. (For a picture of this arrangement, see www.mgagnon .net/velo/potence-double.en.shtml.) Other, somewhat lighter-weight alternatives are the very sturdy Thorn Accessory Bar and the less substantial but more flexible Minoura SwingGrip. The Thorn mounts the same way an extra stem does, and the Minoura typically attaches to the stem or steerer with a built-in clamp.

Stems

There are two major categories of stems—the quill type used on traditional road bikes and early moun-tain bikes, and the threadless variety found on nearly all new bikes. Each type comes in a range of diame-ters, lengths, and rises. Because new bikes come with threadless headsets, most of the discussion in this book assumes that you will have one of those. The stems made to fit threadless headsets are also usually referred to as threadless.

A threadless stem is an arm that projects from the steerer (steering tube) and holds the handlebar. It has clamps at each end, at right angles to one another, one for the steerer and the other for the handlebar. The clamp sizes must match the diameter of the steerer and the bar. The other dimensions are the reach and the rise. Reach is the horizontal distance, measured center to center between the two clamps, and it is normally given in millimeters. The rise is the angle at which the stem meets the steerer—a stem that extends straight forward has a 90-degree (or 0-degree) rise. A stem with a 120-degree rise will position the handlebar higher, and it can also be flipped on the steerer to place the handlebar lower. Typically, spacers fit over the steerer to determine the vertical position when the stem is clamped to the steerer. The number and thickness of spacers may be small if the manufacturer has cut the steerer to a fixed size. Ideally, if the steerer is uncut, the height of the stem and hence the handlebars can be adjusted by moving the positions of the spacers and the stem.

Steerer extenders are used to mount the stem higher if the manufacturer has cut the steerer too short, thus allowing the stem to be mounted at the right height for you. Changing stems or adjusting the mounting height is a standard way to fine-tune the fit of the bike, as described in Chapter 10.

Two specialized types of stems are adjustable and suspension stems. Adjustable stems can be purchased or rented from a bike shop, and they allow you to change the reach and rise in order to obtain the optimum dimensions for a fixed stem. Suspension stems provide shock absorption and can be an excellent addition to a touring bike. Unfortunately, they are very hard to find in the correct size for modern bikes. The best one, the Softride Powerstem, is no longer manufactured.

10

Adjusting Bike Fit

You can approach bike fitting in a number of different ways. Local bike shops will certainly be willing to fit you to a bike if you are buying one from them. If they use sophisticated fitting systems, though, they will probably charge you for it. Opinions differ widely on how good the various fitting systems are; the "Bike Fit and Frames" section under Resources, at the end of the book, provides references. For the beginner, however, any fitting system will at least include measuring specific parts of your body and applying those measurements to the major frame dimensions. Even if you decide later that some subtle adjustments need to be made, you'll have started with something close to what you need.

It's important to keep some perspective on the whole issue of fit. Longtime tourists sometimes indulge in endless discussions about the nuances of fit, but for most cyclists the objective is simply to get a bike that is about the right size, do a little fine tuning for the first few thousand miles of riding, and then simply enjoy the bike. The nuances only become important if you have some specific problem you need to solve or if you just like to fuss with optimum position. This chapter provides a more detailed discussion of frame fit and selection than was introduced in Chapter 5, along with a step-by-step description of adjusting fit without any specialized equipment.

First, a few basics. If you're buying a bike, or re-equipping an older bike, it has to fit you to a reasonable level or you will never be able to ride it comfortably on extended tours. If you can't reach the pedals with the seat at its lowest position, you're definitely not going to be able to use the bike much, especially for long distances. Similarly, if the bike is so small that you have to buy a special, very long seat post and stem extension, and your knees still hit the bars, no adjustment will make the bike a reasonable fit.

When you're buying a bike from the folks at a local shop, they should have bikes for you to take trial rides on, and they should take basic body measurements if you're going to order a bike from them. Find out if they are willing to swap out components (such as stem and cranks) free of charge, if it proves necessary to correct the fit. If you've paid for a bike-fitting session, you should have lots of leverage on this issue. When trying out bikes, it can be valuable to find one that fits well, even if it isn't suitable for touring, because you can use it to determine preliminary frame dimensions.

Checking a frame's dimensions is critical and ensures that the bike will fit you within a reasonable range. Body dimensions vary a lot. One average-looking person who is 5 feet 9 inches tall may have legs 3 inches longer than another equally average-looking person of the same height. The first person will do better with a bike that has a longer seat tube, a shorter top tube, and perhaps longer cranks, even though the two are the same height.

Once you have a bike with the right geometry for the touring you want to do (see Chapter 5) and it is approximately the right size, you can make several small adjustments and accessory changes for an exact fit. These include seat height, angle, and fore-aft adjustments; stem height adjustments or inversions (inversion for threadless headsets only); bar or brake-lever adjustments; a new seat post for better adjustment or increased height; a new stem for adjusting reach (or height); new bars for better positioning; and longer or shorter cranks.

Choosing a Frame for Fit

Most people will want to have a bike with a standover height that allows standing comfortably astride the bike with both feet on the ground. Most mountain bikers want about 2 inches of clearance. If you measure your pubic bone height (as described under "Frame Size" on page 56) with your normal riding shoes on, you'll want a standover height at least an inch less. You'll want to verify this based on the methods described in the following paragraphs before ordering any frame.

Suppose that you've looked at other issues and decided that, based on geometry and features, you're considering a Trek 520 and a Surly Long Haul Trucker, but you can't ride either of these locally. What is the right size? You can start with a bike that fits to compare dimensions, or you can use one of the fitting systems.

If you currently have a bike that you think fits well, you might start with its measurements and compare it to the Trek and Surly in similar sizes. However, you need to make sure you are comparing apples to apples. Measuring the "size" of the bike and the top tube length can be done in several ways. Check the manufacturers' specifications and make sure you understand how they measure. Generally, you want to look at the seat tube length, measured the same way, and the effective top tube length (see Drawing 13 on page 87), intended to normalize toptube measurements, regardless of slope.

One way to approach frame fit is to start with the most common fitting system used by bike shops—the Fit Kit, now in use for 25 years. The basic process is based on a few body measurements and a calculation of suitable frame measurements from them. There are variations, extra tools that can be used, and different philosophies of use by different shops, but the basic kit measures pubic bone height and torso or trunk length (see Drawing 27 on the next page), and comes up with a recommended size (seat tube length) and a range of top tube lengths with corresponding stem

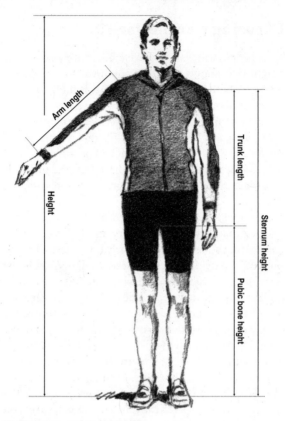

27. Body measurements for bike fitting.

reach lengths. (Your forward lean and arm reach will be determined by the effective top tube length plus the stem reach. It will also be influenced by your choice of handlebars.)

Most local shops will charge $20 to $40 for a Fit Kit fitting, often good for credit if you buy a bike. A more elaborate version of the process, using an adjustable bike, will cost two or three times as much. Extras include features like an adjustable stem that you rent to fine-tune the fit later, positioning of shoe cleats, crank length testing, and the like. Talk with your local bike shop owner to see what it offers, what it recommends, and what the costs and possible credits are.

If you've had a Fit Kit measurement, ask to see the results and compare the top tube suggestions with the effective top tube lengths of the bikes that you are considering, preferably the ones in the middle of the range. Write them down. This will give you a chance to fine-tune the fit and avoid getting a stem that is too long or too short, and it will allow you to change handlebars if you later decide to do so. Make sure that the listed standover height is in the right range, and do a sanity check on the size—if it's way out of line from the Fit Kit figure, double-check your measurements.

This recommendation is based on the belief that top tube length is the most important factor in choosing the size of a frame. While not universally accepted, it is held by quite a few experts on bike fit (including the late, great Sheldon Brown, Grant Petersen of Rivendell Bicycle Works, and the folks at Surly Bikes). Thus, if you have a road bike that feels comfortable, measure the effective top tube length and the stem reach, and then compare these to the top tube lengths of the bikes you're considering, preferably allowing for an intermediate stem reach in the neighborhood of 80 to 100 mm. That is, start with the formula

$$\text{old effective top tube length} + \text{old stem reach}$$
$$\approx \text{new effective top tube length} + 90 \text{ mm}$$

and determine the near matches in the bikes you're considering.

You'll want to be careful when using this approach. If the seat tube angles of the bikes you're considering are very different, this can throw things off, and so can a large difference in seat tube lengths (bike sizes). A smaller seat tube angle moves the saddle back, effectively lengthening reach. A much shorter size (measured the same way) means that the seat post will extend higher and the seat will be farther back. Head tube angle and stem mounting height and rise also have some effect. Overall, however, adding the top tube and the stem reach should give you a good start.

What if you haven't had a Fit Kit measurement and you don't have a road bike that fits you? Take the measurements shown in Drawing 27 on page 196 (don't worry about trunk length—it can be calculated by subtracting the pubic bone height from the sternum height.). Then go to Wrench Science's Web site at wrenchscience .com or Tiemeyer Cycles at www.tiemeyercycles.com/ fit.htm, and use their fit calculator to get a recommended frame size and effective top tube length.

Another approach is to get Bill Boston's Accufit calculator, which runs on a personal computer and costs about $30 for up to two cyclists. You can find it at www.billbostoncycles.com.

Step-by-Step Fitting Adjustment

Start by thinking a little about what you are trying to do in fine-tuning the fit of your bike. You want to set things up so that when you are riding for long distances you are in the most natural and comfortable stance possible.

Your weight rests on five points of pressure: your feet (2), your rear end, and your hands (2). Your feet are well designed to bear your weight, though continuous unnatural spot pressure may require some accommodation. Your butt can bear your weight with little problem when you are sitting still on a soft surface, as at dinner or in front of the TV, but for riding, things are a bit trickier. Your hands are not suited to bearing much weight—since evolving from four-legged animals, we've adapted to using our hands for grasping and manipulation, so they are sensitive to pressure and not well adapted to bearing weight and pressure for long periods.

You are probably not a racer, and thus your legs are not likely to be well trained to bear all your weight for many hours, while still pedaling at a high cadence. Still, you want most of your weight to be borne by your legs and feet, with as little as possible on your rear end, particularly when you are building up your mileage and toughening up your seat.

Try standing in the middle of the room and leaning forward as though you were cycling. Your posterior moves back. If you try standing with your back against the wall and assuming a cycling position, you can't do it without falling forward onto your hands. To stay on your feet (or on your pedals) your butt has to move back to balance your weight. Otherwise, most of your weight will rest on your hands. This is not a sustainable position when you are touring. Your hands can't tolerate the weight for hours on end. (Some racing styles do rely on this sort of position. Sprinters move their weight well forward onto their hands, but only for short periods of time. Time trialers and pursuit riders often use a low position, shifting most of their weight forward, but to do this they use time-trial bars with arm rests.)

You should have your saddle positioned well behind your feet, so that excessive weight doesn't rest continuously on your hands. There are sensitive nerves running through your palms, and chronic weight-bearing is likely to result in discomfort, numbness, and pain. Continuing to abuse your hands without attention can result in long-term injury.

Your basic riding position when touring should be leaning forward from the seat at a comfortable angle. When you put pressure on the pedals, nearly all your weight should rest on your feet. Your abdominal muscles and back should keep you from putting excessive weight on your hands. Your elbows should be slightly flexed. Most tourists spend the majority of their time with their hands near the center of the bars, on the brake hoods, or on the curves just above the brake hoods. However, the lower positions on the drops, or forward on the drops where the brakes can be grasped, should still be comfortable, although this isn't the usual position for touring cyclists. These are the most aerodynamic positions when riding on the flats, and the most stable ones in descents. They should be comfortable and not stress inducing. Straight mountain bike bars don't allow many positions, which is why those who prefer more upright riding posture like having alternatives, such as Euro touring bars. At a minimum, bar-end extensions should be used with straight bars to provide some variation.

Position is also a function of age, conditioning, and inclination. Younger riders, and those in training for racing and sport riding, are often happier down on the drops. (The low position does interfere with inflating the lungs, so those with better cardiovascular condition will be more comfortable.) At the end of the day, a lot of touring cyclists just prefer a more upright position most of the time, whatever the reason. It is less aerodynamically efficient, but it is easier to take in the scenery.

The objective in fitting a bike is to achieve a comfortable riding position that can be sustained over many full days of riding. As your conditioning improves, you'll be able to ride faster and farther, with less discomfort, but the fit will not change.

The following steps are intended to ensure a proper bike fit:

Step 1: Check the crank arm length. Ideally, you'll have checked this before ordering your bike, but if not, it is still a good idea to verify the length so you know if you have something far from the optimum size. Start with the pubic bone height, as shown in Drawing 27 on page 196 and described under "Frame Size" on page 56. Use Lennard Zinn's formula for calculating crank length:

$$\text{crank length} = \text{pubic bone height (in millimeters)} \times 0.216$$

For tall riders, multiply pubic bone height by 0.210. Many nuances may dictate adjustments; for details, check Zinn's book, listed in the Resources section at the end of this book.

Step 2: Set initial handlebar and seat height. Position the handlebars first; you'll follow by setting the height of the seat to correspond. If you're buying a modern bike with a threadless headset, specify that you want an uncut steering tube if you have that option. (With most bikes you won't have a choice.) With a threadless headset, the stem clamps onto the steering tube at any position up to the top—spacers are inserted below, and possibly above, the stem. If the steering tube is uncut, you have maximum flexibility in positioning the stem, and when you have the fit adjusted, you can get your shop to cut it or do it yourself. Once the tube is cut, the only way to mount the stem higher is to add a stem raiser, which will work but it isn't ideal. (For photographs of stem raisers, see sheldonbrown.com/harris/stems/index.html#raisers.)

Begin by mounting the handlebars you want to use on the bike. Different handlebar styles result in different fits, so if you are planning to use something different, like Euro touring bars or moustache bars, mount them—there is no point in having to go back and repeat all this fine tuning. If you don't have specific preconceptions, start off with average road drop bars. If you have a choice, leave them untaped until you've finished fitting the bike. That way you can fine-tune the position of the brake levers and the angle of the bar, and tape them afterward. If the bars are already taped, just go ahead—you can adjust the brake lever position later if necessary.

Next, take a carpenter's level (it has the little bubbles in transparent tubes to indicate angle), loosen the adjustment bolt(s) on the seat post, and set your saddle dead level. Do this with the bike itself level on the floor or ground. Tighten the bolt(s).

Now you need to get a preliminary seat height. The easiest way is to have someone help you and to mount the bike in a trainer—it is worth borrowing one if you don't have one. If you don't have a trainer, you can put the bike in a doorway and get on it while bracing yourself by holding onto the doorjamb. Wear normal cycling shoes, running shoes, or the equivalent.

Determine a comfortable sitting position on the saddle by leaning forward on the brake lever hoods in a relaxed position, with your heels on the pedals, and slowly pedaling backward. Your legs should completely extend with your heels on the pedals—with the knees extended, not bent—without rotating your hips. If someone is helping you, he or she should watch from behind to be sure that your hips are not rotating sideways as you pedal backward. If you're doing this alone, feel your seat; it should not be sliding from side to side.

Adjust the seat height by getting on and off the bike as many times as required to get the right vertical position. When the balls of your feet, not your heels, are on the pedals your knees will bend slightly at the bottom of the pedal strokes. Use a permanent marker to mark this position on the seat post, so you can return to it. Note that cranks of the wrong length will affect this position. That's why it is best to start with cranks of the right size (Step 1).

Step 3: Adjust cleats on step-in pedals. Before you set the forward-back position of the saddle, you need to have your feet properly positioned on the pedals, which is the purpose of doing this step now. It is easier to do this if the bike is mounted in a trainer.

To begin, the ball of your foot should be over the pedal axle. If you are riding on some kind of platform pedal without cleats, you might want to mark the sides of the soles with a permanent marker where the ball of your foot is. This will allow you to check the position visually in the next step.

If you are using cleats, this is the time to position them. As with all screws and bolts on the bike, lubricate the threads of the bolts first, so that they will tighten properly. Also, if the cleats have been used before, clean any dirt from the hexagonal recesses in the screws, and make sure that your Allen wrench fits tightly. It is much easier to buy a new set of screws than to deal with a stripped screw head.

Position the cleat on each shoe immediately under the ball of the foot (more or less the widest part of the shoe). It helps to draw two reference lines on the shoe soles with a ruler and marker. The two lines should be at right angles and intersect directly under the ball of the foot. One line should run left to right from one side of the shoe to the other and the second line should run down the midline of the sole. Position the cleat at the intersection so that it lines up on the two axes, and tighten the screws completely.

Now clip the empty shoes into the pedals, one at a time. (This will require some effort without your weight on the shoe.) Rotate the shoe and the crank, with the shoe both right side up and upside down. You should be able to see if the shoe is not perfectly parallel to the plane of the bike. Adjust the cleat position and repeat as necessary. Be sure to tighten the cleats each time—if the cleat position slips, you have to start over. Looking from the bottom of the shoe when it is lined up along the crank arm, it is pretty easy to see if the cleat is mounted straight.

Once both shoes are straight, put them on, get on the bike, and make sure they feel right. The geometrically derived positioning described above is a starting position. You have to ride the bike to know if adjustments need to be made. Your knees might be happier if one toe was angled slightly in, for example, or you might prefer pedaling with your feet a little farther forward. Elaborate fitting machines can help fine-tune foot position on the pedals, but if you pay attention, you can work this out by trying the bike out and making adjustments in very small increments, until you have everything just right.

For the moment, just try the shoes on the trainer and adjust as needed until they feel right. Later on, when you are convinced that you have the cleat position just right, use a marker to trace around the cleat and mark the correct position, or scribe it with a sharp point, so that you can reposition it if it is knocked out of line or replace it when it is worn without having to start from scratch.

Step 4: Set forward-back position of the seat. For this step it is best to mount the bike in a trainer, making sure it is level (check with a carpenter's level, as noted in Step 2). You'll also need someone to help you. The helper needs a plumb bob and line—a pocket knife or some similar small weight hanging on a string will do.

Pedal the bike a little until you are comfortably settled in the saddle. Pedal backward for a bit to make sure—you want to be in the most comfortable spot on the saddle. In this position, turn the pedals until one crank arm is pointed straight forward, level with the ground.

Have your helper hold the string against the front of your forward knee, so that the weight drops down along the outside of the pedal. Make sure the bob is hanging straight down. It should pass the center of the pedal spindle. Adjust the seat backward or forward until it does.

Recheck the saddle height from Step 2. Moving the saddle back and forth often changes the vertical position. Also verify that it is still level.

As with the other positions determined in this process, consider this knee-over-pedal-spindle (KOPS) position to be a preliminary one. As you ride during the following few weeks, it is worth moving the saddle backward or forward, no more than $\frac{1}{2}$-inch at a time. With any test adjustments, change only one thing at a time, and only in small increments. After a couple of weeks you'll have all the positions fine-tuned to your liking. The plumb line past the pedal spindle is often stated as an important fitting rule. *It is not.* People with different foot lengths necessarily have different results. The purpose of this adjustment is to find a good starting point.

Note that if you can't move your seat far enough back, seat posts that project to the rear (long-setback seat posts) are available, allowing the seat to be placed farther back and effectively reducing the angle of the seat tube. Nitto makes several models (the Nitto Wayback from Rivendell is the most extreme), and the Grand Cru post from Velo Orange also has a long setback.

Step 5: Set handlebar height and reach. Handlebar positioning is one of the most subjective steps in fitting a bike. It depends on your riding preferences, your age, your conditioning, your size, and the kind of riding you do. As the first step in this fitting process, you set the handlebar height, and then positioned the seat height to match. As a final step in fine-tuning the fit, the handlebar is readjusted.

The ways you can adjust the position of the bar depend on the bike. If your bike has an uncut steering tube with the stem mounted below the top, you have the freedom to move the bar up by adding spacers below the stem and removing them above. If your stem has spacers below it, you can lower the bar by reversing this process. If you don't have the option you need, you may be forced to change the stem. (For older, threaded headsets, the equivalent issue is whether the stem can be moved up or down. There is a limit line inscribed on the stem to show how high it can be safely raised.) For some changes, stem raisers (steerer extender tubes) might be required to raise the bar.

Start by determining the height of the bar relative to your seat. Is it higher or lower? Is it level? If the carpenter's level you used is long enough, run it from your seat to the bar. Otherwise, run a straight board between them and lay the carpenter's level on that. Raise the low end of the board to level it and measure the gap to the bar or the seat. Most road racers and sport riders prefer to set the bars a couple of inches below the seat. Most tourists prefer the bar to be level or a few inches above the seat.

A good start to evaluating the bar position is to ride the bike on the trainer. Warm up for a little while until you are comfortable, and make sure you are sitting at the most comfortable place on the saddle, not pushing back or sliding forward. Sit up in the saddle while pedaling and then lean forward to grasp the bars. All the main positions on the bars should be within comfortable reach; for standard drop bars that includes the center, the side near the drops, the brake hoods, and the drops. (For a mountain-bike-style straight bar, you don't have a choice—the standard position should be comfortable.) You shouldn't have to stretch uncomfortably and should be able to look straight ahead comfortably (as if down the road). You shouldn't have to lock your elbows to reach any of the positions, and your body should be comfortable—neither too arched in your back nor stretched out too far. And, again, your hands shouldn't bear too much weight in any position.

You should have a sense of how the bar position feels at this point. If too much weight is on your hands, you have to crane your neck, you can't breathe comfortably, or your trunk muscles feel stressed supporting your upper body, then the bar is too low. If you're too upright and can't reach an efficient position in the drops, or you have too much weight on your seat, then the bar may be too high. If you have to lock your arms to reach some positions, you tend to move forward on the saddle, and you feel stretched out, then the reach is too long. If you tend to slide back on the saddle, you feel cramped, or your arms are excessively bent, then the reach may be too short.

A friend can help you check the reach with the plumb bob, assuming that the bike is level. Get comfortable on the saddle again, lean forward, put your hands on the drops, and look forward. When your friend holds the plumb string on your nose, the bob should reach the stem about an inch behind the bar. If it is an inch in either direction, the reach is off. The same rule applies for mountain bike bars.

As indicated above, changing the height or reach of the bar may be relatively straightforward or may require a new stem, handlebars with a different bend, or both. One of the best ways to tinker with your position and get things just right is to buy an adjustable stem or rent one from a local bike shop. This allows you to make incremental changes on your rides until you have the right position, and then to get exactly the right fixed stem.

11

Maintenance, Repairs, and Tools

This book confines itself to mentioning some skills and tools that are particularly useful for maintaining your bike, making simple adjustments, and handling problems that might arise on a tour; all of which can be handled with small, easily carried tools. It doesn't, however, make any attempt to teach you to be a bike mechanic—lots of people tour with very little knowledge of how to work on bikes.

How much of a bike mechanic do you want to be? How much you want to learn is a matter of personal preference and necessity. It is quite possible to learn how to do most of the work on your own bike—everything that doesn't require expensive specialized tools. To do this, get one or more of the technical manuals mentioned in the Resources section at the end of the book. Then start doing small jobs on your bike, and build up your abilities.

Every touring cyclist should know how to fix a flat and change a tire, but beyond that it is largely a matter of taste and the kind of touring you plan to do. If you are planning a solo tour in the Canadian Northwest Territories or crossing Patagonia from Chile to Argentina, you would be well advised to learn as much as you can about your bike and how to fix it, and to bring the right set of tools and spare parts. However, if you are planning to do mainly group rides and supported tours and you aren't mechanically inclined, you can just plan to throw yourself on the mercy of the experts on the ride.

There's no point in carrying a bag full of tools that you don't know how to use. With a few exceptions noted below, carry only those tools that you can use. Many of us have learned a lot about bike repairs and how to make them while patching things together on the road after a breakdown, but that isn't the recommended method for learning. If you have mechanical problems on the road that you don't know how to fix, you'll usually rely on a skilled member of your group or hitch a ride to the nearest bike shop. Standing by the road with a front wheel held against your chest often brings out the Good Samaritan in passing drivers.

In any case, the skills of a bike mechanic are usually built up over time, and unless you are very determined and in a big hurry, buying a full package of tools for the home mechanic is rarely justified. Even though you may pay more per tool, it is just as well to pick up tools a few at a time as you need them. As you acquire more skills, you may find secondhand or free items to add to your tool kit. Many touring cyclists carry them in a bag that straps under the saddle so they are always with the bike, even when riding locally with no handlebar bag or panniers. However, spare parts are often specific to your bike, so even if you have an ace mechanic along on the tour and you are all thumbs, you may still need to accumulate a few repair items and bike-specific tools.

Tools and Lessons to Get with the Bike

The best time to buy the tools you need to maintain your bike and get some basic tips on how to use them is when you are buying your bike (assuming you get it from a local shop). Talk with the shop folks about special tools that might be needed to match your equipment. Ask for their help—it's also a good way of getting a feel for how knowledgeable they are and what kind of support you can expect. And you're likely to get a reasonable price on the tools as part of the deal for the bike. By all means bring the bike back to get the prepaid adjustments after the first few hundred miles, but negotiate an agreement that the shop will let you watch and give you some pointers on how to do the same thing yourself. You need to be a little bit pushy to arrange this—after all, the shop has an assembly line in the back to accomplish these tasks, and you'll slow things down. But with a little diplomacy and the leverage of being a paying customer, you should be able to arrange it.

The very first set of tools you should acquire is the set to tighten all the basic connectors on the bike (mostly Allen wrenches). Ask about the tools needed for this when you purchase your bike. You'll also need tools to remove the gear cluster from the freehub (or the freewheel, if you're buying an older bike that has one). Ask about spare spokes and the size of spoke wrench needed for installing them. Getting spare spokes is not a bad idea, though well-built wheels should not suffer broken spokes. Get twice as many right rear spokes, because this is where most spokes break (see "Fixing Broken Spokes" later in this chapter for more details). The spokes and freehub remover are specific to your bike, and you should carry them even on tours where you are expecting someone else to provide mechanical capability.

One or two Allen wrenches should be the right size for adjusting the height of your seat, its angle, and its fore-aft position. Get someone from the bike shop to show you how to do this. You'll need this knowledge to be able to fine-tune your position when you're riding (the best time to fine-tune).

Ask someone in the shop to show you how to adjust the two derailleurs. The derailleurs always go out of adjustment in the first few hundred miles of riding as a result of cable stretch, and the shop will normally tell you to bring the bike back for adjustment. That's fine, but it's also a good idea to know how to do it yourself, and you'll find out what tool is needed (if any) and how to use it. Make sure your shop contact shows you both the cable tension adjustments and the limit-screw adjustments. Cable tension governs where the derailleurs are aligned for particular positions of the shift levers. The limit screws determine how far they can go in either direction, regardless of cable pull (see "Maintaining and Adjusting Derailleurs" later in this chapter for more details).

Ask about adjusting the brakes. There should be in-line barrels for fine-tuning the brake adjustment. If the bike doesn't already have these adjusters, have them installed when you buy the bike. (It is reasonable to take the position that they are standard and the bike should have them as standard equipment.) You'll also want to have the tool(s) for making the cable adjustment at the brake, and the one(s) for fine-tuning the brake pads. Learn how to make all these adjustments when you buy the bike, and you'll be able to do them on the road (see "Maintaining Brakes" later in this chapter for more details).

What kind of tool is needed for removing the pedals? Typically a pedal wrench is needed if they are tight; Allen wrenches or a small crescent wrench can exert only limited torque, and there isn't enough space to use a larger adjustable wrench. How about the pedal caps and any tools needed for servicing the pedals? For servicing and adjusting the hubs? Does the chain have a master link? What is needed to remove the cranks?

Asking these questions will familiarize you with your bike and equipment, and tell you what you need to know to make minor adjustments. Whenever possible, you should get the shop person to demonstrate or, even better, hand you the tool and show you how to do it yourself.

The small combination tools made for cyclists can eliminate the need to carry a number of separate items, but because they have clever, angled arrangements, make sure to check the tool against your bike—every screw and bolt you may need to tighten or loosen. You don't want to find out hundreds of miles from home that the Allen key you need to tighten your seat post or the main bolt on your rear rack won't actually fit because of the angle of the multitool.

Of course, you should have a patch kit, a spare innertube of the right size, and tire irons to change a tire. These are items you should buy immediately from your local bike shop. Another related item you should have in your kit is a tire boot of some kind. This is something that can be attached or glued to the inside of the tire casing to cover any gash or serious puncture in the body of the tire—anything larger than a tiny puncture will provide an opening through which the tube will stretch under air pressure and cause a blowout. Tire maintenance is covered in more detail in "Repairing a Tire" later in this chapter.

Basic Skills to Learn

If you aspire to do some tours that are far from the nearest bike shop, whether in third-world countries or in remote parts of North America, you will really want to acquire some mechanical skills. Without this knowledge, it will be difficult to even put together a well-thought-out repair and spare parts kit.

It is certainly possible to do quite a lot of touring without learning much about maintaining your bike, particularly if you go on supported tours or travel with people who are good at dealing with mechanical problems. However, if you want to be more self-sufficient, you need to acquire some basic bike-maintenance and repair skills, such as learning how to clean and repair a chain, tune the brakes, install new brake blocks, adjust the derailleurs, and replace cables. By learning these maintenance skills you'll be able to make repairs on the road, and you'll gain confidence.

You should get in the habit of regularly checking the tightness of the nuts and bolts holding on the luggage racks, the brakes, the brake levers, the handlebars, the headset, the derailleurs, the shifters, the cranks, the pedals, and the chainrings. The set of wrenches you've acquired will be your primary tools.

The general rule for bolts on the bike—those holding the luggage racks, for example—is that you should lubricate them first and then tighten them firmly. It might seem that oiling or greasing bolts would cause them to loosen more easily, but this is not the case. Lubrication allows the bolts to tighten smoothly rather than moving in increments. They are more likely to stay in place after having been lubricated and tightened firmly but carefully. Standard motor oil and machine or automobile grease work fine, though some prefer anti-seizing compound or special bicycle greases, like Park Polylube or Phil Wood. Don't use vegetable oils, which will break down over time, causing threads to corrode and seize.

Proper lubrication and periodic checking are the standard ways to prevent things from loosening on your bike. Some cyclists and mechanics like to use thread-locking compounds instead of oil or grease for attachment bolts—the most common is one of the Loctite compounds, available in any hardware store. The lighter-duty ones, such as Loctite 243 (in the red bottle or tube), work well to hold bolts in place, as well as lubricating them and protecting them from moisture and corrosion. *Never* use any of the heavier-duty Loctite compounds on bicycle threads; they can make it very difficult to remove a bolt without breaking it. Another way to prevent bolts from loosening is to install longer bolts when there is adequate clearance and to back them with nylon locking nuts, such as those made by Nylok. This technique is handy for luggage racks and fenders.

Performing Standard Maintenance

Keeping your bike clean and maintaining the adjustment of brakes, derailleurs, and bearing sets are the keys to keeping it in good condition and to learning the details of adjustment and maintenance. Developing a routine for handling most of these tasks is the best way to avoid problems. Cleaning and lubricating the chain, keeping the brakes adjusted, replacing brake pads as needed, and readjusting derailleurs whenever they begin to slip out of alignment are the most common maintenance tasks. These need to be done fairly frequently—perhaps every few hundred miles, but at least every week, and every day after riding in significant rain. Make a habit of regularly checking the tightness of all the bolts.

Less frequent checks need to be made of several other parts of the bicycle. You should manually check periodically for variations in spoke tension. If you rotate the wheels and systematically squeeze each adjoining pair of spokes, you'll notice any with low tension. You can get a more precise reading by plucking each spoke—the tone of the vibrating spoke indicates the tension. On a dished wheel, the dished-side spokes will have a higher pitch, but all the spokes on a particular side should have the same tone.

Other items that should be checked somewhat less frequently are the bearing sets in the wheels, the pedals, the headset, the crank arms (for tightness) and the bottom bracket. None of these should have significant play, binding, or hesitation spots when they are turned. Try to get a lesson from your local shop on inspecting them. With caps removed, they should be clean and well lubricated. When the bearings need attention, the normal procedure is to disassemble, clean with a citrus-based solvent, reassemble, and adjust. You can get lessons on each assembly, figure them out, or consult one of the manuals or Web sites listed in the Resources section at the end of the book.

Special tools are needed for some assemblies, and these vary by manufacturer, the type of bearing used, and manufacturing technique. For example, some bottom brackets require a special tool to disassemble, and cartridge bearings that are pressed into place may require specific tools to allow replacement. The tools are generally not very expensive, and learning to service these parts is a worthwhile skill, but you may choose to just have your local bike shop do this work. All the components with bearings should be checked occasionally, depending on how much you ride, ranging from once a month to once a year. You should check all these items before any major tour that will last for more than a week. If any of these critical moving parts don't feel quite right between inspections, they should be checked and repaired if necessary (either by you if you can or by your bike shop). Some experienced cyclists have grease fittings installed in pedals and hubs so that they can inject grease (and force dirt and moisture out) without having to disassemble the parts.

Fine-tuning the adjustment of derailleurs and brakes is a task that you should handle regularly on your rides. When shifting becomes slightly imprecise—indicated by hesitation in shifts or a slight noise from the gears—you should adjust the cable tension to correct the problem. Similarly, as brake cables stretch, you'll need to tighten them with the adjusters so that the brake shoes are as close to the rims as possible without dragging.

Misalignment in the front derailleur manifests slightly differently. You may find that you hear evidence of rubbing or experience difficulty shifting to the largest chainring or a tendency for the chain to fall off the lowest chainring. These are almost always due to stretch in the cable, which simply needs to be tightened slightly. Much more fine-tuning may be required if you have indexed shifting for the front derailleur. It is more common, particularly with bar-end shifters, for the front derailleur to operate using friction rather than indexing, even when the rear is indexed.

Note that if you have indexed shifters that can be switched to friction, as most bar-end and down-tube shifters can, this is an easy fix for many adjustment problems that occur on the road, as when a derailleur is knocked out of alignment. Simply switching to friction makes many problems disappear, because precise cable tension is no longer required.

Maintaining Chains

Maintaining the chain is your most important general maintenance task. This is true for a number of reasons. The chain is exposed, and it almost seems to attract dirt. It is under tension all the time you are riding and can be a major source of friction if it is not clean and well lubricated. It passes over your gears and leaves dirt there. Perhaps most important, if the chain is not kept clean and lubricated, it becomes worn, and a worn chain wears down your (expensive) cogs and chainwheels. You need to develop your own routine, based on your riding and the climate where you ride. It's best to wipe and lubricate your chain after every long ride, every week if you're just riding around town. On tour, try to check the chain every day.

Chain wear. It's important to understand how chain-cog-chainwheel wear works. New chains are constructed with a fixed length, or pitch, between each link, rivet, or roller. This distance exactly matches the distance between the teeth of each of your gears. Because the chain, as it flexes around the gears, has to pivot on the rivets, the rollers turn on and rub against the rivets. The friction thus generated tends to wear the rivets circumferentially. As the rivets wear, the chain lengthens.

If you allow the chain to lengthen significantly, the links become longer, and they wear against the driving edges of the gears because the link length and the tooth spacing no longer match. The gear teeth change shape, and eventually they no longer shift correctly. The insidious syndrome, however, is that the worn cogs and chainwheels work *for a while* with the worn chain, but as they wear, they become unusable with a new chain. They are slowly and subtly ruined. The teeth wear so that the distance between them matches the non-standard length between the links of your worn chain. If you replace a chainwheel or a cog without replacing the worn chain, you'll rapidly ruin the new component. Chainwheels, which are more expensive and usually made from aluminum alloy, will be ruined faster than cheaper rear cogs, which are always made of steel.

One manifestation of chain wear is that the chain works properly when you are in your most-used gear combinations, but in less-used gear combinations you experience skipping, bad shifts, or chain suck—when the chain sticks to the bottom of the chainwheel (see "Chain Suck" later in this chapter for more information). The chain and the gears have worn together in the common configuration, but they don't match in others. If you switch wheels between different bikes after allowing excessive chain wear to occur on one bike, problems can rapidly ripple from one machine to the other. Thus it is important to pay attention to chain lubrication and cleanliness (to avoid premature wear), and to check for wear periodically, so that you replace the chain before it wears down your gears.

When your chain is worn, it lengthens—the distance between one link and the next becomes a little greater, because the contacts between the rivets and the insides of the rollers are worn. Each junction adds a little slop. There are a couple of ways to easily measure your chain for wear. You can use a precise ruler, made for a shop or a draftsperson. Twelve sets of outer and inner links under tension—24 segments—should measure exactly 1 foot. If this measurement is more than $\frac{1}{16}$-inch longer than 12 inches, replace the chain. If you don't have an accurate ruler or you don't want to be bothered, buy a metal or plastic chain wear indicator. This gadget slips onto the chain, and its markers show when it's time to replace it. A number of different ones are available, and they all work. Just remember that they all measure elongation; the chain has to be under tension for you to see it.

Lubrication and cleaning. Experienced cyclists have all sorts of regimens for cleaning and servicing chains. The essentials are to keep the chain clean and to lubricate it regularly. Any good chain lubricant acts as an adhesive to accumulate road dirt. When the dirt stays on the chain, some abrasive bits will work their way into the spaces between the rivets and the rollers where they will grind away at the metal. Other bits of grit will migrate onto the rollers and will cause abrasion between the rollers and the teeth of the gears. Keeping the chain clean minimizes these problems and greatly increases the life of the chain, the cogs, and the chainwheels.

There are lots of good chain lubricants available. Get one specifically intended for bicycle chains. It should be relatively light; the critical aspects are that it should help you to clean dirt from the outside of the chain, and it should penetrate into the space between the roller and the rivet. Roller-rivet contact is the most important surface for lubrication, but it is out of sight and hard to reach. The outside of the roller also needs lubrication because it rubs against the gear teeth, but it is easy to coat with lubricant. The rest of the chain needs a thin film of oil to protect it from rust, but it doesn't actually need lubrication.

Wax-based chain lubricants are a very poor choice. They keep the chain looking clean on the outside and they don't pick up as much dirt as oils, but they don't usually penetrate to the roller-rivet surface, so they don't lubricate the most important parts of the chain. An example of this approach is to heat the chain in paraffin wax, so that it penetrates the links. Even if this reaches the roller-rivet contact, it hardens at working temperatures and soon wears off, leaving those surfaces without lubrication.

When you are lubricating the chain, move it slowly and put a drop of lubricant on each roller; you want some of it to move into the space between the roller and the rivet. Don't lubricate a dirty chain— the oil will wash some grit particles into the interior spaces, so you may make things worse. Wipe all the excess oil from the chain after lubricating. Any extra oil on the outside of the chain just picks up dirt.

When the chain has picked up a lot of dirt, it needs a complete (and messy) cleaning. There are two basic ways you can do this. You can buy a chain scrubber, which is attached to the bottom span of the chain while it is on the bike. The chain scrubber has cleaning brushes and a reservoir filled with solvent, and the chain is cycled through it. If you get one of these, get a good-quality one—it will still be messy to use, but it will work. The cheap ones are also messy to use, and they work poorly.

When the chain needs more than wiping with a solvent-wetted rag, I prefer to remove the chain from the bike, clean it with brushes in a small tray with solvent, and then put it back on the bike. However, I buy chains with master links that make them easy to remove and remount. Other brands of chains require special rivets (see the discussion on the next page), which make them harder to remove and reinstall. If you remove the chain to clean it, it is advisable to reinstall it so that it goes in the opposite direction. Shimano engineers found that this doubles the life of the chain.

The old standbys as solvents for cleaning chains are kerosene and diesel fuel, but these are not environmentally sound and not optimal for your health. If you do get stuck using them in an emergency, put on gloves to minimize absorption through the skin, and use in a very well-ventilated place. *Never use gasoline.* It is volatile and carries the risk of explosive ignition, and it is very bad to breathe the fumes. The best solvents are the new citrus-based ones, which are now widely available. They don't pose a hazard to either your health or the environment. You should buy solvent from a cycling supplier, but if you can't, read the label carefully to make sure it's okay for bicycle chain use. The ones suitable for use on bicycles contain citrus-derived terpenes, not citric acid or water. (The contents should include d-Limonene and not water or citric acid.) These solvents are still flammable, but far less so than any petroleum-based solvent.

Replacing the chain. In addition to keeping the chain clean and well lubricated, it is important to replace worn chains to avoid more expensive repairs. Chains wear internally—on the rollers, bushings, and pins—and this wear is manifested by a lengthening of the links as noted in "Chain Wear" earlier in this chapter.

Replacing chains is cheaper than replacing gears, so it is wise to be proactive. Many cyclists measure their chains periodically (see page 216). Some don't bother measuring; they keep track of mileage and change the chain every 1,000 to 1,200 miles.

To install a new chain, you need to first make sure the chain is compatible with your other components. An older-model chain won't work with a 10-speed system, for example. In general, a narrower chain works with older systems, but not vice versa. The rule is to check the specifications before you buy the chain—there are many nuances.

New chains normally are long enough to accommodate any normal bike—you simply remove enough links to fit your bike. Any chain that is not long enough should be returned. Usually, assuming your current chain is the right length, you just cut the new one to the same length, and then follow the manufacturer's instructions to put the new one together. Modern Shimano chains require the installation of a special rivet; modern Campagnolo chains need a special set of links installed with a special rivet on each end; and current SRAM chains, and some others, are put together with a special master link.

If you're dubious about the length of your old chain, or you don't have it available, thread the new chain directly between your largest chainwheel and your largest cog, without going through the rear derailleur. Find the nearest link with which you could connect the chain (erring on the long side). Add two links (one inch). This is the correct length for the new chain. The two extra links allow enough slack for the rear derailleur. Cut the chain at that point (see "Opening and Closing Chains" below), making allowance for whatever connection method your new chain requires—master link, Campy HD-link, or Shimano special rivet.

Then shift the rear derailleur toward the smallest cog, thread the new chain through the normal chain route, and connect it. Make sure you install the chain according to the manufacturer's specifications. Some specify that it be in a particular direction (Shimano does for its 10-speed models).

Opening and closing chains. Cutting a chain (removing it from the bike or removing some links) requires a chain-link tool (see Drawing 28). This tool is designed to drive a rivet most of the way out of the chain, allowing the links to be separated but leaving the rivet protruding from one side plate. The chain-link tool should have a tool-steel pin, sometimes with a bearing at the tip, which can be centered on the rivet on one side of the chain, and a cradle that holds the chain links on either side so that the spacing between the side links is held steady as the rivet is driven out.

Older chains made for freewheels or freehubs with five or six cogs had reusable rivets. You could drive any rivet out and then reconnect the chain by pressing it back in after links were added or removed. With the much tighter tolerances for modern narrow chains, this is no longer true. Once a rivet on one of these chains is driven out, it can't be reused, so do not use an older chain-link tool on newer, narrower chains. You must use the connection method specified by the manufacturer (often requiring special-purpose rivets) or install a master link designed to fit the chain.

Stiff links. A stiff link binds and doesn't articulate properly as it runs through the bends of the rear derailleur. This may occur if you've ridden in the rain and then let the bike sit without cleaning and relubricating the chain, so that links have rusted. Generally a good job of re-oiling the chain will take care of this problem. Stiff links can also result from chain damage (the chain has come off a gear and been distorted from subsequent mechanical jamming) or from

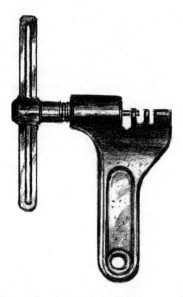

28. A chain-link tool. The two projections within the jaw are the tight-link cradle (left) and the primary cradle (right). If you purchase a chain-link tool, make sure it is specified to fit your chain.

improper installation. In this case it may be possible to loosen the stiff link with a chain-link tool. This must be done with great care, however, and if you aren't carrying a spare chain, you should probably consider stopping at the nearest bike shop and either replacing the chain or buying a spare, just in case. Using chain-link tools on the new, narrower chains is tricky, because the tolerances are so tight.

Loosening a stiff link with a chain-link tool essentially relies on pushing the rivet in very slightly from each side plate, eliminating the binding of the inner plates against the outer ones. This operation was quite straightforward with old-style chains because reusable rivets protruded somewhat on either side of the chain's outer plates. Narrower modern chains are designed to eliminate every bit of additional width. The rivets are expanded at the ends and protrude only a hair, so moving the rivet with respect to the plate can compromise the strength of the chain.

If the stiff link was caused by improper installation of the chain, so that it occurs at one of the special rivets (e.g., Shimano or Campy), you may be able to safely adjust it with the chain-link tool, though you might be well advised to remove the special rivet and replace it with a new one. If the binding results from damage to the chain, you should consider adjustments using the chain-link tool to be temporary emergency repairs (replace the chain at the next available bike shop). Remember that if a chain is weakened, it will usually break when an unusual amount of force is applied. Such occasions normally happen when you are sprinting, accelerating in the middle of an intersection, straining on a hill, or making emergency moves—just the times when you don't want the chain to break.

Modern chains rarely break, except under unusual stress. These chains are very strong. However, because tolerances are so tight, modern chains are harder to repair than their predecessors. If a chain has been damaged, replacing it as soon as possible is advisable.

Master links. As mentioned earlier, some modern chains (e.g., SRAM, KMC, Wipperman) come with keyed master links (see Drawing 29) that can be installed and removed by hand. You simply advance the chain until you find the master link, release it, and remove the chain from the bike. This is easy with a clean chain; finding the master link is more of a challenge when the chain is dirty. The master link substitutes for one link having outer plates, so it must be installed between two inner links (the ones that are narrower and have rollers). Some master links can be installed on the chains of other manufacturers, but check the specifications. Master links are generally specific to the brand and width. Thus the SRAM PowerLink for 9-speed chains is different from the one for their 6-, 7-, and 8-speed chains. Many users of Shimano chains use an SRAM PowerLink to install the chain, rather than the Shimano pin, because the PowerLink is more reliable and easier to remove. This

29. A master link makes opening and closing the chain easy and does not weaken the chain the way removing and resetting the rivets does.

compatibility has been extensively tested in the field, though neither manufacturer acknowledges it. At the time this book was written, only SRAM made a master link (PowerLock) for 10-speed chains, and it is compatible only with SRAM and Shimano chains.

Chain suck. As mentioned earlier, chain suck occurs when the chain "sticks" to the bottom of the chainwheel as the links of the chain fail to release from the lower teeth of the chainwheel. This catching of the chain on the lower chainwheel teeth pulls the rear derailleur tension arm forward, and it can cause nasty chain jams in the chainwheels or messy problems in front shifting. This can cause you to fall over, or at least come to a grinding halt. You must then realign the chain by hand, resulting in skinned knuckles and grease smeared everywhere. It can badly damage the chain and bend or break teeth on the chainwheel. Chain suck most often occurs when you are shifting down with the front derailleur, especially to the lowest ring, and you are pedaling hard, exerting a lot of force on the chain.

Riders often attribute these problems to the front derailleur, and poor adjustment of either derailleur can indeed exacerbate the problem. However, chain suck is almost always caused by excessive chain wear. The worst instances occur when a new chain is used with a worn chainwheel. Generally, the cyclist has allowed the old chain to wear excessively, so that it has ground against the load-bearing edges of the chainwheel teeth. This gives the teeth a slightly hook-shaped profile, and at the bottom of the stroke, they tend to hook the chain, particularly when a new, unstretched chain is installed. In these cases, the remedy is to replace the chainwheels and to ensure that the chain is not worn.

Maintaining and Adjusting Derailleurs

Derailleurs should be kept clean and well lubricated, which is normally just an extra housekeeping chore associated with servicing the chain. Use the same brushes, solvent, and rags to clean all parts of the rear derailleur. Oil the moving parts and wipe off all excess oil.

Learning how to adjust the derailleurs is one of those basic tasks that you should master as early as possible. You can either get a mechanic at the shop where you bought the bike to show you how or work through the process using one of the resources in the Resources section at the end of the book.

A new bike always requires the cable tension to be readjusted in the first few hundred miles of use, because new cables stretch. On indexed shifting systems (ones that click for each gear change), the cable tension has to be correct for the indexing to work. As the cable stretches and the system goes out of alignment, you'll hear the gears making noise in the rear, as though they were trying to shift, or there will be a delay after you change the position of the lever. In front, the derailleur cage will rub against a chain when it shouldn't, or you'll have to push the shift lever beyond the indexed position to get it to shift. (Some bikes are set up with indexed shifting for the rear derailleur and friction shifting [no clicks] for the front derailleur.) With non-indexed (friction) shifters, a stretched cable generally results in not being able to shift to the lowest cog in the rear, because the cable has been stretched and can't exert enough tension to pull the derailleur to the farthest position. (The situation is reversed for Rapid Rise systems.)

If the bike has threaded-barrel adjusters, use them to bring the cables back to the right tension. When they reach their limits, you need to move everything to the slackest position, take some slack out of the cable at the screw on the derailleur itself, and then fine-tune the position with the barrel adjuster.

Learn where the adjustment screws are on each derailleur, and experiment with them while the bike is suspended. You can use a work stand if you have one, or you can suspend the bike from its seat with a piece of nylon webbing hanging from a tree or a solid bracket or hook in the ceiling. This will allow you to move the shifters while turning the cranks, watching the exact effects of shifting.

Details for both derailleurs will vary with your exact model, and consulting the references listed in the Resources section at the end of the book is recommended. In general, however, the rear derailleur has three adjustment screws, sometimes labeled, sometimes not. The "L" screw sets the limit of travel in the direction of your low gear—the largest cog, which is next to the spokes. If it is too loose, your chain can over-shift into the spokes, which is a bad thing. If it is too tight, you'll have a hard time shifting into low gear. The "H" screw limits derailleur travel in the direction of the smallest cog. If it is too loose, your chain can come off on the right side, possibly jamming. This is also not good, but it is less serious than having the chain go into the spokes. Again, if the screw is too tight, you'll have trouble shifting into your highest gear.

In both cases, you adjust the screw so that the bike shifts easily to the gear while the chain is on any of the front chainwheels. It should run smoothly and quietly on that cog, with no tendency to be pushed to either side by the derailleur. If you keep things properly adjusted, there won't be any tendency for the chain to ride off the cogs in either direction during normal shifting.

The third screw is the "B" screw (rarely labeled), which pushes against a protrusion on the rear drop-out and adjusts the angle of the derailleur, thus controlling how far the chain wraps around the cogs. The B screw doesn't usually need adjustment, but it should be checked after the L and H screws are changed. When the chain is on the largest cog, the B screw should be adjusted so that the upper pulley does not rub on the cog.

For the front derailleur, this section ignores height and angle adjustments, which are important when initially setting up the bike or in dealing with mis-alignment after an accident. Like the rear derailleur, the front has H and L limit screws to prevent the cage from moving too far in either direction. These are fairly straightforward to adjust if they need tweaking.

After you've done basic adjustment of the derailleurs with the bike on a stand or hanging, you need to take it out and ride it and check each shift. The chain shifts a bit differently under load than it does on the stand, and you may have to do a little more fine-tuning.

Maintaining Brakes

Like derailleur cables, brake cables on a new bike can be expected to stretch, and brake pads wear with use. Brake cables should each have a barrel adjuster somewhere along the cable or at one end, but not all do. Without barrel adjusters, or when one has reached its limit, you'll have to tighten the cable at the brake, unless you can move post-mounted brake pads closer to the rim.

The method will vary with the type of brake. With a center-pull cantilever brake, which is the most common type for touring bicycles, you'll usually make this adjustment at the pinch bolt where the primary brake cable attaches to the straddle cable. Before unhooking anything, check to see how much slack needs to be taken out of the cable to achieve the right tension. This is bound to be a guess. Detach the straddle cable at the side that is slotted for quick release, eliminating the tension on the main brake cable. Loosen the pinch bolt (you need two wrenches or sockets) and move the clamp up the cable the estimated amount. Tighten everything, reattach the straddle cable, and try things out. You'll probably have to make several attempts to get the adjustment right, though if you have barrel adjusters, you can fine-tune with those, so the pinch bolt positioning only has to be approximately right.

You should get a set of replacement brake pads when you buy the bike or soon after. Allow some time to learn and experiment when you first replace them. Many experienced tourists replace stock brake pads when they first get the bike, substituting high-performance pads for the originals. After all, bicycle tourists carrying a substantial amount of luggage have special braking requirements on long downhill grades. Kool Stop salmon or bicolor brake pads are widely favored as substitute or replacement pads. Pads vary widely with brake models, and you need to buy pads that fit your brakes.

Replacing Cables

Eventually cables need to be replaced. I would recommend that you do this yourself at least once. On long tours, you should have spare cables in your repair kit, and the prospect of replacing one will be far less daunting if you have already done the job at least once.

While housing often lasts longer than the cables within, if you are replacing cables for standard maintenance, it makes sense to do the housing at the same time. Cables and housing are cheap, and the job is labor intensive. For emergency repairs on the road, I carry only spare cables and assume I will reuse the housing or purchase it at a shop.

When replacing cables, although all the parts can be bought separately, it makes sense to get a kit—appropriate for your equipment—for derailleurs or brakes. Derailleur and brake cables are clearly different, and though they look the same, *brake and derailleur housings are not interchangeable*. Modern shift or derailleur housing is specially made to resist compression in order to support indexed shifting. It cannot withstand the forces applied to brake-cable housing.

Any of the resources listed for repair and maintenance will provide a good primer on preparing and routing cables, but Sheldon Brown's article on cables is particularly recommended (see the Resources section at the end of the book).

Truing a Wheel

If you've followed the recommendation to learn to build a wheel that I made in Chapter 7, you'll know how to true a wheel. If not, it is a very good idea to do some experimenting at home to get a feel for it. Ideally, you should work on an old wheel or one on the least valuable bike you have on which the nipples are not irretrievably corroded to the spokes. If you don't have a spare, it is okay to experiment with one of the wheels on your touring bike—just exercise appropriate care not to overdo. You want to change the spoke tension just enough to see how the process works.

If you're truing a wheel at home, beyond a little experimenting, it is best to use a truing stand—purchased, borrowed, or homemade (see Chapter 7). However, it is perfectly possible to use the bike as a truing stand, and that is what you'll do if you break a spoke on the road or knock the wheel out of true by hitting an obstacle. You'll need a spoke wrench in your repair kit that is the correct size for the nipples on your wheels (there are three common sizes). Flip the

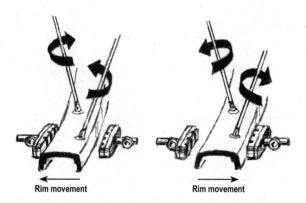

Rim movement   Rim movement

30. Truing a wheel. For each spoke you tighten, you should loosen the ones on either side that pull in the opposite direction. Large arrows show thread movement of spokes; nipples turn in the opposite direction.

bike over and get it in a stable location before starting to work on the wheel. First replace any broken spokes (see "Fixing Broken Spokes" later in this chapter).

Truing a wheel is done by balancing the forces of the spokes on the two sides, which hold the rim under tension, but also pull the rim toward one side or the other. As you adjust the rim to one side or the other, you'll normally work on several spokes, and you'll turn the nipples on one side of the wheel in the opposite direction from those on the other side (see Drawing 30). In general, to adjust a wobble in the wheel, you tighten one to three spokes and loosen another one to three. For a larger distortion, you increase the number adjusted. Before turning each nipple, apply a drop of oil to lubricate the threads.

Always make changes in tension in very small increments, and turn the wheel to determine the effects on the rest of the wheel. Finally, when the wheel is spinning true, squeeze the spokes all the way around in groups of two to four, releasing imbalances that have built up and finding any loose spokes. This will often create some pops, as nipples settle in. After doing this, you'll typically need to tighten a few spokes and make some tweaks in the alignment.

Repairing a Tire

The most common repair that any cyclist has to make is fixing a flat tire, though if you have higher-quality touring tires (see "Choosing Tires" on page 153), you can ride thousands of miles between flats. Tire repair is quite simple if you follow these steps:

Step 1: Remove the wheel. Release the brake and remove the wheel—an easier task for front wheels than for rear ones, particularly if you have to remove the panniers. If you have a double-legged kickstand, you can easily do this with the bike in place, though you might have to remove one set of panniers to redistribute the weight. If you have to lay the bike on the ground, be sure to lay it on its left side after removing the wheel so you don't put weight on the derailleurs or let them dig into the dirt.

If you aren't used to removing the wheels on your bike, there are a couple of small details that are easy to miss. If the brakes have quick releases, either on the brakes themselves or the brake levers, use them. They should move the brake pads far enough from the rim to allow the tire to clear the brakes. Otherwise, you'll need to slip one end of the straddle cable out of its slot, assuming you have cantilever brakes. (For other types of brakes without quick releases, you'll need to loosen the cable.) When you've undone the quick release on the axle and loosened the acorn nut on the other end, the front wheel may not fall out. Most bikes are now made with depressions on the inside of the dropouts, so that you have to spread the fork blades slightly or hit the top of the wheel with the heel of your hand to spring it free. (Many disapproving cyclists refer to these unnecessary depressions as lawyer lips, because they are designed to keep wheels from easily popping out.)

You may have to move the back wheel forward before removing it, depending on the construction of the dropouts. In any case, shift the chain onto the smallest rear cog before you loosen the quick release.

Then pull the derailleur back as you remove the wheel. If your bike has a chain hanger (a small post on the inside of the right chainstay), hook the chain over it so that it stays wrapped correctly around the derailleur.

Step 2: Check the damage and remove the tire. Your strategy for fixing a flat may vary somewhat depending on whether you are at home, in camp, or on the road. In all cases, take the time to think things through before diving in. This will help you keep from getting too dirty or making mistakes.

Before removing the tire, inspect it thoroughly and run your hand carefully around the inside of the tire to try to find the source of the puncture, taking care not to cut your finger on anything sharp. If there is something still embedded in the tire, you'll feel it. Remove it and make note of where it was lodged in the tire. If you find the location of the puncture, mark the sidewall with a permanent marker (useful to carry in your tool kit). Alternatively, you can mark the position of the valve stem on the tire wall, which will allow you to correlate the tube and the tire. Note that if there is an obvious tear in the sidewall or the tread, which probably would have resulted in a loud and sudden blowout, there is no point in going further unless you have a tire boot in your repair kit. If there is a break in the casing, just patching the tube won't work. With a nail puncture, you may have two holes on opposite sides of the tube—you may also have rim damage if a long nail has gone all the way through the tire.

Next you need to push the bead with your thumbs from one side of the tire so that it slips to the center of the rim, the lowest part. This will allow you to more easily lift the bead at the diametrically opposite side of the wheel. You need to do this because the diameter of the bead is less than that of the outside of the rim. That's why the bead stays on the rim.

You should then pull the bead of the tire over the rim on the side from which you are working. Begin working away from the valve stem, because it can get

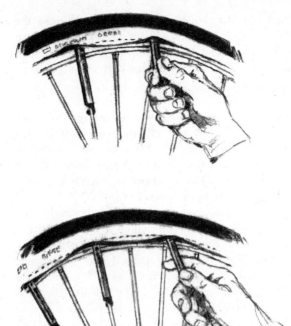

31. Removing a tire for repair.

in the way of your work and there is more danger of pinching the tube in the vicinity of the valve stem. The effort required varies with the fit of the tire and rim, but the process is shown in Drawing 31: lift the bead over the rim with a tire iron and hook the end of the iron over a spoke, then repeat with a second tire iron, and then a third. Then move the middle lever and lift a new section. Each time you insert the tire iron, be very careful to lift only the bead of the tire and to avoid pinching a section of the inner tube.

After you have moved the bead over a foot or so, you can usually just slide one tire iron all the way around the rim to remove the rest. At that point, the tension of the bead will have been relieved. As you are doing this, avoid rotating the tire on the rim, because you want to retain the relative position of the tube and tire so that you can correlate the puncture between the two. After you've removed the bead from one side of the rim, you can remove the inner tube. Be sure to maintain the original orientation—don't flip the tube over accidentally. The valve stem gives a positional location for the tube, and if you've avoided rotating the tire or have marked the position of the valve stem on it, you can match positions on the tire and tube. This can be important, because if the hole in the tube is small, you can check the tire at the same point on the circumference to try to locate the thorn, bit of glass, or other penetrating object that made the hole. Nothing is more frustrating than to patch a hole, get back on the bike, and get another flat 20 miles on due to the same thorn, still embedded in the tire casing!

Step 3: Find the leak and (if needed) boot the tire. If you found the problem when you looked at the tire, look at the same location on the tube and see if the hole is there. If you haven't found the leak, blow the tube up with your pump until it reaches double or triple its normal volume. If you hear a hiss, follow it. If not, rotate the tube past your face and see if you hear the leak or feel the escaping air. If not, visually inspect the inflated tube to try to find the leak. Check the entire surface area of the tube. Some leaks are caused by wear against spoke holes or debris inside the tube. Avoid flipping the tube over, unless you mark the uppermost side. When you find the leak, you want to be able to look at the same location on the tire or rim for the cause, so that you can fix it at the source.

If you can't find the leak with the methods just described, try spreading water on the tube surface, gradually working your way around. If that doesn't work, add a little liquid soap and look for bubbles. You'll eventually find it. (If you can, blow the tube up and submerge it a section at a time in a sink, watching for a line of bubbles.)

When you find the leak, mark it with chalk or permanent marker. Wash the tube off at that location and dry it. Don't try to patch the tube until it is completely clean and dry. Choose a patch large enough to cover the puncture, and roughen an area around the puncture with the sandpaper from your patch kit. If there is a ridge of rubber projecting in the area, it should be sanded flat. (If you are using glueless, self-adhesive patches, follow the directions that came with them.) The roughened area must be large enough to extend beyond the patch you will use, *after the tube has been deflated to its normal size.*

Let enough air out of the tube, assuming a small hole, for the tube to be approximately normal in cross-section, and quickly spread a very thin layer of glue around the whole roughened area. Leave the tube in a place where the glue can dry without accumulating any dirt. While the glue is drying, check the corresponding area on the inside of the tire or the rim strip/rim area. If there is a thorn, piece of glass, tack, or other protrusion penetrating the tire, remove it. If there is a rough spot or an exposed spoke hole along the rim and the puncture is on the inside of the tube, fix the problem area.

Another common form of tube failure results from a pinched tube. This occurs when a length of tube is caught under the bead or folded back onto itself during mounting. The air pressure and the fold cause concentrated stress and wear, and the tube fails. Pinch failures are usually obvious because of longitudinal marks where the fold or pinch area of the tube occurred.

One particularly treacherous source of punctures is wire from steel-belted radial car or truck tires. These are almost invisible and can stab your fingers just by brushing them, especially when they project on the inside of the tire. One precaution you can take is to carry a cotton swab in your tire repair kit and use it to run around the inside of the bicycle tire in both directions. The cotton will catch on any embedded wires, which then can be removed with pliers. You can find these wires with your fingers, but that could be much more painful.

Punctures on the inside of the tube are typically the result of a section of the rim tape shifting out of place and allowing a spoke hole or a burr to cut into the tube. Finally, look for *snake bite punctures*—two holes on opposite sides of the tube where it was pinched when you rose over an obstruction. Snake bites are the result of insufficient tire pressure on trails or rough pavement. Look for possible tire damage at the same location as the snake bite puncture in the tube.

When you have discovered tire damage (not just a punctured tube), you need to put a boot on the inside of the tire before patching the tube. Many experienced riders like to use sections of old tubular (sew-up) tires for boots. A very serviceable and lighter modern alternative for small breaks is a rectangle of Tyvek from a packing envelope flap like a FedEx envelope. Tyvek doesn't stretch, so just remove the paper portion from the envelope flap and the adhesive will hold the boot in position. Old-fashioned boots are usually glued in place, but the glue doesn't have to secure the boot, which is held in place by air pressure after the tire is reinflated. The cement is only used to position the boot while everything is assembled. Tyvek boots are only usable for short tire breaks—a half-inch or less. Material from a tubular tire or the wall of a thin, high-pressure road tire is needed for larger breaks. Feather the edges of any thicker boot you make. Ridge-like edges will wear through the tube.

Having a boot is critical. If the tire casing is torn, the inflated tube will work its way through the opening and quickly cause a blowout. However, a boot repair is only temporary. You'll feel a bump when it goes around, and it will wear through the tube eventually. If you are carrying a spare tire, use it.

If you have a spare tube, you may want to install it instead of patching the damaged one. The same applies to a spare tire. Don't ignore other steps, however. If a thorn is protruding through the tire and you don't find it, it will create another leak, whether you patch the old tube or install a new one.

Step 4: Patch the leak. Assuming the tire doesn't have major damage, you're ready to patch the tube. If it will hold air at all, blow it up to normal size, and check the cement with a clean, dry finger. It can be tacky to the touch, but there should be no liquid cement. If there is, it has not dried properly, and you need to wait. Once the cement is dry, remove the backing from the patch and press the patch firmly onto the cemented area of the tube. Work out any wrinkles. Dust the patch area and then the whole tube with talcum, which you should carry in your repair kit.

At this point, especially if you did not already find the source of the puncture, you should run your fingers around the inside of the tire (still half mounted on the rim, though you can easily remove it if you choose). Feel for any irregularities or foreign objects, and remove them if necessary. Remember, be careful of the wires mentioned earlier. Pour a tablespoonful of talcum in the inside of the tire casing and rotate the wheel to distribute it around the inside of the tire, adding more talcum as needed. The idea is to create a low-friction, absorbent contact between the tube and the inside of the tire, so that the tube slides easily to a natural position when inflated at high pressure.

With the tube inflated to approximately normal size, insert it in the tire with the valve protruding through the valve hole in the rim. You want the tube to assume its normal position, without any folds or distortions. You may then need to deflate the tube a bit to allow you to work the bead back over the rim.

Push the bead over the rim near the valve stem, and work it over the rim in both directions from the valve stem. When a significant length of bead is seated, push on the valve stem to be sure that it is clear and that none of the surrounding tube will be pinched. Continue around the wheel, pushing the bead on with your thumbs, and taking care that none of the tube is pinched under the bead. Usually, it is possible to completely install the bead manually, but this varies with the tire-rim combination and with your manual dexterity and strength. You may have to pry the last few inches of the tire bead over the rim with tire irons. If so, be very careful not to pinch the tube.

Begin inflating the tube, and then inspect the tire and the rim all the way around on both sides to ensure that the beads are evenly seated. All visible circumferential references should be symmetrical. Most tires have ridges, molded marks, lettering, and embossed designs that will show if the bead is unevenly seated. These should all be a uniform distance from the rim. If they aren't, deflate the tire slightly and press the bead in appropriate places to ensure that the seating is uniform.

Finally, inflate the tire to full pressure, and check again that the bead is seated correctly all the way around the tire. When all is well, reinstall the wheel and make sure it is inflated to the correct pressure. Continue on your way.

Once you are comfortable with repairing tires, a puncture will not delay you for long, though you may decide to find more robust tires for the next tour. Tire repair can be enormously frustrating, particularly if you make mistakes and experience another flat. Over time, however, you'll gain enough experience to avoid repeated flats.

Some Emergency Road Repairs

The critical emergency repair skills for the touring cyclist are really just basic skills associated with bicycling. If you know how to interpret noises of complaint that your bicycle is making, then you will usually be able to anticipate mechanical problems before they occur. If you have the tools to adjust your bicycle along the road, you'll avoid nasty surprises. The more you learn about making adjustments yourself rather than relying on mechanics, the more you will be able to anticipate and avoid or fix minor mechanical difficulties. Perhaps most important, if you've performed basic mechanical tasks on your bike, you'll understand the issues of handling them on the road. To take a specific example, if you've never removed a gear cassette from a rear wheel, you won't understand either the importance or the operation of a Hypercracker as a substitute on the road (the Hypercracker lockring tool is discussed in the next section). Apart from generalities, however, there are a few specifics that are worth mentioning here.

Fixing Broken Spokes

Many experienced cyclists tour for years with never a broken spoke. Well-built wheels are a major reason for this kind of success, but riding skill and luck are also important (if you know how to ride lightly on your wheels, you can reduce the stress on them). Regardless, when you encounter broken spokes, whatever the root cause, you need to deal with them. To do so, you need to have the right tools and repair items, as well as adequate knowledge.

Most broken spokes are the result of poorly built wheels. The best wheels are tightly constructed to distribute stress evenly around the circumference, so that no single spoke is subjected to excessive stress. There is a reason why master wheel builders like Peter White can unconditionally guarantee their wheels!

Broken spokes can also occur as a result of circumstances (you hit a rock with your front wheel on a high-speed downhill run), misuse (touring with heavy luggage on a wheel that was designed for unloaded sport riding), or other miscalculations.

The simplest situation you might need to handle is a single broken spoke that occurs not too far from your destination for the day. A single broken spoke on a wheel that has 36 or more spokes can be managed by a quick wheel adjustment entailing no major delay. As shown in Drawing 32, you can simply wrap the spoke around one of its neighbors and adjust the tension of the neighboring spokes to bring the wheel into true. This is, however, always a temporary solution, and it may not work when more than one spoke breaks in the initial incident. One reason that touring cyclists prefer 36-, 40-, or 48-spoke wheels is that they easily

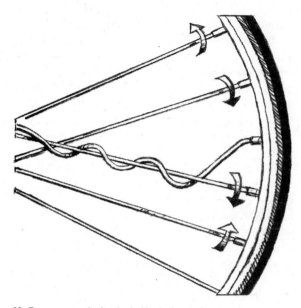

32. Temporary repair of a wheel with a broken spoke.

allow this kind of repair. With a 24- or 28-spoke wheel, much more tension would be put on adjoining spokes to bring the wheel true, and they would be far more likely to break in turn.

The best solution on the road, if you are suitably equipped both with hardware and skills, is to replace the broken spokes, either permanently or temporarily. Let's first consider fixing the problem properly, and then proceed to temporary solutions.

A permanent fix for broken spokes, of course, is to replace them altogether. A typical touring bike has spokes of three lengths—the front-wheel spokes, which have equal length and tension on either side; the left rear spokes; and the right rear spokes, which are shorter and tensioned more tightly than those on the left, because right rear spokes must accommodate the gears on the right side of the rear wheel. That is, the rear wheel is *dished*—squeezing the gears into the space between the hub flange and the right drop-out means that everything else has to move left. The resulting geometry dictates that the right (drive-side) spokes of the rear wheel are shorter and under higher tension than the left-side spokes (assuming the same cross pattern). Therefore, broken spokes usually happen on the right (drive) side of the rear wheel. That's where the maximum stress is.* Most touring cyclists who carry spare spokes have bikes that use three spoke lengths, but most of the spare spokes they carry will be for the right rear.

Completely fixing a wheel with broken spokes requires replacing those spokes and then retensioning the wheel. This is easy to do (if you have the replacement spokes and the spoke wrench) on the front wheel and the left rear. On the right rear, however, where most broken spokes actually occur, things are harder. Because of the position of the gear cluster on the right rear, it is hard to thread replacement spokes through the hub flanges, and usually impossible without removing the gear cluster.

This combination means that to deal with broken spokes on the right rear side, you need either an improvised solution (FiberFix replacement spokes, described below) or a way to remove the gear cluster. Both solutions are reflected in the suggested road tool kit (see "Tools for the Road" on page 411). To remove the cassette (gear cluster) in the shop, you would use a lockring tool made for your cassette (freewheels and different brands of freehubs use different tools). A substitute that can be used to remove Shimano cassettes is the Hypercracker lockring tool, available from Harris Cyclery. Assuming that you can thread the spokes through the holes in the hub, you can usually use the existing nipples that remain in the rim holes and avoid having to remove the tire. Be sure to thread the spokes so that each head is on the same side of the hub flange as that of the original spoke. Screw the nipples for any

* Note that this discussion emphasizes standard touring bike configurations. Bikes equipped with disc brakes, like many modern mountain bikes and a few world-touring-style bikes, have dished wheels front and back, and the implications for spoke lengths and replacement are complicated.

replacement spokes to approximately the right tension before changing the tension on any other spoke. Then true the wheel, using the bike as a truing stand.

For temporary repairs that don't require removing the cassette—always an uncertain task without a shop and all the right tools—there is a clever solution that is lightweight, inexpensive, and easy to carry in your repair kit. FiberFix replacement spokes are made from aramid fibers (Kevlar or an equivalent), which are as strong as steel under tension. Just follow the directions that come with them, then true the wheel. The hardest part of the job is removing the old spokes if they are on the right side of the rear wheel. For that, you may need diagonal wire cutters and some hand strength.

Repairing a Broken Rear Derailleur Cable

All cables on your bike are subject to breakage, though if you keep up with maintenance, you should usually be able to avoid this problem. The solution, of course, is to replace the cable with a spare from your repair kit (see "Replacing Cables" earlier in this chapter). If it is late in the day and you're near your destination, however, you may decide to improvise. A rear brake cable is typically not critical as long as you ride with appropriate care. If the front brake cable breaks in moderate terrain, you might be able to ride safely with only the rear brake, but be very careful and do not attempt any significant downhill grades. If you encounter one, you need to fix the cable or walk. Breaking the front derailleur cable will be an annoyance, but for most derailleurs, the chain will go onto the smallest chainring and the bike will at least be rideable. If necessary you can adjust the limit screws to move the chain in the front onto a different chainring.

If the rear derailleur cable breaks, most bikes will go into the highest (smallest) gear in the rear, which may be impossible to use if you have to do some climbing to reach your destination. There are two quick fixes for this. The H limit screw may have enough range to

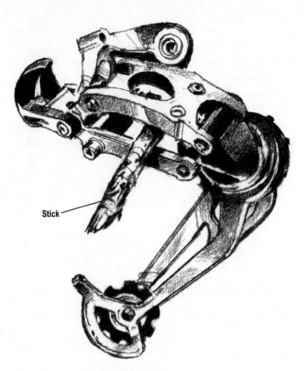

Stick

33. Fix for a broken rear derailleur cable.

reach a rideable cog. If not, insert a small stick between the parallel plates of the derailleur, holding them apart just like the cable tension does, as illustrated in Drawing 33. With an appropriate-size stick, you'll be able to hold the rear wheel up and rotate the pedals to shift into an intermediate cog that can get you to your destination.

12

Clothing and Rain Gear

Clothing for bicycle touring must, above all, be functional and versatile. You want to stay comfortable on the road, be presentable off the bike, and carry as small a pile of clothes as possible to cover all your needs. As with many aspects of bicycle touring, there are lots of ways to accomplish this; this chapter discusses a few of them.

Basic Clothing and Headgear

The basic principles of dressing on a tour are similar to other outdoor activities. Make sure to have the protection you need. Many wear long sleeves to protect against the sun, even in hot weather, in which case a lightweight, loose-woven fabric like seersucker may be just right for a shirt. Use layers to add insulation or wind protection, rather than carrying a heavier top or bottom. Using layers also allows you to use the same garment for multiple purposes. A long-sleeved merino wool top can be presentable enough in a restaurant or a museum, can be a good top to put on after you arrive in camp (so that you can pull off your sweat-soaked jersey and wash it), and can provide an extra layer for riding on a cool morning.

Fabrics are a matter of personal preference and budget. Most of the standard bicycle clothes designed for sport road riders are made of Lycra or similar nylon fabrics. Many outdoors people favor layered clothing made of some variation of polypropylene. These synthetic fabrics have a lot of advantages for outdoor use. They are lightweight and compact, and they dry quickly after being washed. They don't retain moisture next to the skin, causing abrasion and chilling at the wrong time. Some of the high-tech versions have layers that wick moisture from the skin so that evaporation occurs at the outer layer—clothes don't get as wet from perspiration, and a number of other characteristics are improved. One of the high-tech synthetics that garners particular favor in hot weather is CoolMax.

The performance of the best outdoor fabrics contrasts most with cotton. In general, cotton clothing is a bad choice for outdoor activities, including bicycling. When it gets wet from rain or perspiration, cotton is abrasive to the skin, and it chills the body badly when temperatures drop. It takes a long time to dry out, and when it is wet, it is very heavy. You should therefore minimize the cotton clothing you include in your touring outfit. One exception would be a lightweight, loose-fitting seersucker shirt for use in hot weather, though the new lightweight woven synthetics are a good alternative, and many of them are well designed for both outdoor use and wear in town. Many have well-designed vents and may incorporate sun protection.

One disadvantage of synthetic fabrics is that they tend to acquire a significant odor from perspiration, and this odor is not completely removed by laundering. Given this and the availability of much-improved wool products in recent years, many touring cyclists and other outdoor enthusiasts are rediscovering the advantages of wool for many garments. Wool has all the advantages of the best synthetics (wicking, warmth in damp conditions, low abrasion), dries almost as quickly, and is much less prone to acquiring an offensive odor. Tights and jerseys made with of fine merino wool from Australia or New Zealand using modern methods are completely itch-free for nearly everyone. Merino wool is used in the best-quality nonsynthetic outdoor clothing; Icebreaker, Ibex, and Portland Cyclewear are manufacturers that get consistently high ratings. However, such garments tend to be rather pricey.

Less upscale wool products have many of these advantages, but they may be itchy, and some cyclists will find them intolerable. Keep in mind, however, that wool jerseys and shorts were the garments of choice fifty years ago. They are still perfectly serviceable, as long as they don't bother your skin. Also note that wool should be washed in cold water. Anything warmer may cause your costly garment to shrink to an unusable size.

Helmets

European cyclists are often amused at the fact that most American cyclists wear helmets. Nearly all studies agree that helmets save lives, however, and I strongly recommend that you not ride without one.

Regardless of how skilled you are as a rider and a reader of the intentions of drivers, when you are riding on the road, you are surrounded by vehicles that are much bigger and heavier than yours. If you're a skilled rider, you can anticipate many mistakes that drivers may make, but sometimes there is nothing you can do to avoid being hit by a car or to control your subsequent trajectory.

A helmet gives you a much better chance of escaping serious injury or death if you are hit, as well as in falls resulting from other causes. Buy a good helmet, replace it when it is excessively worn, and wear it religiously. For a contrary view on helmets, take a look at www.cyclehelmets.org.

In general, helmets sold in the United States during the last decade have all had to meet fairly rigorous safety standards, so you're not likely to encounter a really unsafe helmet, unless you buy one that doesn't really fit your head and be easily knocked off in a crash. The helmet should fit your head well, the straps should be comfortable, and when it is secured, it

34. Don't even think about riding without a helmet. This one has a removable visor.

should not easily rotate off your head in any direction. People's heads are shaped differently; choose a helmet that fits yours.

Helmets are sold with and without visors, and cyclists vary in their feelings about them. Most are removable, so you can take it off if you don't like it. Some find visors helpful in reducing glare on occasion. Technically, both visors and the snap studs to which they are mounted present extra projections on the outer shell, which can catch on rough surfaces during a sliding crash, but the same is true of other projections and the edges of ventilation holes. The safest helmets are those with rounder shells and modest ventilation, but none of these issues is nearly as important as structural integrity, a good strapping system, and good fit. If you find visors helpful, use them; if not, take them off. Helmet covers are advisable for cold and wet weather (see "Helmet Covers" later in this chapter). The best source for the nuances of

35. Cycling jerseys are cut long so that they cover your lower back even when you are bent over the handlebars. The rear pockets are a helpful place to carry items you might need while riding.

choosing helmets is the Bicycle Helmet Safety Institute at www.bhsi.org. As mentioned earlier, the contrarian view is well argued at www.cyclehelmets.org.

Jerseys

Most touring cyclists wear bicycling jerseys, even if they search out more subdued designs than sport riders favor. Any upper body wear that is suitable for outdoor activities can be fine for cycling, and there are advocates for all sorts of combinations. If you already have a good set of layers that you use for hiking or backpacking, there is no reason not to adapt them for bicycle touring.

There are a few advantages to jerseys made specifically for cycling, however. They are cut longer than most shirts, so when you lean into the handlebar drops, the back doesn't ride up above the top of your shorts. A lot of riders find the pockets in the rear to be very useful. Things don't fall out when you lean forward, and the pockets don't hang awkwardly when you are riding, so they are a handy place to put glasses, cameras, bandanas, snacks, and the like. It's a matter of personal preference, though, and if you use a handlebar bag, you may not need the back pockets. General-purpose wool and CoolMax jerseys are cheaper than the cycling ones.

Shorts and Underwear

Standard bicycle shorts today are tight Lycra versions of the wool racing shorts of 50 years ago. They extend fairly far down the thigh so that they don't ride up and bunch, possibly irritating your inner thigh and crotch as you pedal over many miles. They are padded in the saddle area with what is called a chamois—traditional shorts had a suede pad, and the very best ones were made from the leather of the chamois, an Alpine animal related to goats. No chamois has been made from actual chamois leather for a very long time, but the name persists. The chamois in modern cycling shorts is made from various laminates of synthetic material. The objective is the same—to provide contact as frictionless and absorptive as possible, with a little padding, so that the cyclist does not suffer abrasion or irritation from long days of riding.

Several alternatives to standard road bike shorts are widely used. Let's begin with standard cycling shorts, however, because the majority of cyclists, including touring cyclists, use them. They are not designed for modesty, and many riders feel embarrassed to wear them into restaurants, roadside cafes, and the like. A simple solution to this problem—if it is a problem for you—is to simply carry a pair of light baggy nylon shorts to pull on over the bike shorts when you are off the bike. Modesty is easily served, and if you want to be more fashionable, you can simply put some effort into choosing the overshorts.

Hybrid garments, called "skorts," are available for women. They are bicycle shorts with short skirts on the outside.

Most touring cyclists do not wear underwear underneath cycling shorts. The reason is simple. The whole purpose of the chamois is to provide a contact surface that absorbs moisture and does not chafe the skin. Underwear defeats the purpose. Cotton underwear becomes wet and abrasive. Regardless of the material, it introduces seams and ridges that cause saddle sores after many miles. Hence, most riders, male and female, wear their cycling shorts directly against their skin. This preference is not universal, however. Some riders use CoolMax or polyester underwear under their riding shorts and find this very satisfactory.

An alternative to road bike shorts is the "baggy" cycling shorts favored by many mountain bike riders. These shorts are available with sewn-in chamois, removable chamois, or no chamois at all. This style of shorts has both advantages and disadvantages for tourists. The less revealing fashion statement is welcome to many. You'll have to try loose shorts for yourself to see whether they allow you to ride without bunching up and causing friction. They usually have an inner short that incorporates the chamois, and the combination works fine for many cyclists. Another nice feature for touring is that mountain bike shorts typically have several pockets, which is particularly handy when you are off the bike. It's important to experiment for yourself. Keep in mind that mountain bikers typically work as hard as road riders, but they usually ride far fewer miles, so mountain bike shorts may or may not work for you. Note that there is again a divergence of opinion on whether underwear is desirable.

One disadvantage of baggy shorts for touring is that they tend to be heavier, bulkier, and slower drying than standard road shorts. If you decide to carry two pairs of mountain bike shorts, in addition to wearing one, it will probably add significant weight and bulk to your luggage. You can get around these problems by a judicious choice of baggy shorts that are tailored from lightweight nylon, but you'll have to shop carefully. Catalog stores rarely bother to mention these characteristics.

Another alternative is to wear shorts that don't have a chamois over very lightweight bicycle shorts or underwear that incorporates the chamois. These inner bike shorts come in several weights and styles. There are some brief styles designed for both men and women, though most people prefer the ones that are longer, like bicycle shorts. They come with chamois or pads in various weights and they are made by several manufacturers, but the most widespread is Andiamo, which is sold by a number of U.S. outlets. Andiamo makes a number of the mid-thigh-length versions, with various padding thicknesses. Note that there is no uniform terminology. Some shops refer to the mid-thigh-length versions as "briefs."

I've found that these inner shorts with chamois work well with baggy cycling shorts that are tailored to have no seams in the saddle area. They can also be used with lightweight convertible pants not specifically designed for cycling—the kind that have zip-off legs. This yields an extra pair of shorts that can be turned into full-length pants and worn with normal underwear off the bike. The other advantage of inner shorts is that in cooler weather they can be combined with tights, knickers, or long pants that are not specifically intended for cycling. One has to be careful about garments with seams, but a wider range of clothing can be used for cycling. And inner shorts can be washed separately (and dried more quickly). One disadvantage to the Andiamo inners combined with separate tights or pants is that the combination may be too hot in warm, humid weather.

Shoes and Accessories

As discussed under "Pedals" on page 130, choices of shoes and pedals are intimately linked. There are several major considerations in choosing a shoe/pedal combination that suits you. If you like the positive foot positioning and efficiency provided by cleats that click solidly into the pedals, you need shoes that work well with this system. You might be able to find some that also allow reasonable walking, but chances are you'll have to carry different shoes for walking.

If you prefer to be able to move your foot on the pedal to reduce numbness and injuries that can result from positive foot positioning, you will have more flexibility in choosing the shoes you use on a particular trip. You will sacrifice some efficiency in pedaling and may risk certain other more injuries (positive positioning prevents injuries for many cyclists).

Regardless of your pedal preference, other footwear requirements of your trip may fit with your cycling requirements or they may require additional footwear. If your SPD-compatible shoes will work for walking in public places, then you might not need additional shoes for a tour where you are visiting a lot of museums. However, if the cleats project enough to hit hardwood or stone floors, they might not be okay in a museum or a church.

Similarly, if you are planning to do some day hiking while bike touring, your SPD-compatible shoes may or may not work. You need to do some testing and make sure. In general, the stiffness that is needed to protect your feet from many SPD-compatible pedals will probably make the shoes unsuitable for extensive hiking.

SPD-Compatible Pedals and Shoes

The majority of touring cyclists today prefer to ride with SPD-compatible pedals and shoes, because they find that it is just easier to pedal long distances with the feet automatically placed in a fairly efficient position. Such shoes are relatively light, are efficient for riding, provide good foot support, and are comfortable for long intervals on the bike, as long as you've taken the time to find a pair that fits well. Typically, these same cyclists carry a set of flip-flops, Tevas, or slip-ons to wear when they reach their motel or camp. This provides the relief of a change of shoes and, typically, some footwear that is socially acceptable and non-hazardous when you are off the bike.

Despite of all the claims to the contrary, most cleats project a little beyond sole treads, so if you walk down a hall in your bike shoes, you hear a click-click-click. Cleats are not friendly to hardwood floors, and they can cause nasty slips on polished stone. For hiking, they can be problematic as well.

If you are using SPD or similar pedals, you need shoes or sandals that are set up for SPD-compatible cleats. Eggbeater pedals require SPD-compatible shoes, so if you like them, you'll have to buy the shoes to use them. But, because they provide a small clip area, they also require shoes that have quite stiff soles. If you choose shoes that have more flexible soles, even if they have SPD drilling, they will be very uncomfortable after a long day on eggbeater pedals. Eggbeaters and some other small SPD-compatible styles have a very small contact area through which force is transmitted, so if the sole of the shoe is flexible, the pedal will dig into your foot, and this will become progressively nastier as the day wears on.

In addition to cycling shoes, certain sandals come drilled and with mounting plates for SPD-compatible cleats. There are models made by Shimano, Lake, and Keen. Many experienced cyclists wear cycling sandals even in cold or wet weather (with Gore-Tex or neoprene socks). A good fit is just as important with sandals as with shoes. For camping and light hiking, some people like sandals a lot, while others find that they too easily accumulate debris.

Compatible Footwear for Platform-Style and Similar Pedals

The main alternative to a step-in shoe-and-pedal system is to use the most comfortable and suitable shoes for a particular tour combined with platform pedals, which give you a larger surface area and may use pins or straps to achieve some positive positioning and efficiency. A clear advantage of the non-cleat approach is that you can use a variety of shoes with the same pedals—presentable walking shoes if you are visiting cathedrals and museums, light hiking shoes if you're doing a lot of hikes, or a range of sandals if they suit your fancy. You will have to make a choice between step-in and platform pedals to start, and then experiment with other alternatives over time.

If you are touring with platform-style pedals (see "Pedals" on page 130), with or without Power Grips, you have a wide range of footwear choices. Nearly any footwear you find comfortable for outdoor activities can be pressed into service—sandals, light hiking shoes, or running or walking shoes. Make sure you try them out on long training rides, however. Cycling exerts continuous pressure on a few areas of the foot, unlike the cyclical and more varied pressure of walking or hiking. The surface area of the platform pedals you choose will also affect shoe comfort level. Pedals with a smaller contact area or a few ridges of contact require stiffer soles; otherwise you feel the imprint of the pedal ridges in the soles of your feet by the end of the day. Pedals with a larger contact area are comfortable with a wider range of shoes (but they may have poorer traction in wet or slippery conditions).

Road-Style Pedals and Shoes

A few touring cyclists use road-cycling shoes and cleats. If you are used to them and have the equipment, this may make sense, but you'll need to carry sandals or other walking shoes, because road-cycling shoes with cleats are not designed for walking even short distances.

Gloves

Standard cycling gloves for warm weather have half fingers and leather or synthetic palm covers, so that you can reach down to the tires and allow the surface to brush against your palm while riding, to dislodge glass fragments or thorns (this works only if you don't have fenders). The leather palms also reduce injury if you fall, since you instinctively reach out with your palm to protect yourself. The partial fingers are desirable in hot weather so that your fingers don't sweat into a closed bacterial bath. Trail riders often prefer full-fingered gloves for extra protection.

The amount of padding that is desirable in your gloves is a matter of personal preference. Some padding is standard, and it is definitely helpful in reducing pressure on the nerves that run through your palms. Gloves with gel inserts provide somewhat better padding, but not everyone likes them. Many cyclists choose to add padding to the handlebars instead. If you get gel-cushioned gloves, pay attention to the quality. In some of these gloves, the gel bunches up after some period of use and creates more rather than less pressure on the nerves running through your palm.

Headbands and Bandanas

Touring cyclists have varying strategies for keeping sweat from dripping into their eyes during hot riding conditions, or for cooling their brows. Carrying two or three terry headbands or bandanas is usually effective. When one is saturated, you can wring it out and fasten it on top of your luggage to dry out.

Eye Protection

Sunglasses are important for touring, and if you don't wear glasses normally, you may also want a pair of clear or lightly tinted glasses to protect your eyes from windblown grit in low-light conditions. If you wear contacts, riding without glasses can result in getting grit in your eyes and sometimes in having the wind catch the edge of a contact. Get good-quality sunglasses; cheap plastic lenses don't adequately protect against some ranges of ultraviolet light. Most cyclists find wraparound glasses to be most effective for protecting the eyes. Polarized lenses with UV-filtering coating are generally advisable.

Clothing and Gear for Cold and Wet Weather

Always be prepared for the weather variations that you are likely to encounter on your tour. It is not uncommon to encounter hot weather during the middle of the day, and chilly conditions in the afternoon or early in the morning. Anyone doing tours that cross high mountain passes needs to be prepared for cold conditions and occasional snowstorms. Most problematic are conditions that are both cold and wet.

However, most touring cyclists need to be prepared only for occasional cold. Many of us regularly commute during genuinely icy conditions, but few choose to do anything that would be considered a bike tour in really cold conditions, so the discussion here is confined to occasional cold weather riding. For truly frigid cycling, consult www.icebike.com.

A few very lightweight, low-volume items can make an enormous difference in keeping you comfortable. A windproof top shell and a pair of pants are invaluable. Thin nylon ones are cheap and serviceable.

Returning to the general topic of preparation for occasional cold weather, an additional base layer can add more warmth in dry conditions and serve as a spare if you encounter chilly rain. This layering approach is always advisable for touring. When packing, you can add a few items for extra warmth when needed. For a more temperate tour, you take the same set of clothing but subtract a layer or two.

Depending on the season and location of your tour, here are some other useful items for layering:

- a hat that will fit under your helmet

- a wool or synthetic pull-on shirt and tights ("base layer" in many catalogs)

- leg warmers and arm warmers—essentially knit tubes of wool or synthetic material that you can pull over your limbs to provide a little extra warmth, and then remove when riding; keeping your knees warm is also important to prevent injuries

- lightweight booties that can be pulled on over your shoes—if you use cleats, the soles have to have openings cut for them (some booties are waterproof—see "Capes and Booties" later in this chapter)

- a down or synthetic insulated vest

Keeping Hands Warm

Warm gloves or mittens are a must for cold-weather touring. Wool and synthetic pile are both effective, and windproof shells may be advisable. Mittens are much warmer than gloves, but you need to find a combination that allows you to shift and brake without interference. For colder conditions, a superior alternative is poagies (also known as poggies or pogies), mittenlike shells that wrap and attach around the handlebars, allowing easy insertion of the hands; they are derived from whitewater paddling. They are excellent for winter commuting but are rather specialized items for touring. Only shell versions without insulation would be likely candidates to carry on tour. Cycling poagies are not commonly available items—they appear and disappear in various manufacturers' lines. Some of them are reviewed and linked at www.lobsterglove.com. One good source is www.barmitts.com. Recently, most suppliers have been small makers in Alaska: Bike Toasties from Apocalypse Design (www.akgear.com), Expedition Poagies from Epic Designs (www.Epicdesigns-ak.blogspot.com), and (moving to Michigan) Moose Mitts at www.trails-edge.com/retail/moosemitts/moosemitts.htm. For a similar, relatively inexpensive approach, go to www.drybike.com, which emphasizes the shell design that is most appropriate to touring.

Helmet Covers

Whether you use a rain hood or not, you should carry a lightweight, waterproof cover that stretches over the top of your helmet. A useful piece of rain gear, it will often let you ride comfortably in the rain without pulling up the hood of a jacket or rain cape. Your ability to look around will often be enhanced. In addition to shedding rain, a helmet cover can be helpful in cold weather as well, reducing ventilation around your head when you don't really need or want it.

Rain Gear

No rain gear can possibly achieve the performance for which everyone hopes—to keep all rain out, provide enough ventilation without allowing perspiration buildup, protect against wind chill and wind-driven rain, and protect against spray from tires. Experienced touring cyclists have their own preferences, but technique plays an important role in the effectiveness of rain gear (keeping down the build-up of sweat, for example), as do the conditions in which one normally rides, and other equipment.

Speaking of equipment, if you are going to ride much in the rain, you need to equip your bike with fenders (see "Fenders" on page 161). The additional spray from the road on rainy days is likely to overwhelm rain gear that might otherwise work fairly well. It also covers the gear with a lot of dirt, which degrades the performance of fabrics that combine some breathability with water resistance.

First consider the fabric used for any rain gear—typically some kind of coated synthetic material or a laminated layer that resists the passage of water. The cheapest and lightest material is nylon with urethane coating. It is relatively waterproof, at least when it is new, but the moisture that constantly transpires from your skin is likely to condense easily on the slick surface next to your body, and when you are actively sweating, which is rather common when you are cycling, you'll soon be soaked with moisture from inside your raingear.

A great advance for outdoor enthusiasts was the invention of Gore-Tex laminated materials, which have a layer with very small pores. In the right conditions, the pores are too small to allow liquid water to pass through, but they are permeable to water vapor, so the fabric "breathes." At best, however, all breathable fabrics have limitations as cycling rain gear. The most important is that, when significant rain sheets on the outside of your jacket and pants, it forms a barrier to the passage of moisture, regardless of the breathability of the fabric itself. Second, even if rain is not forming an exterior barrier, if you are sweating, you'll produce moisture faster than the vapor can pass through the breathable fabric, and sweat has to evaporate to a gaseous state before it can do so.

Solutions to these problems are incorporated into the best rainwear. The most important are vents strategically placed to allow enough air circulation to carry the moisture generated by your body to the outside. The best and most widely accepted raingear designed specifically for cycling is from Showers Pass (www.showerspass.com). Other popular (and less expensive) raingear is made by O2 and Nashbar.

Rain jackets and pants. The best rain jackets have vents designed with cyclists in mind, taking advantage of the air flow you create while you are riding, but with closures to seal the vents when the rain is blowing in. There are many other subtle design features. A fuzzy inside fabric surface can reduce interior condensation. Tailoring that takes cycling positions and air circulation into account can promote increased air circulation, reduce condensation, and minimize accumulation of moisture. The most extreme ventilation is provided by a rain cape, which creates one large vent below your rain protection (see "Capes and Booties" later in this chapter).

In general, for the best touring rain jackets, look for an actual rating of the waterproofness of the fabric (measured by resistance to pressure from a column of water) and vapor permeability measurements. Seams should be sealed, and preferably taped. Vents should be well designed for cyclists, and there should be a long tail at the back to provide adequate coverage from spray in riding positions. Get a jacket that is roomy enough for layered clothing. A tight-fitting aerodynamic jacket may be advantageous for sport riders dealing with afternoon showers, but it is not versatile enough for touring. Hoodless jackets should have high collars that can be fastened tight to keep rain from dripping down the back of your neck, and a soft inside collar helps to prevent chafing. Some people like hoods. If you wear one, it has to fit inside the helmet so that it doesn't interfere with turning your head and checking traffic. If you use a helmet cover, you can usually get by without a hood.

Another approach is to get a far less expensive jacket that is reliably waterproof but lacks the sophisticated features just described. Such jackets are lighter in weight, much cheaper, and may be adequate in parts of the world that get less precipitation. Avoid those that are really not designed for rain beyond a brief shower.

Similar considerations apply to rain pants. The best ones are designed for cycling; they have vents and are tailored with extra room at the knees so that they don't bind when you are pedaling. Because there is less opportunity for sophisticated ventilation, and because dirty spray affects the legs more, many riders eschew the highest-quality rain pants and opt for cheaper waterproof designs. Still, the hierarchy of the best rain pants is similar to that for jackets—Showers Pass, O2, and Nashbar.

Some advocate a different kind of leg protection, called Rainlegs, sold in the United States by Wallingford Bicycle Parts. These cover the front of your thighs and knees—the area that gets wet first in the rain. Rainlegs are a great idea for commuting but are not likely to provide adequate protection for touring any distance in the rain.

Capes and booties. One alternative approach for your primary rain protection is a cycling cape, which is essentially a rain poncho cut to fit a cyclist and with thumb loops in front to hold the front of the cape out as far as the handlebars and reduce the tendency for the wind to blow the cape to the rear. A cycling cape is inexpensive and provides lots of ventilation below, but it also provides a sail to catch the wind, and it cuts off your view of the pavement directly below. Some cyclists swear by rain capes; others hate them. Campmor is the principal U.S. camping gear retailer that sells cycling capes. Capes are also available from European suppliers, who cater to commuters in a region with more rain and more daily cyclists than the United States.

Finally, don't forget about foot protection. Many advocates of cycling sandals either carry neoprene socks or use wool socks combined with Gore-Tex socks. This allows you to keep your feet comfortable without carrying too much extra stuff. If you use non-cycling sandals on platform pedals, the same approach will work. The alternative approach is to carry a pair of lightweight waterproof booties. Booties can be made from lightweight fabric to break the wind and trap warm air. You don't need the more expensive and bulky insulated booties unless you're expecting very cold weather. If you are worried about colder weather, an inexpensive method is to carry wool socks large enough to go over your shoes and cover those with lightweight fabric booties. If you use cleats, you'll need to cut openings in the soles of the booties—they will no longer be fully waterproof, but they will still work.

13

Lights and Locks

This chapter discusses equipment that may not be needed on some tours or may be essential for your safety (lights) or the security of your bike (locks). Lights are important for safety if there is any possibility of your riding in twilight or dark (and there is nearly always a possibility). Most tourists will want at least some security device to safeguard the bike when stopping at a restaurant or a store, and for tours that include urban areas, real locks may be a necessity.

Lighting Systems and Reflectors

This discussion of lights concentrates on the basics. Specific systems have undergone enormous change in the last few years, as much more efficient light sources and batteries have become available. This rapid rate of change seems likely to continue, so detailed recommendations of specific systems would soon be obsolete.

As a bicycle tourist, lights may be important to you for three different purposes:

- making you visible to motorists so that they don't run you down

- illuminating the road or the path ahead when you are riding

- providing light for bike repairs, making camp, doing chores, and finding your way around the campsite

Reflectors can be very useful for the first but not for the other two. Your need for lights for any or all of these purposes will depend somewhat on the kind of touring you do.

Seeing and Being Seen

The most critical aspect of lighting—and the sole purpose of reflectors—is to reduce the likelihood of being hit by a car. As discussed in Chapter 3, there is always a problem, even in broad daylight, with drivers who simply don't see cyclists because they aren't attuned to the necessity. This is much more of a problem at dusk and in the dark.

Many touring cyclists make it a practice not to be caught out on the road late in the day, much less at night. This rule is usually feasible when touring in the summer months: start early in the morning, and time your day so that you reach camp or lodging well before dusk. This will give you long days of riding during midsummer, more than enough to tire you out. If you're touring during the shorter months, however, you'll have to plan on shorter riding days to avoid twilight. And there are always circumstances under which you may be caught out on the road as the light wanes.

Touring always involves dealing with unexpected contingencies—surprises are part of the attraction of traveling by bike. If you encounter a headwind for a long stretch, need to patch a tire in the afternoon, end up in a long conversation with some local residents, or ride farther than you expected without finding a good camping spot or lodging, you may end up riding later than you had planned. Even if you aren't late, conditions such as rain, fog, or blowing dust can reduce visibility so that having lights to attract the attention of automobile drivers becomes advisable.

In general, you should consider strategies to make yourself visible to drivers as part of the standard set of equipment and skills for touring. Bright colors; reflective clothing, equipment, and attachments; and lights can all be useful, along with riding skills.

There are two types of lighting requirements: emergency lighting intended for use on infrequent occasions and lights for those who regularly find themselves riding when the ambient light is poor.

How Good a System Do You Need?

Bicycle commuters need to be seen and may need good lights to see the path ahead. Typically, however, they use lights going to work in the morning and returning in the evening, and electrical outlets are available in each place, so lights using rechargeable batteries are often an economical and environmentally sound choice. The batteries have to have enough capacity to stay bright for the entire trip, perhaps both coming and going, along with enough reserve to handle a flat tire. All this means that you can probably get by with relatively inexpensive, lightweight lights.

Randonneur riders, who typically ride through the night on some events, have much more demanding lighting requirements. Those who can afford them often get dynamo hubs, which provide reliable lighting with no need to purchase or recharge batteries (see "Dynamo Systems" later in this chapter).

Most touring cyclists do not have these requirements. I recommend organizing your tours so that you normally finish your days when there is still plenty of light. This ensures that, if you are doing credit-card touring, you reach your accommodations early, and if you are camping, you have time to set up camp in the daylight. If you follow this guideline, you need a light for camp if you're traveling self-contained, and bike lights only for emergencies and unforeseen delays.

Reflectors

Reflectors are cheap, lightweight, and can provide a lot of extra visibility for the touring cyclist. They increase your safety margin, so it is reasonable to say that you can't have too many of them. All bikes sold in the United States come with some legally required reflectors already installed. If you choose to remove any of them, because of weight, aesthetics, or because they obstruct some mounting point for equipment, you should replace them with reflective tape, which works just as well and weighs even less.

If your panniers, bags, and rain gear don't have reflective strips or panels, it is a good idea to add them. You can get 3M Scotchlite reflective material at many locations. Stick-on patches and tape, along with vests and the like, can be obtained from www.reflexsafety .com and at many cycling suppliers and organizations. The day-glo yellow version also improves visibility during the day. If you prefer something a little more subdued during the day, the white/silver style is unobtrusive in daylight but is just as visible at night. Tape can be used on pedal edges, forks, fenders, racks, helmets, and other locations.

Vests, triangles, or sashes of brightly colored reflective material can be a valuable way to make yourself visible at night and during the day. A vest weighs only a few ounces and can be worn night or day when conditions might result in drivers failing to notice your presence.

Reflectors are an enormous aid when car lights are pointed toward you, but don't rely on them too heavily, because they won't help you in some situations. For example, if a car's lights are directed away from you until you are near each other it may be too late to avoid an accident. If you are riding on a parallel bike path, the driver might not see you until you join one another at an intersection. You need to think about lights as well.

Choosing Lights for Riding

Lights come in a wide variety of technologies and styles. Headlamps can be mounted on the handlebar, front rack, fork, stem, fork crown, fender, headset spacer, or helmet. You can use one or multiple headlamps, and they can be flashing or steady. A similar range of options applies to taillights.

Two basic types of lamps are used for bike lights. LED technology has improved so much that very bright lights can be made with low power requirements (so they drain batteries much less quickly), and this technology is rapidly coming to dominate the market for cycling lights. LED light sources last a very long time, so burned-out bulbs rarely need to be considered—the LED will probably last longer than you do, though other parts of the light, like the switch, will be less durable. LED lights use arrays of diodes. A disadvantage is that designers have less control over the pattern of the beam than they do with a halogen or krypton bulb, and the beam pattern of an LED light is almost never adjustable.

Halogen or krypton lamps, the other choice, do burn out eventually, but they can also be very bright and quite efficient. The designer can control the beam pattern with a high degree of precision, and some lights are set up so that the user can control the beam within a given range of variation. You need to carry a spare bulb for a halogen lamp, and to know how to replace it when fumbling in the dark.

Flashing versus steady lights. Flashing lights generally are better than steady ones at attracting the attention of a driver, but they make it harder for the driver to judge the distance. This is true for both headlamps and taillights. Blinking lights are obviously poor for seeing what is ahead of you. (Incidentally, blinking lights are illegal in some jurisdictions, but safety should probably be your main consideration.) Some cyclists try to work around this complication by using one blinking light and one steady one.

There are arguments regarding colored vs. white lights. Many experienced cyclists use red or orange lights in the rear and white ones in front, either blinking or not, because it is the standard vehicle convention, and confusing a motorist is the last thing a cyclist should want to do.

Where to mount lights. Many cyclists like helmet-mounted lights: you direct your head where you want to look, and the light is there. However, the light source is fairly high, which can be less effective than a light mounted low, and it is harder for a motorist to see and calibrate your position.

When using a single headlamp, it's best to mount it on the front rack or on the fork. One trick is to make your own mount to go on the hoop of a front rack, hollowing out a short segment of a 1-inch wooden dowel to fit on the rack tubing, which allows the light to be mounted with a standard handlebar clamp. When you're touring, it can be stored in a pannier. Another very nice arrangement for lightweight lights is to use a Cronometro Nob attached to the fork blade—it's intended as a computer mount, but it works fine for lights that aren't too heavy.

To see the path ahead, you want a beam that is bright enough and well enough focused so that you can see clearly for 150 or 200 feet. When you're riding at a moderate speed, this will allow you to see objects that you won't hit for about 10 or 15 seconds. It certainly won't allow you to make a high-speed descent safely.

The brightness of lights and the beam shape and pattern are complicated subjects and will not be discussed in detail here. If you want to investigate the nuances, Peter White has good discussion at www .peterwhitecycles.com. In general, it is best to mount the headlamp fairly low and to have a beam that extends fairly far ahead (meaning that it can't be too wide) but is not so narrow that you can't see anything to the sides 20 feet ahead (the tunnel effect).

One approach is to use two headlamps, one with a wider and the other with a narrower beam. Some people like to use a helmet-mounted light with another light mounted on the bike. For touring, some riders use a rack-mounted headlamp and carry a very bright small flashlight for a second light. The flashlight is an ideal camp light, and it can be used with a headband as a camp headlamp. It can also be used with a handlebar mount as a spare bike headlamp.

Batteries

Power sources for lights also vary, and battery technology is progressing as rapidly as light sources. Ignoring dynamo systems for the moment, you have a choice between disposable and rechargeable batteries and, in the case of rechargeables, between custom battery packs and lights taking batteries with standard sizes.

In general, rechargeable batteries are more economical in the long run and more environmentally sound than disposable batteries. However, for touring, rechargeable batteries are only suitable if you will be stopping frequently at locations with access to electric power, and staying long enough to charge them. If you are stopping at inns, restaurants, or convenience stores occasionally for long-enough intervals, and you aren't shy about asking to use a plug, this will work. You can top off the charge pretty reasonably if you're stopping for a meal but not if you are just buying a can of soup and a head of lettuce. Commercial campgrounds usually have electrical plugs available somewhere. If you are traveling long stretches in remote areas, however, you had better have lights that use disposable batteries. Then you can buy a few extras when you stop at a store, and you don't have to worry about having no light after the sun goes down. Some very good lights come with custom battery packs and chargers, so they are useless if you run into a stretch of the tour where you can't find a place to plug in your charger. On a credit-card tour, this might not be an issue, but if you are camping it can be a major impediment.

If you are using disposable batteries (usually alkaline ones), it makes sense to consider other electronic devices you're carrying. If your GPS, camera, flashlight, and computer use the same type of battery, spares are easier to buy and carry. Using the same type of battery won't always be feasible; it's just worth considering. Typically, suitable lights using disposable batteries will take size AA. Non-alkaline, "standard" batteries (zinc-carbon and zinc-chloride) can be used in a pinch in lights that recommend using alkaline batteries, though they won't last as long.

Rechargeable batteries are convenient and inexpensive to use in the long run, providing you can charge them. If you're not sure, it is wise to use lights that can take either rechargeable or disposable batteries that you can buy at a roadside store. The three main types of rechargeable batteries that are practical for bike lights are alkaline, nickel metal hydride, and lithium ion, and each has unique characteristics and idiosyncrasies:

Rechargeable alkaline. These batteries are relatively inexpensive, reliable, and fairly easy to find. Of the types discussed here, they have the lowest capacity (you have to recharge them more often). They have a "memory" for charge, which means that it is advisable to discharge them completely every few charges so they don't acquire a lower capacity before their usable life should be over. Despite their lower capacity, rechargeable alkaline batteries retain their charge for a long time, which can be very helpful for the touring cyclist. When you pull that light out of the bottom of your pannier where it has been sitting for two weeks, it is really nice if it actually works. Because they produce the same voltage as widely available disposable batteries, you can easily pick up spares if you feel the need.

Nickel metal hydride. Nickel metal hydride (or NiMH) batteries have a considerably higher capacity than rechargeable alkaline batteries, if they begin fully charged. However, they lose their charge relatively quickly when they are stored. After two weeks in your pannier, they won't have much charge remaining. One other idiosyncrasy of NiMH batteries is that they need to be run through several charge-discharge cycles before they reach full capacity. Make sure to do this to new batteries at home before you leave on your trip. NiMH batteries develop a slightly lower voltage than alkaline batteries, but they are close enough to be interchangeable for flashlights. Some GPS units may have a special setting for NiMH batteries to adjust for the voltage difference.

Lithium ion. Lithium ion batteries have the highest capacity of the common rechargeables, and they are the most expensive. They retain their charge fairly well—they won't fail you after a couple of weeks in your pannier, though you should make sure that they are at full charge before you leave home. Because they develop a different voltage than alkaline batteries, they are not interchangeable, and they won't be available at the crossroads convenience store in a rural area.

Chargers. One other important thing you should pay attention to when buying lights with rechargeable batteries is the type of charger required. Chargers are designed to accommodate specific types of batteries. You want a "smart charger," one with electronics that sense the charge in the battery and adjust the voltage applied. The cheaper chargers can overcharge the battery if they are connected for too long, ruining batteries rather quickly.

Combining Camp Lights and Bike Lights

If you are camping on your tour, you'll want to be sure to avoid carrying extra special-purpose equipment when it isn't necessary. Portable lights can be combined in a number of ways. I use a battery-powered headlamp for my bike, either with rechargeables or regular batteries, depending on the tour. I carry a high-capacity lithium-ion-powered flashlight that serves as a spare headlamp, with a handlebar mount and a headband for use in camp. It's best to carry an extra set of lithium ion batteries, just in case. A small but powerful flashing LED light is ideal for the rear of the bike. A setup like this is quite lightweight, even if you are carrying chargers.

Dynamo Systems

If you regularly commute long distances or do randonneur riding, you might consider a dynamo front hub with a lighting system to match. A good dynamo supplies enough power to run very bright lights when riding at a relatively low speed—somewhat faster than walking. Good dynamos (the best is the SON) are reliable, efficient, and add an imperceptible amount of drag to the hub. They are also quite expensive (hundreds of dollars). If you are in the market, take a look at Peter White's Web site (www.peterwhitecycles.com). "Bottle" dynamos, driven by friction against the tire sidewall, are a cheaper alternative.

Of course, the dynamo power is not available for camping, for patching tires, or when you are standing at the side of the road, so auxiliary lights are often needed.

Choosing and Using Locks

As with lighting, you need to carefully consider specifics for your tour before you decide what kinds of locks you need. This section discusses the trade-offs between weight and security.

Urban Environments versus Typical Touring

If you use your touring bike for regular commuting in urban areas, college towns, or other places where bikes are frequently stolen, you'll need some pretty heavy duty locks to secure your bike, and even then you can't rely on locks alone for security. And if you are touring in such areas, you may need to lock your bike securely. Some hostels in Europe, for example, do not have interior storage space and are situated in urban areas where you would not want to leave your bike without a good lock.

In those circumstances, it's best to carry a high-security U-lock and a fairly substantial armored cable. Two separate locking systems give you a way to secure valuable parts like the front wheel, to attach to more than one anchor, and—most importantly—to use separate systems that will discourage a thief. The easiest way to break a U-lock is different from the easiest way to cut a cable, and having to do both will take more time and different tools. Nevertheless, it is important to realize that serious bike thieves can break any lock. Don't leave a valuable bike out overnight in a high-crime area.

Doing a good job of locking the bike is more important than the locks themselves. Anchor the bike to something solid, and pay attention to the way it is locked. If you walk through any college campus, you'll find many bikes that are locked with a U-lock that goes around the down-tube and the front wheel in such a way that all a thief has to do is to undo the quick-release on the front wheel and lift the bike, lock, and wheel up to carry them all away. No tools required!

The most secure way to lock a bike using a U-lock is not intuitively obvious. Pass the lock around the rear wheel within the rear triangle and then around a solid metal anchor. Even if the lock doesn't include a frame tube within the U, there is no easy way to remove the bike, unless the U-lock itself can be broken. Undoing the quick release does not allow the bike to be removed without cutting the wheel apart—not an easy task.

Finally, if you have a bike with expensive wheels and you can't always secure both with your locking system, you should consider replacing the quick-releases with a keyed system. MEC (Mountain Equipment Co-op) sells a relatively inexpensive one; Peter White sells a much more effective type. (In both cases, you need a special tool to remove the wheel, so don't lose it if you're on tour.)

Fortunately, this level of security is often unnecessary on bicycle tours. If you are on a credit-card tour, you can usually bring your bike into your room for the night; just be sure you are careful not to leave grease or scuff marks. On occasions when you can't bring the bike into your room, make sure there is a secure place to park it before you check in—a locked storeroom or the equivalent. When you are camping, you don't generally have to worry about serious thieves. Casual theft can be prevented with a modest lock or by incorporating the bike in your tent supports so it can't be removed without waking you.

Situations where a lock is really needed usually occur when you stop at a restaurant or a store. Even if you can keep the bike in sight, it may be wise to lock it. After all, your gaze is bound to stray, and you might want to use the bathroom. These circumstances don't usually require massive security, just enough to discourage the mischievous or save someone from a moral lapse. For such situations, it is useful to have a way to genuinely secure the bike, locking it to a solid anchor—though this will not protect it against a serious thief with a power grinder and a pickup truck.

Moderate Security on Tour

For the kind of situations described above, some touring cyclists simply carry a fairly lightweight cable and lock—just enough to keep reasonably honest people from losing their moral bearings. A good combination is a 6-foot-long 12-mm cable with a fairly secure lock. This kind of lock weighs about 12 ounces—heavy, but not unmanageable. While not providing big-city security, it gives you the flexibility to lock the bike fairly safely in a lot of different situations. A U-lock of the same weight would be more secure when locked to a solid pole, but it would not reach in many of the circumstances one encounters while touring. A cable can anchor the bike to telephone poles, racks, or metal posts, and a 12-mm cable is not easy to cut with normal implements. Others use a shorter cable and just run it through the wheels and frame when there isn't a rack or metal post available.

Note that the lightweight locking approach entails several advantages when you are stopping at restaurants or roadside stores. You'll typically carry your handlebar bag or whatever you use to contain your valuables. The bike and panniers constitute a pretty heavy package, and if the front wheel can't be turned, nobody can ride off on it, or even wheel it off very easily, because it can't be steered.

Some tourists have a trick that they use in lieu of any lock at all. On bikes with quick-release levers on the brakes (not on the brake levers), they adjust the brakes so that they ride with the quick releases open. (This makes them useless for their intended purpose.) When they stop at a roadside stand or restaurant, they flip the brake quick releases, locking the wheels with the brakes.

Of course someone knowledgeable about the nuances of good bikes could see what was going on, but most would simply find that it wasn't possible to roll the bike away. A passerby might rummage through your panniers, but if you carry your wallet, camera, and GPS in your removable handlebar bag, they probably won't find anything in which they are interested.

You can complicate the possibility of someone walking off with a pannier by using nylon zip-ties to provide an extra attachment to the rack. If you're doing this, carry a package of zip-ties—they weigh almost nothing. (Don't rely on any of these minimalist techniques in third-world cities. In much of the third world, you can rely on honesty and good will. But when you're in urban high-crime areas, thieves will take anything, and they are far more astute than their counterparts in developed countries.) Personally, I'm willing to carry at least a modest cable lock to secure the bike, even on tours in rural areas of the United States. If nothing else, it reduces the paranoia when I stop at a roadside convenience store.

Consumer Issues with Locks

It is very difficult to compare locks for any of the characteristics you should consider before buying them. Clearly, you want to look at relative security compared with weight and price. Neither of the major bicycle lock manufacturers that dominate the market in the United States—Kryptonite and OnGuard—provides the information to evaluate either in a useful way. (Both make very good locks.) Neither one, nor any shop or online dealer, lists the weights of the locks, and they don't respond to information requests on this issue. Because many of their customers go to great lengths to reduce weight, the missing information is unforgivable.

On the security front, the situation is almost as bad. A number of European countries have testing and certification standards that are based on objective comparisons, and both American lock companies advertise that their products meet many of these standards, but they only use the information as advertising fluff—they don't mention which of their products have passed which tests. Both Kryptonite and OnGuard have their own internal rating methods, which they do list with each lock or cable, so you can compare security between two locks from the same maker, but you can't compare weights, and you can't compare products between companies.

Past performance does not inspire confidence. In the early 1990s, news of the ability to open most U-locks with a 10-cent ballpoint pen spread like wildfire over the Internet. As it turned out, the manufacturers had known about the vulnerability for several years but had done nothing to deal with it. Only after the bad publicity surfaced did they redesign the locks and offer to replace defective ones. Do not buy old secondhand U-locks that use cylindrical keys—they all have this defect.

14

Racks, Luggage, and Trailers

Whether you are relying mainly on bed and breakfasts and other paid accommodations, or are on a self-contained tour, you need to have luggage that attaches to the bike, and it is always a challenge to fit everything you need. Just as with backpacking, kayaking, or any other self-propelled sport, there never seems to be enough room for everything you might need. The challenge is to reduce the number, size, weight, and volume of the things you need, so that you are self-sufficient with fewer items. Finding exactly the right balance is immensely satisfying—light and compact, yet sufficient for all the requirements you encounter on the tour.

In considering your choice of panniers and other means to carry your load—which may include other kinds of luggage, racks mounted over the front or rear wheels, and even a trailer where conditions suggest one—it makes sense to get containers with sufficient volume. After all, then you can take more gear when you need to, but you still can use the same panniers and other bags for lighter loads. Many panniers have compression systems (see Drawing 2 on page 11), so that you can reduce the volume when you aren't carrying as much gear.

Unfortunately, this strategy flies in the face of the universal law that stuff that must be carried expands to fill the available volume (a problem with trailers). Therefore, the first rule of packing for bike touring is: *Reduce the load and volume first!* Though it is quite possible to take enjoyable tours while carrying far too much stuff, it is really worth trying to reduce volume and weight as much as possible. With all self-propelled sports this is a matter of balance, personal style, skill, self-discipline, and budget. As we see have seen, most equipment choices are a trade-off. For example, you want your raingear to be waterproof, comfortable, breathable, durable, lightweight, and inexpensive, but you have to choose your priorities. It is worth noting that even the most vociferous advocates of trailers observe that one problem with them is that they encourage their users to carry too much stuff—it is always easy to throw a little more into the voluminous bag on the trailer.

Some experienced touring cyclists argue that weight is less critical for bicycle touring than for backpacking. After all, when you are traveling on level roads, the bike rolls along with about the same level of effort, even if you add 20 pounds. Extra volume increases wind resistance, but extra weight requires extra effort only when accelerating—there is a little extra road resistance, but not much. The backpacker, by contrast, has to actually carry the pack and deal with its weight at each step.

This is true to a degree, but if you ride on a lot of hilly terrain and cover a lot of miles, consider that you are using a lot of energy moving that load up hills. If you are riding a long day in the mountains, you will certainly be climbing thousands of feet, cumulatively perhaps between 10,000 and 20,000. Extra pounds in the luggage will definitely matter. Even on the flats, the extra effort required to get the load moving after every stop does add up over the length of the day.

Volume matters everywhere, because it correlates with wind resistance, the major energy drain when you are touring. As a result, you should get bags that are big enough to carry your equipment (and keep it dry) but should reduce the weight and volume of the equipment you need to carry as much as you possibly can. If you really have enough self-discipline when packing, getting relatively large packs is the best strategy, because they allow maximum flexibility. But if you are like most of us and lack self-discipline, getting packs just large enough for the trip you are planning may be the right choice.

Racks and Loading

Racks should provide a solid attachment between your bike and the bags you are carrying. They are important for any cycling tourist who does not use a trailer instead of panniers and other bags. The typical arrangement for luggage is the one shown in Drawing 2 on page 11: two sets of panniers with pairs on the front and back, perhaps supplemented with a handlebar bag and one container on top of the rear rack.

Ideally, you should purchase the racks with your bike, so that the mounting arrangements and size match up. Perhaps you'll get a price break, but this is not critical. If you buy racks later, just investigate the mounting features carefully.

Distribute the Load

Your bike will ride a lot better if you distribute the load between the front and rear axles. This means that ideally you should have panniers and racks on both front and rear. When people have only one set, it is usually mounted on the rear, but bike handling is usually better if a single set is mounted in front.

In general, you should try to carry at least half the weight in the front panniers (and perhaps a handlebar bag or a rack-top bag). Try to pack denser items like food, flashlights, fuel, and tools in the front panniers. The rationale for this is that putting all the weight on the rear wheel, which is already carrying most of your body weight, makes the bike handle poorly. (Many analytically-inclined touring cyclists argue that 60 percent of the luggage weight should be in the front.

Optimal distribution will vary with bicycle design and rider, however.)

An exception is mountain bikes equipped with a front-suspension fork. There are a few front racks that can be attached reliably to a suspension fork, but only small panniers or strapped-on stuff sacks are likely to work on this type of rack.

Note that some racks, particularly front ones, are "low-rider" racks, like the top rack in Drawing 36 and the rack shown in Drawing 37 on page 283. Originally designed by Jim Blackburn, these have the advantage of keeping the weight on the front wheel low to the ground, which makes for a much more stable ride. Some tourists object that low-rider racks can't carry sufficiently large panniers, so they defeat the principle of even loading. Others do not consider this to be a problem, but you may want to experiment a bit. Cyclists who like to carry a rack-top bag instead of a handlebar bag dislike some low-rider racks because they don't have a top platform (see Drawing 37 on page 283). The size pannier you can put on low-rider racks depends on both the pannier design and the mounting system. If you carry heavier items in the front panniers, even if they are relatively small, you should be able to avoid significant problems.

Clearance and Mounting Issues

As discussed in Chapters 4 and 5, any road bike designed for touring should have mounting braze-ons for racks both on the dropouts and on the fork and seatstays. Ideally, there should be two sets of eyelets on each of the dropouts to mount fenders and racks. Various clamps and brackets can be used instead of braze-ons and eyelets, but if you are buying a road bike specifically for touring, it should have these fittings.

Because mountain bikes are often missing rack mounts, manufacturers of high-quality mountain bike racks have significantly improved the hardware for mounting without braze-ons. Good examples are the

Rear extension keeps
rear of pannier from
swinging into wheel

36. Bike racks for panniers. Top: a front rack made by Nitto. Center: an
Old Man Mountain rear rack with rear extensions that allow panniers to be
mounted farther back. Bottom: a Blackburn rear rack.

systems from Old Man Mountain, but other manufacturers are rapidly improving their mounting systems, and most high-quality racks now come with several alternative sets of mounting hardware. These can also be used when adapting bikes not specifically built for touring. Both bikes and racks have widely varying construction details, so the many possible mounting issues can often be solved by using different brackets and mounting hardware. For example, bikes that have mid-fork braze-on fittings for mounting racks do not use uniform dimensions from the braze-ons to the front lugs. If you are ordering racks via mail or the Internet, be sure to check everything you can about compatibility and verify that you can return the rack if it doesn't fit.

Racks for panniers have to fit on the bike and allow proper clearance for the bags. Aside from issues associated with mountain bikes that have fork suspension, and especially rear suspension systems (see "Basic Differences between Mountain Bikes and Road Bikes" on page 68), the most common clearance problem is between your heel and the front edge of a rear pannier. This is most likely to be an issue on bikes with short chainstays, such as mountain bikes and road bikes designed for racing or club riding (see "Recommended Frame Dimensions" on page 100).

If you buy your racks and panniers with the bike, you can check this clearance by loading the panniers and riding the bike; if there are problems, ask the folks at the bike shop to make adjustments. If you are adding the equipment to your bike, there are several ways to deal with the problem, which can be combined::

- Get rear panniers with lower front edges that slant backward at the bases or that have a narrower front-to-back profile. Volume can be added by making the panniers taller, deeper, and projecting farther to the rear.

- Get a rear rack with a rear extension that projects backward, like the one shown in the center of

Drawing 36 on page 279, so that the pannier can be mounted farther back without swaying into the wheel. This rack also has a mounting plate and attachment brackets designed to allow adjustment of the pannier position.

- Get panniers with a mounting system that allows you to easily adjust the position for mounting on the rack, so that the panniers can be reliably hung far enough back to clear your heel. Many of the best modern designs have hardware that clamps on rack rails to allow this adjustment—Arkel, Ortlieb, and Lone Peak are examples.

Get Sturdy Racks

If you are planning long self-supported tours, particularly in remote areas or rough terrain, you should get racks that are as strong and durable as possible. People have toured successfully in difficult terrain for years with aluminum racks, but properly designed steel racks are stronger, more durable, and more easily repaired. Cheap racks made from tubular aluminum with no side-to-side bracing are likely to sway at the worst times, and they may also break on a tour.

The best racks are made from welded aluminum alloy rod or from chromoly or stainless steel tubing. With proper bracing, they can be very stiff, preventing swaying. Examples of different types of bracing can be seen in Drawing 36 on page 279 and Drawing 37 on page 283. The bottom example in Drawing 36 shows a rack with rear struts that slant inward at the top, providing triangular bracing against side-to-side deformation. The front racks shown in Drawing 37 have an inverted U-shaped brace (hoop) that stiffens the rack.

Good racks to compare include those from Bruce Gordon, Tubus, Old Man Mountain, Nitto, Jandd, Surly, and the higher-end Blackburn racks. Old Man Mountain racks are especially designed for mountain bikes. Another company that specializes in racks designed for mountain bikes is Delta Cycle.

Panniers and Other Bags

Panniers are the standard luggage for most touring cyclists. They leave your body free and ventilated, don't put extra weight on your crotch, and keep the extra weight you are carrying low and well attached to the bike, which is the most stable way to carry it. When they are well chosen and properly packed, they do not degrade the bike's handling. Backpacks are generally not well suited to cycling, because they don't have these characteristics. (Mountain bikers on routes like the Great Divide Trail sometimes use relatively light backpacks to supplement either a single set of panniers or a BOB trailer.)

As mentioned at the beginning of the chapter, choosing the size of your panniers is a bit of a trade-off. If they are too small, you'll end up strapping too much stuff awkwardly to the tops of your racks, where they catch the wind and rain, are inconvenient to manage, and present a hazard of straps or other fasteners being caught in the bike's moving parts.

On the other hand, panniers that are larger than you need are unnecessarily bulky and will probably be filled with more stuff than you need to take. (Extra room generally gets filled with things that "might come in handy.")

Everyone has to come up with his or her own ideal compromise. If you are planning to do self-supported trips over thousands of miles or in remote regions, you probably want the largest panniers available (over 2,500 cubic inches for rear pair, and over 1,800 cubic inches for the front pair). Ratings of panniers' volume should not be taken too literally. Manufacturers use different standards, and the actual volume they contain will depend on your arrangement and how much you stuff into each bag or squeeze on the top, so volume figures should be considered only as the most general guide.

Your style of packing and the things you need to carry have a lot to do with what you can carry in a particular style of pannier. The models with lots of pockets and compartments are really handy for some packing

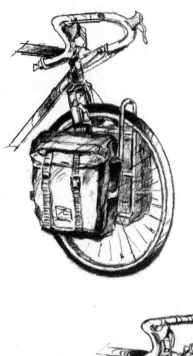

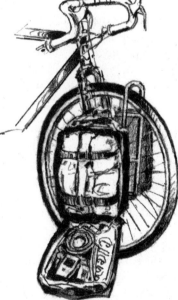

37. A panel-opening pannier in the lower example and a more common top-opening one in the upper example. The rack is a low-rider rack made by Bruce Gordon, stiffened by a hoop over the wheel.

Racks, Luggage, and Trailers

styles. Otherwise, they may just waste a lot of space. Some cyclists would rather have panniers like those made by Ortlieb, which consist mainly of large spaces that you must organize yourself. (To be waterproof, Ortlieb panniers avoid the seams required by pockets and partitions. Hence, each pannier is just a single large compartment.)

Similarly, construction style radically affects what you can pack. Some people love zippered side panels (see the bottom example in Drawing 37 on page 283), because you have immediate access to everything (as long as you've organized it neatly). Others prefer a top cover that has straps on both sides, so that it can be expanded flexibly upward—when you need to transport the groceries you've just purchased to the campground, for example.

Construction Details

The best panniers are very rugged and will last many years and many thousands of miles. Less well made models cost less but will wear out more quickly, and will generally force you to tolerate a few design deficiencies.

Here are some important design and construction features:

- Stitching and seams should be sewn so they don't unravel or pull out easily. They should be double- or triple-stitched along critical lines, edges should not be left exposed, allowing fabric to unravel, and major seams should be sealed and taped or bound (or welded in the case of waterproof panniers).

- Zippers, if used, should be heavy and of high quality. The edges to which they are sewn should not be unbound fabric edges, which will unravel in a year or two.

- The mounting system should be solid and well engineered. It should provide positive attachment to the rack that won't be knocked loose by road shocks or a stray bump from your heel. Shallow hooks over the rack, held down only by shock cords or springs—a setup that was standard a few years ago—are now indicators of lower quality.

All this is not to say that you must go out and spend hundreds of dollars on panniers to enjoy bicycle touring. There are less expensive bags that perform decently. However, they will probably not last nearly as long, and they will be more prone to fall apart on the road, as thin nylon fabric fails and unbound seams come apart.

Waterproof or Not?

At first thought, this seems a silly question—why would you *not* want waterproof panniers? The question is a bit more complicated than it seems. Many people find that zippered panel openings, or extensible covers, along with a lot of zippered pockets, are pretty convenient for packing and organizing gear. However, zippers are not waterproof and sewn-on pockets require seams that allow water penetration. These features can be water-resistant but not waterproof, so you rarely see them on truly waterproof panniers.

Truly waterproof panniers, like Ortlieb's entire line or Mountain Equipment Co-op's Aqua-Nots, consist basically of single large compartments. Some cyclists are quite happy with these, but others find them to be a real nuisance. Finding items in these large spaces can be difficult because you can't organize anything in pockets or compartments. This is particularly irritating when you pull into a campground in the rain and have to unpack the whole pannier to find the first few things you need. And if some water does get into a waterproof pannier, it stays there until you pour or sponge it out—assuming it isn't soaked up by your down jacket.

Many nonwaterproof panniers are quite resistant to penetration by moisture, and most tourists find them perfectly adequate, particularly when supplemented by waterproof or water-resistant stuff sacks for some equipment and by rain covers that can be put on the outside during real downpours. Truly waterproof panniers (like Ortlieb) are usually very durable and fairly heavy. Advocates come up with other means of organization, such as colored stuff sacks to substitute for pockets and compartments.

Pannier Makers

The undisputed leader in making waterproof panniers is Ortlieb, but Mountain Equipment Co-op (MEC), Topeak, Nashbar, and Novara (marketed by REI in the United States) have gotten good reviews from some users for their waterproof models.

Some of the best water-resistant panniers with well-arranged pocket systems are those made by Arkel, Lone Peak, Bruce Gordon Cycles, and Jandd. Brule Mountain Gear (www.panpack.com) and Nashbar make panniers that can be converted into backpacks for easy travel on public transportation or hiking side trips.

Less expensive bags can also give very good service, though they won't last as long as the best-quality ones. Usually less expensive bags are made from lighter fabric, so the weight of the panniers may be significantly less but durability will probably suffer. Experienced tourists have been quite happy with panniers from Nashbar, REI, and MEC. Be sure to evaluate your prospective panniers according to the criteria listed above, paying particular attention to the attachment system and quality of construction.

Handlebar Bags

Most touring cyclists use panniers to carry the bulk of what they need on a tour, but other accessory bags are also widely used, particularly handlebar bags. After panniers, these are the most commonly used bags. They provide storage space for small items that you need to reach while you're riding and are typically used for money, passports, wallets, snacks, cell phones, and a rain jacket. Map cases are often mounted on the top and may be part of the bag.

The traditional mounting method using leather straps around the handlebar interferes with an important hand position, so it is uncommon today. The two alternatives are mounting systems that attach to the handlebars (or handlebar extensions—see "Handlebar Real Estate and Extensions" on page 190) or a front rack. Some who have front luggage racks with a top platform simply mount the bag there, though with that solution slightly deeper bags are often used. Traditionalists, particularly Francophiles, favor décaleurs, which are small racks that support the handlebar bag and attach to the headset, fork crown, or other locations. Velo Orange, Wallingford Bicycle Parts, and Rivendell Bicycle Works sell variations of these racks, as well as traditional bags.

Most touring cyclists who use handlebar bags have models with mounting systems that clamp to the handlebars and hold the bag a few inches to the front, usually with a quick-release system that makes it easy to remove the bag when you leave the bike for a few minutes on forays into stores or restaurants. Such bags are made by all makers of panniers, and they are usually bought at the same time. Note that only lightweight items should be carried in the handlebar bag. Otherwise it will bounce when you hit a bump in the pavement. The mounting systems are not intended to hold much weight.

Some tourists avoid handlebar bags because of the space taken up by mounting systems (see "Handlebar Real Estate and Extensions" on page 190) or because they feel that the weight degrades bike handling. These choices are a matter of personal preference.

Saddlebags

Saddlebags were standard equipment for traditional English cyclists, and a few people still favor them, either as a substitute for panniers or as a supplement.

Many Brooks leather saddles are equipped with slots for mounting saddlebags, or bag loops can be attached to the saddle rails. Large saddlebags are typically used with special racks similar to décaleurs but mounted to the seat post. Most touring cyclists do not favor saddlebags to carry much weight or volume, but there are dedicated advocates. Small saddlebags, which are widely available, can be very useful for carrying tools. This provides convenient access, and the tools are on the bike for day rides when you aren't carrying panniers.

Strapping Stuff On

The temptation to just strap things onto the rear rack, and to the front if your front rack has a platform, should be controlled. That said, people doing expedition-style tours in remote corners of the world often have to do this. It also can be convenient to use the rear rack for specific items, such as a tent and sleeping bag, contained in a waterproof stuff sack. This works if you don't have to carry extra water (see "Water: Carrying, Storing, and Purifying" on page 312) or a bear barrel (see "Carrying Food in Bear Country" on page 317) on the rear rack.

If you are strapping items on the rear rack, get straps that fit, which will hold the load securely and don't have loose ends to catch in moving parts. Take time to get the right set of straps for the job. Haphazard use of bungee cords is not a good idea. Bungees should only be used for relatively light, compact items; too often they turn out to be the wrong length, are not strong enough to hold the load steady, or their hooks easily become caught in moving parts. When elastic cords are appropriate, it's better to buy a length of shock cord, fuse the ends against raveling, tie one end to the rack, and have a standard way to fix the other end. Alternatively you can make or buy elastic cords or straps that are the right length and strength for the specific job and have end fasteners that connect solidly to the rack.

If you regularly carry a tent and sleeping bag on the rear rack, you may want to get an appropriately sized waterproof bag designed for that purpose. Ortlieb makes some good ones.

Trailers

The alternative to panniers for carrying gear is a trailer. Mountain bikers traveling routes like the Great Divide Trail prefer to use trailers, because they cause fewer problems than rack-mounted luggage on single-track trails. They also work without great difficulty when attached to bikes with full suspension. (Note that only specialized single-wheel trailers are favored for this type of trail use. These attach to the rear axle and track right behind the rear wheel of the bike, and advocates find that they bounce less than rear-mounted panniers (though not everyone agrees).

Trailers also have a considerable following among tourists who stick to the pavement. Advocates like the way the bike handles with a trailer. Others do not. A variety of trailers are available, many designed for city use rather than touring. Burley trailers are widely used and come in a variety of designs, mostly two-wheel. By far the most popular trailer for touring, however, is the single-wheel BOB (short for beast of burden), shown in Drawing 38 on page 290, which comes in two models, the Yak and the Ibex. BOB trailers attach to the rear axle area with a bracket and a cotter pin. Usually, those who use them for touring buy a waterproof haul bag designed for the trailer. These have quite a large volume—enough that it is easy to take far too much stuff.

Note that for touring on the road, BOB trailers have the advantage of closely following the bike, but they rely on the bike for lateral stability. Tourists who like two-wheel trailers, such as the Burley models, favor them for their inherent stability, even when detached from the bike, but a two-wheel trailer requires the cyclist to pay attention to the route of both wheels behind—the right wheel may drop into gaps at the edge of the road. Any trailer can cause some problems in this respect, and

38. A mountain bike with a trailer for luggage. Some cyclists prefer trailers even for rugged trails.

the touring cyclists who prefer them make up a distinct minority—most are firmly in the pannier and rack camp.

It is easy to park the bike with a BOB, as long as there is enough room. You angle the bike with respect to the trailer, and the combination is usually stable. Detaching the BOB quickly is harder, because you have to remove the cotter pin, and the trailer is awkward to handle when disconnected. Moreover, even more than with waterproof panniers, you need to come up with a system for packing things in the single large bag that rides in the BOB. There is no built-in compartmentalization, so if you don't have a system, you'll end up pawing through a mountain of stuff looking for some small item—the flashlight, for example. Finally, any trailer greatly complicates getting to and from a tour, unless you are starting from home. An extra carton is required to ship the trailer, and manhandling it into a vehicle or onto a train is a nightmare.

If you do tour with a BOB, add a cotter pin to your list of spare parts to carry. Users have many stories of endless searching for a lost cotter pin among the pine needles of a campground.

15

Camping Gear

Many touring cyclists prefer to camp on most trips. Camping gives you maximum flexibility in many regions, particularly those where commercial accommodations are few and far between, and it can be a very economical style of travel. If you plan to rely on camping during your bicycle tours, however, you'll need camping gear. You may already have serviceable equipment for backpacking or other self-propelled activities that will serve well enough for bike touring, but this chapter covers equipment from the point of view of the long-distance cyclist.

Tents and Other Shelter

Most touring cyclists who carry their own shelter tend to prefer tents, though tarps are quite practical in the conditions usually encountered when bicycling, which most of us confine to circumstances without a lot of blowing snow. Tents make it relatively easy to hunker down in bad weather, to protect against insects at night, and to obtain some privacy when spending the night in a crowded campground.

If you already have a lightweight tent that you use for backpacking or mountaineering, you'll probably use it for bike touring as well. It may be less than optimal, but it will almost certainly work well enough to start. If you're shopping for the perfect tent for self-contained cycle touring, however, there are a number of considerations. This section concentrates on features and design considerations for tents.

Size and Weight

Light weight and compact packed size are more important for cyclists than for backpackers. You don't have to heft your pack after every rest stop when you are bicycle touring, so a few extra pounds are not of much importance on the flats, though you do have to do some work to get them moving whenever you've stopped or slowed down. In terms of overall exertion, however, you can climb many more vertical feet when bicycling in the mountains or hills than you can when you are hiking. Any extra weight has to be schlepped up all those hills. On the other hand, weather conditions encountered by cyclists are typically less extreme than in many other outdoor activities, so the extra weight required for all-season tents is unnecessary. As with all aspects of camping, balancing weight against other factors is subjective.

When you're comparing weights, it is important to compare apples to apples. If you're shopping at local stores, it is wise to bring a small scale so you can actually compare the weights of two tents you're considering. Catalog weights are often overoptimistic—by a lot—and it can be quite tricky comparing tents from different manufacturers. Large suppliers of lightweight outdoor equipment like REI and MEC, which carry a number of different brands, can often be useful in making choices, because they provide comparison tables and make some effort to normalize the entries, but many retailers just reprint the manufacturers' weight claims.

In comparing tents, you also need to look at the floor area and shape, the inside height at places where you'll be sitting or crouching, and the roominess. Many cyclists prefer to take a nominal "two-person" tent for solo touring to have a reasonable amount of room for gear and moderate comfort. Similarly, quite a few couples or others touring with a companion opt for a "three-person" tent. The number of people for which a tent is rated often reflects either serious optimism on the part of the manufacturer or a commitment to significant intimacy for anyone who purchases the tent on the basis of advertising. Check the actual layout of the tent floor and the vertical profile of the tent.

Desirable Features and Design Constraints

You'll decide how to balance various tent features based on your own experience, your priorities, and the type of touring you plan to do. Will you be dealing with significant heat, cold, wind, or rain? Will you need to worry about insects? Here are some considerations that may guide your choice of tent.

Features like vestibules should be considered: they can provide extra room for storing gear, cooking in bad weather, and separating wet gear from dry. For a reasonably waterproof tent, sealed seams in the fly or roof are essential. If the tent has a waterproof floor, it will be easier to find a location to pitch it where you will be dry.

If you're getting a tent, rather than a tarp or similar shelter, good insect protection is an important feature. Campers using tarps and similarly well-ventilated shelters need to take a separate piece of netting to use when the bugs are bad, but tents should provide good built-in insect protection—it is one of the important reasons to choose them. If the tent uses a design that is fairly tight to the weather, well-designed vents are critical for both hot conditions and wet ones. Tents with a lot of netting are more comfortable in warm weather and can provide good shelter against rain if the fly is well designed, but they won't offer much protection in cold, windy conditions.

Don't ignore the color of the tent. Pale colors that transmit some light are a lot more pleasant when you are sitting out heavy rain. Very dark colors are much hotter when the sun is beating down, and they are depressing over long periods of precipitation. And if you do some camping in spots where you would prefer to be relatively inconspicuous, a bright day-glo orange will not be helpful.

Many details in the design and construction of tents should be considered; we'll focus on a few of them here. Most important is the basic shape of the pieces of fabric. Simple A-frame tents require that each hanging line, like the ridge line, be cut along a catenary curve. This is the curve that a suspended cable would take, given a particular tension and suspended weight. Modern freestanding tents have many catenary curves, forming a complex geometric structure. The first freestanding tents, based on the geodesic domes of R. Buckminster Fuller, were made in the late 1970s, mainly by Sierra Designs.

The main canopy (the roof) can have single- or double-wall construction. Double-wall tents use a waterproof top layer, usually a fly—essentially an upper roof that sheds rain or snow—and an inner layer that allows water vapor to pass through. Other double-wall constructions suspend the inner canopy from the outer one and have no separate fly. Single-wall tents try to avoid condensation by using either vents or a breathable fabric like Gore-Tex, or both.

There is no perfect solution to the problem of condensation inside a tent, which sometimes can get you and your gear quite wet. This is a bit less of a problem in moderate temperatures, because condensation is caused when the warm moisture-saturated air inside the tent comes in contact with the cold tent fabric. Condensation is exacerbated when that fabric also has a very smooth surface, as most coated, waterproof fabrics do. Rain cools the tent wall, and it also raises the humidity outside, so air circulation helps less. And when it is pouring rain outside, even breathable fabrics present an essentially complete barrier to water escaping the inside of the tent by vapor transport.

Construction and design details are important. The surfaces and lines of support for the tent should be uniformly tight when the tent is properly pitched.

Sagging fabric will flap in the wind, indicating that too much stress is concentrating at a few points. Strong, evenly sewn seams are critical for longevity; they should either be folded over or have the fabric edges heat-fused, preferably both. Zippers should be of high quality, with large enough teeth or coils to resist jamming; those on sloping outer surfaces should be protected with weather strips. Floors should extend a few inches up the tent walls to keep out splash and water rivulets. Seams on the roof, fly, and floor should be sealed with seam sealer or taped with a waterproof tape permanently bonded to the seam.

Freestanding and Non-Freestanding Tents

Many of the best modern tents have "freestanding" designs (see Drawing 3 on page 15). They use flexible poles that fit into fabric sleeves or attach at a number of points on the tent wall to form a freestanding structure, sometimes a dome, more often a more complex shape. Freestanding tents have a number of advantages. Well-designed ones are very strong, because the shape of the tent distributes stress evenly and reduces sagging. They allow more flexibility in the choice of tent site, because they don't rely on guy lines or stakes to hold them up—only to anchor them against the wind. So you don't have to carry a bunch of bulky stakes.

Once you are used to the tent, it can often be set up and broken down very quickly. (Until you are used to it, the reverse is true. Setting up the tent can be like putting together a frustratingly complicated wooden puzzle.) Because stress points in the fabric are minimized, most mild-weather tents come with a lightweight net canopy to provide insect protection and ventilation, and a rain fly to keep out the rain in all but the most severe storms. Well-designed freestanding tents often allow you to pitch the fly alone, so that you can carry the fly, the poles, and a few stakes and lines when you don't need a full shelter. For this purpose, the footprint (see "Tent Accessories" later in this chapter for more on footprints) usually serves as a ground cloth.

The ability to pitch the tent with few stakes and guy lines is a major advantage at some wilderness campsites, and it is enormously helpful when you are stuck camping on the gravel pads that are common in a lot of developed campgrounds these days. Those gravel pads are intended to keep heavy vehicles from sinking into the ground. It is often difficult, if not impossible, to drive tent stakes into the surface, unless you are carrying spikes and a sledgehammer.

Freestanding tent designs do have disadvantages. They are expensive. They can't be pitched without poles, and the poles are fragile except when holding up the tent. If you aren't careful, the freestanding capability can be deceptive—if you don't anchor the tent, it can literally blow away, particularly when your gear is not inside the tent. Big Agnes makes some freestanding tents that are well suited to bike touring.

Quonset-type tents, which are shaped like half-cylinders or half-cones with tapered ends, are slightly less convenient than freestanding tents but weigh less and are quite weather-tight. They require one or two anchors at each end, and usually a few side anchors to withstand serious wind. Most tents of this type are mountaineering tents, and they are likely to be on the heavy side for bike touring, but Warmlite tents of this design are among the lightest and roomiest available. A heavier but less expensive tent of this type is the Kelty Crestone 2. Some models from Tarptent fall into this category, and they are very serviceable, light, and economical. This type of tent tends to have less headroom than a comparable freestanding tent.

There are many other, mostly older, styles of tents, which run the gamut from very good to inadvisable. Most are variations on A-frame tents, typically with two poles forming an inverted V at the front of the tent and a single pole at the rear. Several factors have greatly reduced the number of these simpler designs, including widespread copying of freestanding designs, the increased popularity of backpacking, and the availability of cheap overseas labor to cut and sew the complicated patterns of freestanding tents.

It is still well worth looking at these simpler A-frame tents, however, because they can combine very light weight with a lower price. They also are robust and flexible in the ways they can be pitched. If you accidentally step on one of the poles of your freestanding tent and break it beyond repair—unfortunately easy to do—you may have quite a difficult time turning the remnants into a reasonable shelter. With many non-freestanding tents, improvising a fix, such as using a stick or tying a guy line to a tree branch, is quite simple. And you can easily replace the pole on the road—you don't need a custom part. For do-it-yourself tourists, A-frame designs are easy to lay out and sew, whereas freestanding tents require detailed patterns.

A-frame tents do have some disadvantages. They require a number of stakes and guy lines to set up, and some of these need to be in particular positions. You have much less flexibility in picking a tent site because of the stake and attachment points required. A-frames often weigh more than the best freestanding tents. Finally, for a given floor plan and apex height, there will be less room to sit up or crouch in the tent, and the walls will sag much more, especially when they are weighted by moisture or a little snow.

Tent Accessories

Vestibules—additional sheltered areas that cover an area extending out from the door(s) at one or both ends of the tent—are useful for storing some of your equipment, particularly wet gear, and giving you more room inside. They are part of some tents and can be added to others, either permanently or with zippers, so they only have to be carried when you want them. They are particularly useful when the main tent is on the small side, and they help you get in and out in foul weather without tracking a lot of rain and mud into the main living area.

Tents are expensive, so most campers carry a ground cloth or "footprint," a small ground cloth cut to fit the shape of the tent floor. A footprint reduces wear on the tent floor. It also allows you to isolate dirt and moisture rather than having to roll it up with the tent. Footprints are available for most tents, but usually they are overpriced. Cutting to size a piece of Tyvek, a material commonly used in house construction, or a cheap tarp provides an alternative that is just as good and can be discarded without regret when it becomes too worn. Tyvek is relatively stiff, and therefore rather noisy when used for camping. There's a softer variety but it's hard to find. You can toss a sheet of the stiff Tyvek in the washing machine for a cycle or two to make it softer and quieter.

Tarps, Tube Tents, and Bivy Sacks

There are lighter, cheaper, and simpler alternatives to carrying a tent, assuming that you are traveling in seasons and locations without much snow and ice. Most of us don't do a lot of bike touring in winter, even if we commute year-round. Occasional snow at campsites near the Continental Divide is not usually a big problem. If you're an experienced camper or you're willing to put up with a little discomfort as you learn, a tarp and a ground cloth, perhaps supplemented by a length of mosquito netting, may be all you need to camp on many bicycle tours.

Tarps. Tarps can be pitched in a variety of ways, all relying on some combination of anchors available around the camp site, supplemented with stakes and parachute cord that you bring. Some ingenuity is often required. Grommets attached every three feet or so along the sides of the tarp make pitching more convenient, but it is perfectly feasible to tie a cord to the tarp without a grommet. Either use a sheet bend (illustration at www.en.wikipedia.org/wiki/Sheet_bend or www.en.wikipedia.org/wiki/Double_sheet_bend), into which the fabric is tied directly, or use a pebble or other small object placed on the tarp and tied off with the cord. That is, if you need to anchor a fabric tarp where there is no built-in attachment point, just put a pebble on the fabric, push the pebble into the surface to form a bulge, twist it off, and tie the end of the guyline around the twist. Commercial alternatives like Sierra Designs Grip Clips do the same thing, providing a mechanism for gripping the tarp. Various clever attachment devices are also available at camping stores.

Sophisticated tarps like the ones made by Kelty which are cut with a catenary diagonal for more stable pitching are available, but most tarp campers want simplicity and low cost, and a tarp with a catenary cut moves into the price range of tents. The lightest, best-quality tarps are made from nylon coated with silicon-based waterproofing (silnylon). An 8-by-10-foot silnylon tarp made with 1.1-ounce ripstop nylon weighs less than a pound. Combined with a ground cloth, parachute cord, and stakes, it should still be under 2 pounds. The standard blue rip-stop polyethylene tarps available at very low cost at many hardware, building supply, and discount stores will weigh twice as much, but they serve quite well and are much cheaper. The 8-by-10-foot size will work for one person, though many use larger sizes so they can dispense with a ground cloth by folding one end under or can cover the bike with the upper end, using it as a support. Some cyclists carry a couple of lightweight poles to help rig the tarp.

Bivy sacks. Bivy sacks are small shelters, usually intended for one person, that give you a place to crawl in with just your sleeping bag. If you have experience using one for ultralight backpacking or climbing, you'll know whether one will work for you. If you don't, a tarp or very light tent will provide a lot more room and be significantly cheaper.

Tube tents. Tube tents are an inexpensive way to get started. They are plastic tubes available from camping suppliers that you can pitch by stringing a length of parachute cord between two trees or other anchors. The bottom is held down by your gear.

Hammocks. Hammocks designed for camping are favorites of a few enthusiasts. The ones designed for lightweight camping are made by Hennessy. If you expect to bicycle in treeless areas, they are not a good choice, because it is hard to find a place to hang them.

Sleeping Bags and Pads

The choice of a sleeping bag tends to be rather subjective. Some people are comfortable sleeping in close-fitting bags, while others are not. Some people are quite comfortable in a bag that is rated for 15 degrees warmer than what they are experiencing. Others need a bag rated for 20 degrees colder. If you have a lot of experience with camping and backpacking, you'll know where you fall in the spectrum. If you don't have this experience, try out some bags in a shop specializing in this kind of equipment, and take into account how your metabolism compares with that of other people. If you normally need more blankets than anyone you know, get a warmer bag. Conversely, if you are typically the warmest person in the room, you'll be able to get by with less insulation in your sleeping bag.

Your needs depend a lot on the trips you are planning. If you are traveling where the temperatures don't get very chilly, you might just start with a lightweight bag with a zipper and a little synthetic insulation, but if you are doing a ride in the high mountains in spring or fall, this will not be a happy solution. Check the temperature ranges for the areas where you are planning to ride, and try to figure out the temperature rating required for your sleeping bag.

If you participate in other self-propelled outdoor activities, you probably already have a sleeping bag, and you can just use that one on bicycle tours, at least for a while. The optimum bag for bike touring, however, emphasizes light weight and minimum packed size. Because bicycle touring is generally a mild-weather activity, you may want a lighter bag than the one you bought for cold-weather trips. A winter down bag that is comfortable for chilly nights in the mountains will be rather heavy and bulky for most bike touring.

For light weight and compressibility, a quality down bag is far superior to anything else. They're quite expensive, though, and are worthless if they get wet. Many bicycle campers, particularly those who don't need low-temperature bags, choose a bag with synthetic insulation. They are less expensive, retain some insulating qualities when wet, and are much easier to dry.

All the major suppliers of lightweight outdoor equipment have extensive lines of sleeping bags. REI and MEC are good places to start.

Pads also evoke a lot of disagreement. Thermarest pads have been one of the standard solutions for a long time. They are a cross between a pad and an air mattress, consisting of a foam pad enclosed in an airtight cover. After you unroll a Thermarest (or equivalent), you open the valve, letting the foam pad expand and inflate the cover. Then you add a few breaths of additional air and close the valve. You can also buy attachments that allow you to turn the pad into an imperfect, but usable, camp chair. The most luxurious pads available now, however, are the air mattresses that have some down or synthetic fill. They are warm and very comfortable, and some are very light.

Another option worth considering is sleeping bags with built-in pads. These sleeping bags have insulation on the top and sides but don't bother to put compressible insulation in the bottom. Instead, the bottoms of the bags are envelopes for mated pads, usually of the type just described. Warmlite and Big Agnes both make this kind of sleeping bag. Some users are wildly enthusiastic, others not so much.

Extra Clothes

If you are camping for most of your trip, you need to pay some attention to clothing for camp. Changing out of perspiration-soaked riding clothes is always a welcome luxury, and either hanging them out to dry or washing them is usually one of the first things you want to do when you arrive in camp. And if you get caught riding in inclement weather, you'll need a change of clothes to get dry and perhaps warm again.

The kind of camp clothing you bring will naturally depend on late afternoon and evening temperatures. A typical rider may carry a light wool pullover, a hat, a pair of light pants with zip-off legs, underwear, and wool tights. Where evenings are chilly, add a down vest. A rain jacket serves as both jacket and windbreaker, and rain pants serve the same purpose for your lower body. Consider a crushable hat with a wide brim to shield you from the sun. For chilly evenings, very light synthetic or silk gloves can be useful. Everyone has his or her own preferences. The main criteria are that everything you take should be multipurpose, light in weight, and easy to pack.

Stoves and Cooking Gear

If you are planning on camping most of the time on your tour, you will probably find a stove to be a necessity, unless you can remain cheerful on a diet of cold food and beverages. You need to establish both your approach to and your skill at cooking with available ingredients before you can consider what kind of stove and cooking kit to use.

While most camping skills are directly transferable from backpacking to bicycle touring, cooking is different. Even in regions where stores are few and far between, as in the desert Southwest of the United States, you'll still usually pass places where you can buy food, though fresh vegetables and other healthy foodstuffs may be hard to come by. Thus, while backpacking cuisine often consists mainly of reconstituted dehydrated food, cooking on bicycle tours is typically a matter of improvising good meals from whatever is available at the grocery store, farm stand, or convenience store that you pass in the afternoon. Cooking on tour is discussed more fully in Chapter 18.

On backpacking trips, water often needs to be boiled to eliminate possible contamination. On many bicycle tours, you can count on being able to get potable water at a tap and carry it into camp, or use purification methods. When this is true, you can carry less fuel and your stove does not need the capacity to boil a lot of water.

Your style of cooking will also dictate your needs for a stove. Are you happy heating up some soup or ramen, eating a couple of pieces of fruit, perhaps a salad, and a granola bar, and making a cup of tea or coffee? Or do you like to cook a meal from fresh ingredients when you can find them? Several different types of stoves are described here.

Stove Trade-Offs

Choosing stoves inevitably requires a number of trade-offs, and you need to think about your own needs before going much farther. First, your destination is critical. If you are flying to the start of your tour, you won't be able to carry fuel, so you have to be able to find it at your destination. Fuel availability varies widely—typical isobutane/propane cartridges are easy to find in much of the United States and Canada, but not in many other places; alcohol is available almost anywhere, if you know how to ask; other fuels vary in availability, and most are tricky to find without researching both availability and vocabulary. (How do you ask for white gas in Puerto Montt, Chile?)

Second, different types of stoves and fuels have different advantages, as discussed later in this chapter. If you are likely to need to boil a lot of water, you'll almost certainly end up choosing a white gas or multifuel pumped stove, but if you only want to be able to make tea or heat water for ramen, other stoves will work equally well. If you like to cook meals that require adjusting the burner, you won't want a stove that burns either like a blowtorch or not at all.

Finally, the type of trip matters. As indicated in the discussion of fuels, availability varies, and fuel that is economical for a weeklong tour may be rather expensive and inconvenient over a month or six weeks.

Fuel Types

Three main categories of fuel are used in stoves intended for self-propelled camping. Traditional backpacking stoves use white gas, and modified (multifuel) versions can also burn automobile fuel, kerosene, or diesel fuel. Other backpacking stoves use pressurized cartridges containing propane or isobutane. Finally, many minimalist campers use alcohol stoves. Each of these choices has particular advantages.

White gas is the workhorse fuel. It produces a lot of heat for the weight carried, and stoves using it can burn very hot, so it is the best choice if you may need to boil a lot of water. It is also the most inexpensive per ounce, so it can be very economical if you purchase the quantities you need along the way, but that is sometimes difficult—cost per ounce is irrelevant if you have to buy a large container and discard most of it. White gas is always the preferred fuel for multifuel stoves.

Cartridges of propane and isobutane stand out when it comes to convenience. You just attach the cartridge, turn the stove on, and light it. You don't have to transfer liquid fuel and worry about spilling it, and the flame is adjustable. However, this is the most expensive fuel per ounce, you can't refill the cartridges, and it has more limited availability.

Alcohol is the third alternative. It is less toxic than petroleum-based fuels, it is widely available, and it can be carried in plastic containers rather than requiring specialized metal ones. It is generally more expensive per ounce than white gas, but it is more likely to be found in containers of practical size at convenience stores, so it may prove less expensive in the end. Alcohol stoves generally are not very adjustable, nor are they pressurized, so alcohol is not suitable if you need to boil a lot of water or want to do more elaborate cooking.

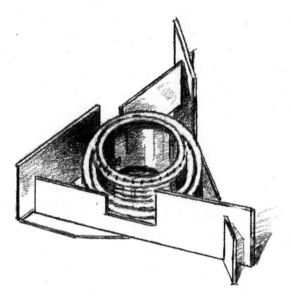

39. The Trangia Westwind, a commercially made alcohol stove.

Fuels like canned heat and flammable tablets, both widely available in surplus stores, are used by a few touring cyclists for cooking, but they are generally more suitable for emergency use, so they are not considered here, nor are stoves designed to concentrate heat from twigs or other roadside fuel.

Alcohol Stoves

A popular alternative for cyclists, as for ultralight backpackers, is the alcohol stove (see Drawing 39). They come in a variety of models and are lightweight, simple to operate, quiet, and very efficient. Some come with stands, windscreens, heat concentrators, and pots; each model has its devotees.

An alcohol stove is usually on or off—you can't bring water to a boil and then simmer the dish you are making. These stoves are perfect for cooking simple dishes—heating soup or stew, making pasta or rice dishes, sautéing, frying, and heating water for tea or coffee.

As with all equipment, it is best to learn how to use your stove at home before taking it on the road. You'll be much happier at the end of a long, tiring day if you can get a meal going quickly without spending time fussing with the stove. Each type of stove has idiosyncrasies, but alcohol stoves generally just need to be filled and lit. It's important to establish a stable location with wind protection before you light one. Most alcohol stoves are not easily moved once they are started. The alcohol flame is nearly invisible in daylight, so it is easy to make the dangerous mistake of thinking that the stove is not burning. The fuel is not nearly as volatile as white gas, however.

Experiment at home when it is windy. You may need to buy or make a windscreen to operate the stove in windy conditions. Lightweight camping catalogs will list inexpensive commercially available windscreens, typically made of heavy aluminum foil so they can be folded flat for packing. Brasslite makes some excellent alcohol stoves, which are accessible on the Web at www.brasslite.com. They also burn hotter than most alcohol stoves, and some have provision for a flame that adjusts—but not by much.

Making your own alcohol stove. You can buy alcohol stoves, but quite a few people choose to make their own. Very simple and super-lightweight alcohol stoves can be made from aluminum cans; a number of instruction sets can be found on the Internet. Two Web sites to check out are www.zenstoves.net and www.pcthiker.com/pages/gear/pepsiGstoveinstruct .shtml. Brasslite also has instructions for making your own stove, following their design, which can be found at www.brasslite.com.

Fuel choices for alcohol stoves. One great advantage of alcohol stoves is that the fuel is cheap (compared with propane or butane canisters) and widely available, and it can be carried in plastic bottles. On a long trip, you can stop at a hardware store and get another bottle of fuel with little difficulty or expense. Alcohol stoves are clearly the most environmentally friendly choice for bike camping.

A disadvantage is that the fuel is not standardized. The best fuel is ethanol (ethyl alcohol), but because of federal regulations, the only way to buy pure ethanol is in glass bottles at liquor stores, where you pay an exorbitant price (Everclear is a common brand). What you can buy at hardware, building supply, and similar stores is denatured alcohol, which is ethanol mixed with methanol or other poisonous additives so it can't be consumed without causing severe side effects. Unfortunately, formulations of denatured alcohol vary widely, and their performance as fuel is quite variable. One widely available brand in the United States and Canada is S-L-X, which is sold in paint and hardware stores as a shellac thinner and marine-stove fuel. It comes in 1-quart steel cans, so if you carry a liter plastic bottle with a good seal, you can refill it pretty easily and discard the can, which pours very badly. This brand is half ethanol and half methanol. Since all denatured alcohol is poisonous, be careful to avoid breathing the vapor, and never cook inside your tent.

Methanol, available as Heet gas line antifreeze (yellow bottle), will also work, but it is even more poisonous than denatured alcohol, so you need to be really careful to avoid breathing the fumes. Keep skin exposure to a minimum with any fuel. However, none of the alcohol alternatives is as toxic as white gas, gasoline, or kerosene. Isopropanol, sold as rubbing alcohol, does not burn as well (lots of soot), and often has enough water that it won't burn at all, so it is a last-resort alternative. Denatured alcohol is often known as methylated spirits in English-speaking countries outside North America.

Note that alcohol stoves are often hard to extinguish, so they are typically just left to burn out. If you gauge the fuel perfectly, the stove will burn out just as your dinner is ready, but this doesn't always work out, and smaller alcohol stoves often have to be refilled and restarted before dinner is done.

Cartridge Stoves (LPG Canister Stoves)

For convenience within the United States, cartridge stoves (see Drawing 40) are hard to beat. Most hardware and camping stores carry canisters of fuel for them. They are very easy to use and provide reasonable heat output, and their flame can be reduced to a simmer. Fuel, a mix of isobutane (or butane) and propane, is more expensive than alcohol or white gas, however, and you can't count on obtaining it outside the United States and parts of Canada. The canister cannot be refilled, and if you start a trip with a partially used canister, you don't know how much fuel you really have.

Cartridge stoves are probably the simplest and most convenient stoves for bike touring. They are readily adjustable from very hot to a simmer. The cartridge can be detached easily without loss of fuel. The fuel is not ideal for conditions below freezing, but that is not an obstacle for most bicycle camping.

Cartridge stoves are the most expensive type to operate. Although the steel canisters can be recycled, this is not likely to be feasible on tour, so they just turn into trash when they are empty. A canister setup will be a little heavier than an alcohol or white gas stove, and the weight penalty is higher if you're carrying a partly empty cylinder along with a replacement. In most respects, however, cartridge stoves work very well for bicycle touring. They require less care to use safely, because you never have to handle liquid fuel, and it is easy to turn the stove off and move it as necessary.

There are some situations that would make cartridge stoves a bad choice. If you are going to remote areas where there are few stores or on tours outside the United States and Canada, cartridges may not be available, and you are not allowed to take them on a plane, so you can't carry fuel with you if you are flying to your tour. It is not legal to mail them, so you can't have them sent general delivery to post offices, like other supplies.

40. Typical cartridge (canister) stoves. Both use cartridges with valves that are self-sealing, so the cartridge can be removed. Butane cartridges are more widely available than mixed propane and butane, but either can be used with most stoves.

The simplest cartridge stoves are made so that the fuel canister acts as the stand, like the top example in Drawing 40. This can be somewhat unstable with a larger pot or in tricky cooking situations, so if you are considering this type, look at the kits that include a wider base that fits on the bottom of the cartridge, or buy one separately. A better solution, like the bottom example in Drawing 40, has a stable pot stand and a separate fuel canister.

Note that while all canister stoves have the same kind of valves, so that any cartridge screws onto any stove, the fuel mixtures are different between brands. When you can, it is best to use fuel that is intended for your stove. Some users have reported occasional clogging or stoves that burned too hot when using a different manufacturer's fuel. If you're using a different fuel than that intended for your stove, be careful, but on the road you'll use the cartridges you can find, and this doesn't usually present a problem.

White Gas and Multifuel Stoves

If you want a stove that has high heating capacity but can also be turned to a simmer, you should consider pressurized liquid-fuel backpacking and mountaineering stoves, either exclusively using white gas, such as Coleman fuel, or having multifuel capacity. The latter is important if you're traveling outside the United States.

White gas stoves have been the most commonly used stoves for lightweight camping for many years, and they have many advantages. Multifuel versions (see Drawing 41) are somewhat more expensive and complicated stoves that can also burn a variety of fuels, such as kerosene and automobile gasoline. The additional versatility can be very useful when you are traveling in less developed parts of the world, where white gas may be hard to find—even the local term for it may be problematic. The multifuel models tend to be a little crankier, however, so you should learn to use the stove beforehand and carry a servicing kit. Kerosene is not as volatile as white gas or gasoline, and priming the stove is trickier. Otherwise, they operate the same way as white gas stoves. Note that white gas is the preferred fuel for any of these stoves, multifuel or not, because it burns cleaner than any of the alternatives. Other fuels are more likely to require cleaning the jets and other maintenance. In spite of this they are a godsend when you are traveling in some remote areas.

White gas stoves generally have a high heat output; they boil water quickly, and they typically can

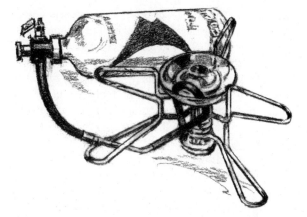

41. A pressurized multifuel stove that will burn white gas, kerosene, diesel fuel, or even leaded gas.

be turned down to a simmer. You can easily tell how much fuel you have, and on many models the fuel bottle also serves as a reservoir for the stove. They are the cheapest to operate, as long as you can find fuel in reasonable-size cans. (Unleaded gasoline should not be used in a stove designed for white gas; it will result in rapid carbon buildup. It can be used in multifuel stoves.)

White gas stoves are fairly easy to operate, though those who've never used them will want to practice a little in the backyard before camping with one. Typically, the stove is pumped up to pressurize it, a little fuel is released into the burner area, and this is ignited with a pocket lighter. As it burns it preheats the burner, so that when the stove is turned on there is a steady, adjustable flame. The traditional versions, like the original Primus stoves, don't have pumps but generate their initial pressure when the stove is primed.

Cooking Gear

With all the stove types discussed above, you can also purchase complete cooksets built around particular stoves, which may include windscreens, heat exchangers, a pot holder or other accessories, and pots made to work together. Some makers of complete systems are Jetboil, MSR, and Primus. These are more efficient, but they are also much more expensive and less versatile. When touring alone, you may take the same stove but will probably carry different-sized pots than when cooking with others; the perfect set for a solo traveler will be different from that needed for a group of four.

You can, however, buy cooking gear separately and much less expensively at a camping store or a secondhand store. What you need depends on your cooking style. If you're happy with very simple meals, you may be able to get by with a single pot that holds less than a quart and is very compact. I carry two larger pots, so that I can heat water for tea or coffee and, in the second pot, make a meal that may simmer for a while. Two pots also provide versatility in heating water for dishwashing. Some cyclists carry a lightweight skillet. Camping pots normally don't have handles, so you'll need a pot gripper. Try to pick a simple but versatile set of utensils. There are lightweight ones available in camping stores. Most groups carry shared pots, together with a bowl and a cup for each individual. Carry all the needed accessories in your cook kit—butane lighter, pot scrubber, utensils, liquid soap, and perhaps a glove for handling hot items.

Water: Carrying, Storing, and Purifying

The amount of water you need to carry and possible requirements for treatment depend completely on where you are riding. In many parts of the United States, you can plan on filling your water bottles conveniently at roadside establishments. Municipal water supplies can usually be assumed to be safe, so you can fill your water containers with confidence at almost any tap. In these circumstances, you just need a few water bottles and the discipline to drink regularly, before you are thirsty. If you're camping at primitive campgrounds or stealth camping, you'll need containers large enough to hold water for the evening and morning so that you can stock up where water is available and then carry it to your campsite.

By contrast, on some rides in the southwestern desert regions of the United States, you'll have to drink a lot to avoid dehydration and overheating, and roadside convenience stores can be far apart. Carrying enough water requires both foresight and the right equipment. You can easily require a quart of water every hour when you're riding in hot weather.

If you are riding on backcountry roads or trails and relying on streams for water, you'll have to treat or boil the water to avoid waterborne pathogens. In underdeveloped countries, you may be able to buy water or other liquids, depending on your route—the commercially bottled ones are usually safe—but tap water often needs to be treated. If you purchase water or other drinks, verify that the seals are intact.

Carrying Water

Depending on how many water bottle cages you have on your frame, you might be able to carry a little over 2½ quarts of fluids. Even if your bike has three cages on the frame, the largest bottles that will fit are 1-liter (just over a quart) ones, and the position of the cages often limits the size that can be used. Some people ride with hydration packs, which generally have a capacity of 2–3 quarts, but many tourists prefer to carry extra water on the bike rather than on their backs. On most tours you can carry several extra 1-liter bottles in your panniers, but desert tours require a lot more water. A rigid 3-liter PVC bottle for soda drinks is lightweight and can be securely fastened to the top of a rear rack with a length of shock cord.

Hydration bags (the plastic bladders used in hydration packs) can also be carried inside panniers and filled at the last water source before camp. Folding plastic jugs may be useful for carrying water around camp, but they aren't of much use for camps where there is no water source. A tough hydration bag can be hung on one side of the rear rack instead of a pannier. The strongest ones are Dromedary Bags from MSR, which are made of Cordura nylon fabric laminated to a waterproof liner. A 4-liter bag will fit on one side of a rear rack, though you'll lose a little capacity at the top. Carrying a hydration bag on one side of the rear rack makes that side unavailable for a pannier, of course, so to utilize this solution you would need to be travelling without one rear pannier or using a combination pannier-backpack that you can carry on your shoulders after filling the hydration bag.

Treating Water

In most bicycle touring, you resupply with water when you pass roadside establishments, organized campgrounds, and the like, so the issue of treating water doesn't arise. In underdeveloped countries, you may rely on bottled water for drinking and boil tap water when you are cooking. However, there are some trips where you'll need to use either streams or tap water that you can't trust. In those situations treating water before you drink it is very important.

This section considers only pathogens in water. Chemical pollution is a completely different issue. It usually has an industrial source, though there are a few arsenic-contaminated springs in the desert Southwest. (These rare arsenic occurrences can be identified visually—other organisms are also poisoned by arsenic.) For industrial pollutants, beware of streams that are below industrial facilities or mines.

The three types of pathogens that occur in drinking water are protozoa, bacteria, and viruses. A related problem is particulate content. Cloudy water requires more vigorous treatment against pathogens than clear water, because microorganisms can bind to the suspended particles. Thus, it is always best to prefilter cloudy water before treating.

The most reliable means of eliminating pathogens is boiling. Water that has been at a rolling boil for at least a minute at sea level, three minutes above 5,000 feet, and five minutes above 10,000 feet is safe to drink. While this is often not practical because of the fuel needed for large amounts of drinking water, if you are camping and have to use a nearby stream, it can be a reasonable solution. Make a full pot of tea, and fill a water bottle with the tea you don't drink immediately. But don't cheat—the water has to be at a full boil for the requisite time, not just simmering with a few bubbles on the bottom.

Filters are the most popular treatment method for backpackers and travelers in underdeveloped countries. The better ones can handle significant volumes of water, and they don't introduce chemicals that taste bad and may produce side effects. You should be aware that filters are not all equivalent. The higher-end ones have prefilters to remove silt and other particles before they reach the microfilter. Microfilters that filter to 0.2 microns remove some important bacteria that pass through 0.5 micron filters. (The filter specifications indicate the largest size particle that will pass through, so a 0.2 micron filter is more effective than a 0.5 micron one.) Neither of these filters removes viruses, which are generally much smaller than protozoa or bacteria. The better filters, like the MSR Hyperflow, are very effective for most uses, but they will not remove viruses either.

Water purifiers are typically filters that also use iodine resin or another method to kill viruses and a carbon filter to remove certain chemical contaminants. The most widely accepted lightweight purifier is the First Need XL. Conservative testers like the U.S. Centers for Disease Control have not yet tested the claims of these purifiers, nor the chlorine dioxide and ultraviolet light systems mentioned below.

Chemical methods are probably the most appropriate for infrequent water treatment when using water from streams is a worry. Iodine and chlorine have long been used, with iodine being the more effective. The taste of iodine is distinctive, and most find it unpleasant. (If the alternative is bicycle touring with a bad case of diarrhea, you should be able to put up with the taste.) Iodine tablets, such as Globaline, Coughlan's, and Potable-Aqua, can be found at lightweight camping stores. Follow the manufacturer's directions, and pay attention to expiration dates.

The most popular new chemical treatment for drinking water is chlorine dioxide (ClO_2). It is unstable, so it is carried in 2 bottles and mixed just before you use it. It is effective against many pathogens, has no unpleasant taste, and breaks down rapidly enough that it won't kill the bacteria in your gut that help you digest food (causing diarrhea). The most popular product is Pristine ClO2 water treatment. Note that while it is marketed as being effective against protozoa (cryptosporidium and giardia), some reports in the scientific literature indicate that protozoa are resistant to the treatment.

Note that chemical treatments are less effective in cold water and water with particulates. Silty water should be allowed to settle or be filtered before treatment, and you should allow extra time and extra chemicals if water is cold or still cloudy.

The latest water treatment method is ultraviolet-C light, generated with a small battery-operated device with which you stir the water for a short time. The water has to be clear (some devices are sold with prefilters), but water temperature is not an issue, as it is with chemical treatment. The commercially available models are quite lightweight and are made by SteriPen.

Carrying Food in Bear Country

Bears present a significant problem in some areas. Bears forage actively for food, and any food you are carrying could easily become a meal for a bear while you are tucked away in your tent. When you're bike camping in bear country, you need to pay special attention to food storage. Having a tent or a pannier ripped open by a bear in search of carelessly stored food can ruin a trip. It can also be deadly for the bear, because bears that learn to go after human food often end up being destroyed by wildlife managers. You should take particular precautions in bear country in late summer and fall. The average black bear getting ready for hibernation has to consume approximately 40,000 calories a day, so it becomes a single-minded food-finding and eating machine.

Bears are intelligent; they have eyesight similar to ours and an extremely acute sense of smell. In places frequented by campers, the bears have learned to defeat casual preventive measures. When you see expensive outdoor refuse containers with bear-proof lids on your tour, they should be a clue that you need to pay attention. In some national forests and parks in the West and some state lands in California and Montana, you are *required* to have approved bear-proof containers when you are camping. There are places all over the United States where bears can pose a significant problem, even in Florida.

When you are camping in bear country, it is very important to keep your food and all scented toiletries well away from your tent for safety. To avoid unpleasant incidents, you also should store food and toiletries in a bear cache. An organized campsite may have bear caches available. These are typically metal boxes with latching mechanisms that bears can't open.

When a bear cache isn't available, most people hang food and toiletries in a stuff sack or a pannier suspended from a tree, well off the ground and some distance from the trunk or branches. Take a 100-foot length of synthetic cord, such as parachute cord, tie a weight to one end, and toss it over a suitable tree branch. Then tie your bag to one end, haul it up, and tie off the other end. The bag should be at least 10 feet off the ground, 6 feet from the trunk, and 4 feet below any branches. It should also be at least 100 feet from your tent. Note that while this will work fine in most places, bears in some locations have learned to outsmart us humans—which is why some land managers now require bear-proof containers.

If you're traveling much in bear country, particularly if you are stealth camping, the best solution is a bear barrel or canister (backpacker's cache) made of ABS or other composites and available from light-weight camping suppliers. You can strap a bear barrel to the top of your rear rack or use the lighter-weight Ursack (www.ursack.com). The Ursack is made from lightweight, flexible, "bullet proof" fabric and is used in the same way as the bear barrel. All these measures are valuable in protecting your food from smaller mammals, from mice and voles to raccoons.

Whatever protective measures you use, camping practices are the most important factor in avoiding bear problems. Cook away from your tent. One very effective method is to stop and cook an hour early, and then move on before you camp, so that your camp is free of food and cooking odors. Do not put any food or equipment that has been in contact with food in your tent. Be careful about items like toothpaste, insect repellent, and sunscreen; they should be in the cache, or at least well away from your tent.

Touring

16

Trip Planning, Route Finding, and Precautions

Whatever style of tour you want to take—either relying on conventional accommodations or using the self-contained approach where you're mostly camping out—good planning is critical to experiencing a trip that's enjoyable, relaxing, and safe. This chapter concentrates on some of the issues that are common to credit-card touring and self-contained travel. It covers planning, finding your way, and staying safe. The following two chapters cover issues specific to touring using commercial accommodations (Chapter 17) and self-contained touring, where you carry camping gear on the bike (Chapter 18).

Wherever you are and whatever your style, your bicycle and your unusual mode of traveling may provide a social introduction. People may think you're weird, but few are likely to be hostile, apart from the rare character in a pickup who throws a beer can in your direction. Most people are friendly toward bicycle tourists and curious about their stories. Many will invite you to dinner or provide helpful local advice. Even where language barriers exist, pointing and pantomime will get you a long way.

Take the time to say hello to the people you meet or who are camped next door in a campground. It will make your tour more interesting, and it will be helpful to the next cyclist who happens along.

Planning the Trip

Bike touring encapsulates some of the most captivating aspects of travel, and planning a trip is rewarding in its own right. Experienced touring cyclists have varying preferences for planning a trip. Your initial planning should include the style of your trip (essentially, where will you be sleeping at night?), estimated mileages you plan to cover, your equipment requirements, and the expected costs. Beyond that, the scope of planning can vary a lot. You can choose to pore over maps for weeks and create a detailed itinerary, while researching natural history, interesting places along the way, and side trips you might make; or you can draft a preliminary route in one evening and then navigate the details from the seat of your bike.

Trips to the far corners of the world, of course, require the most planning, but they can also be the most fun to plan. Poring over maps, guides, travel narratives, and other information about faraway tours is an adventure in itself, and it makes the final tour far more interesting. You develop a feeling for the places where you plan to tour, a list of things you want to see, and at least a general idea of the likely costs.

Many cyclists prefer to lay out a general plan for the trip and then decide on specifics as they go along. Anyone can do this successfully, but it is recommended that for your initial tours you plan things fairly thoroughly. You'll still find lots of occasions when you have to adjust your plans because of contingencies, miscalculations, or interesting experiences that you hadn't anticipated. Every bicycle tour is full of surprises, but for your first few tours it is good to have some structure in which those surprises can occur. Later on, when you've gained some experience with the distances you can travel under various circumstances, and you know how to find accommodations in strange places and routes around unexpected closures, you can act more spontaneously and take on freeform trips with confidence. In any case, don't become so wedded to your program that you can't step outside the box.

If you're just starting out as a bike tourist, you might plan a few short trips close to home and then move on to longer ones as you gain experience and confidence. Or you might begin by planning a much longer trip, and then travel the first couple of legs of the route as an introduction. For instance, plan a four-week self-contained trip starting from your house that you want to take in the near future. Then follow the first or the final section of the route on a weekend or a one-week trip. This will give you a good idea of whether your planning, equipment, and training are adequate before you embark on the longer trek.

Equipment requirements depend on the type of touring you are doing, so they are discussed in more detail in the next two chapters. Some generalized equipment lists are included in the Resources section at the back of the book. However, coming up with the details and necessary modifications are what planning is for. If you are doing a tour in populated areas with a lot of retail establishments, the water containers that fit on your bike may be more than adequate. If you are planning a tour in the deserts of the intermountain American West, you'll need to put a lot more thought into this issue. Similar considerations apply to maps (paper or electronic), repair kits, and a host of other issues.

Planning for Different Touring Styles

Some cyclists, especially those touring roof to roof, plan their trips completely beforehand, making reservations in advance and holding to a particular schedule. This method may be a necessity if you're traveling in a popular tourist area during the busy season, because otherwise it may be impossible to find a place to stay.

Others may prefer to do some advance preparation but leave the details flexible. This approach allows for adjustments based on weather, physical conditioning, route changes that suggest themselves along the way, and interesting adventures that may pop up during the tour. Pick a general route, plan the overall mileage you need to cover each day, and take some maps and lists of possible places to stay or camp. These can be adjusted on a day-to-day basis. Depending on the circumstances, you can call a day or two in advance for reservations or just wait until you arrive in town in the afternoon to find a place to stay.

How this works in practice depends on where you are touring. If you are staying in rooms for let in Europe or *pensións* in Latin America, you will probably do fine as long as you have a few addresses and phone numbers in a particular town and it's low season. If the first place you try is full, the host or hostess will have friends and will be willing to call around to find you another place. This is often the case—though a bit less reliably—at mom-and-pop motels in the less-populated parts of the U.S.

Self-contained tourists usually can be more flexible in their planning. You might start with a set of detailed bike maps like those covering the Adventure Cycling routes (see "Printed Maps" later in this chapter for more information). These include detailed routes, locations of supplies, paid accommodations, and campgrounds along the route. If you take one of these routes, you can also be sure that the people you see along the way will be used to cyclists because so many use them. There will still be plenty of surprises, ranging from poor routing and closed stores to changes resulting from road construction or temporary closures.

Another possible starting point is to peruse some day-by-day tour narratives at one of the Web sites listed in the Resources section, particularly www.crazyguyona bike.com, which includes journals from nearly every style of touring imaginable. If one of them inspires you, you have a good start in planning your own trip.

Estimating Daily Mileage

When you're planning a tour, you need to estimate the daily mileage you can cover. After you've done a few long tours, you'll have a good idea of the distance you can ride each a day with maximum enjoyment. For your first tours, however, it is important to be realistic and avoid trying to cover excessive distances. You should start by keeping track of your normal training and recreational rides, at least some of which should be rides carrying your touring gear on the bike. You should also do at least a couple of weekend tours carrying your gear before embarking on a tour lasting two weeks or more. If you are planning to do a fully loaded tour crossing the United States, you need to do some short tours with *all* your gear.

You'll need to experiment and think about your physical conditioning and what you enjoy, but for your first longer tour, you probably should plan on daily distances that are one-third to one-half what you can cover comfortably on a typical day ride. On a long tour, you won't enjoy yourself if you are desperately pushing to finish each day. You'll be tired for a few days, and then your pace will pick up as your conditioning improves and you fall into a routine, but you will also have to deal with weather, occasional fatigue, interesting diversions, and other unanticipated changes in plan. If a pass over the Rocky Mountains is closed by an avalanche, you might have an interesting stay in a nearby town, but your schedule will inevitably change.

To the degree that you can, it is also a good idea to plan some options. If you've planned 60-mile days, try to figure an alternate, equally satisfying route that will require 45-mile days. Don't forget that a lot of rain, days of headwinds, or mechanical troubles can drastically change your plans. If you've planned with some flexibility, such hazards don't have to ruin a trip. In fact, they will make it more interesting, but only if you haven't chained yourself to an ironclad schedule. On trips of two weeks or more, allow for an occasional day for rest, doing laundry, and walking around town.

Finding Your Way

Studying maps in anticipation of a long tour is one of the great pleasures of bicycle touring. That pleasure is greatly enhanced these days by the availability of information on the Web. Where it was once quite difficult to find out what places were worth visiting near some small town in the United States, Chile, or the Czech Republic, a Google search is now likely to bring up a wealth of information, and some of it will even be accurate.

You can plan your trip using paper road maps, specially prepared bicycle maps, or commercially available trip-planning map software, like DeLorme's Topo USA or Garmin's City Navigator. Or, if you have access to a reasonably fast Internet connection, you can use the free maps and software available at maps.google.com (see "Google Maps and Google Earth" later in this chapter for more information). GPS units that include detailed maps and mapping software can also be purchased.

Printed Maps

Finding maps of the right scale and with the right information is the first challenge. The appropriate scale varies a good deal, depending on the location. If you are carrying the maps on tour, you need a map scale that will not require a trailer just to hold the maps. In addition, a full set of very detailed maps is quite expensive. Paper maps that are printed at a useful scale can be voluminous. For example, one of the Adventure Cycling transcontinental routes (Transamerica, Northern Tier, or Southern Tier) is likely to comprise a dozen maps, and you would probably supplement those with some local maps (Yosemite National Park, Cincinnati, Black Hills, or whatever). Most transcontinental cyclists break them into packets and have a friend mail them general delivery to intermediate post offices.

You'll want to start with maps of about state scale. For those, often the free state maps produced the Highway Department or Transportation Department are the best. Many states even produce bicycle-oriented maps. Some of these are listed in the Resources section, but it is always worth contacting the Department of Transportation or the Department of Tourism of the state in which you are interested. The Internet makes finding them much easier than it used to be. Persistence pays off. State employees are usually over-worked and underfunded, but the information is often there, and you'll find lots of helpful people if you try.

As you proceed to more detailed planning, maps that have more detail are essential, because state-scale maps don't usually show a lot of the roads that are most suited to bicycle touring. In Utah or Nevada, you may well find that a state map has all the roads of inter-est clearly marked; in more populous areas, this will definitely not be true. For many parts of the country, some of the best road maps with the right level of detail are produced by AAA, and these are free to members. Bicycling organizations in individual states are also good sources of information. Finally, the state-by-state atlases published by DeLorme include topographic information and have a useful scale for bicycles. Try the one for your own state or a nearby one that has good possibilities for bicycle touring.

Coming closest to ready-made tour plans are the various bicycle touring maps. The pioneer ones for the United States are those compiled and published by Adventure Cycling Association (see page 437), origi-nally known as Bikecentennial—it did its first tour and route across the United States in 1976, in commemo-ration of the bicentennial anniversary of the country. This route crossed from Oregon to Virginia, cover-ing approximately 4,250 miles. It was then ridden by around 2,000 cyclists. Although updated, the route is still a popular transcontinental tour.

Adventure Cycling (ACA) now publishes guides and maps for a score of long-distance touring routes. These include three transcontinental routes, many long-distance regional tours, several fascinating and scenic historical routes (Lewis and Clark Trail, Underground Railroad), in addition to the Great Divide mountain bike route, which parallels the Continental Divide from Mexico to Canada. Many permutations of the transcon-tinental routes are possible, using some regional tours. To see Adventure Cycling's mapped tours on a map of the United States, go to www.adventurecycling.org/routes/nbrn/NBRNFeb07.jpg. Overall, the organization has mapped nearly 40,000 miles of bike routes in the United States.

Even if you are not planning to follow one of ACA's routes, it is worth buying the maps to take a look at the information provided. ACA tries to follow low-traffic roads, deal with issues like river crossings (many major bridges are closed to bicycles), and provide information on camping, motels, and bed-and-breakfast establishments. Going through one of the ACA packages provides an education on what you need to plan your own route. Some cyclists prefer to shorten some of the ACA routes by taking shorter, more direct, more heavily traveled roads in some places, but the ACA routes provide excellent examples and a lot of detailed information. Note also that the ACA routes are available free to GPS users (see "GPS Systems" later in this chapter).

Many other maps and guidebooks oriented to cyclists in the United States, Canada, and overseas are also available. Several are listed in "Map Sources" on pages 437–445, and quite a few others are available. Some are free, either electronically or in print. Others are a bargain for the small cost at which they are offered.

The computer-based maps described below in connection with GPS systems are often a real bargain and are generally quite up-to-date. Every map, printed or computerized, has mistakes, oversights, and outdated information, but even if you are planning to use computer-based maps and a GPS for your final planning, starting off with some large-scale paper maps is usually a good way to achieve an overview.

Google Maps and Google Earth

You may prefer to avoid technological solutions and their myriad complexities. If so, you should rely on paper maps for getting around and skip this section and "GPS Systems" later in this chapter. This choice is a matter of personal preference, and there is a large contingent of touring cyclists who studiously avoid the intrusion of computer technology on bicycle touring generally.

However, by using Google Maps on the Web, you can create a personal tour route fairly quickly, from a weekend trip to a transcontinental one. It may take you a few hours to learn the interface—since it is Web-based, it doesn't follow standard rules—but the possibilities are remarkable.

To give a quick example, open Google Maps (maps .google.com) in a Web browser, zoom in to the location of your house or enter your address as a starting point, right-click and pick the "Directions from here" option, zoom out a little, choose a place perhaps 50 miles away from your home, place the cursor on it, right-click and choose "Directions to here." Repeat this process as many times as you like, selecting "Add a destination" each time. Google Maps will draw a route and list directions for the entire route you have just defined. Clicking the "Avoid highways" box at the top left of the directions will change the route to avoid interstates and other high-speed roads. By choosing the "Walking" option to the left of the "Get directions" drop-down menu, you'll get a route that is very close to an optimal routing for cyclists. It will automatically avoid restricted-access roads, like most interstate highways.

In addition to adding new points, you can click and drag the location bubble on the map to a new end location. Note that the "Walking" option is new at the time of this writing and coverage is still spotty. (The option is still far from perfect in dealing with restrictions in non-urban areas—tunnels, bridges, and other areas of concern for cyclists.) As with all mapping, you need to maintain a healthy skepticism and realize that the maps are mainly oriented to drivers, not cyclists. Restrictions on bicycles are rarely noted, and bike paths and pedestrian/bicycle underpasses or bridges are usually missing from the database. Most importantly, features that are mapped change constantly (roads, trails, buildings, restrictions, and intersections), so maps are always out of date. This is inevitable, so you'll have to make allowances. Updates that affect drivers have far higher priority for map-makers (print-based or electronic) than those that affect only pedestrians and cyclists, so you should assume that maps will nearly always be more obsolete for the cyclist than the motorist. This is not to imply that electronic resources are not useful to touring cyclists. On the contrary, they are invaluable, and they are generally more likely to be up-to-date than paper maps. However, as with paper maps, you should never assume that the information you find is wholly reliable. Use it as a guide, and figure out what is real based on your own observations. In this respect, finding your way is like other aspects of cycling—it is a window on the real world. Don't be misled by the expectations that others have provided. Believe your own observations, and act accordingly.

You can search for motels, campgrounds, or restaurants at locations along your route in Google Maps, and their locations will show up on the map, along with addresses and phone numbers. Ratings and sometimes pricing from commercial rating companies are also available with a click. Of course, you have to treat this information with a grain of salt, but that is true of any map, guidebook, or other source. You can print maps and directions from Google Maps, save them to your personal folder, share them on the Web, view the route on satellite photos or terrain view, and export them to Google Earth.

The free version of Google Earth (downloaded from the Web) shows you an amazingly rich view of terrain, roads, and a wealth of other information. You save files in .kml format, which is used to display geographic data in an Earth browser like Google Earth and Google Maps. These saved files can be used with GPS receivers (see "GPS Systems" below), so you can create a preliminary route in Google Maps and either print maps or transfer routes by hand to other paper maps. You can also transfer the route to a GPS and use it with any maps that you've bought for the GPS or that came with it.

All this may be enough technology to send you screaming for a decent collection of paper maps, but the possibilites of connecting these technological solutions are important for anyone who is so inclined.

Google Maps and Google Earth are not limited to the United States. Want to create a preliminary route to ride from Regensburg, Germany, to Budapest, Hungary? You can do it. On the other hand, Google Maps knows nothing about bike paths along the Danube (no cars allowed), so they won't appear on the route you generated. You can refine the Regensburg–Budapest route manually, using the aerial photography, but you won't know anything about what is open or closed, and there are deficiencies in the satellite views. Technology provides you with wonderful possibilities, but you have to accept that it has weird and arbitrary limitations and inaccuracies. Sometimes you'll have to revert to old-fashioned research to resolve the issues.

Coverage is also highly variable. Argentina is a blank slate in Google Maps at the time of this writing. In Google Earth, Argentina at least exists, though the satellite images are far more rudimentary than those covering the United States. Another interesting example is the Yucatán Peninsula in Mexico. You can find Mérida in Google Maps, and Tulúm as well, but even though the major roads are mapped, Google Maps doesn't have a clue how to create a route between them, even for automobiles. These two examples show that satellite imagery, maps, and routing databases are distinct. They are all imperfect and variable in coverage and quality, and the coverage and resolution can be quite different between the various datasets, creating anomalies that are inexplicable to the average user, who doesn't know how the underlying software works. In the example cited, a major highway links Mérida and Tulúm, but Google Maps' routing database doesn't know it is there, so the routing algorithms aren't able to utilize it. These anomalies change on a daily basis in electronic databases, as well as on paper maps. Don't put too much faith in the magic of technology or the data on the Internet. Human intelligence and analysis are still required!

You know these limitations intuitively when you are looking at paper maps, because you have learned to read them. Maps can be out of date, incomplete, or just wrong, and all of us have encountered instances when they were inaccurate. The same is true of computer databases, and they tend to integrate many pieces in ways that are deliberately concealed from the user (when everything is accurate, you don't want to know the details). There are always lots of errors and deficiencies in the underlying datasets, but you only care about them and notice them when they affect you. All the same problems exist in commercial mapping software, including paper maps and routing databases built into GPS receivers. In particular, even commercial routing programs that have options to create bicycle routes often do not catch bicycle restrictions on roads, such as major routes that are closed to bicycles because of tunnels.

The point is that all compendia of human knowledge are imperfect, and maps are excellent examples. Many people have had enough unfortunate experiences with paper maps to understand their limitations intuitively. Electronic maps and databases are just as inaccurate, but many people don't sense this immediately, because they have an inordinate faith in electronic systems, and they are oblivious to the actual source of whatever data they are viewing on a screen.

GPS Systems

If you want the ultimate ease in planning routes and locating yourself along the way and you favor technological solutions, a global positioning system (GPS) will suit you perfectly. If you are a traditionalist, you're not technologically inclined, or you'd just rather plan things out on paper maps, you should skip this section. There are many advantages to old-fashioned paper maps.

This book will not detail the multiplicity of GPS options, which change almost daily so that detailed recommendations would be obsolete by the time you read this book. If you already own a handheld GPS, you'll want to look at what software and maps are available to create appropriate routes and waypoints to be loaded into the device you already own. If you have a newer unit that has built-in or loadable maps, you should check to see what additional options are available in loadable maps for your receiver. Recent GPS models can be loaded with maps that are extremely good and very detailed (but also rather expensive).

GPS technologies, especially the features of available receivers, change constantly. The most sophisticated modern models include built-in or loadable maps and programming that allows the user to request a route from A to B, using roads with specific criteria and calling up instructions and visual maps along the way. Older GPS units are capable of determining your location, storing planned routes, and directing you to the next waypoint.

As electronic gadgetry converges in function, you can now get cell phones, MP3 players, and GPS units in combined packages. Smart phones are already appearing with GPS built in or added, combined with mapping services transmitted over cellular nets, but the practical utility, reliability, and receiver quality remain to be evaluated. Just keep in mind that the functionality of each service has to be judged independently.

How GPS Works. All GPS units receive signals from 24 satellites operated by the U.S. military, each orbiting approximately 11,000 miles above the Earth. The satellites broadcast microwave signals that can be used by a GPS receiver to calculate its position on the Earth's surface, using a worldwide coordinate system and very precise time data. A GPS receiver (the unit you purchase and carry, technically abbreviated GPSr) is both a microwave radio receiver and a computer that can process the signals from the satellites in view, calculate your position, and in the case of the newer units, plot it on a displayable map. The GPS unit can store positions, routes, tracks, and maps so that you can plan your routes in advance and then follow them on your tour.

GPS Capabilities. To get an idea of the possibilities at the time of writing, take a look at the DeLorme GPS PN-20 with Earthmate and Topo USA software or the Garmin Colorado 400t, which comes preloaded with U.S. topographic maps. These GPS units weigh only a little over 5 ounces, and each has U.S. or some other street maps built in, along with more limited world-wide maps. Associated software allows you to plan routes in advance on a computer,* and then load those planned routes into the GPS. That is, you can load a group of maps onto your computer, use software combined with your own preferences to plan your tour, and then load the tour route into the GPS unit, which you mount on your handlebars. With an older GPS unit, you'll have waypoint data, so on the tour you'll know the distance and direction to the next waypoint. With the newest units, you'll have a map on which your position, the next waypoint, and the roads between will be displayed. In other words, you'll not only have the map at your fingertips, you'll also have your route plotted on the map and turn-by-turn directions along the way, if you want them.

The combination is a technology geek's delight. However, those who aren't technologically inclined are likely to find them frustrating, and advertised features may not work as described or may only be available

---

* Mac users who can't or don't want to use a Windows virtual machine like Parallels will want to examine the Mac OS alternatives carefully before deciding on a GPS/mapping software package. GPS manufacturers generally are oriented toward Windows-based PCs and provide Mac OS support that ranges from none to poor. Garmin is the best in this respect. For conversion issues, go to www.gpsbabel.org, which provides programs for converting formats and manipulating GPS data that run on a number of platforms. Linux users will find virtually no native support from GPS manufacturers.

at extra cost. Basically, when everything works, you can create a route by picking a starting and an ending point on maps displayed on your computer, plus any intermediate locations you want to go through. You can set criteria such as staying off interstates—critical for routing a bike tour, but not included in all routing software. You get the route on the map, a GPS route, maps, and elevation profiles for climbs. Routes can be loaded into your GPS unit for the tour. If you have the right combination of software, maps may be loadable onto the GPS as well. All these same functions can be achieved on the GPS unit itself, which is a powerful special-purpose computer, but doing the routing on the GPS will take much longer than on a PC because of its limited interface (no keyboard, small screen, etc.) and reduced computing power.

This combination of maps, GPS, and routing can provide remarkable convenience and map accuracy, but you have to decide whether the entire high-tech package appeals to you and whether it is worth the expense and the trouble. GPS maps and routing are a huge convenience when they work, but things can go wrong. Don't forget, for example, that dead batteries mean dead maps.

Finally, computerized GPS systems entail the typical frustrations of all modern computer systems. Marketing campaigns promise particular capabilities, but you find that there is always a gotcha. You bought the GPS unit with built-in maps and an interface with your computer, together with a routing system that works on that computer. And you find that the maps you bought for the GPS don't work on the computer—unless you pay an extra $600. This will not be a surprise to anyone who is knowledgeable about modern technological systems.

GPS features and systems. A variety of additional features on some GPS units are favored by some tourists, ranging from heart rate and cadence monitors to barometric altitude sensors. And the prospect of combining GPS with a cell phone will appeal to many. In all such cases, the quality of the maps on the GPS should be evaluated on their own merits, independent of other packaged features. The many auxiliary features, like cadence and heart monitors, are not discussed in this book. The only function considered here is route-finding, and for that purpose, positioning and map-ping capabilities are the important features.

One disadvantage of the DeLorme PN-20 illumi-nates a major problem with all GPS systems on the mar-ket today. Only U.S. maps are available for the PN-20—it is called the Earthmate, but it is really the USmate. A similar triumph of marketing over accuracy is typi-fied by Garmin's "North America" products—named by someone who either doesn't know or doesn't care that Mexico is part of North America. Garmin markets maps covering some parts of Mexico, but they are not included in the North America packages.

While all GPS makers support the ability to export and import GPS waypoints, routes, and often tracks in transferable formats, every unit with maps (built-in or loadable) uses proprietary mapping formats. Thus, if the GPS you buy doesn't have or doesn't accept maps for an area you are planning to tour, you are out of luck. You can use third-party mapping software to plan tours and generate waypoints or routes, but you can't get maps that will load into your GPS unless they are provided by your manufacturer, a cooperating third party, or someone who has cracked the manu-facturer's format and produced purportedly compat-ible maps.

GPS units can be very useful without built-in maps. Some tourists use PC mapping software to cre-ate routes and load them onto older GPS units, which don't have the capability to display maps. You can use any GPS to locate yourself by coordinates or along a route that you have preloaded, but the built-in map fea-tures of a newer GPS unit will be worthless without the manufacturer's maps. You also often have to dig pretty deep to find out just what is really included in adver-tised maps. (Note that newer units typically have faster and more accurate positioning features. The technical details aren't discussed here, but don't assume that all GPS circuitry is the same.)

At the time this is written, of the major GPS makers, Garmin has the best worldwide map coverage; Magellan has maps for a few areas outside the United States; and DeLorme has extremely good coverage of the United States but none elsewhere. Mio, which was first established in Asia and Europe, has models for a number of regions worldwide and claims it will offer maps for additional areas via SD card—a removable memory card. Note that when you purchase maps for GPS units, the shelf life is limited. Some free updates may be provided, but others require an additional purchase. Maps that you buy are often locked into a single GPS unit, so if you buy a new receiver from the same manufacturer a few years later, you may have to buy a whole new set of maps.

Despite the skepticism expressed in this section, the mapping information you can carry in a modern GPS is truly breathtaking, and it is very cost-effective. Using the old-style planning method, you can spend a lot of money on paper maps and still find errors and segments that are unpredictably out of date. Frequently, with GPS and computer-based map systems, you can download updates, often free for products you've purchased and registered. Try that with your paper set of USGS maps of a region of the United States or Ordnance Survey maps of Great Britain!

Mapping information and routing databases are very expensive to create and maintain. The GPS manufacturers and mapping software developers provide enormously valuable information for reasonable prices. However, given the proliferation of proprietary formats, typically using cartographic data that began as taxpayer-funded government mapping, it is to be hoped that those businesses will move toward common standard formats so that you don't have to buy a new GPS when you are heading to Europe or Latin America.

It is also worth noting that route files for all the Adventure Cycling routes are available free for downloading from their Web site. If you have mapping software and maps loaded on your GPS, this effectively means you have maps for the Adventure Cycling routes, along with planned routes, turns, campsites, restaurants, and motels. The routes also match paper maps that can be purchased from Adventure Cycling.

Staying Safe on Tour

By and large, bicycle touring is a pretty safe activity, with traffic being the principal hazard. Traffic danger can be minimized by developing good riding skills. You can also plan tours on rail-to-trail routes that are completely free of motor vehicles. Spills can occur anywhere, however, so you should carry a first aid kit and have some basic first aid skills, as discussed in "First Aid" later in this chapter. And one hazard can be a major issue at times—dogs.

Dealing with Dogs

Local dogs, which have an instinct to defend their territory and to chase moving cyclist-sized organisms, can present a major hazard in some circumstances. Most situations can be handled with a little knowledge and the right attitude, but there are times when these are insufficient. On those occasions it helps to be prepared. The hazards arise from the fact that you are pretty vulnerable. You need your hands to steer, your feet may be clipped in, and in any case outrunning the dog(s) and keeping your balance requires you to keep your feet firmly on the pedals, not flailing to the side trying to fend off a dog. You won't have anything that you can grab to fend the dog off, unless you've attached it somewhere specifically for the purpose. A frame pump is often pressed into service, but it isn't usually very good for discouraging a biting dog, and you'll almost certainly ruin the pump if you try.

The hazard is that a dog can easily clamp down on a foot or ankle or get tangled in one of your wheels, causing you to crash. If there are several dogs, this possibility is exacerbated, and it is quite common for there to be more than one. Dogs are as instinctive about running in packs as they are about chasing prey.

There are a number of strategies for dealing with dogs you may encounter in rural areas. (This book won't discuss problem dogs in your own neighborhood, except to note that the real problem is with the owner and that is what has to be handled. Try talking with the owner, and if that doesn't work go to the police or animal control officers.) Typically, along rural roads, the owner won't be nearby and may not be interested in calling off the dog, so you should assume you have to deal with the problem yourself.

If you are on the flats or on a downhill and already past the dog, you can probably just ride away from it. Dogs are usually pretty fast in a sprint, but their speed doesn't last long, and they lose interest as they get farther from their territory. You can't count on these factors, however, so don't exhaust yourself, and use the time to plan your next tactic if outrunning the dog doesn't work. For a dog lunging at you from the front, you have to call on your emergency bike-handling skills.

Talking to the dog in a firm, confident voice will often do the trick. "Get up on the couch, now, Rover!" or "Go back to the chicken coop, Fido!" can get your voice in the right range. Panic is likely to have the wrong effect, and aggression can work either way, causing the dog to slink off or go after you with renewed vigor.

If these strategies fail, your remaining options depend on your preparation. If you are unprepared, the best possibility is usually to dismount on the opposite side from the dog and keep the bike between you and the dog. Picking up stones and throwing them (or pretending to pick up stones and throw them if real stones aren't available) will often work. Once you are standing on the ground, you're less vulnerable, and you can usually work through the situation.

The best defense you can carry is a pressurized canister of pepper spray. Again, it has to be clipped where you can easily get it when you're riding—otherwise it is worthless. Halt is a moderately effective type of spray intended for mail carriers, cyclists, and runners that can be purchased from cycling supply houses. Unfortunately, the formula has been diluted somewhat, and while it usually works, it is not as effective as it could be. Far more effective is full-strength pepper spray, intended for disabling human attackers or as bear spray. It works, it won't permanently injure the animal, and it is justified in dealing with any dog that persists in attacking a bicyclist.

If you get pepper spray, it is important to practice using it beforehand, just in case you ever need it. With Halt, get an extra canister for practice, and only carry an unused, fully charged one on the road. Suppliers who sell full-strength pepper spray also sell inert practice canisters, and you should get one of those to use for practice. Try it in the backyard first, then try it from the bike, aiming for the area that would be occupied by an attacking dog. Spraying into the wind will obviously accomplish the opposite from the intended purpose, and worse. Along with the spray and the practice canister, you should get neutralizing wipes to use on your hands, and you should carry them next to the canister, just in case you get any spray on your hands or some is carried back by the wind. In an actual situation, don't ever spray into the wind; wait until you have a clear shot. An attacking dog that is hit in the face with pepper spray will have time to regret its mistake, and it may be less likely to go after the next cyclist who comes down the road.

First Aid

Except for a few cycling-specific issues, I will not spend much time on first aid, nor on first aid kits. This is not because they are unimportant. Acquiring good first aid skills is strongly recommended for bike touring. Taking standard Red Cross first aid courses is a good way to start, supplemented by any outdoor emergency medical training sessions (often oriented toward climbers, backpackers, and river runners) that are available in your area. If you trained in first aid or emergency medicine years ago, you should take a refresher. If you want to learn some of the issues beyond standard first aid, which assumes that emergency services are readily available, a good place to start is the most recent edition of *Medicine for Mountaineering* by James Wilkerson.

The first aid kit is a very important item to carry, but it has to be tailored to your tour and your skills. Carrying a large kit filled with items you don't know how to use is not helpful. One of the best ways to prepare for dealing with emergencies on a trip is to put together a first aid kit. You will then know exactly what is in your kit, along with the intended use for everything. If you are doing a long tour in the Northwest Territories or the Australian Outback, you'll need a more complete first aid kit and set of skills than you would in populated parts of the United States.

Two issues are worth calling out because they are specific to cycling: road rash and saddle sores. A spill on a bike is likely to result in abrasive wounds over some surface of skin. Scrub the wound and get the dirt and grit out as soon as possible. This is painful, but it becomes more painful the longer you wait, and if you go to an emergency room, they will need to do exactly the same thing. Betadine-impregnated swabs are a good thing to have in your first aid kit for cleaning wounds. Just make sure to ask whether anyone in your group is allergic to iodine. Betadine is a water-based iodine preparation, and it is an excellent disinfectant that does not sting, so it doesn't induce any additional pain. Take the time to get all the grit out of the wound— otherwise it will have to be done later, when the wound would otherwise be healing. Materials with non-stick surfaces are important for bandaging road rash. Sterile trauma burn dressings work well.

Saddle sores can form from combined friction, bruising, and infection. The most important treatment is prevention. Take care of your sitting anatomy, change your shorts, and don't let sores develop. Early treatment is the next-best alternative, beginning with keeping any developing sores washed and cleaned with an antimicrobial solution. If you want to continue to ride, cleanliness is the most important prescription. Cyclists have all sorts of recommended topical treatments. One is to use antiseptic cream after washing and to cover any sores with polyvinyl chloride film, which is used for covering burns. A roll of this film will be sufficiently sterile if you cut off a couple of inches from the exposed end before cutting the length you need.

Cell Phones

If you always carry a cell phone, then it won't occur to you to tour without it, and you will be well aware of issues associated with keeping it charged. Coverage, or lack thereof, may be less familiar. Many touring cyclists don't like carrying cell phones on tour; this is a matter of personal preference. A phone can be useful in emergencies, and the convenience of cell phones when you are touring is undeniable—for example, for calling ahead to check accommodations as pay phones disappear from the landscape and pay phones coupled with usable phone books fade into history.

However, cell coverage is often spotty along the best touring routes. If you carry a cell phone, consider it to be a convenience that may or may not work when you need it most. And if you aren't used to carrying a cell phone, remember that you also have to carry a charger and work out a routine to ensure that you use it.

If you're considering picking up a cell phone just for touring, look for plans that allow you to prepay for anywhere, anytime minutes that don't expire for the longest time possible and that roll over if you purchase more before expiration. Plans change constantly, and signal coverage varies between carriers. Internet research will help, but prepaid plans are the ones phone companies are least interested in selling, so persistence is required.

For travel outside the United States, it is important to know that different national systems use different frequencies and protocols (encoding schemes), so you need to check on the standards where you are going unless you are planning to just buy a prepaid phone at your destination. Most U.S. systems, like Verizon and Sprint, use the CDMA protocol, which is incompatible with most of the world. T-Mobile and AT&T use GSM, like most of the world, but phones from these carriers are still often incompatible because of the frequencies used.

The most versatile phone is a quad-band unlocked GSM phone (not tied to a particular service). This can take SIM cards purchased locally and will work almost everywhere. The SIM card is what gives the phone its number (on a GSM phone), so if you want a number at which friends and family can reach you without calling them every time you change, you'll need a SIM card from a U.S. service that supports international calls. It will need to be activated for international service, and you'll want to find out the rules and charges. You should also be prepared to iron out the wrinkles that will inevitably occur. Or you can buy a SIM card locally in each country you visit. This is usually the cheapest alternative, but you will not have the same phone number. A map of worldwide GSM coverage can be found at www.coveragemaps .com/gsmposter_world.htm.

A good source of basic information on international cell use, together with cost-saving tips, can be found at www.thetravelinsider.info/2002/0308.htm. On choices for touring in remote places, see www .triumf.ca/people/oram/cycling/ta_electronics.html.

Dealing with Weather Surprises

Apart from wind and rain, which you expect on a tour, events occur that you can't just grit your teeth and ride through. If you are doing a tour down the Atlantic Coast and a hurricane is heading up to meet you, it's time to change plans. If you see severe weather building up in the Midwest, you should immediately seek shelter, perhaps in an underpass. Then, if you actually see a tornado coming, you can retreat into the ditch with your bike.

During fire season, forest fires can also create situations where you have to change your plans as gracefully as possible. Diverting to a different route may be all that is necessary. On other occasions, you may just have to abort the trip.

17

Roof-to-Roof and Supported Tours

This chapter discusses some issues specific to tours that are not "fully loaded," that is, where you aren't carrying your shelter, cooking gear, and the like. Even if you enjoy doing self-supported tours, it can sometimes be a pleasant change to travel with less gear, perhaps with the chance to take a shower at the end of the day and to enjoy your evening meal without having to shop and do all the preparation.

Touring Roof to Roof

Even hard-core self-contained bicycle touring enthusiasts are likely to make some trips using conventional accommodations, a style often referred to as roof-to-roof or credit-card touring. In some populated areas, camping can be difficult or impossible, or it may require more chutzpah than you are willing to summon. There are, for example, a number of segments of the eastern seaboard of the United States where camping possibilities are quite limited. Many heavily populated regions in Europe provide few possibilities for camping. Some hardcore campers still manage to do guerrilla camping in such locales, but even many experienced campers find the approach unappealing.

Other reasons why many touring cyclists prefer to stop at motels, guesthouses, or other paid accomodations include the opportunity to take a shower and wash some clothes. Cyclists who want to cover a lot of ground while carrying a minimum of weight may prefer not to carry camping equipment and to avoid the need to shop for dinner and pick up enough water for cooking and rehydration. Several hours a day may be saved when you don't have to shop, set up and strike camp, and perhaps go out of your way to reach a camping spot. Other cyclists find it pleasant to take at least some trips where the day begins and ends with a comfortable bed, a hot shower, a secure place to leave the bike, and a convenient restaurant.

There are many kinds of tours that just work better when you stay in paid accommodations. If you want to tour the cathedrals of southern England, stop at historic cities, and take in some museums and Shakespearean plays, you will probably find that staying at bed and breakfasts fits with the experience and the schedule far better than trying to camp. Even many self-contained touring cyclists plan to stop at a motel every four or five days to clean up and get organized, or they do so along stretches of the tour where campgrounds are hard to find, such as urban areas.

How Much Will It Cost?

Tours using publicly accessible accommodations will vary a lot in cost, depending on your finances and preferences but also on where you are touring. You're going to pay a lot more on Cape Cod or in the Napa Valley than on state highways in Utah.

If you've followed one of the general planning methods described in Chapter 16, call or email a few places where you're thinking about staying and find out their room rates. Call a few restaurants where you might eat and ask for the prices of the entrees. Figure out how you'd like to eat. Some people always stop in restaurants, some always cook, and others do a little of both.

For example, on one trip that my wife and I did in England, we stopped for a pub lunch around noon, but restaurants opened too late for my wife's blood sugar, so we would pick up salad materials at a store in the afternoon and fix a salad at our B&B room in the evening. No stove was needed, just bowls and utensils. On most of my tours, even if I'm staying in motels, I usually get my food from grocery stores and cook at a picnic area or a park. Of course, this means that I carry a stove and a pot, even if I'm not camping out. If it is raining, I may stop at a restaurant, unless I'm camping.

For trips to other parts of the world, you'll probably have to consult guidebooks for at least some of your expense estimates. The Rough Guides, the Lonely Planet books, and the Moon travel guides are three series that tend to cover the range of accommodations and eating spots suitable for touring cyclists. See the Resources listings for other sources, such as cycling clubs abroad. They often have excellent lists of accommodations like bed and breakfasts and rooms for let. The Cyclists Touring Club in the United Kingdom is a good example.

Once you've done a little investigation, it should be quite straightforward to budget for your trip. If you are doing a long trip or going to a remote area, don't forget to budget for contingencies.

Don't Get Caught 50 Miles from the Next Roof

The most important aspect of preplanning your trip is to get essential information and to take it with you. Depending on where you are, this may consist of lists of accommodations and phone numbers in particular towns. In many parts of the western United States that are particularly attractive for bicycle touring, distances between motels and between sources of food and water can be long. If you aren't carrying camping gear, you don't want to leave a road junction and head for a motel that is 25 miles down the road at 3:00 p.m., only to arrive there at 5:00 p.m. and find it boarded up and out of business. Use your lists, call ahead to make sure the place you are headed to is open and has room, and avoid nasty surprises. If you don't have all the information with you, ask the locals, and keep trying until you find someone who actually seems to know the answer.

Of course these same rules apply when you are traveling abroad. If you are staying in rooms let out by locals, they will usually know everyone nearby who does the same thing, so be sure to ask. Even if there is a language barrier, sign language, pointing, and pantomime will work, as long as you have an attitude that induces people to want to help.

Plan appropriately for food and water. In areas of the western United States where water sources are spaced far apart, be sure to carry enough water containers (see "Water: Carrying, Storing and Purifying" on page 312), and fill them when you have a chance. Carry purification supplies, just in case. Stock up on food as well. Follow the suggestions offered under "How Much Will It Cost?" earlier in this chapter to make sure that the gas station where you are planning to fill up your water containers is still open. In the desert Southwest or in central Patagonia, running out of water is a serious situation.

Hostels and Other Low-Cost Accommodations

In many parts of the world there are extensive networks of accommodations for self-propelled travelers, variously referred to as hostels, backpacker accommodations, *hospedajes, residencials, pensións,* and so on. These facilities typically provide dormitory-style accommodations and sometimes semiprivate rooms for couples or foursomes, usually with shared bathrooms and shared cooking facilities. The implications of specific names vary a good deal with the country and the region, but if you do some planning in advance, you can arrive equipped with a set of addresses and phone numbers for a particular town, and even when they have no vacancies, proprietors will direct you to another place. If you speak the language well enough to be able to handle telephone conversations, you can call your destination when you reach a town. If you don't speak the local language, and if the proprietor of a destination cannot accommodate you, he or she will usually volunteer to phone a friend who also rents rooms, giving you directions that you might be able to understand. (It helps to have a pencil and pad handy to offer them as you try to understand rapid-fire instructions.)

The international youth hostel network has largely withered away, especially in the United States, but it is still worth checking into (see page 435). The convention for hostels was that travelers, mostly but not exclusively young, brought sheet sacks for bed linen and arrived on foot or by bicycle to find an inexpensive dormitory-style accommodation. The number of affiliated hostels in the United States has dropped to less than a hundred, and many states have none at all, so this is only an option for a few trips in the United States. In Europe, about 1,800 hostels are affiliated with the organization known as Hostelling International USA, so staying at a hostel may be practical on some trips. You can check locations online to see if any are located on or near your route. If so, it may be worth becoming a member of the organization to have access to European hostels.

Whether you are interested in this alternative is also obviously a matter of personal style and comfort, but hostels have the special advantage of connecting you automatically with both inexpensive places to stay and a support network you would never find otherwise. They don't discriminate on the basis of age or race, and you'll meet wonderful and interesting people with phenomenal linguistic capabilities if you try them out. Membership is inexpensive.

Apart from the youth hostel network, many parts of the world have large networks of pensións and similar facilities, which usually consist of rented rooms in private residences. They are typically somewhat more costly than the youth-oriented facilities just mentioned, but they are still inexpensive and provide an invaluable entrée to the local culture, coupled with more privacy than a college-like dormitory. This network of accommodations is widely available in underdeveloped countries, both in urban areas and on popular backpacking and student-travel routes. Travel guides like Lonely Planet, Rough Guide, and Moon list many of these accommodations.

The Warm Showers List

Another approach for accommodations is the "Warm Showers List," a network of thousands of cyclists worldwide who offer one another mutual hospitality. If you sign up for Warm Showers, you agree to host cyclists passing through your area on the basis of mutual convenience and advance agreement. In turn, you have access to contact information for other members of the Warm Showers List. The list has been in operation for 15 years, and it can be a great resource for many touring cyclists. It can be found at www.warmshowers.org.

If it fits with your life and preferences, the Warm Showers List gives you a great opportunity to meet cyclists touring through your area, hear stories about their trips, and enrich your tours by meeting local people who know the area, while saving money on accommodations.

Don't Carry Too Much

I've encountered quite a few credit-card bicycle tourists who carry an awful lot of stuff. It is easy for anyone to slide into this habit, but one of the major advantages of this style of touring is that your bike shouldn't weigh too much. You still need to have tools to deal with mechanical issues. You need a couple of changes of clothes, rain gear, and various odds and ends, but you should put a lot of thought into reducing the load as much as you possibly can. "What to Take" on pages 408–413 includes a checklist of possible items, but it is intended as a memory jogger. You should take only the items on it that you actually need.

Clothing should be multipurpose and as lightweight as possible. If you are going to visit museums or other locations where you don't want to wear Lycra bicycle shorts, carry a pair of pants that will serve for both spare riding bottoms and civilized society, or carry a light, no-wrinkle travel skirt to put on over your shorts (see Chapter 12 for more details).

Similarly, if you are doing some cooking while credit-card touring, you should carry minimalist cooking gear—a very light stove, a single pot, a bowl, and lightweight utensils, like the Lexan ones. While many decisions on whether to carry this or that piece of equipment reflect preference and style, when you are packing, it is always wise to go back to the basics:

- Carry enough water. For the bicycle tourist this means having containers to carry enough for the area where you are riding. It may also mean carrying some filtration or purification items (see "Treating Water" on page 314), but if you are doing credit-card touring, you only need to be able to carry a day's supply of water at most, plus emergency supplies. In many areas two or three water bottles are sufficient. You just need to fill your water bottles whenever the opportunity arises. On tours of sparsely populated routes in the desert Southwest, even credit-card tours, you may need to carry well over a gallon of water. You'll use a gallon a day to stay hydrated, and you need to carry enough extra for emergencies, including being prepared for store closures (if the gas station went out of business, the water tap won't be working).

- Bring enough food to get you to the next source of supply, plus some emergency food.

- Carry clothing to protect you from the elements. Depending on the locale and time of year, this may include rain gear, extra clothing for warmth, and a spare set of riding clothes to wear while your primary clothes dry. There are lots of other needs, but start with what you need to survive and keep riding. Consider everything else to be luxury items, and pare ruthlessly. You may need extra footwear, depending on your choice of pedals or shoes and the purpose of the trip, but try to minimize extra footwear.

- Assemble a minimal repair kit (see "Tools for the Road" on pages 411–412), and adjust it for real necessities, as well as your bike and your own skills.

Supported Tours

Of all the styles of touring, supported tours require the least planning and experience on your part. Modern supported tours encompass an enormous variety of approaches to touring. There are large-scale events all over the United States, often connected to charitable causes, which provide opportunities to take part in rides where you cross a state or wind through it with hundreds or thousands of other riders, some participants camping and some staying in motels.

At the other end of the spectrum are club trips and tours organized by small commercial enterprises that provide varying levels of support. These range from tours that prearrange accommodations and provide contacts in case of problems; to small-group tours with an expert cyclist/mechanic/translator/fixer in Italy, or rural China, or over mountain bike routes in Mexico; to fully supported tours with a motor vehicle (the sag wagon) that carries your luggage and picks up anyone who has mechanical difficulties or runs out of steam. Many companies cater to relatively inexperienced cyclists. Others, such as Pac Tour, specialize in long, fast, difficult tours for strong riders but provide full support.

These days, more and more commercial organizations that run supported tours are set up to supply bikes. This approach has become quite popular for casual tourists, and it is likely to win over more experienced cyclists, as the combination of well-equipped rental bikes converges with the increasing expense and difficulty of transporting your own bike. If you are happy with a small group tour and want to go to Italy, you may be willing to forgo your perfectly fitted bike in exchange for the ease of flying without having to worry about your equipment, together with a savings of several hundred dollars that you can apply toward the cost of the supported trip.

Choose the supported tour that you feel meets your touring desires. If you prefer solitary travel or small groups, the big rally-style events with hundreds or thousands of participants may not appeal to you, though many people really enjoy them. You get a chance to mix with a diverse group, ride with whoever is moving at your pace on a given day or climb, and take advantage of some group protection from traffic and other societal pressures. These events can be a lot of fun, and you can meet a lot of people who share your interests.

Another interesting approach is to organize a group of friends to go to someplace different and use a local tour company to plan the details. A good example is Bike China Adventures (see page 449), which runs small group tours in China. You pick one of their routes or let them know what you want to do, negotiate the price and dates, bring your bike or have them provide one, and then pull together a group of friends for the tour. Or, if you are cycling solo or have only a couple of companions, you can join one of their tours.

Large Events

There are dozens of very popular large events throughout the United States, ranging in length from a few days to a couple of weeks. A list of some of them is included in the Resources section. The organization and services provided vary, but typically a van hauls your gear (subject to a weight limit, and usually a single duffel). You carry what you need during the day and decide whether you will camp or stay in motels. You can usually either cook in camp or eat in restaurants. The daily distances and elevation gains are all listed well in advance, but for planning training before then, you can look at the itinerary of a previous year to determine the level of difficulty.

People riding in such events usually sort themselves out into affinity groups with a similar pace. A group of serious sport riders is always in front setting a fast pace, with various other levels spaced out along the road. Depending on the organizers, the level of support you can expect is usually clearly described on the Web site (sag wagons, water stations, and so on).

These large tours are nearly always run by a core of dedicated volunteers. Often the proceeds go to a worthy cause. Usually they are very well organized, but there are inevitable glitches. You should be philosophical about these, particularly if you haven't volunteered to help next year.

Smaller Groups

Small- and medium-sized group tours are the specialty of many commercial and not-for-profit organizations. Many are listed in the Resources section. These range from tours with a specific flavor and emphasis that might have 20 riders or 75, to tours that have 10 or 15 riders. It is easy to find anything from a mountain bike ride in Mexico's Copper Canyon or the red rock country of Utah to a cultural tour of Provence or a gourmet trip through northern Italy.

If you browse through the Web sites listed in the Resources section, you'll get a feel for the variety available, and a few cost no more than what you would pay if you planned the trip yourself. For a taste of the variety, take a look at all the tours offered in a given year by Adventure Cycling, a not-for-profit organization that has been organizing tours for over three decades.

Most organizations are small businesses run by touring enthusiasts. They vary in style and quality of services (and competence), but nearly all are small operations trying attract customers, so if you see one that does almost the sort of tour you'd like at close to the right price range and you want to organize a group of friends to go, you will almost certainly be able to persuade the tour company to accommodate you.

For tours abroad, one huge advantage to supported tours is increasing every year: as this book is being written, some international airlines will still take your bike if it's within the standard baggage allowance. Even with these airlines, though, it is hard to know in advance what the rates will be. Bike handling is also deteriorating, so the risk of damage is high and getting higher. If your bike is damaged, you face the hassle of fixing it at your destination or possibly an aborted trip, together with extra baggage costs and the prospect of getting your bike repaired when you get home (see Chapter 19 for details on packing and shipping bikes).

Now, all these hazards and expenses shouldn't be taken too seriously—after all, these sorts of stories have always been part of the romance of travel! Nevertheless, the attractions of arranging things with an outfitter that will supply bikes reasonably close to what you want are greater every year. The commercial tour operators get some fairly good deals on bikes from major bike companies, so they often provide decent bikes for a reasonable price. You'll have to decide their level of competence and responsiveness by e-mail, but that is really no different from arranging for a hotel room, and it is part of the adventure of travel.

Self-Guided Tours

A number of companies (some are listed in the Resources section) have regular tours that are not guided and provide no support on the road. Instead they arrange accommodations on a specific itinerary. This can be particularly helpful in Europe—you get a nice itinerary and you know what you will pay, but you travel on your own with the companions you choose. The exchange rate is locked in when you pay. The company arranges the accommodations, and you know that the places where you are staying will be prepared to deal with bikes.

Get Details in Writing

The level of support is generally specified in tour descriptions, but this may be done in an artful manner. Make sure you understand exactly how things will work, and make sure that all the details are put down in writing. (You should carry these details with your travel documents.) What accommodations are included? What kind of bikes? Will there be a support vehicle? Will it carry your luggage? Will you have a guide? Is he or she a competent translator? A competent mechanic? What meals and drinks are included? What transfer fees (airport to start of trip and back) are included? If your operator is arranging flights, what fees are guaranteed when you pay your money? Are exit fees included? (Many countries charge a substantial cash fee when you leave. If you don't pay, you can't leave.) Some of these questions don't apply to domestic tours, but the point is the same: make sure you understand exactly what is included and what is not. Print out any e-mails you receive in answer to questions and put them with your travel documents.

The kinds of issues just listed are standard aspects of international travel, but it is always wise to anticipate as many of them as possible. Unexpected charges and costs abound, and the prudent traveler should be as prepared as possible. An experienced tourist will be ready for the unexpected, but she or he will also encounter fewer unexpected problems than a novice.

Mountain Bike Tours

Supported mountain bike tours are increasingly popular, and both commercial companies and not-for-profit organizations offer more of them every year. Even more than road tours, a supported mountain bike tour is a very different experience from one done on your own. The difference between carrying all your own gear on the Great Divide Trail—pulling off to pick up resupply packages at local post offices or shopping for supplies at backcountry stores—and doing a supported ride where everything is brought in by Jeep to the camp-site is huge. Both may be fine experiences, but they are quite different, and each entails its own set of ethical considerations. (If supplies are being brought in by motor vehicle, this may or may not be an appropriate use of preserved wild lands, and by going on such a trip you are subsidizing that type of use.)

Like tours you plan yourself, mountain bike tours can be all-trail trips or a mixture of paved roads, rugged dirt roads, and single track. An example of mixed routes is Adventure Cycling's Denali Adventure, a self-supported trip that finishes at Denali National Park (formerly McKinley National Park). Several other mountain bike trips run by the same organization are essentially all on trails.

Remote Self-Supported versus Catered Trips

Whether mainly trail trips or mixed trail and road, organized tours can be self-supported (you carry your gear, and possibly part of the group food) or catered. For example, the Adventure Cycling trip in 2009 to Wyoming is a trail-riding trip and participants camp along the way, but meals are cooked in a group, and luggage and food are transported by van. In other cases the meals may be completely catered. Many commercial mountain bike trips have similar logistics—you camp at night, but you carry only your day gear. This approach has obvious attractions. You simply have to decide whether it is the experience you are looking for.

Environmental Ethics

One important issue you should consider when choosing supported mountain bike trips is whether the organizer complies with local environmental rules. Unfortunately, a significant number of mountain bike outfitters bring tour groups into environmentally sensitive areas without complying with local requirements. It is a good idea to ask your outfitter whether she or he is complying with the regulations of the areas visited on the trip. When in doubt, call the land management agency or the local Sierra Club chapter or group and ask. Mountain bikes and large groups can have significant environmental impacts on native wildlife and plant communities, and it is important to interact with them responsibly.

18

Self-Contained Touring

For many die-hard touring cyclists, self-contained touring is the ultimate bike-touring experience. They don't acknowledge that you have experienced a real bicycle tour unless you have camped with equipment carried on the bike. While not everyone is such a purist, there is a special attraction to trips on which the nights are spent fixing dinner on a small stove and sleeping under the stars or the forest canopy. And, of course, your touring dollars can stretch further on this style of tour.

Even bicycle camping trips, however, can vary widely in character. Bike camping in relatively populous regions, where drinking water is readily available on most days and you can shop frequently for groceries, is very different from remote treks where you have to carry a lot more on the bicycle. Cyclists also differ sharply in how big a load they are willing to carry for what they consider to be comfort and convenience. Some experienced tourists rarely travel with less than 60 pounds per person, while others hardly ever have more than 20, with exceptions for water and food when traveling in arid or remote regions. This chapter discusses some of the essential skills and equipment, as well as the differences in style, among experienced touring cyclists.

One of the best ways to try out self-contained touring is to work out some short trips near home. In

42. Camping along your route can be a good option for inexpensive travel in rural areas.

many locations, you can do this from your doorstep, getting off the busy roads after a few miles and making your way to a state park or federally owned preserve that you can reach in a few hours' ride. If you live in a truly urban area, of course, this may require a drive or a ride on public transportation to get to a reasonable starting point.

Much of the idea of such trips, however, is just to get out into the countryside for a short time and explore what it's like to camp from a bike with minimal need for elaborate equipment, knowing you can get yourself home without disrupting a major trip. Even if you're an experienced backpacker or river runner, this kind of camping can take getting used to. The folks at Rivendell advocate what they call Sub-24-hour Overnight (S24O) trips. In many areas, you can ride up into the mountains or into a rural area on a Friday afternoon or evening, camp overnight, and then ride home the next day. If you can manage such trips where you live, it makes a nice break and is a great way to learn bicycle camping. It requires only minimal camping gear, because major unexpected weather changes are unlikely. You can get by with a couple of small panniers, a saddlebag, or a bag that fits on your rear carrier. Food preparation also can be minimal, and you will know in advance how much water you need to carry. How far and hard you travel to get to your campsite is up to you: the hard-core might ride 50 miles after work to a campsite, while those with more moderate ambitions can usually find one within a 20-mile radius from home or from the end of the bus line.

Where Can You Camp?

More places than you may think. If you are an experienced lightweight camper, it is possible to find places to camp apart from organized campgrounds in many regions. Surprisingly, this is often possible even close to urban centers. This style of camping is variously known among practitioners as stealth camping, guerrilla camping, or wild camping.

Stealth Camping

The circumstances for stealth camping vary widely. In most national forests, particularly in the West, it is perfectly legal to camp in undesignated campsites (referred to as dispersed camping in Forest Service regulations), providing you obey a few rules. Typically, you may not make a campfire, and you need to be more than 100 feet from any water source, road, trail, cliff base, or archeological site. Special regulations apply in some areas, so you should check the rules in advance. During high fire hazard conditions, national forests may be closed. Technically, fire permits from a district office are required for camp stoves at all times for dispersed camping. These are free, but the district office may be many miles off your route. You should never build actual fires when stealth camping. Carry a stove and minimize your impact.

When you are doing dispersed camping, pay attention to signs. Even though "No trespassing" signs are not always accurate, it's better to avoid places that are posted as such. Inholdings (privately held land within a national park or forest) are fairly common and it is never wise to get into disputes with local residents, even if you know that a particular parcel is public land. Many other public lands, such as areas controlled by the Bureau of Land Management and many state forests, have similar rules on dispersed camping, but you should check when you are planning your trip. Local caretakers do not always know the rules, but diplomacy is always a better strategy than confrontation if the question arises.

In small towns, ask at a restaurant, convenience store, or the police station about a good place to camp. You'll often be directed to a park or someone's backyard. If you're in a rural area with fenced or posted land, riding down to a ranch or farmhouse and asking will frequently get you permission and often a good deal of hospitality. When there is a house in sight, asking is almost always the right approach. The only potential disadvantage is an encounter with the family dogs, but this is usually not a problem if you are friendly and confident. A dog will know if you are hostile or afraid (see "Dealing with Dogs" on page 337).

Where houses are not visible, discretion is usually sufficient, but pay attention to livestock. Find a place that is inconspicuous and leave early. Be very careful of fire. Don't build campfires, and use your stove very carefully. In bear country, try to cook and clean your dishes before you reach your campsite. Make a hole with a small plastic trowel for any human waste, and then bury it. Burn toilet paper before burying, if it is safe to do so. If you follow leave-no-trace camping practices, you'll also avoid unnecessary confrontations.

Interstates and other large highways frequently have spacious and deserted rights of way. In wooded areas, these often include excellent locations for stealth camping. You probably will not be traveling along these highways, but as you cross them or travel parallel to them, look for good campsites. You'll usually want to stop well before dark, set up camp in an inconspicuous spot, and cook supper. If you are caught out late, it may be quite easy to find a spot that does not attract attention, but you should leave as soon as your campsite is no longer cloaked in darkness. You can always postpone breakfast until you've ridden for an hour or two. If you are stealth camping, you have to be sure to pick up food and water well in advance. The best locations for wild camping are usually far from the nearest source of supplies.

Designated Campgrounds

There are thousands of designated campgrounds all over the United States, both privately operated and publicly run by agencies ranging from national forests and parks and the Bureau of Land Management, through various state agencies, to local municipalities operating town parks with camping facilities. Researching the ones along your touring route is part of the planning process, which is enjoyable if you start well ahead of time. Anticipating the tour is an important part of the experience.

In general, private campgrounds are oriented toward recreational vehicles and cars or pickups towing travel trailers. They offer amenities like "full hook-ups"—electric and plumbing attachments at the campsites, which are of no use to the bicycle camper but add significantly to the expense of staying. The prices at such campgrounds often exceed the cost of an inexpensive motel, so it is a good idea to check prices ahead. Campsites emphasize gravel or concrete pads intended to hold heavy vehicles but poorly suited for pitching a tent. On the other hand, such campgrounds usually have decent showers, bathrooms, and sinks, so they are good places to clean up and do laundry. If you are lucky, there will be a few tent sites off in a corner, which are likely to be quieter and offer a little more privacy than those next to RVs.

Federal and state parks and forests are mixed. Some are similar to private campgrounds. Others are simpler and more suited to bicycle camping. Prices are similarly variable, and it is always worth checking the cost of various federal, state, and Canadian passes. The rules for these have changed almost annually for the last few years, so they won't be summarized here, but generally the federal passes cover admission and sometimes a discount on camping fees. State parks vary widely in their friendliness to bicycle campers, reservation requirements, and the cost of passes.

Some state parks have a policy of not turning away bicyclists arriving at the end of the day, but this varies widely, and even where it is the rule, not all employees are aware of it. Diplomacy, as usual, is likely to produce better results than knowledge of the rulebook. There is always the possibility that a camper on a bicycle will be directed to an unofficial corner that is more suitable for tent camping than a regular campsite.

When planning your trip, carefully check the policies on making reservations. Popular areas, like state parks along West Coast highways and campsites in national parks, are usually booked far in advance. Surprises are inevitable, but advance planning is always advisable. Make reservations where they are accepted. When something doesn't work out, be prepared to stealth-camp or retreat to a motel.

Note that the preceding paragraphs emphasize the situation in the United States and Canada. Circumstances and attitudes vary widely in the rest of the world. A good way to get a general feel for a particular country is to search www.crazyguyonabike.com and similar sites for the country you're planning to visit and read the trip logs you'll almost certainly find there.

Camping Skills

If you aren't experienced in lightweight camping, you should develop your skills before undertaking an ambitious multiweek tour on which you are camping all or most of the time. In many parts of the country this is not too hard to manage. Plan some local weekend trips to camping areas that can be reached from home in a day's ride or less. In many Western states, this is simply a matter of heading toward a national forest or state park. In the Midwest there are many routes and camping areas within relatively easy reach even of major urban centers.

On other short trips (such as S24O) you can try out equipment and techniques in a fairly familiar and known situation. You know what kind of weather to expect; you carry only a few more clothes than you would on a day ride; you don't have to worry about whether you can find supplies; you're close to home if you need to bail, and so on. Such trips are a perfect test bed for trying out equipment, building confidence, and learning camping techniques. If your sleeping bag isn't quite warm enough, you only shiver for one night. If you aren't too happy with your new one-pot recipe or the stove doesn't work well, it is not a big deal. You don't have to carry gear for all the conditions that you might encounter on a transcontinental tour. You know the weather forecast before you leave. And if your work allows you only limited leisure time, you can acquire a lot of experience without ruining your annual vacation. Instead, you're prepared for that long vacation tour.

You can test camping techniques on S24O trips. Want to try going very lightweight with minimal equipment? S24O trips won't completely reveal the consequences when you transplant these techniques to a month on dirt roads in Patagonia, but they will at least give you a good idea. And if you want a better idea, try an S24O trip with minimal equipment when the weather forecast is not so good. It won't replicate the experience of cycling for a month in bad weather, but it will at least give you a basis for making decisions.

For developing camping skills, of course, all lightweight, self-propelled sports share a large common basis of skills and equipment. Hiking the Appalachian

Trail, doing a self-supported kayak trip of Desolation Canyon on the Green River, and backpacking the Torres del Paine circuit in Chile are very different, but they all build the kinds of camping skills you need on long, self-supported bike tours.

Setting Up Camp

The biggest differences between bicycle camping and backpacking are the process of finding a campsite and the types of campsites you may use. If you're stopping at organized campsites, you'll want to try to find a spot that is actually suitable for a tent, but you need to be prepared to settle for a gravel pad if necessary. If the campground is full and it is late, you may have to try to negotiate for a spot off to the side to avoid riding on in the dark.

Around small towns, unless there is a municipal park that is designated for camping, you need to make a few friends and ask for recommendations. If you stop at a restaurant or a grocery store, just ask about a place to camp. You'll often get a suggestion and sometimes the offer of a backyard. Often the next best possibility is just to go to the local police station or sheriff's office. If you get a suggestion there, you can at least figure that you probably won't be woken up in the night by a suspicious officer. Churchyards and cemeteries are often good possibilities, but it is important to ask permission.

The best routine for touring is to stop early and set up your camp in daylight, start cooking, and have plenty of time to relax and get things in good order. Still, there will be times when things don't go as planned—a couple of flat tires, 20 miles of headwind, or just an interesting conversation at a rest stop. On those occasions you'll be very glad if you've practiced setting up your tent or tarp at home so that you can do it without thinking about it, even in the rain or the wind. You should know the number and position of anchors that you need, so that you can pick out a good spot for the tent or other shelter quickly, clear any debris from the floor area, put down your ground cloth or tent foot-print, and set up the shelter.

Perhaps even more important than practice is organization. All the things you need to set up camp—flashlight or headlamp, rain gear, warm clothes, tent or shelter components, and kitchen—should be in the places you expect, so that you aren't pawing through your panniers looking for a tent stake or a lighter. On a relaxed day, you might change your shoes and socks, then start a pot of water boiling for tea. Then set up your shelter and lay out the pad and sleeping bag, and change from riding clothes to something comfortable for camp. Finally, it's time to move whatever should go in the tent and tidy everything up on the bike.

If you're in bear country and you don't have a bear-proof container, find a place to set up a bear cache and toss the line up, so that you can haul the bag up when you've finished cooking (see "Carrying Food in Bear Country" on page 317 for more tips on staying safe). Then it is time to relax, do any necessary bike main-tenance, read, catch up with a journal, or just enjoy the scenery. Note that even if one isn't worried about bears, there are lots of other critters that will be happy to chew their way into a pannier, so many of the same procedures are still a good idea—all food in a secured bag, all dishes and utensils washed, and toiletries out of the tent.

Staying Comfortable

In addition to a change of riding clothes and rain gear, you should carry some comfortable camp clothing (see "Extra Clothes" on page 301). Depending on the season and area, you should have sun protection, camp clothes that are comfortable but lightweight, and enough sup-plemental clothing to keep you warm on cool evenings, even after a couple of days of bad weather.

In rainy conditions, the key to maintaining rea-sonable comfort is keeping your camp clothes and your sleeping bag and pad dry. This is mainly a func-tion of being careful when you are breaking camp and packing. Stuff your sleeping bag and camp clothes in waterproof bags in the tent, and put on the day's riding clothes. Then put on your rain gear, start packing the bike, and pack the tent last, in a way that doesn't get everything else wet. Roll the ground cloth afterward, so that the dirt from the bottom doesn't get on everything else. If you have sunny weather at lunchtime, roll out anything that is wet and let it dry in the sun.

Meals on the Road

Where food is concerned, bike touring is not like backpacking. Most of the time when you are bicycle touring, you will be buying your supplies at stores along the road. If you are doing a long trip on remote roads in Canada's Northwest Territories, for example, you may be shopping and cooking like a backpacker, concentrating on dehydrated foods and getting supplies for a couple of weeks at a time. For most cycling tourists, however, both the cooking style and the supplies are quite different.

Even in remote parts of the western United States, where you may easily travel 100 miles between convenience stores, you probably won't be carrying more than a couple of days' worth of food between shopping opportunities. Chances to resupply with water are likely to be nearly as far apart, and water is the heavy part of your evening meal, so even if those crossroads stores in Utah carried freeze-dried backpacking meals (they usually don't), it would be a waste of money to buy them. Why spend a lot for dehydrated meals that take a long time to cook, when you must also get the water to rehydrate them at the same store?

Instead, bicycle campers can usually get at least some fresh ingredients, and often a variety of groceries. Hence, the cyclist can improvise much more than the backpacker and can usually plan on much more variety. Some choose to stick with a very simple menu that just requires adding boiling water, but it is usually possible to make quite imaginative meals when you are bicycle camping, ranging from stir-fry to quickbreads.

Food Sourcing—Learn to Improvise

On most bicycle tours, you won't often be more than a day's travel from a place to buy food. To feed yourself well on tour, you need to be flexible and imaginative. If the locale and the season are right for roadside vegetable stands, they are a great source of delicious and nutritious food. You can stock up at a vegetable stand in the afternoon and devise a menu for the evening on the basis of what is available, possibly supplemented by a little fish, meat, or cheese from a local market. Adding grains or other starches that you've bought at a market will provide a nutritious and enjoyable meal.

In the absence of vegetable stands, a neighborhood grocery store is the best bet, with convenience stores as a last resort. Fortunately, in really remote areas with no grocery stores, convenience stores are more likely to have a few somewhat fresh vegetables and some meat, unlike similar establishments in more populated areas.

However, when you are on rural roads, you will not find the variety or selection of food that we have become accustomed to, with vegetables brought from halfway around the world and fish flown in from the coast. If you are lucky there will be a few fresh vegetables. If there is also some meat, poultry, or passably fresh fish, figure out a recipe while you are shopping and improvise. For non-vegetarians, there is always a selection of canned tuna, salmon, chicken, and meat that can be mixed into a meal. Cheese is also always available, and it is a tasty addition if you are not vegan.

Flexibility is the key. If you can only deal with fixed recipes you've derived in advance, you will be endlessly frustrated, and you won't eat very well. The key is to learn to make reasonable meals from what you can typically buy at a convenience store, and when you encounter something special, whether it is a steak from a 7-11 cooler, a trout you caught in a roadside stream, fresh produce from a vegetable stand, seafood from a seaside fishmonger, or the odd canned delicacy found by chance in a small town with a unique ethnic population, turn it into a gourmet opportunity.

Nutrition and Cooking on the Road

For both vegetarians and non-vegetarians, it is always possible (and inexpensive) to devise a combination of complementary proteins that is tasty and nutritious: rice, beans, and corn tortillas; garbanzo beans (chickpeas) and rice; peanut butter sandwiches. For non-vegans, milk products together with pasta (macaroni and cheese, for example) are a good source of complete proteins.

Moreover, the experience of vegetarians over the years shows that as long as you eat an adequate variety of foods, you'll get all the nutrients you need, including protein. If you take in enough calories and get sufficient variety, you'll end the tour much healthier than you were at the beginning. Whole grains are not always easy to cook on tour, because they usually take a long time to cook, assuming you can find them on the way. This is one reason to have a stove that can simmer. On days when you get into camp early, you can use raw brown rice or something similar as a base for a meal. Buy enough for a few meals when you encounter a grocery store that is well stocked, and then cook it when the opportunity arises.

Canned soup along with a fresh salad can make a good dinner. Barring medical restrictions, the high salt content of most canned soups and stews is not really much of a worry when you are sweating on the road all day. You should make sure that you get adequate potassium, because sweating depletes your potassium supply, particularly when your sodium intake is high. Orange juice and bananas are both good potassium sources, as are potatoes, tomato paste, and yogurt.

You need to develop a few flexible cooking techniques and carry the tools to use them when you are bicycle touring. Many tourists are happy to eat cold meals a lot of the time and carry a very small stove and pot or container for heating soup, coffee, tea, or whatever. Others prefer to take a little more weight and enjoy some flexibility in cooking varied meals from what they can find along the way. To follow this approach, carry a 2-quart pot (larger with a group of three or more), one smaller pot, and sometimes a small skillet, together with a stove that will boil water in the pot and that can be adjusted to simmer. These allow you to cook pasta, rice, lentils, or potatoes, and to do stir-fries or sauté vegetables, meat, or fish when they are available.

If you are happy with heating whatever canned food you can buy at the convenience store, you can manage with the lightest stoves and smallest pots. A little more weight buys you a lot of flexibility, if you have some culinary imagination.

19

Getting Yourself and Your Bike to the Tour

The most appealing way to get to a tour, of course, is to ride there on your bike. There is a special attraction to tours that start and end at your doorstep, but this is not always feasible—for example, if you live in an apartment on New York's Upper East Side. This chapter discusses some of the issues associated with getting you and your equipment to and from the tour.

I consider various transportation alternatives, and it's worth noting that, except for some tours within the United States, most journeys to the tour starting point begin with air travel. And unless your itinerary allows you to simply pedal away from the destination airport, some intermediate stage of travel will be involved for you and your bike also. This chapter also discusses options for getting from one leg of a tour to one where bicycling isn't practical. And because nearly all tours except those close to home involve packing and shipping your bike, those important topics are covered as well.

By Car

Driving can figure into a tour in various ways. The simplest scenario is when you drive to your starting point but arrange a loop route for your tour, so that you ride back to the same place you started. That way you don't have to worry about shuttling the car from your starting point to your destination.

Planning for this kind of tour is fairly straightforward. Your only real problem is likely to be parking your car safely for the time you're on tour—not usually a worry for a weekend but possibly of some concern during long tours. One solution is to make arrangements with a motel or commercial campground where you stay to let you leave your car there and to keep an eye on it—this works better with small mom-and-pop operations than with large chains.

If you are doing a long trip that ends many miles from your starting point, you'll have to explore other possibilities, which will vary with the route, the number of riders, and a host of other variables. You might arrange a shuttle for your car, rent a car for at least one person to retrieve your vehicle, or have a driver take a train or bus back to the starting point.

While trains and buses are often practical and economical alternatives for getting to or from the terminus of a tour in much of the world, in the United States they are not usually very reasonable possibilities. Even when it is environmentally unsound, using a car to get to the beginning of a tour is often the only practical and economical alternative in the United States, simply because we subsidize automobile travel and other travel alternatives have become (amazingly!) less and less bicycle-friendly. Thus, taking a car, even a one-way rental with a drop-off fee, can turn out to be cheaper and more practical than any other way.

Every trip is different, so the important thing to keep in mind if you are using a car to get to or from a trip is to plan for it. It is easy to ignore important details if you are used to regular car use. If you plan on driving several cyclists in any normal passenger vehicle—even a large van—the bicycles, the riders, and their touring equipment will take up a lot of space. It is easy to overlook how much if you don't check and agree on arrangements in advance. Think about efficient packing and how you are going to carry your bicycle(s). While it's usually easy to get a couple of bikes and touring luggage into even a compact car, protect it with heavy, disposable plastic bags or sheeting to avoid grease stains on the car. If more than two people are involved, the space required expands geometrically. If the vehicle capacity is marginal, you may decide that it is worthwhile for a number of people to ship their panniers to the destination in advance, rather than discovering at the last minute that you need to drive three cars rather than one.

If you're driving your own vehicle, you probably have a suitable bicycle rack. If you are renting a car and more than two riders are traveling in it, you may have to think things through. Is it possible to rent a roof rack? Because few modern vehicles are well designed for racks and reserving a rental car rarely guarantees the model, this can be a problem. Ski racks are readily available for an extra charge in some parts of the country, and if your bike is boxed, it may be relatively simple to carry some suitable line and tie the box to an available roof rack or ski rack, providing it is well-constructed and solidly attached to the vehicle. The main point is to plan ahead and then be prepared for surprises. Rental car agencies are not always reliable in providing promised equipment beyond an economy, compact, or full-sized car. I've had a friend arrange for a four-wheel drive with a roof rack, and then arrive concurrently with a hurricane to be provided with a two-wheel-drive vehicle with no roof rack when he had to navigate dirt roads in tropical storms. Rental car agencies are unreliable, and they are worse internationally.

Of course, there are many touring situations where you'll find yourself relying on cars in one way or another, ranging from taking a taxi, van, or shuttle from an airport to being met by friends in their own cars. Improvising and flexibility are often the key to getting by. Vans and shuttles can often handle a boxed bike without huge problems, though you may have to exhibit a bit of humility, since you'll probably be taking up more than your share of space and effort. It is often useful to have prepared a few nylon straps (climber's webbing works well) and strategic holes through the bike box, so that you can easily carry the bike over long stretches of pavement and up and down staircases. However, you may also have to consider taking the bike and other stuff out of the box to fit into a car. Large taxis might accommodate the box, but in places where most taxis are compacts, this is unlikely. Unpacking the bike (and whatever else you put in the box), getting yourself organized, and getting things into a small car is a major challenge. Think things out in advance as much as you can, but be prepared to deal with significant obstacles.

Finally, you may find yourself at the side of the road in circumstances where the most practical solution to an unexpected problem is to get a ride from a passing motorist, preferably one with a pickup truck. For example, if you have mechanical problems you can't fix on the road and are far from the nearest town and bike shop, hitching a ride may be your only alternative. Or you may encounter bridges on which bicycles are not allowed. It's best to research this issue in planning your route, but surprises do happen. Be ready to hitch a ride and to make things as easy as possible for your benefactor. Get your luggage off the bike beforehand, and be ready to quickly toss everything into the stowage area.

By Bus

Buses are often the best way to get around in many parts of the world. They are cheap, they go everywhere, they give you an opportunity to meet interesting, friendly, intelligent people, and you'll never have an issue taking your bike in parts of the world where everyone uses the bus. You may have to put up with a little anxiety as your bike is tossed up on the rooftop luggage rack, along with chicken cages, agricultural implements, and miscellaneous bags of stuff, but it will be a lot safer than when it is subjected to the mechanized baggage-handling machinery of "developed" countries on its way to being put on a plane.

The most friendly countries for the bicycle tourist catching a bus are places like Guatemala and some African nations. Things go downhill as development goes up. Most European countries are far more bike-friendly than U.S. cities, but specifics vary widely and you shouldn't make any assumptions. Do your research before leaving home.

Sadly, in much of the United States, bus systems are currently not very well supported or developed. In some urban areas, buses are a perfectly reasonable means of getting out of the downtown congestion. In many metropolitan regions, buses are equipped with bike racks and bike transport is included in the fare (as long as the racks aren't already full—during rush hour bike space may be tight). But schedules and routes give no consideration to bikes as a means of transportation. So, for example, bus routes that might be useful to get to the start of a tour at the edge of an urban area or to bring you into an urban center from the periphery often run on very limited schedules strictly oriented toward rush hour commutes. This is fine if it fits your schedule, but it may not. As an example, if you've reached downtown Denver and you'd like to start your tour from a peripheral city like Morrison or Lyons, there are good bus routes and the buses have bike racks, but you'll only be able to catch a bus at the end of the day, not in the morning. (The buses are scheduled to bring people into Denver in the morning and take them home after work.)

There are many useful regional bus systems, but they are hard for outsiders to find and use, and support for bikes is inconsistent. You can often find efficient and cost-effective service between larger cities, but this is not easy information to find for an out-of-state visitor. You'll need to exercise your Web search skills to find available service, but this can be a real challenge. Searching for "Foster City" or "San Francisco bus" will get you to SamTrans, and if you then go to its site map you can find out about the system's bike racks, but it is not simple. Similarly, if you search for "Colorado Springs Denver bus," you'll find FrontRange Express, which runs buses between Denver and Colorado Springs, and if you then go to the FAQ you'll find the fares, schedule, and bicycle capacity, but you have to do a little work. Service from Boston to Hanover, New Hampshire, can be found pretty easily, and the Dartmouth Coach rules for carrying bikes are a few clicks away. Want to get from Boston to Cape Cod? You'll have to work a lot harder both to find the bus company and to ascertain the (quite vague) rules on taking your bike. The Internet certainly makes finding regional bus routes easier than it might otherwise be, but they remain obscure and hard to find. And they are not typically bicycle-friendly.

Buses for longer-distance travel in the United States have become a pathetic remnant of a once-useful system. Nationally, only Greyhound remains, its routes a wan remnant of the original network, and even though its remaining customers are generally low-income, prices are high. The Greyhound system can still be helpful to get to many places that are not served by rail or airline, and in the United States you can take your boxed bike as checked luggage for no additional charge.

Greyhound is a useful way for you to get from the nearest airport to the more remote start of a tour, and its luggage provisions are reasonable. For example, I can take a bus to many attractive starting locations in New Mexico or Utah that are not accessible by commercial airlines, and then follow interesting tours back to my home base in Boulder, Colorado. But there is no Greyhound service to Boulder; I need to get to Denver first, and many towns in New Mexico and Utah that were once serviced by bus have been abandoned by public transportation. So the bike becomes the main connecting vehicle: to reach a tour by bus, I have to pick from one of the few remaining terminus spots for a start or end point. Mostly, the bus doesn't go there anymore.

In Canada, except for a few specific intercity routes, the situation is even worse than it is in the United States. You cannot take your bike (except folding bikes in their cases) as checked luggage on Greyhound in Canada. If you are traveling via Greyhound in Canada, you need to box your bike and ship it via Greyhound (or other carrier) before boarding your bus.

By Train

Trains ought to be the ideal way to get a bike tourist and bike from urban centers to desirable starting points for a tour in the countryside—and in some parts of the world, they are. Unfortunately, train systems in too many places have been allowed to decay, or they simply don't accommodate cyclists very well.

For example, I'd been planning a tour of some of the wonderful cycling routes that have been established in Quebec—2,500 miles in all—so I investigated the possibility of getting to and from the trip via Amtrak. I can get to Denver either by bike or on the local bus, which has bike carriers. I thought that I could take Amtrak to Toronto and then use Rail Canada to Montreal to start the trip. Amtrak, however, won't let me take my bike past Chicago, so I had to abandon the idea and go back to the airlines.

This section reviews some of the opportunities and barriers in using trains to access bike tours. Rail systems vary greatly depending on nation and region.

In the United States

Despite the experience just recounted, there have been some signs recently that trains may become a reasonable method of travel for cyclists trying to get to and from tours in the United States that are far from home. While the airlines have been making it progressively harder and more expensive to fly with a bike, Amtrak (and Rail Canada) have been slowly moving in the opposite direction, making it modestly easier and cheaper to travel with your bike. These are only trends, and it remains to be seen how things will work out—in the past, U.S. trains have been abysmal in accommodating cyclists. We don't yet have high-speed trains in

North America, Amtrak covers little of the country outside the Northeast, and train fares are not yet competitive with air travel, even ignoring extra costs for food and other incidentals.

On some of its major routes, Amtrak has begun to make taking your bike almost convenient. You can sometimes get a carton from Amtrak at modest cost and then check the bike through on the train you are taking for a very reasonable surcharge. A few Amtrak trains are even equipped to allow bikes to be carried onboard without being boxed—an approach that is common in Europe. If you are traveling between cities that have checked baggage service among the amenities shown on Amtrak's Web site, you can ride to your local Amtrak station, buy a large bike box for $10, make a few easy adjustments to the bike (like turning the handlebars), and send the bike as checked baggage for an extra $5. Just get another box for the return trip and you're all set.

However, there are still major gotchas that could pop up. If the amenity is not available, you can't take your bike *at all*. At the moment, you have to do a bunch of research to determine at which stations the bike-check amenity is available, and you can't always rely on what you find out. We can only hope that Amtrak continues in a positive direction and actually makes rail travel useful in the United States, as it is in Europe and many other civilized countries, including many "underdeveloped" ones. A nationwide policy is needed to make trains bike-friendly in both the United States and Canada.

In Canada

Canada's rail system crosses the continent along the southern populated margin adjacent to the United States, with important hubs in British Columbia, Manitoba, and Quebec. It extends through the Maritime Provinces, with separate connecting lines to a few locations farther north: there is a line in central Canada to Churchill on Hudson Bay and one to Prince George and Prince Rupert in northern British Columbia. Much of Canada is bereft of rail access, however, like its provincial southern neighbor. Rail Canada's Web site, www.viarail.ca, has links to a map of Canada's rail system, though the site itself is not well designed, and it is often hard to find useful information. For information on taking bicycles, go to www.viarail.ca/planner/en_plan_baga_volu.html, where you can access both fees and information on which trains carry bikes. For other information, there are hardly any links, other than to schedules, but there is a search box on the home page.

In general, you can check your bike (packed in a box) between destinations in the Canadian system, but not all scheduled trains have checked baggage service, so you have to do some real research to plan your trip. However, this is easier than with Amtrak in the United States. If you pack your bike in a carton, it will cost $20 as checked baggage, regardless of the number of connections. You need to verify your route, however, to find out whether baggage can be checked between your points of departure and destination. A bicycle box is free at stations that accept checked baggage. Of course, you need tools to turn your handlebars and remove the pedals, and it would be wise to bring some of the other packing items mentioned under "Packing Your Bike" later in this chapter.

The Canadian rail system accepts bikes in heavy plastic bags as checked luggage but requires a damage waiver, so this is not recommended. To find out whether bags can be checked on a particular route, you start a reservation for the route on a particular date, and then click the information link to determine whether checked bags are accepted.

In Europe and Elsewhere

Europe has a well-developed rail system and often has provisions for taking bikes without disassembly and at rates that are not exorbitant. Thus it is quite possible to plan multileg trips that are joined by train—ride for a week in one region, and then take the train to your next starting point. Rules and tariffs vary widely, however, so you need to do your research in advance. And the best deals for Americans, like the Eurail Pass, are often not practical if you are traveling mainly by bike, because they are generally based on giving you unlimited train travel in a particular region for a specified amount of time.

Rail service in other places varies widely, as does the feasibility of using it for transportation with your bike. In South and Central America, you are far more likely to use buses or planes—developed rail systems that cross between countries are rare. Rail systems in Africa and Asia are highly variable, often dependent on colonial history. In places where passenger service is well established, trains are likely to be so crowded that using one with your bike will be quite a challenge.

Australia and New Zealand both have trains connecting a number of major cities; Australian trains connect the corners of the continent. Different companies operate trains in both countries, and their rules are inconsistent. Some New Zealand trains allow you to travel with your bicycle without taking it completely apart or boxing it. Checked luggage allowances are generally permissive enough that you could box your bike and take it on any of the passenger trains. Because the rules are different for each train operator in each country, you'd need to check the specifics for the connection you are planning in either Australia or New Zealand.

Air Travel

Because one of the main attractions of bicycle touring has always been that you can carry your own transportation to some faraway, fascinating location and then pedal away into a unique travel experience, air travel to or from a tour holds a particular attraction. Indeed, for many years the most common way for touring cyclists to get to the beginning of a faraway tour, return from the end, or both, has been via airplane. After all, whether you are planning a tour of Central Europe,

Patagonia, northern Canada and Alaska, or Africa, you will probably not have the time, funds, or inclination to get on a tramp steamer or take a camel caravan to the beginning of the route or from the end.

The chief issue you will usually face as a touring cyclist is getting your bike and equipment to the beginning of a tour, and/or getting it back from the end. In general, this has traditionally meant solving the problem of bringing your bike as checked luggage on a plane, train or bus. For Americans, who have had marginal train and bus service for years, this has usually meant, *What are the tricks for flying with your bike?* Taking a bike on the plane has been a challenge and a significant expense for decades, but until recently, overseas flights were actually easier and more economical than domestic flights, because for decades the tariffs and rules for bikes that were tightly regulated internationally were a free-for-all domestically.

The issues associated with air travel have become more complicated and the prices higher and less predictable because of a combination of security issues, fuel costs, and the corporate management problems of the air carriers. As a result, if you need to take a plane, you need to incorporate the expense and possible rule changes into your planning, rather than simply assuming that you'll take your bike as luggage and perhaps pay a few extra dollars in oversize baggage fees. Airlines rules for carrying bicycles and other excess baggage have become so variable day-to-day and so arbitrary that it is virtually impossible to know what you'll encounter. Every attempt to track the rules and fees (see "Rules and Practicalities" later in this chapter) has failed, because of constant changes and the fact that an agent will assess different charges on any given day.

Air travel with your bike is still feasible and it is the only practical way to reach many excellent touring destinations, but it is well worth thinking things through in advance, and it is important to assume that you may be subjected to a significant surcharge when you check in, with no practical alternative.

Even some of the best solutions for frequent travelers, like take-apart bikes and folders (see "Folding and Take-Apart Bikes" on page 76), can be problematic, because the extra charges and the rules for dimension and weight limits change constantly and are subject to arbitrary interpretation by gate agents.

Be sure to carefully read "Packing Your Bike" later in this chapter. And keep in mind the rules about prohibited items as you are getting things together. Make sure that anything like knives, scissors, and multitools are in your checked baggage; you don't want them confiscated at the security checkpoint after you have already checked your baggage. Liquids in containers above the 3-ounce limit also need to be in the checked baggage.

Almost anything pressurized is banned in both checked and carry-on baggage, as is just about anything that is seriously flammable, regardless of the container. Never pack or carry fuel or CO_2 canisters or cartridges. Deflate your tires. If you have a mountain bike with pressurized shocks and you can deflate them, do so; if they can't be deflated, you may have a problem. Note that many items may not actually pose a hazard: inflated tires definitely don't, but deflating them is a fairly ironclad rule, so be warned.

The key to having good touring experiences when traveling by air today is to do plenty of advance planning and then to be relaxed and flexible on the trip—good strategy for travel in general. Good diplomatic skills are often the most important items for air travel. It may be helpful to have a printout of the airline rules for taking a bicycle, but in the current world of travel, it is equally important to present the document to the gate agent in a nonconfrontational and friendly manner.

Rules and Practicalities

The best overall reference for airline rules on bikes is the International Bicycle Fund's page at www.ibike.org/encouragement/travel/bagregs.htm, but it is nearly impossible for anyone to keep up with changes these days, so use this location as a starting point and check the airline's Web site before starting to budget. Even then, be aware that there are often contradictory rules in different places on the same airline's Web site, and assume that the rule is *buyer beware!* For many years, the very experienced traveler, pilot, and bicycle tourist Jim Foreman tracked the rules for carrying bicycles on different airlines on his Web site. He has uncharacteristically thrown up his hands and given up.

If you are taking your bike as checked luggage, be sure to verify the baggage rules for the airline while buying tickets. There are a lot of nuances. For example, you will probably have to sign a damage waiver, no matter how well the bike is packed. If the airline loses the bike, they'll probably have to compensate you, but the limit will be far less than the bike's value, and if you miss your tour, there won't be anything you can do about it. Also, there may be extra charges for exceeding the weight limit, for exceeding size limits, or for taking a bicycle. You may well be charged all three! In these days of e-tickets and Web purchases, you would have a hard time getting a ticket along with a paper document that actually specified the rules and tariffs to which you are agreeing. The best you can do is to carefully check the baggage regulations and fees at the time you purchase the ticket, print them out and highlight the relevant passages, and carry the printed pages with your travel documents. If an airline representative then wants to charge some outrageously different price, you'll at least have a basis to make your case. Be prepared to be philosophical, however, and recognize that persuasion is likely to be more efficacious than confrontation.

If you buy your tickets for the entire trip as a single purchase, you'll usually avoid having new rules and fees imposed for each leg, but beware of possible problems. If you are charged oversize or overweight fees for each leg of a trip, the costs can add up. In general, the rule is that if you're making the whole flight on one ticket, you should have uniform rules and tariffs applied, and they should be those of the least restrictive or lowest charges, but it pays to be prepared and to pay attention when you arrive at baggage check-in.

"Code-sharing" arrangements between airlines have added additional complications (you're flying on one airline, but it may also have flight numbers for another airline). People have reported a lot of variation in how they were charged, depending on the possible permutations. These variations are not supposed to occur, but as a practical matter you have no recourse.

Consider the advantages of direct flights, when they are available, if you are taking your bike as checked luggage. There are fewer opportunities for it to be damaged or to go astray. You only have to worry about one moody baggage clerk. Despite the colorful tales of "baggage apes" who delightedly mishandle bags, most damage to both checked baggage and shipped bikes occurs as a result of automated baggage-handling systems. If your bike carton or a package ahead of it catches in a turn, many other bags and cartons can back up behind or fall on your bike, and rather large unanticipated forces can be applied. These are far more likely to cause damage than one baggage handler tossing the bike, however carelessly. Hence, a direct flight greatly reduces the chances of both damage and misdirection.

Transportation Security Administration (TSA) inspection is one of the major complications today when you take your bike as checked luggage. The section titled "Packing Your Bike" later in this chapter was written with this in mind. Depending on the airport, you may be able to smooth the process and gain some peace of mind by accompanying your bike to the TSA inspection—ask at the check-in counter and stay very calm, whatever the process. Obviously, it is in your interest for the carton to be retaped correctly and for any loose parts to stay well secured in the box.

Domestic versus International Flights

In general, domestic tariffs change more rapidly and are far more arbitrary than international ones. Some international carriers still have relatively bike-friendly policies. A few years ago the international carriers all abided by a set of agreements that in the end meant that, within the weight and number-of-bag limitations, passengers could take a bike as checked luggage without additional charge, and this policy also applied to domestic legs of a trip on a single ticket. Those days are gone. Some international flights will accept your bike without additional charge. The same airline may charge you a high surcharge on the return flight, for no discernible reason. Plan things as well as you can, but don't be surprised if they turn out differently than you expected. Still, most international carriers have more reasonable policies than the U.S. airlines. And international airlines based abroad are generally more bike-friendly. A few international carriers will still take your unboxed bike as luggage with no extra charge. No U.S.-based international carrier still does this.

If you happen to be going to a location that is remote enough to require a small plane for the final leg—various islands and out-of-the-way places in Africa, Asia, Alaska, or northern Canada—you need to carefully check the weight and size limitations when you arrange the flight. These planes don't have large cargo areas, and they have very tight weight limitations, so be prepared.

The biggest issue specific to international travel is customs. When you take your bike as checked luggage, you typically go through immigration first when you enter the destination country, then you pick up your bags and clear them through customs. This is usually surprisingly efficient, and in most of Europe you have to clear customs only at the first port of entry. If you have connecting flights to EU countries, you normally only go through customs once.

On your return to the United States, you clear immigration at the port of entry, pick up your luggage, including your bike, clear customs, and then put the luggage on a conveyor belt to be put on your connecting flight. This belt may not be able to accommodate your bike box, and you may have to deal with a few complications to get it checked through. So, it's prudent to avoid tight connections at port-of-entry airports.

An Aside on Folding Bikes

A reasonable response to many of the issues raised in this chapter would be: *Why didn't you just get a folder?* Most touring cyclists have not yet converted to folding bikes, but as the cost of fuel continues to rise, the ever-increasing burdens of transporting conventional touring bikes around the world suggest that touring cyclists should seriously consider folding bikes for international travel (see "Folding and Take-Apart Bikes" on page 76). Many other issues remain, but the advantages of a Bike Friday or one of its competitors that will fit within current airline luggage regulations present a serious challenge to conventional touring bikes.

A minor point is that if you have a folder in an airline-legal case that fits normal weight requirements, don't bother to mention the fact. Some representatives of a few airlines have imposed a "bicycle" or "sporting goods" surcharge for folders that met every luggage limit. There is no reason to tempt fate by bragging about your bike. Even if asked about the contents, "bike parts" is a truthful answer. (This is not a common problem, but it has been encountered by a number of cyclists.)

If you are thinking about a folding bike as an alternative, you need to consider all the equipment issues for folders, particularly any nonstandard components that are hard to replace in remote areas. Some of the ride complications of smaller wheel diameters can be alleviated with fat tires, but the issues associated with tire and wheel replacement need to be considered.

Most folders with 20-inch wheels (see "Folding and Take-Apart Bikes" on page 76) take BMX-compatible tires, which are almost as widely available worldwide as MTB-compatible 26-inch tires. The same argument applies to rims. You won't be able to find ideal tires or rims in Sri Lanka, but you can probably find something that will work and will allow you to confidently travel with fewer replacement parts.

Should You Ship Your Bike?

Whatever form of travel is used to get to a tour, most touring cyclists have to arrive at their starting points with their bikes. Renting or buying a suitable bike at the start of the tour is rarely feasible, except possibly for those taking package group tours. For the truly intrepid, it is possible to buy whatever local variety of bike is available and use it to travel the country of choice, but it implies a different travel experience than the one generally discussed in this book. Chinese, Thai, and Indian utility bikes are admirable in their own right, but you're not likely to want to tour on one.

There are exceptions, and they are well worth considering. Local bike-touring entrepreneurs can sometimes be found who can set you up with reasonable touring or expedition touring bikes for far less than you would pay to ship your own. The same person is likely to know everything there is to know about touring in his or her region, she'll have the issues of readily available spare parts well researched, and she will be an extremely valuable and interesting local contact. This situation is the rare exception, however, and it is a gamble that you may or may not want to take. Anyone running a business catering to adventure tourists in remote parts of the world is likely to be interesting in more ways than one. He or she is living on the edge, and you may or may not want to incorporate his or her adventure into your own.

As indicated in the discussion of air travel earlier in this chapter, in the last few years, the combination of security and bureaucracy issues, airline industry chaos, and increased fuel costs for airlines have made the normal solution of taking your bike as checked luggage more expensive, less reliable, subject to constantly fluctuating fees and rates, and increasingly frustrating. As a result, more and more touring cyclists are concluding that even when they fly to their destinations, it is cheaper, more reliable, and far more hassle-free to ship their bikes directly to the start of the tour rather than trying to take them as checked luggage. Shipping the bike directly can also be a good alternative if you are traveling by rail or bus, but the details vary and are much more specialized, so this section considers it mainly as applied to air travel.

Advantages to Direct Shipping

There are several principal advantages to shipping the bike directly:

1. It may be cheaper. Airlines increasingly charge fees that are exorbitant and based on arcane rules. Even if you carefully research the rules in advance, it may not do any good when you arrive at the check-in counter.

2. You can insure against loss and damage with a shipping company, with reasonable expectation of recovering your loss. Airlines will require you to sign a confiscatory waiver limiting their liability to far less than the cost of the bike. You can't pay extra to insure it for its full value.

3. Many touring cyclists believe that direct shipment is far more reliable than shipment via checked baggage. This belief is anecdotal; no reliable studies have determined the issue one way or another.

4. Shipping companies have established a good record in the last few years for getting things to their destinations at the times promised (you do have to know the details of the promises). Airlines have done less well, and they are rarely willing to make any promises.

5. Costs are more predictable and transparent. Airline charges have become notorious for daily changes, even for passengers with conventional bags and

travel plans. Airline charges are in a constant state of flux, and it is impossible to plan a trip with a reliable understanding of what it will cost. If you ship your bike directly you can choose to spend more if necessary to meet your schedule at the beginning of the tour and save money by using a lower rate on the way back.

6. The carrier can pick up the bike box from your house and, in many cases, deliver it to your final destination. (If both are business addresses, it saves money with some carriers.) If you ship early and have someone receive the package before you arrive, you can also save money.

Note this important caveat for international travel: You are unlikely to have any real trouble clearing your bike through customs when you take it as checked luggage, but there can be major issues and delays if your bike has to go through customs without you. Be sure to research this issue carefully before shipping your bike internationally. You may need to use a customs broker, and this may be worthwhile if you get good service.

For shipping internationally, you'll save yourself a lot of headaches if you research the shipping possibilities and customs requirements well ahead of time. One possibility is to ship to the airport where you will arrive, so that you can clear your bike through customs yourself. Shipping companies may act as customs brokers, but you need to carefully research their services and charges in advance. You might be able to ship to a friend, a member of the bicycle touring community, or a bike shop in the city to which you are traveling. Bike shops are often quite familiar with customs issues in their own countries. To begin researching the issues, the Web sites for FedEx and UPS are a good place to start, and searching the bike list archive is invaluable (see the Resources section at the back of the book).

If you are shipping directly you have to choose between carriers, and you'll encounter widely varying opinions on their relative merits. Still, if you're willing to do the research, you can get far better, more reliable, and more consistent information about the services of the U.S. Postal Service, UPS, and FedEx than you'll ever be able to obtain on United Airlines, American Airlines, or any of their competitors.

Touring cyclists have had excellent experiences with all the major shipping carriers. There are also plenty of horror stories for each carrier, but there is good evidence that smart consumers can avoid many problems from the start. This is not a perfect situation, but it is far less frustrating than the one that increasingly prevails with the airlines.

There are many nuances associated with shipping, and only a few can be discussed here. Check the details on insurance. It may cover far less than the name implies. Get written evidence of the value of your bike before shipping—a letter from your local bike shop should do. If you have that evidence, any insurance claim arising will be easier to pursue.

The U.S. Postal Service is worth considering. You can buy the services you need—insurance, delivery confirmation, and the like. You can send a box to be held for pickup to post offices anywhere in the Unites States. However, the weight cannot be over 70 pounds, and the length plus girth can't exceed 130 inches.

Note that in many locations in the United States, some local drivers are far better at finding addresses than those who work for other companies. If you live in a rural or once-rural area, you probably know which companies perform best. If you are shipping to a friend or a bike shop in a rural area, ask them. It is generally wise to avoid contract shipping and receiving locations—the ones that take USPS mail, UPS packages, and so on. If something goes awry, you'll have a hard time getting anyone to take responsibility. Be aware that Federal Express is actually made up of several companies, with different organizations and delivery services. FedEx Express is not the same as FedEx Ground, and the latter does not have as good a reputation for on-time delivery. FedEx Ground is quite a bit cheaper, however, and it may be fine if you can ship early for pickup at the local office.

Pay close attention to the carton dimensions and the weight limitations when you get a shipping quote. If you stuff your panniers and camping equipment into the carton, you may go over a weight limit, and if the sides bulge out, you may be charged for a larger size, particularly if you are shipping via UPS. Also, check the tariffs carefully, and do your measurements. Charges are often based on a combination of weight and dimensions.

Packing Your Bike

Whether you are bringing your bike along as checked luggage or arranging to have it shipped to your destination, you'll usually need to pack it up beforehand. There are exceptions—rail lines with accommodations for rolling a bike on and placing it in a rack or hanging it from a hook, airlines that accept bikes in plastic bags with only the handlebars turned and pedals removed, and buses in remote areas where the method is to tie the bike on the roof with the livestock and other stuff. But most of the time, if you are flying to the start of your tour or taking a train or bus, you'll need to pack your bike in a case or carton. This section will concentrate on typical touring bikes. Tandems, recumbents, folding bikes, trailers, and take-apart bikes have special problems or advantages, and they aren't covered here.

Normally, whenever you're shipping your bike or packing it for public transportation, you'll get a standard bike carton from a local shop prepared as described below in "Boxing the Bike." Some exceptions are covered elsewhere: hard bike cases are described under "Commercially Made Cases and Alternatives" below, and custom containers developed for particular shipping options are discussed under "Other Options for Shipping Your Bike" later in this chapter. Finally, as described in the paragraph immediately below, you can reinforce a standard bike carton.

Typical bike shipping cartons are designed to hold a bike that is partly disassembled but with the rear wheel attached to the frame in the normal way. One extremely serviceable substitute for commercially made bike cases is a regular bike shipping box reinforced with corrugated plastic, which goes by trade names like Coroplast and Correx. You can buy this material in sheets at many business supply stores large enough to carry packing materials, at some building supply stores, and through the Web. It is lightweight, relatively cheap, and easy to cut with a standard utility knife. Its advantage is that you can use it to reinforce a normal bike box, adding extra panels at critical spots and even building in reinforcing cross-structures to strengthen the box using glue, tape, or slotted connections. Effectively, you build your own custom reinforced case. The materials are inexpensive, but you have to decide how much your own labor is worth. You also need to calculate whether the relatively small additional weight and volume required will cause you to inch past one of the shipping restrictions discussed below. A very simple way to get better reinforcement from a standard carton, at the cost of more weight, is to get a second, slightly larger bike box and double-box your bicycle.

Commercially Made Cases and Alternatives

In the past, with good luck, it was possible to use a soft, padded bike bag, but baggage handling has gotten worse as it has become more mechanized, and soft, padded carriers are unacceptably risky now. Similarly, the heavy plastic bike bags that are recommended and sold by some airlines provided a convenient alternative at one time. Some cyclists argue that while the heavy plastic bags provide less direct protection, the visibility of the bike inside the bag and the ease of handling make up for these deficiencies. A few (non-U.S. based) international carriers still allow (and sometimes promote) this plastic bag option (you may have to reserve a bag ahead of time), but it is not recommended.

There are excellent hard-shell bike cases that are useful for some travelers. They provide superb protection and ease of packing, though they are not cheap. They are only worth considering if you travel a lot with your bike, weight surcharges are not a major consideration, and your destinations allow you to store the case for your return trip.

An alternative cardboard container that may be available free from some bike shops is the one used by Cannondale, which your shop should be able to provide if it is a Cannondale dealer. Cannondale boxes are wider, but shorter in both the other dimensions. Cannondale uses heavier cardboard and a different packing system than other bike cartons. Both wheels must be removed, the frame suspended from an internal "pallet" to protect the dropouts, rear derailleur, and other delicate parts, and both wheels placed to the side, separated from the frame by a cardboard divider. The smaller overall dimensions may result in lower shipping fees both by airlines and commercial shippers. Cannondale boxes have also been reported to be very useful for shipping disassembled BOB trailers (up to two trailers to a carton).

Boxing the Bike

This section describes in detail a step-by-step procedure for packing your bike. It involves taking the bike partly apart, so practice is critical. Do a few trial runs to learn how to pack the bike, to make sure you have all the tools available, and to develop a list of packing materials. It will take you at least a couple of hours to pack the bike on your first try. Once you've had enough practice, you'll be able to do it in 15 or 20 minutes.

Don't forget that you not only have to pack the bike beforehand, but you need to be able to put it back together in some airport or railway station far from home, and then repack it to come back. It is embarrassing to demonstrate your incompetence at a crowded terminal in Europe or Latin America, and it is extremely problematic if you find halfway through that you don't have a critical Allen wrench to attach your handlebar or seat to the bike. Moreover, in case the airlines do not treat your bike well, you'll want to know exactly what is missing or misaligned, so that you can deal with the situation as efficiently as possible.

Step 1: Measure the bike. Measure the bike beforehand, so that you can ask your local shop to save a box of the right size. Partly disassemble the bike, as described in Step 3, and measure the length and height the carton must accommodate. Also do your research on critical dimensions required by the airline or shipping service you are considering. A few inches of additional length or girth can be very expensive, because of the way the charges are calculated (see "Air Travel" and "Should You Ship Your Bike?" earlier in this chapter). The critical measurements to be sure your container is large enough are (1) the height of the top of the seat tube above the ground with the rear wheel on the bike, and (2) the length from the back of the rear wheel to the front-most part of the bike (with the handlebar and front wheel removed and the fork rotated, if that works on your bike).

Step 2: Gather your supplies. Ask the shop to open the lid of the box without cutting it (pulling it back from the fasteners) and to save all the little specialized protectors and spacers that were used to protect the bike that was originally packaged in it. These normally go in the trash, but they are invaluable in packing your bike. They typically include a plastic front drop-out spacer (substituting for the front axle), derailleur protectors, and the like.

In addition, you'll need a couple of rolls of 2-inch packing tape and some lengths of tubular foam pipe insulation, available in hardware and building supply stores. You also need a roll of fiberglass strapping tape if you're packing your bike for an airline. Some use this for everything, in which case you would need more. The foam pipe insulation is used to protect the frame tubes and fork blades; generally you can use a

2-inch outside diameter, but a size larger or smaller works fine. You'll also need some heavy-duty ziplock bags (gallon-size bags are most useful) and a few straps. The straps can be heavy-duty zip ties from the hardware store, old toe-clip straps, or any comparable straps you have lying around. Miscellaneous packing material, like foam, bubble wrap, or old towels, also comes in handy.

Step 3: Clean the bike. Next clean the bike thoroughly. You don't need to clean it meticulously, but if you are like most of us, the bike will need some cleaning. If the drive chain is grimy when you arrive, you'll get a lot of black grease on you as you reassemble the bike. This is not a fun way to start the tour.

Step 4: Prepare the bike. First remove any panniers and other bags, water bottle cages, tire pumps, the front wheel, the pedals, the front luggage rack and fenders, if any, accessories like headlamps and computers, and the seat and seat post. Shift the gears so that the chain is on the largest chainwheel in front and the largest cog in the back. (The large-large position ensures that the rear derailleur is retracted as far as possible, and the chain provides some protection for the vulnerable teeth on the large chainwheel.)

Put all the hardware together in a pile, and put all the attachment screws back in their sockets on the frame, screwing them moderately tight so they don't loosen and fall out. Put the front-wheel skewer with the quick-release and hardware in the pile of loose parts.

Turn the cranks so the left one is parallel with the down tube (angled forward and up). Tape lengths of foam tubing around the down tube, the top tube, the seat tube, and the chainstays, cutting open one side of the tubing when necessary. Place the front wheel against the left side of the frame, strapping the tire to the top tube at the top, working the left crank between the spokes, and then padding, taping, and strapping so that everything is held together tightly without any rubbing of metal on metal or metal on paint.

Remove the handlebar and swing it around with the cables still attached, so that it fits as well as possible into the left side of the bike and front wheel. Removal technique depends on your equipment. For most modern threadless headsets, you open the clamp around the handlebar, remove the bar, and then screw the clamp back together. For older threaded headsets with quill stems, you usually loosen the expander bolt and remove the whole stem from the steerer tube. With this type, you may also need to loosen the clamp and rotate the handlebar in the stem clamp.

Once you have the handlebars positioned, pad and strap them to the frame and the front wheel. If you can turn the fork backward, do so. Put the substitute axle, with end caps if you have them, between the fork drop-outs, and make sure it is solidly in place, taping if necessary. Substitutes include a surplus quick-release and a retired hub, an old axle with suitable nuts, a piece of threaded rod with nuts, or homemade wooden spacers with attached studs and nuts. The most important thing is to have a rigid spacer solidly installed between the fork dropouts, so that the fork can't be compressed and bent by having weight put on top of it while the wheel is removed. End caps on the substitute axle provide additional protection.

Step 5: Protect vulnerable parts. Tape foam tubing around the fork blades and the head tube. If you got a pile of plastic and cardboard packing items with the bike box, there will probably be one piece that slips over the derailleur end of the rear quick release to protect it. Securely fasten padding and cardboard spacers around the derailleurs, improvising if you don't have ready-made items. The better these items are protected and braced, the better chance you have of avoiding a scramble to fix, replace, or realign critical parts of the bike at the beginning of your tour. You want to protect your bike from any potential rough baggage handling.

When you put the bike in the carton, it will rest on the fork tips. You should protect them. The plastic doodads that were in the box you got from your local shop may have some molded pieces to do this. If there were none, you can improvise a small (2" × 2" × 6") block of Ethafoam with holes carved for the fork ends. This ensures that the fork ends won't break through the carton and be damaged. Ideally, it should be integrated with the front spacer or axle between the front dropouts.

Step 6: Package the loose parts and tools. Now package and attach the loose parts and tools you need to put the bike back together. If you are packing to ship the bike separately, rolling things like pedals and tools into a towel and then taping the bundle solidly into a space in the frame is best. It is critical to make sure such packages are really secure; if they come loose, they will unroll, and important small items will escape their captivity through the grip holes or holes made during shipping. Before they escape, they will ding your paint to remind you of your negligence.

For modern air travel, most of this packaging should be done with bubble wrap and ziplock bags. Since these are transparent, TSA baggage inspectors are less likely to look inside, probably defeating your carefully constructed anchor system. That is, if the inspector, instead of seeing a rolled-up bundle in a towel, which he or she may feel a duty to unwrap, sees a pair of pedals wrapped with bubble wrap, secured in a ziplock bag, and taped to the frame padding, your packing job is more likely to remain intact. Similarly, instead of leaving your tools inside their usual fabric pouch strapped to the frame, you might be better off taping them with clear packing tape to the foam tubes, and putting the empty tool pouch in a pannier pocket. Make the TSA inspectors' lives as easy as you can by making things visible with a cursory glance.

Step 7: Load the bike into the box. The whole bike should now be a stable unit that you can pick up and slide into the carton, subsequently padding it with foam, panniers, or cardboard to keep it from moving inside the carton and to prevent the projecting hard parts from breaking through the carton.

Other cycling-related items may fit into empty spaces in the bicycle box, but find out beforehand what the shipper's regulations allow you to pack with it. Possible items include clothing, panniers, helmet, cycling shoes, camping gear, and so on. Do not include expensive electronics, and be very careful not to inadvertently toss in prohibited items like fuel canisters or bottles of liquid fuel. Any bottles that have been used for fuel should be washed out and dried so they no longer smell of fuel.

This whole step is fraught with opportunities for last-minute mistakes. Measurements and weights of bike cartons are the subject of a morass of constantly changing regulation and fare minutiae. Throwing the tent into the bike box at the last minute may subject you to a $200 surcharge at the airline check-in counter, where you are ill-equipped to open the box and adjust your baggage. Similarly, stuffing the helmet in before you transport the carton to UPS may bow out the sides of the box, causing the clerk to increase the measured dimensions of the box, sending it into the next size/weight category, and also costing you a large premium. Again, you may have no time for adjustments if you are shipping the box at the last minute.

Step 8: Seal and label the package. Follow the important sealing and labeling rules below, any of which could make or break your trip. Because Murphy's Law is a constant companion to the adventurous traveler, it behooves you to pay attention.

- Seal all edges of the carton with wide, sturdy packing tape, with the important possible exception of the top.

- Seal the top the same way if you are shipping by commercial carrier. If you are taking it as checked luggage on a plane and you can't accompany it to inspection, as described in "Air Travel" earlier in this chapter, seal the top with a series of cross-strips of fiberglass packing tape so that it is obvious how an inspector should open it. Make sure this top opening is constructed of overlapping flaps of cardboard that can easily be cut and retaped without requiring much effort. TSA employees have wide discretion to open your bike box without spending a lot of time thinking about it. Make their job easy.

- Carefully consider the identifying information you should put in the main addresses on the box. Your home address is not sufficient. If your bike takes a different plane than you do, you don't want it to go to your home address, unless the trip has already been cancelled or postponed and you just want the bike back. Typically, you want something like:

  Name: Frieda Pedaler
  Home address: street, city, state/province,
      zip/postal code, country, phone, e-mail
  Destination address(es): Hotel X, street,
      state/province, zip/postal code, country,
      phone, e-mail

- If you are carrying a cell phone that will work at your destination or you have an e-mail address you can access while traveling, you should identify it prominently. Don't expect harassed and over-worked lost-luggage people to read the fine print.

- Carefully and clearly mark this primary identifying information in heavy indelible ink on the outside of the box and on the inside of the box, on the sidewall below the top flaps, so that it won't be accidentally torn away. It is easier to do this before you pack the bike in the box. Put the same information on a luggage tag attached to the bike frame.

  In addition to the primary information, print out an itinerary that covers where you plan to go if you haven't yet received your bike. When checked luggage goes astray, you want the baggage people to be able to find you, rather than sending the bike to your home or to the hotel you left several days before. This needs to be a custom itinerary constructed for the purpose. Your cycling plans are not relevant—you won't be following them until your bike arrives! Tape this itinerary in a prominent place on the outside of the carton. It needs to be easy to find but not easy to confuse with your primary contact information. You can either put it in a plastic envelope, or cover it with clear packing tape.

- It is also useful to tie the carton with nylon or polypropylene rope. The idea is to provide a good grip for baggage handlers that won't slip off and that will generally make it easier to handle. Go around the length once and the girth twice, with stable knots at all the rope junctions. As with TSA inspectors, you want to make things easy for baggage handlers.

- If you are flying, partially deflate the tires. There is a persistent myth that the low pressure of the air cargo hold can cause bicycle tires to explode, and some airline employees are concerned. In fact, the physics don't support this hypothesis, but it is not a battle worth fighting.

- Other labels may be useful to put on the box. For example, if you are leaving the carton in a guest house or a bike shop for the duration of your tour, it may be worth putting a large legend in the local language noting that the box is not trash and it is being saved for a returning (paying?) guest. Don't add to the noise for your initial trip; you can write these labels when you arrive. (Put the text on a sheet in the box, along with a large permanent marker pen, so that it is easy to create the labels when you arrive.)

Note that, in addition to the advice given here, there are several excellent resources, in print and on the Web, offering advice on packing a bike (see the Resources section at the end of the book). In an era of soaring fuel costs and shifting transportation economics, things change constantly, so you need to verify the current situation for every aspect of getting your bike to your tour.

Other Options for Shipping Your Bike

In addition to taking your bike as checked baggage and shipping it via common carrier, several specialized services have appeared recently, and they are worth considering. Shipbikes.com is specifically oriented to cyclists; it makes a special bike container (the AirCaddy) with a triangular cross-section, built to meet the requirements of FedEx Ground, UPS, and the airlines (airline requirements for shipping, not checked baggage) and designed to hold the bike with minimal disassembly. You just take off the front wheel, lower or remove the seat, and rotate the handlebars. You may also have to remove racks and fenders to fit the bike in. Then you clamp the fork ends into the mounting hardware, fold the AirCaddy top over, and seal the container with tape. The AirCaddy is not cheap (around $100), but it is durable enough that it should be good for a number of trips. It is expensive enough that you don't want to throw it away, so you need to deal with storing it or shipping it to your end point, but it folds flat once the bike has been taken out, so this is far less of a problem than with a hard-shell case. In Europe, you might have a chance of getting it stored for a reasonable charge (storing and shipping hard-shell cases, or even bike cartons, can be *very* expensive in Europe).

Shipbikes.com has an arrangement with FedEx Ground to ship bikes within the United States. You make shipping arrangements directly from the www.shipbikes.com Web site, arranging pickup and delivery, getting a price, and receiving a shipping ticket for FedEx via e-mail. By several reports, it is significantly cheaper than taking the AirCaddy to a FedEx Ground location yourself. So, if you're planning on making several trips in the United States, the AirCaddy may be the most economical solution for you. The AirCaddy has room for other touring equipment, but be watchful of the 60-pound weight limit. The AirCaddy weighs at least 20 pounds, and your touring bike with racks and fenders will not leave a huge weight margin for other equipment—you'll probably have to limit yourself to a few bulky, lightweight items.

Another possibility is Sports Express (www.sports express.com), which provides a variety of shipping, pickup, and delivery services, including rates for tandems and recumbent bikes.

Two Travel Scenarios

All the cautions and tales of woe in this chapter might be enough to put you off altogether from doing any traveling to a faraway tour, but I hope that is not the case. Traveling to interesting places to bicycle-tour is a pleasure, and it can be a great adventure. All the caveats are simply intended to help you avoid major glitches, so it seems worth mentioning a couple of specific scenarios—one hypothetical, one real.

Patagonia in My Dreams

One trip on my short list is a combined cycling and backpacking trip to Patagonia, the enormous southern projection of South America that is divided between Chile and Argentina and along which the crest of the Andes runs. I've backpacked there and traveled around, but I've never done a bicycle tour there.

Patagonia has continental dimensions, so one could never do a tour *of* Patagonia, only various trips *in* Patagonia. The distance from one end to the other is more than twice the distance between New York and Los Angeles, most of it is uninhabited, and it includes some of the most arid deserts and one of the largest icecaps in the world.

Preliminary investigations are promising. One of the best ways to get to the southern tip of Patagonia is on LAN, the Chilean national airline, which flies from Los Angeles, New York, and Miami. LAN still allows two checked bags with reasonable weight limits and dimensions, so without the bike, I would have no baggage charges. The boxed bike (they also allow unboxed ones) qualifies as sporting goods, so even though it is oversized, I'll only be charged $100 for an extra bag, and I'm going to fly literally a quarter of the way around the world, to Punta Arenas at the southern tip of Chile—as close to the South Pole as the panhandle of Alaska is to the North Pole. From Los Angeles this journey covers approximately 90 degrees of latitude, so $100 excess baggage charge is pretty reasonable.

I'll basically take a backpack and the boxed bike. I'll probably ship the bike to Los Angeles by FedEx Ground and take a domestic flight with my backpack as checked luggage. Then I'll fly LAN to Punta Arenas, take a bus to Puerto Natales, stay in backpacker accommodations, and store the bike there. I'll take the bus to Torres del Paine National Park, backpack for a week or so, and then take the bus back to Puerto Natales. I'll then bicycle to Calafate, Argentina, store my bike again, and take the bus into Los Galciares National Park in Argentina, where I'll backpack for another week before taking the bus back to Calafate.

At this point, advance planning will be useless. There are several Argentinean airlines that I could use to fly north from Calafate to Trelew, but reservations can't really be made from outside Argentina, so I'll have to arrange things in Calafate. The attractive side of that situation is that though I'll have to negotiate in my less-than-perfect Argentine Spanish, ad hoc arrangements are a lot easier than in the United States. The price will probably be reasonable. Most likely, I won't find a bike box (not a lot of bike shops in Calafate), so the bike will have to be loaded directly.

From Trelew, I plan to bicycle a dirt road to a huge penguin colony at Punto Tombo, then around the Península Valdés, which is mostly paved, to see the fur seals and other marine life,. I'll also visit the major paleontological museum at Trelew (there are colossal finds of dinosaur fossils in Patagonia), and then bicycle up the valley past some of the Welsh settlements (yes, Welsh! from Wales—there were once more speakers of Welsh in Patagonia than in Wales) in the Chubut Valley before crossing back west to Chile and riding north to Bariloche in the gorgeous lake district. Finally, I'll bike to Puerto Montt, from where I can take another LAN Chile flight to Los Angeles or Miami.

While this is still a fantasy trip, I already have enough information to make it a reality. It is probably too ambitious, and I'll have to be satisfied with half my initial itinerary. Once I figure out my schedule and budget, I can start paring it down. Nonetheless, once you've planned a few trips and actually done the tours, it is straightforward to come up with the basic outline and budget for the next one. Then you can work out schedule details and enjoy the fun part—finding the best maps, reading about the history and natural history, and refining your plans.

Central Europe with Mark Boyd

For a second example, let's look at a trip taken in the summer of 2008 by the inveterate touring cyclist Mark Boyd. (Mark's Web site, with many photographs and tour logs, is listed in the Resources section at the end of the book.)

Mark has toured extensively in the United States on his Cannondale, but during summers he often tours some infrequently visited regions of Central Europe. Given the complications of transporting bikes these days, Mark built up a Surly Long Haul Trucker with the plan of using it on tour in 2008 and then storing it with a friend, so that next year he can simply fly over and have a bike waiting for him in Europe.

Mark flew British Air and was not charged for the bike (though it was not treated gently, and he had to make some repairs in Budapest). This in itself is a good lesson in preparation. Mark is experienced and methodical, so I'm sure that the damage could not have been prevented with better packing or foresight.

Nonetheless, he rode from Budapest through the Balkans, Bulgaria, Romania, Ukraine, Poland, and the

Czech Republic to end in Germany in a little over two months. He stayed primarily in small hotels and reported varying quality for the price (though they were certainly cheaper than in more fashionable parts of Europe).

For this kind of adventurous touring off the beaten path, one has to be flexible in one's expectations; guide-book coverage and Web searches are of limited utility for planning lodgings in the remote corners of Bulgaria and Ukraine. Nonetheless, Mark had a remarkable tour and covered the route he had planned. And he now has a touring bike in Europe.

Resources

What to Take

Every trip is different, and so are people's preferences, so the following lists are a starting point at best. In particular, they don't include the various vocational, educational, or special-interest extras you might want to take along. You have to decide which and how many of those to take, both to fulfill your goals on the trip and to suit your own interests. Are you more interested in taking a computer to post a trip journal to the Internet every day or two, or a bird book, binoculars, and butterfly and plant guides? The space and weight constraints of bicycle touring require that you choose among many possible extras.

Credit-Card Tours

Small first aid kit (see "First Aid" on page 339)
Toiletries and medications in small stuff sack
Travel alarm
Cable lock
Insect repellant
Suntan lotion
Lip balm with sunscreen
Bilingual dictionary for the place you're visiting—mail
   home and buy a different one, as needed
Wallet and passport
Ziplock bags in several sizes (for credit-card receipts,
   toiletries, tea bags, and other items)

Small electric water-heating coil (for making tea in hotel rooms)

Lexan cup

Small Lexan plate and utensils (for meals made from items purchased at a grocery store or deli)

Repair kit (see "Tools for the Road" on page 411)

Camera, spare battery, and spare memory cards or film

Charger for camera battery

Small notebook and pen

Flashlight, handlebar clamp, extra batteries, and charger (works as bike light if necessary)

Bike tail light

Reflective vest

Glasses case for regular glasses or sunglasses (can hold the pair not being worn)

Spare prescription glasses

Dishcloth, dish soap

Rain jacket, pants, and booties

Down vest and windbreaker

Lightweight wool tights to wear under pants when needed

Cycling shoes or sandals (worn when riding)

Sandals for off-bike wear

Address book

Pants with zip-off legs

Lightweight long pants

Two presentable shirts

T-shirt

Bathing suit

GPS with maps (and extra paper maps bought along the way and mailed home)

Bandana (for sweat and protection against breathing swarms of insects)

Two pairs of cycling shorts

Baggy nylon shorts to go over cycling shorts when not riding

Two cycling jerseys

Lightweight wool pullover

Two pairs of off-bike underwear

Two pairs of cycling socks

Two pairs of off-bike socks

Light stocking cap
Silk or synthetic gloves
Crushable sun hat
Clothesline
Three water bottles on bike
Extra water containers as appropriate

Supported Tours

Start with the "Credit-Card Tours" list, some of which may be carried in a duffle rather than on the bike. The repair kit can be reduced if you have good mechanical support, but it still needs to include everything specific to your bike, such as the right lengths of spare spokes and a cluster remover that fits your cassette.

If you are camping, add the appropriate items from the "Self-Contained Tours" list, such as tent, sleeping bag, and pad, though most of it will go in your duffle rather than being carried on your bike. Gear for cooking and eating depends on the type of support.

Self-Contained Tours

To the "Credit-Card Tours" list, add the following:

One extra set of cycling clothes
One pair of cycling undershorts (underwear) with
    chamois (supplements non-cycling pants so they can
    be used for riding)
Extra wool pullover
Wool socks
Tent
Sleeping bag
Pad
Stove and cook set
Fuel bottle or canisters
Parachute cord (100 feet)
Bear bag or Ursack (when needed)
Straps for rear rack

Tools for the Road

As with all lists, adjust for your own bike, skills, and circumstances. Tools preceded by an asterisk (*) should be taken on longer trips.

Patch kit with unopened tube of glue, or pre-glued patch kit
Tire irons—steel, aluminum, or nylon
Tire boots
Small container of talcum powder, such as an old-fashioned film canister
Tire pressure gauge for the valve type you are using
Two spare inner tubes
Adapter for Presta valve to allow filling at gas station air hose
Replacement brake pads
Multitool knife (Leatherman, Victorinox, Gerber, etc.—one of the smaller ones, preferably weighing less than the bike)
6-inch crescent wrench
Allen wrenches (hex keys)—can be replaceable ends to a single socket handle or multitool attachment
Phillips and straight-blade screwdrivers—can be replaceable ends to a single socket handle or multitool attachment
Small bottle of oil for chain
Hand wipes, sealed in individual envelopes
Small tube of degreasing hand cleaner
Two pairs of nitrile gloves to protect skin from solvents or just to stay clean during repairs
Short length of chain for spare links
Miniature chain tool
Spare spokes, particularly right rear, carried on frame
FiberFix replacement spokes (available from Peter White or Harris Cyclery)
Spoke wrench
Hypercracker lockring tool (available from Harris Cyclery)
Set of spare cables for brakes and derailleurs

*Three hose clamps (for repairing miscellaneous items, like luggage racks, frame attachments, and tent poles
Nylon zip ties
Razor blade—one of the old-fashioned kind with a reinforced back
Tape—try rolling moderate lengths of duct tape and fiber-reinforced packing tape onto a length of plastic tube, such as the barrel of a discarded pen
Small permanent marker
Tire pump (on bike)
Folding spare tire
*A few feet of soft steel wire
*Spare screws for selected attachments, such as luggage racks
*Selected small sockets, with single T-handle that attaches (when this is carried, Allen keys and screwdrivers are carried as attachments to this handle and the separate ones are left at home)
*Well-protected small tube of superglue
*Spare batteries for any lights and electronic gear
*Diagonal wire cutters
*Small tube of grease
*Small channel-lock pliers
*Sewing kit for clothing and camping gear

Additional Tools to Use at Home

Acquire these as you need them.

Chain whips
Cable and housing cutter
Cone wrenches
Pedal wrench
Wheel truing stand
Dishing stick
Citrus-based solvent
Rags
Miscellaneous screwdrivers
Miscellaneous wrenches
Bicycle stand or improvised equivalent

Chain cleaner (such as a small disposable basin and a
    brush)
Chain wear checker
Crank puller
Bottom bracket tools
Chain tool
Chainring nut wrench
Grease—one of the high-quality waterproof bicycle
    greases

Books and Articles

Bicycling has a long history and a voluminous literature, so only a small sampling is listed here. Books preceded by an asterisk (*) are particularly recommended.

General

Effective Cycling, 6th ed.
by John Forester (Cambridge, MA: MIT Press, 1993)
One of the classics for useful and provocative opinions on a variety of issues ranging from cycling safety through technique and equipment recommendations to mechanical and riding advice.

Zinn's Cycling Primer
by Lennard Zinn (Boulder, CO: VeloPress, 2004)
A useful reference for bicycle fitting and setup, training and conditioning methods, and maintenance, by the technical editor of *VeloNews*.

Bicycling Science, 3rd ed.
by David Gordon Wilson (Cambridge, MA: MIT Press, 1993)
A thorough treatise on the physics and mechanics of the bicycle; includes a chapter on the history of the bicycle.

Bicycle: The History
by David V. Herlihy (New Haven, CT: Yale University Press, 2004)
An excellent history of the bicycle.

Bicycle: Bone Shakers, Highwheelers, and Other Celebrated Cycles
by Gilbert King (Philadelphia, PA: Courage Books, 2002)
Another history of bicycles and cycling.

Around the World on a Bicycle
by Thomas Stevens
Originally published 1887, this account of Stevens' three-year ride around the world, starting from San Francisco in 1884, is available in numerous editions, most recently in a 2001 edition by Stackpole Books. Volume 1 of the original can be downloaded from the Internet at www.gutenberg.org/etext/5136. Volume 2 can be downloaded from documents.scribd.com/docs/1vzc9mr4g91zn3q8wscj.txt.

Adventure Cycle-Touring Handbook
by Stephen Lord (Hindhead, Surrey, UK: Trailblazer Publications, 2006)
This handbook concentrates on travel in remote areas.

The Road That Has No End
by Tim Travis (Indianapolis, IN: Down the Road Publishing, 2004)
Tim and Cindie Travis have been traveling the world by bicycle for several years. This book tells the tale.

Shop/Repair Manuals

Barnett's Manual: Analysis and Procedures for Bicycle Mechanics, 5th ed.
by John Barnett (Boulder, CO: VeloPress, 2003)
The most complete bicycle repair reference book.

Zinn and the Art of Mountain Bike Maintenance, 4th ed.
  by Lennard Zinn (Boulder, CO: VeloPress, 2005)
Zinn and the Art of Road Bike Maintenance, 2nd ed.
  by Lennard Zinn (Boulder, CO: VeloPress, 2005)
Two excellent manuals for novices by longtime frame builder and senior technical writer for *VeloNews*, Lennard Zinn.

Big Blue Book of Bicycle Repair
by C. Calvin Jones (St. Paul, MN: Park Tool Company, 2005)
The Bicycling Guide to Complete Bicycle Maintenance and Repair: For Road and Mountain Bikes, 5th ed.
by Todd Downs (Emmaus, PA: Rodale Books, 2005)
Two other worthwhile books for working on bicycles.

Wheel Building

The Bicycle Wheel, 3rd ed.
  by Jobst Brandt (Palo Alto, CA: Avocet, 2003),
    www.avocet.com/wheelbook/wheelbook.html
The Art of Wheelbuilding
  by Gerd Schraner (Denver, CO: Buonpane Publications, 1999)
Wheel Building, 4th ed.
  by Roger Musson (2008), only available as an ebook from www.wheelpro.co.uk
Three excellent books on bicycle wheels for those who want to delve into the details or learn to build wheels with better-than-basic knowledge. The first book also has a superb analysis of the physics/engineering of the bicycle wheel.

C. J. Burgoyne and R. Dilmaghanian, "The Bicycle Wheel as a Prestressed Structure," *Journal of Engineering Mechanics* 119, no. 3 (March 1993), pp. 439–55.
For anyone interested in the technical details of bicycle wheels as prestressed structures.

Small Wheels for Adult Cycles
by Tony Hadland
Originally published in *Cycling Science* in 1997, and available on the Web at www.users.globalnet .co.uk/%7Ehadland/page15.html. Discusses the use of small wheels.

Frames

The Paterek Manual for Bicycle Framebuilders
by Tim Paterak (www.timpaterek.com.)
Very few of us are likely to develop the background to understand the technical details of building frames. If you want to delve into the subject, this book is the definitive guide.

Information on the Web

The Web is an excellent source of diverse information on bicycle touring, ranging from discussion groups to data on equipment to the opinions of experts. In the case of bike touring, those experts often have very different points of view. Because the Web is dynamic and ephemeral, some of the links listed here are bound to have disappeared or moved by the time you read this book, though they were accurate when it went to press.

General

Bicycle Quarterly
www.vintagebicyclepress.com/vbqindex.html
Bicycle Quarterly publishes articles on a range of topics ranging from technical analyses, test reports, and history to particular aspects of cycling, such as randonneuring. The Web site offers a selection of past articles.

Sheldon Brown's Bicycle Technical Info
sheldonbrown.com
Brown's well-thought-out (and strong) opinions on nearly every aspect of cycling are found here. Also includes extensive repair information and links to hard-to-find equipment items at the shop with which he was associated, Harris Cyclery. Sadly, Sheldon died

in early 2008, but his pages are maintained by his colleagues at Harris Cyclery.

John Forester's Web site
www.johnforester.com
Forester concentrates on some of his long-time crusades in the areas of bicycle safety and legal issues. He has been active in these areas for half a century and was the creator of the Effective Cycling educational program, which was the official system of the League of American Wheelmen until a falling-out a few years ago. For his comprehensive views on cycling, the best source is his book, *Effective Cycling*, mentioned earlier in the "General" section under "Books and Articles," but the Web site summarizes a number of his arguments.

Frequently Asked Questions on Cycling
draco.acs.uci.edu/rbfaq/FAQ
A compendium of answers to questions that have been posed to the rec.bicycles group.

Ken Kifer's Bike Pages
www.kenkifer.com/bikepages/index.htm
The late Ken Kifer's bicycle pages are still very useful, and they continue to be maintained by Ken's friend Riin Gill. (Kifer was killed by a drunk driver in 2003).

Jim Foreman's Web site
jimforeman.com
Jim's site has a wealth of useful cycling tips, stories, and opinions. Nobody should miss the story of Chuck's Motel.

Leave No Trace: Center for Outdoor Ethics
www.lnt.org/programs/index
Here you'll find general principles for minimizing impact and using the land ethically, particularly when camping or riding on trails.

Tony Hadland's pages
www.users.globalnet.co.uk/%7Ehadland
Interesting bicycling history and various specialized
topics can be found here.

Dave Moulton's Bike Blog
davesbikeblog.squarespace.com
For various fit issues, technical design questions,
and cycling history, don't miss Dave Moulton's blog.
Moulton began racing in the 1950s, and he is a legendary frame builder.

Web-based forums
bikelist.org
This is a Web site that includes links to the Listservs of
a variety of bicycling organizations. You can either join
the lists or just view their archives without joining.

Searching for Answers to Cycling Questions
search.bikelist.org
Web site that allows you to search the archives of all
the Listservs on bikelist.org, including the touring list

Tandem Discussion Group
hobbes.ucsd.edu/tandem
A Listserver run by Wade Blomgren.

Multilingual Bicycle Vocabulary and Terms
bemi.free.fr/biciklo
This site has translations for many bicycle terms in a
score of languages.
   And for technical terms for bicycle parts and the
like, there is a spreadsheet of 450 bike mechanics'
terms in nine European languages on the Park Tool
site: www.parktool.com/repair/readhowto.asp?id=152

Ready to Ride Long-Distance Cycling Site
readytoride.biz
This is a randonneur-oriented site by David and Evan
Rowe, which emphasizes athletics-centered long-
distance cycling.

Touring

Alex Wetmore's Bicycle Pages
www.phred.org/~alex/bikes
Alex has interesting discussions on a lot of cycling and especially touring issues..

Mark Boyd's Bicycle Touring Web Site
www.cs.unca.edu/~boyd/bicycling.html
Mark is a very experienced bicycle tourist, as well as an active poster on the touring list. His Web site includes lots of equipment tips, as well as logs and photos of his many, many trips. He carries a computer and a camera on tour and updates his Web site as he goes.

Crazyguyonabike: A place for bicycle tourists and their journals
www.crazyguyonabike.com
Neil Gunton's site hosts hundreds of tour journals, a number of articles, and thousands of photographs.

Bicycle Touring 101
bicycletouring101.com
Jamie Noble's Web site has a wealth of useful information on touring.

Touring—The Internet Bicycle Touring List
www.phred.org/mailman/listinfo/touring
This touring listserver is an invaluable resource for all kinds of information, from descriptions of routes to spirited discussions of equipment choices. If you ask a question on the list, you will probably receive several responses from people who are all very experienced but who have quite different styles and opinions. Members of the list (the Phreds) often offer places to stay overnight for fellow touring cyclists.

The Fully Loaded Touring Gallery
www.fullyloadedtouring.com
This Web site includes lots of good photos of many sorts and styles of trips.

Adam K's Cycling Site
www.adamk.ca
This Web site has excellent advice on touring subjects, as well as logs and photographs of many of Adam's tours, particularly in western Canada.

Cyclotour Guide Books
www.cyclotour.com
Cyclotour publishes a number of excellent cycle touring guidebooks, particularly for the Great Lakes region, eastern Canada, New Zealand, and the French canal system. Their Web site also has some useful articles.

Bicycle Lifestyle
groups.google.com/group/bicyclelifestyle
Peter Jon White's moderated Google Groups forum on touring and other cycling topics. Peter discusses the purpose of the forum and how to sign up at www .peterwhitecycles.com/bl.html.

There are innumerable other individual and collective Web sites with good narratives and photographs of wonderful bicycle tours and meditations, and they cannot all be surveyed here. A few particularly good examples are:

The Spokesrider
spokesrider.com
John Gorman's blog about his various tours and rides with lots of links to related Web sites.

The Blayleys, John and Pamela
www.blayleys.com/articles
A collection of touring tips on topics such as cycling in Ireland, tandems, winter riding shoes and pedals, and lots more.

Tamia Nelson's Outside Up North
www.tamiasoutside.com
Tamia Nelson is an outdoor and natural history columnist in Alaska. Her site has a wealth of good advice on bike touring and camping.

Bike Designs and Outfitting

Circle City Bicycles
www.circlecitybicycles.com/tourbike.htm
Good discussion of touring bikes.

Commuting/Touring Bicycles
www.faughnan.com/touringbike.html
John Faughnan's discussion of commuting and touring bicycles is well worth reading.

Bike Fit and Frames

Rivendell Bicycle Works
www.rivbike.com/article/bike_fit/fit_sizing_position
Includes useful and straightforward ideas about bike fitting that are worth perusing.

Peter White Cycles: "How to Fit a Bicycle"
www.peterwhitecycles.com/fitting.htm
White's "How to Fit a Bicycle," one of the classic essays on bike fitting, is available at his Web site.

Dave Moulton's Bike Blog: "A Different Thought on Frame Sizing"
davesbikeblog.squarespace.com/blog/2006/2/27
/a-different-thought-on-frame-sizing.html
Master frame builder Dave Moulton shares his wisdom on sizing and fit.

Jim Foreman.com: "Bicycle Size and Fit"
jimforeman.com/Stories/bikefit.htm
A good practical summary of bike-fit rules from Jim Foreman, who has ascended to the role of Grand Old Man of U.S. bicycle touring.

Harris Cyclery: "Revisionist Theory of Bicycle Sizing"
sheldonbrown.com/frame-sizing.html
A practical analysis of bike fit from Sheldon Brown.

Women's Bicycle Fit Part 1
www.myra-simon.com/bike/womens-fit.html
An excellent discussion of bike fit for women by Myra
VanInwegen.

Women's Bicycle Fit Part 2
www.blayleys.com/articles/womensfit/index.htm
Pamela Blalock also has some useful comments on
women's bike fitting.

Bicycle Queensland: How to Set Up and Measure for
    Correct Bike Size
www.bq.org.au/cycle-info/education/bikesize.shtml
Another useful source for bike fitting.

Framebuilders: Amateur and professional bicycle
    frame building
www.phred.org/mailman/listinfo/framebuilders
The Framebuilders' forum on proper frame building.

Frameforum.net
www.frameforum.net
Another frame building forum.

Klein
web.archive.org/web/19980201062345/www.
    kleinbikes.com/Technology/Myth/Debunking.html
An archived version of the bike-fitting views of legendary frame builder and mountain bike pioneer Gary
Klein.

Bill Boston Cycles
www.billbostoncycles.com/bicycle_fit.htm
Description of Bill Boston's Accufit system, together
with discussion of specific fit problems.

Georgena Terry on Bicycle Design
www.terrybicycles.com/faq/index.php?action=artikel
    &cat=2&id=5&artlang=en
The founder of Terry Bicycles discusses bicycle fit and
bike design for women.

Sheldon Brown on Frame Sizing and Fit
sheldonbrown.com/frame-sizing.html
The late Sheldon Brown was one of the most knowledgeable authorities on touring and cycling generally.
These are his recommendations.

The Myth of "KOPS," An Alternative Method of Bike Fit
sheldonbrown.com/kops.html
Keith Bontrager discusses the problems with the standard rule of thumb for positioning the knee over the
pedal axle.

For discussion of performance-related issues, take a
look at bikefitting.com.

Wheel Building

Sheldon Brown's article on wheel building
sheldonbrown.com/wheelbuild.html
An excellent primer on wheel building, with illustrated
step-by-step instructions.

Halem Spoke Length Calculator
www.geocities.com/d_halem/wheel/wheel.html
    (just close the password dialog window)
Dan Halem's spoke length calculator.

Wheelpro spoke length calculator
www.wheelpro.co.uk/spokecalc
Roger Musson developed this spoke calculator and
claims it's perfect.

Harris Cyclery spoke calculator
sheldonbrown.com/rinard/spocalc.htm
Damon Rinard's free spoke length calculator.

Epstein spoke calculator
www.appliedthought.com/danny/Spoke
    /SpokeCalculator.html
Danny Epstein's free spoke length calculator.

Technical Issues

Analytic Cycling
analyticcycling.com
Tom Compton's Web site has a wealth of data and calculation tools for all sorts of issues from gear charts to tire resistance to forces exerted on a rider. If you are performance-oriented or you want to explore esoteric technical issues, you should wander around this site.

Harris Cyclery: Sheldon Brown's Gear Calculator
sheldonbrown.com/gears
A handy gear calculator from Sheldon Brown.

Alex Wetmore's Bicycle Pages—Stem Geometry
alex.phred.org/stemchart
A very useful calculator/visualizer for stem lengths and angles of the head tube and stem at Alex Wetmore's site.

Maintenance

Bicycle Maintenance Tips
www.cccts.org/BicycleMaintenance.html
This is a good basic list.

Park Tool
www.parktool.com/repair/index.asp
An excellent resource on bicycle repair, this Web site includes a bicycle diagram set up so that you can click on any part of the bike to jump to recommendations for the components there. It contains detailed procedures for most common repair and maintenance issues.

Chain-Suck: In a Nutshell
www.fagan.co.za/Bikes/Csuck
In a more specialized vein, this site provides the definitive story on chain-suck, presented by Jonathan Levy.

Ultralight Self-Contained Camping Equipment

Adventure Cycling Association article on ultralight
   cycling
www.adventurecycling.org/features/ultralight.cfm
Informative article by Aaron Teasdale from *Adventure
Cyclist* in August 2006, based on a tour of the Great
Divide Trail and oriented toward extended mountain
bike tours. Aaron's packing lists for ultralight cycling,
plus gear sources, can be found at www.adventure
cycling.org/features/ultralightpackinglist.cfm.

Backpack GearTest
www.backpackgeartest.org
Its claim to give "The most comprehensive interactive
gear reviews and tests on the planet" is accurate.

BackPackingLight
www.backpackinglight.com
Online magazine that is considered *the* source for reliable lightweight backpacking information. Much of its
content is equally applicable to bicycle camping.

Gossamer Gear
www.gossamergear.com
Online source of ultralight outdoor gear.

Online forum on ultralight cycling
sports.groups.yahoo.com/group/ultralightbiking
Biking resources for ultralight biking and touring.

Travel Issues

Travel with Bicycles (Air/Rail/Other)
www.bikeaccess.net
George Farnsworth has compiled an amazing amount of
useful information on bike rental, trains, airport issues,
post-9/11 travel issues, and other helpful items for many
parts of the world. These are reports from various travelers, so you need to take the time to wander around the
site, but there is a lot of very helpful miscellany.

International Bicycle Fund: Airline Travel and Baggage
 Regulation for Bicycles
www.ibike.org/encouragement/travel/flying.htm
www.ibike.org/encouragement/travel/bagregs.htm
The International Bicycle Fund is an organization
that promotes cycling for transportation and touring,
worldwide, particularly in Africa. They publish guides
to touring in a number of African countries and a useful (inevitably outdated) booklet called *Flying with Your
Bicycle*. All publications can be ordered from their Web
site. These URLs point to their attempts to maintain an
accurate list of bicycle rules and fees for the major airlines. Sadly, this has become an impossible task; the
Web site is still useful, but it cannot keep up with the
airlines' constant changes.

Travel Insider on Baggage Allowances
thetravelinsider.info/travelaccessories/airlinechecked
 luggageallowances.htm
This site is a useful compendium of airline policies and
practical tips, though it is not oriented to cycling. It is
more up-to-date than any of the bike-specific sites.

The same site has several useful articles on cell
phones for international travel, avilable at www.thetra
velinsider.info/2002/0308.htm. This Web site has
links to the other seven articles in the series. Remember
that these articles are oriented to travelers in urban
areas. Cyclists in remote areas can easily encounter
places where there is no signal, regardless of other factors. Cell coverage in third-world countries is sometimes better than in developed ones, but you can't
count on this observation.

Bikes on Public Transportation (United States only)
www.bikemap.com/bikesontransit
Information on using public transportation with
bicycles can be found here. Steve Spindler has col-
lected a database of very useful information, including
Web addresses of public transportation entities in the
United States and summaries of their policies for carrying bikes.

Touring in the Third World

The International Bicycle Fund (www.ibike.org) has a good deal of information on traveling in less developed countries, particularly in Africa. Stephen Lord's book (*Adventure Cycle-Touring Handbook*) is a good source of advice for touring in the third world.

Several of the touring Web sites listed earlier in the chapter have journals of tours in the third world that are full of useful information.

Tim and Cindie Travis's Web site
www.downtheroad.org
If you're considering traveling in less developed regions, you should visit Tim and Cindie Travis's Web site. The couple left their jobs, sold their stuff, and started biking around the world in 2002, and they are still pedaling. They have developed many practical opinions on equipment and other aspects of remote travel in diverse cultures. They have two books available as e-books.

Many other good sources of information can be found in some of the repositories of touring accounts listed in the "Touring" section above. Another very good set of information can be found in the accounts of Peter Saint James, also in the "Touring" section. You can find these by going to search.bikelist.org, choosing "Touring" in the "List to Search" box, and then entering "Latin America" as a search string. You'll get posts from a number of knowledgeable members, but I'd particularly recommend reading Peter's posts for information on touring in Central and South America from the point of view of a *norteamericano*.

History

Metz Bicycle Museum
www.metzbicyclemuseum.com/History.html
The Metz Bicycle Museum, located in Freehold, New Jersey, has a fine collection of nineteenth-century bicycles. When navigating the Web site, note that "New Bicycles" does not refer to anything of the kind; it links to new acquisitions. None of the bicycles in the museum are "new." The Web site does have in its collection many photographs of interesting machines which provide a fascinating history by themselves.

A Short Illustrated History of the Bicycle: From 1817
    to the early twentieth century
www.crazyguyonabike.com/doc/?o=3Tzut&doc_
    id=1889&v=H7
While nowhere near as detailed and accurate as Herlihy's *Bicycle*, listed in "Books and Articles," this Web account is just what its title implies, a short illustrated history of the bicycle.

The Wheelmen
www.thewheelmen.org
The Wheelmen describe themselves as "dedicated to the enjoyment and preservation of our bicycling heritage." They publish interesting historical studies, organize annual meets for enthusiasts of antique bicycles, and set up occasional tours with big-wheelers. The Web site lists publications available for sale and has many fascinating historic photographs. Its photographs of modern big-wheeler events, with helmeted riders pedaling side by side with riders in period wool caps, are worth the price of admission.

GPS and Electronic Map Navigation

Air Force description of GPS system
www.afit.edu/about.cfm?article=233&a=news&sh=GPS
This is an excellent (and free) history and discussion of the GPS system for the technically inclined by an Air Force think tank.

GPS Resource Library
www.gpsy.com/gpsinfo/
This site includes a wealth of information and numerous links to tutorials and other educational material.

A Practical Guide to GPS/UTM
www.dbartlett.com
Don Bartlett's useful introduction to using GPS systems.

Trimble
www.trimble.com/gps
A good GPS tutorial for those who want a practical introduction.

Specific Receiver Information and Reviews
www.gpsinformation.net
This site, maintained by several knowledgeable enthusiasts, has a wealth of reviews, buying guides, and other information.

Dale DePriest's Navigation and GPS Articles
www.gpsinformation.org/dale
Dale DePriest has miscellaneous technical information and comparisons between Garmin and Magellan, with some discussion of other products.

Geobiking
geobiking.org
Bob Prehn has some general information on using GPS receivers and downloadable files in various formats for a number of trails and routes, mostly in the Greater Denver area. He discusses using Google Earth in conjunction with a GPS receiver and a bike.

Bike Routes using Google Maps
www.bikely.com
A collection of bike routes from around the world, ranging from short rides to tours of thousands of miles. Routes are displayed and created with Google Maps, and can generally be saved in GPX or KML format so they can be used on your computer with commercial or free mapping programs or loaded onto your GPS receiver.

Creating Routes for Use with GPS
www.bikeroutetoaster.com
This site uses Google Maps to create routes, which can then be downloaded for use on your GPS. It is Garmin-oriented, but it is not too hard to use for other receivers.

Organizations

This section includes a number of clubs and a few other institutions of particular interest to touring cyclists. These are not-for-profit organizations with goals related to bicycle touring. Some are devoted to developing trails or routes, others to more general concerns, such as safety.

Note that several organizations listed here and in the "Map Sources" section beginning on page 437 have developed long-distance trail systems—crossing America, traversing a major north-south landmark, or following a similar route. Every one of these efforts is a major service to self-propelled travelers, but some—like the Adventure Cycling routes or the Katy Trail in Missouri—are established tours you can follow with little additional research. Others are at least partly aspirational. It's important to ascertain the real status before planning your trip.

The difference can be easily reduced to practical terms. The Continental Divide Trail—generally following the Atlantic-Pacific watershed divide along the spine of North America—has been worked on by dedicated people and groups for many years but is far from complete. Many people have hiked the route, but there are numerous gaps where the proposed route traverses private property and other complications that affect cyclists and equestrians more than hikers. It is impossible to buy a map of the "trail," much less a guide to supply points, accommodations, and the like.

A good contrast is the Adventure Cycling Association's Great Divide Trail. It generally parallels the Continental Divide, but it does not follow it nearly as closely as the Continental Divide Trail. However, the Great Divide Trail *is a trail*. It is well defined, you can buy maps and guides, and where it goes is clear.

Adventure Cycling Association
See the listing below under "Map Sources."

American Discovery Trail Society
www.discoverytrail.org
The American Discovery Trail Society is devoted to promoting the American Discovery Trail, a coast-to-coast non-motorized trail (walking, biking, equestrian, etc.) covering 6,800 miles in 15 states (there is one route east from California, splitting in two from eastern Colorado to Ohio and then rejoining to form a single route to Washington, D.C., and the Maryland shore). Much of the trail is unpaved, but it doesn't generally require a mountain bike, depending on the alternatives you choose. The society has map kits, detailed directions, and directories of accommodations available on its Web site. This is an interesting route for transcontinental cyclists to follow, but it is still far from being a trail.

Bicycle Helmet Safety Institute
www.bhsi.org
The place to go for ratings of helmets and advice on what features to look for and what to avoid.

Continental Divide Trail Alliance
www.cdtrail.org/page.php
This group is devoted to creating a non-motorized trail following the full length of the Continental Divide from Mexico to Canada.

The Web site is quite useful for travelers, both in delineating the proposed route and in communicating the difference between existing segments and those still in limbo.

Cyclists' Touring Club (CTC)
www.ctc.org.uk
The United Kingdom's official cyclists' organization, CTC traces its history to 1878. It is the oldest cycling organization in the world. The CTC Web site has a wealth of information, publications (including route maps), and advice. CTC also publishes *Cycle Magazine*.

Hostelling International USA
www.hiusa.org
The American affiliate of the International Federation of Youth Hostels.

BBH World Traveler Accommodation, New Zealand
www.bbh.co.nz
BBH (Budget Backpacker Hostels) manages more than 350 hostel-style accommodations for self-propelled travelers in New Zealand. Sleeping arrangements range from single rooms to dormitory-style sleeping. You do your own cooking, and prices are reasonable. The Web site also has good general information on spartan traveling in New Zealand. You can make reservations or buy a BBH card through the Web site.

League of American Bicyclists
www.bikeleague.org
The League of American Bicyclists has almost as old a pedigree as the CTC, having been founded in 1880. It was still the League of American Wheelmen when the original edition of this book was published, but has since changed its name to remove the sexist implications. It has long been the most important cycling advocacy group in the United States and played an important role in paving roads; it continues to advocate for bicycle safety. At its founding, it lobbied against attempts to ban bicycles from roads and park paths and spearheaded demands for a federal highway program, leading what became known as the

Good Roads Movement. The American Automobile Association was modeled after the League. It also publishes *American Bicyclist*.

Randonneurs USA
www.rusa.org
Randonneurs USA promotes randonneur events in the United States. Randonneuring is long-distance, unsupported, (mostly) group-cycling endurance events. Traditional randonneur riding eschews support vehicles. Any repairs/help must be accomplished using local resources or tools carried by the cyclist.

Audax Australia
www.audax.org.au
Another good source for randonneur philosophy and information. Audax riding is generally used synonymously with randonneuring and randonnée riding, though the original French meaning was slightly different.

Map Sources

This section mainly lists sources for state maps and routes, together with international maps intended specifically for cyclists, along with extended bike trails. It also includes some nongovernmental U.S.-specific sources and state-specific sources. Hence, for Illinois, both the free state map and a privately published source are listed.

Note that many states do not publish bicycle maps, either on paper or electronically. Other states may have escaped my attention or published information after this book went to press. For state information not covered here, it is always worthwhile to check the Web sites for the specific state Departments of Transportation and Tourism. Even states that do not publish bike maps will generally send paper highway maps on request.

Adventure Cycling Association
www.adventurecycling.org
Originally called Bikecentennial, the Adventure Cycling Association publishes maps, routes, and *Adventure Cyclist* magazine, and its Web site has a wealth of information on long tours in the United States. Adventure Cycling tours include several transcontinental routes (Transamerica, Southern Tier, Northern Tier), north–south routes on both coasts (Atlantic and Pacific), numerous regional routes (Allegheny Mountains,

Adirondack Park, Great Parks, Great Rivers, Grand Canyon, Western Express, etc.), a number of interesting trips with historical themes, such as the Underground Railroad and the Lewis and Clark routes, and trail routes for mountain bikes, like the Great Divide Trail, which parallels the Continental Divide.

Note that in addition to offering a map set for each of its trails, Adventure Cycling has large-scale maps showing each trail location on its Web site, and it provides free downloadable GPS tracks for each of its routes.

Commercial Map Supplier
www.omnimap.com
This is the most comprehensive Web site for maps and cycling guides worldwide. Their search facility is annoying, because they limit results to 35, so you have to refine your search *before* you know what they have, and the logical operators don't work correctly. Their selection is huge, however.

Arkansas

Arkansas Bicycle Routes
www.arkansas.com/outdoors/biking/
    selected-trips.aspx
The Arkansas Department of Parks and Tourism's list of relatively short recommended tours (up to 80 miles).

Arkansas State Highway System Map
www.arkansashighways.com/Bike/Bicycle_ADT.pdf
The Arkansas state highway map with an overlay of bicycle suitability criteria in PDF format.

Illinois

Biking Illinois: 60 Great Road Trips and Trail Rides
www.bikingillinois.com
The best information on cycling in Illinois is in David Johnsen's book *Biking Illinois*. His Web site (listed above) is the "DVD bonus footage" of the book.

Illinois Department of Transportation
www.dot.state.il.us/bikemap/state.html
Free online bike maps, by region. You can also order
paper maps oriented toward cycling.

Illinois Department of Natural Resources
www.dnr.state.il.us/lands/Landmgt/Programs/
   Camping
Information on camping on public lands in Illinois.

Iowa

Bike Iowa
www.bikeiowa.com/asp/trails/trails.asp
Has links to a number of central Iowa trail systems.

Iowa Department of Transportation
www.iowadotmaps.com/msp/pdf/current/
   stmapmain.pdf
Iowa transportation map in PDF format.

Missouri

Bike Katy Trail
www.bikekatytrail.com
This Web site has maps of the 225-mile-long Katy Trail
across Missouri.

New Mexico

New Mexico State Highway Department
nmshtd.state.nm.us
From this site, follow the links to the maps of bicycle
routes.

New Mexico Touring Society
www.nmts.org
The New Mexico Touring Society has many tours in
New Mexico, and the Web site has descriptions and
maps.

New York

New York Department of Transportation
www.nysdot.gov/divisions/operating/opdm
   /local-programs-bureau/biking
Information on state bicycle routes and maps. Note
that many cyclists recommend using country roads
rather than following the official routes.

New York, Vermont, Quebec

Lake Champlain Bikeways
www.champlainbikeways.org
Information on the 363-mile route around the lake and
the many shorter side loops that make up a system of
over a thousand miles.

North Carolina

North Carolina Department of Transportation:
   Division of Bicycle & Pedestrian Transportation
www.ncdot.org/transit/bicycle/biking/biking_intro
   .html
Features regional, local, and urban maps.

Oregon

Oregon Department of Transportation
www.oregon.gov/ODOT/HWY/BIKEPED/maps
   .shtml#ODOT_Bicycle_Maps
Bicycle maps and information.

Cycle Oregon
www.cycleoregon.com
Cycle Oregon organizes supported weekend and weeklong tours, and the "past rides" section of the Web site
provides useful ideas for planning tours and maps of
various routes they cover.

Pennsylvania

Pennsylvania Department of Transportation
www.dot.state.pa.us/BIKE/WEB/tour_routes.htm
Pennsylvania's bicycle routes.

Wisconsin

Wisconsin Department of Transportation
www.dot.state.wi.us/business/publications/roadmap
    .htm
The state department of transportation does not itself
publish state bike maps, nor does it have state highway maps online. However, you can order a free state
highway map from the Web site above.

County Bike Maps–Wisconsin Department of
    Transportation
www.dot.wisconsin.gov/travel/bike-foot/countymaps
    .htm
Wisconsin does have the best set of bike maps of any
state or province in North America available online,
however. They are available county by county in PDF
format at this Web site.

Bicycle Federation of Wisconsin
www.bfw.org
The state bicycle map is published in eight sections. They
are not online. Paper copies can be ordered from BFW.

Bike 4 Trails
www.bike4trails.com
Wisconsin has several state trails, which are available
here.

Wyoming

Wyoming Department of Transportation
www.dot.state.wy.us/Default.jsp?sCode=homqu
Wyoming bicycling information and a state bicycle
map can be found here.

Australia

Australia is a continent (you knew that, but it is easy to overlook the consequences). With a population of about 20 million and an area of 3 million square miles, the population density is quite low, and nearly all those people are concentrated near a few cities along the coast, so most of the continent is very lightly populated. The proportion of touring cyclists in the population, however, is certainly far higher than in the United States, and there are clubs in every population center. Some are listed below, after map sources.

Royal Automobile Association
www.raa.net
Publishes road maps, which are free to members of other national auto clubs.

Westprint Heritage Maps
www.westprint.com.au/maps.htm
A source for maps of Australia, both paper and electronic.

The Map Shop
www.mapshop.net.au
A good source for maps of Australia, including the set of nine trail maps for the famous Mawson Trail mountain bike route, which covers 500 miles from Adelaide to the outback town of Blinman in the Flinders Ranges. The Map Shop also sells all government maps of Australia.

Bicycle Australia
www.woa.com.au/ba
Bicycle Australia is the national bicycle touring organization and is developing the Around Australia bicycle route. The site includes information on a number of tours.

Bicycle Federation of Australia
www.bfa.asn.au
The Bicycle Federation of Australia is the principal national organization of bicycle touring enthusiasts.

Sydney to Perth
www.theridersofoz.com
A narrative of the 3,800-mile trip along the southern edge of Australia, including a detailed guide to crossing the Nullarbor Desert.

Canada

Like the United States, many but not all Canadian provincial departments of transportation provide free highway maps, though few, if any, have bicycle-specific ones. Other sources are listed after some provinces.

British Columbia
www.hellobc.com/en-CA/TransportationMaps/Maps
    /BritishColumbia.htm?S=N
British Columbia has some good detailed regional maps available online at this location.

Manitoba
www.gov.mb.ca/mit/map/index.html
Manitoba has detailed online maps at this location, as well as a link to information on provincial parks (of which there are also many online maps).

Ontario
www.mto.gov.on.ca/english/traveller/map
Ontario has extensive maps available online at this location.

Saskatchewan
www.highways.gov.sk.ca/sask-maps
Saskatchewan has online maps at this site.

TransCanada Highway
www.transcanadahighway.com/general/maps.htm
This Web site has online maps for all Canadian provinces and territories. They are not detailed but can be useful for general planning.

MapArt Publishing Company
www.mapart.com
MapArt is the main commercial publisher of Canadian maps.

Cycle Canada
www.cyclecanada.com
Cycle Canada, developed by Bud Jorgensen, publishes a number of bicycle routes in various regions of Canada. It sells map and directions packages for a number of tours.

Atlantic Canada Cycling
www.atlanticcanadacycling.com
This Web site has useful general touring information and a lot of good advice on routes in the Canadian Maritime provinces. They sell some excellent guidebooks for routes in this region.

Vélo Québec
www.routeverte.com/rv/ang
The Route Verte (Green Route) in Quebec bills itself as "the longest bicycle route in North America" and comprises 2,500 miles of bikeways linking all parts of the province of Quebec. It includes linked primitive roads, paved shoulders, old tow paths, and rail corridors, all signed and meeting uniform safety standards, and including certified accommodations ranging from campsites to bed and breakfasts and hotels.

France

Travel France: Your Online Guide to French Maps and Books
www.france-travel.co.uk/htm/maps_of_france.htm#cycling_maps
Wide variety of maps of France.

Great Britain

Ordnance Survey Maps
leisure.ordnancesurvey.co.uk
The Ordnance Survey maps are the standard for maps
of Great Britain. Their online store provides a source
for these, as well as GPS maps for Garmin units using
Ordnance Survey data. (All are available elsewhere as
well, sometimes at lower prices.)

The National Byway
www.thenationalbyway.org
The National Byway Trust promotes the National
Byway, a series of routes that make several loops
through England, Wales, and Scotland.

Scotways
www.scotways.com
Scotways is a nonprofit organization dedicated to
maintaining and providing information about rights of
way and trails in Scotland.

Sustrans
www.sustrans.org.uk
The Sustrans Web site has information about cycling
routes in Great Britain, with links to sources of free
online maps for many locations.

Japan

Japan Cycling Navigator
www.japancycling.org
Lots of information on bicycle touring in Japan, including bike paths, but you have to dig deep for it.

Online Shopping

There are, of course, thousands of bicycle shops and specialized suppliers on the Web, and it would be pointless to try to catalog them all. They can be located with a search engine, particularly if you are looking for a specific item. The locations listed here (in alphabetical order) are those that are comprehensive or have some special resources, or that have given me excellent service. The selection is necessarily arbitrary.

Bike Nashbar
nashbar.com
Nashbar is one of the largest Web and mail-order cycling suppliers.

Harris Cyclery
harriscyclery.com
Harris is a smaller supplier, but it carries many hard-to-find items and the site has important technical information. It posts the articles of the late Sheldon Brown.

Jenson USA
jensonusa.com
Jenson carries a wide range of standard components and accessories at competitive prices.

Mountain Equipment Co-op (MEC)

mec.ca

MEC is Canada's most important supplier of equipment for self-propelled outdoor activities. The Web site includes useful information on many topics relevant to touring and bike camping. MEC has house brands in camping gear and touring equipment.

Performance Bicycle

performancebike.com

One of the major cycling suppliers, Performance Bicycle has a range of house brands for many items, in addition to standard components.

Recreational Equipment, Inc. (REI)

rei.com

Recreational Equipment is a co-op, one of the major U.S. suppliers for self-propelled outdoor sports. The Web site has helpful articles and equipment comparison charts.

Rivendell Bicycle Works

www.rivbike.com

A unique shop in the San Francisco Bay Area, Rivendell builds elegant lugged steel frames; it also carries many unique parts and accessories, publishes a newsletter of great interest to touring cyclists, and offers a variety of useful articles on topics ranging from bike fit to cycling philosophy on its Web site.

The Touring Store

www.thetouringstore.com

A small operation specializing in racks and bags.

Wallingford Bicycle Parts

www.wallbike.com

The best source of information on Brooks saddles and carrier of all available models. They also carry touring bags and racks and an interesting assortment of other cycling paraphernalia. They offer a 6-month return policy for Brooks saddles.

Tour Organizers

In the last few years, the number of businesses and nonprofit organizations specializing in bicycle tours has grown from a very small number to thousands. Only a few can be listed here, but they are representative of the variety now available, which range widely in the types of tours supported, costs, and general style.

Alaskabike
www.alaskabike.com
Road tours in Alaska and the Yukon.

Adventure Cycling Association
www.adventurecycling.org
This group offers supported and self-contained road tours in the United States and is the developer of the original U.S. transcontinental bike route and many others since.

Back Pedal Cycle Tours
www.backpedaltours.com.au
Supported tours in South Australia.

Backroads
www.backroads.com
Road tours (mainly) in Europe, North America, Latin America, and Asia.

Bicycle Adventures
www.bicycleadventures.com
Road tours in North America, Hawai'i, and New Zealand.

Bike China Adventures
www.bikechina.com
Guided small-group tours in China, supported or not, using your bike or a rental. Mostly uses mountain bikes due to marginal road conditions.

The Bicycle Tour Company
bicycletours.com
Primarily support for group trips, mainly road.

Bike Riders
www.bikeriderstours.com
Road tours, including some self-guided tours, throughout North America and Europe.

Bike Saint Lucia's Jungle Biking Adventure
www.bikestlucia.com
Mountain bike tours (day trips) in Saint Lucia, Lesser Antilles, and the Caribbean.

Bike Vermont
www.bikevt.com
Road tours in New England and Europe. One of the oldest commercial tour organizers.

Ciclismo Classico
www.ciclismoclassico.com
Road tours in Europe and New England.

Cross-Canada Cycle Tour Society (CCCTS)
www.cccts.org
A nonprofit organization of touring cyclists that organizes and presents reports on tours throughout Canada, some adjoining parts of the United States, and occasionally abroad.

CTC Cycling Holidays
www.cyclingholidays.org
Road and mountain bike tours throughout Europe, northern Africa, Australia, China, Southeast Asia, and India, sponsored by the venerable Cyclists Touring Club.

Escape Adventures
www.escapeadventures.com
Road and mountain bike tours mainly in the United States and Latin America.

Euro-Bike & Walking Tours
www.eurobike.com
Road tours mainly in Europe and New Zealand. One of the oldest commercial tour organizers.

Europeds
www.europeds.com
Mainly road tours in Europe and California.

Experience Plus
www.experienceplus.com
Road tours (mainly) in North America, Latin America, and Asia.

Getaway Adventures
www.getawayadventures.com
Road tours in California wine country and Hawai'i.

Great Explorations
www.great-explorations.com
Road tours in North America, Europe, and Asia, including self-guided packages.

Known World Guide Service
knownworldguides.com
Mountain bike tours in New Mexico.

Marty Jemison Cycling Tours
www.martyjemison.com
Road tours in Europe and the United States.

Mountain Bike Highlands and Islands
www.mbhi.co.uk
Mountain biking in the Scottish Highlands. Also provides routes for self-guided trips.

Nichols Expeditions
www.nicholsexpeditions.com/biking.htm
Road and mountain bike tours in Europe and Latin America.

Pac Tour
www.pactour.com
Specializes in long, fully supported road tours with high daily mileages.

Southwest Trekking
www.swtrekking.com/services/mountain_biking.html
Mountain bike tours in Arizona and Mexico.

Student Hosteling Program
www.bicycletrips.com
Road tours for teenagers throughout North America and Europe.

Western Spirit Cycling Adventures
www.westernspirit.com
Road and mountain bike tours in the United States, Central America, and Mexico.

Supported Large Tours

BicycleTour
bicycletour.com
A list of tours large and small.

National Bicycle Tour Director's Association
www.nbtda.com
Another list of tours. For older browsers and computers, go to www.nbtda.com/FullList.asp.

Biking Bis
www.bikingbis.com/blog/_WebPages
   /Charitybicyclerides.html
A list of rides supporting charities.

www.bikingbis.com/blog/_WebPages
   /statebicycletourindex.html
A list of long tours, particularly across states.

Index

Numbers in italic indicate an illustration

systems for, 167; cable travel in, 168–71; caliper-rim, 166, *172*; cantilever, 54, 62, 68, 109, 166, *172*, 174; centerpull, 166, *172*, 173–74; disc, 40, 54, 70, 75, 166, 240*n*; hydraulic, 167, 169; in-line adjusters for, 178, 210; levers for, 175–77; mechanical advantage in, 168–71; mounting posts for, 109, 174; pads for, 166, 210, 213, 226, 227, 411; quick releases on, 171, 175, 227, 230, 273; reach of, 54, 173; sidepull, 162, 166, 170, 171, *172*, 173; for tandem bikes, 166; V-type, 54, 70, 109, 162, 166, 170, *172*, 174–75

braking, 33–35, 164–66; importance of front wheel in, 165; on mountain bikes, 41, 165–66

braze-ons, 50, 62–63, 74, 109, 169, 177–78. *See also* bosses

brazing, 105; vs. welding, 102, 105–07

brevets. *See* randonneuring

bridge, 89

brifters, 109, 136, *136*, 176

Brompton folding bicycles, 77

Brown, Sheldon, 151, 197, 228, 418, 423, 425, 426, 446

Bruce Gordon Cycles, *60*, 61, 97, 108; panniers, *11*, 286; racks, *283*

Brule Mountain Gear panniers, 286

bungee cords, 288

cable play, in brakes, 169

cables: brake, 109, 169, 177, 227–28, 411; derailleur, 109, 116, 225, 227, 228, 241, 411

cable stops, 109

cadence, 29, 30, 36–38, 39, 43, 75, 117, 198, 334, 335

camping: in designated campgrounds, 362–63; dispersed, 360; gear, 291–318; general techniques, 358–70; leave-no-trace, 361, 419; skills, 363–67; stealth, 14, 313, 317, 360–62, 363

Cannondale bicycles, 59, 111, 404

Cannondale shipping boxes, 393

carbon fiber, in frames, 113

cassettes, 116, *116*, 120, 130

caster, 62, *86*, *87*, 99–100, 100*n*

catenary curves, in tents, 294

cell phones, 341–42

chainrings (front gears, chainwheels), 51, 52, 67, 68, 74, 75, 114, 115, *115*, 116, 118, 119, 120, 121, 122–23, 124, 125, 126, 127, 128, 129, *129*, 135, 212, 214, 215, 216, 217, 219, 223, 224, 226, 241, 395; diameter of bolt circle, 128; wear on, 127, 215–16

chainwheels. *See* chainrings

chains, 125–27; breakage of, 222; cleaning and lubrication of, 126–27, 216–18; cutting (separating), 220;

About the Author

Raymond Bridge is the author of numerous books on natural history, travel, and outdoor activities, including *America's Backpacking Book, Freewheeling: The Bicycle Camping Book,* and *The Geology of the Denver Area.* He is also a leader in local conservation work near his home in Boulder, Colorado, and a volunteer naturalist for Boulder's Department of Open Space and Mountain Parks, monitoring cliff-nesting raptors and other wildlife, and leading school groups on local trails. An experienced touring cyclist and outdoor enthusiast, Bridge contributes articles to cycling magazines and has served as unpaid mechanic for a women's cycling team. He has traveled to many parts of the world to bicycle, hike, and scuba-dive. His next major bike touring expedition is planned for Patagonia.